English

English

English

contents

special help

Vitamix recipes

cereals

quick breads

yeast doughs

(continued on next page)

contents

yeast doughs

dry rubs

About the Blades and Container

The Vitamix machine comes with our standard **wet** blade container. Although the recipes in this book can be made in the wet blade container, for best results Vitamix recommends use of the dry blade container. Additional containers with wet or dry blades may be purchased separately.

⚠WARNING		
	**Rotating Blades Can Cause Severe Injury.** **DO NOT** reach into the container while the machine is running.	

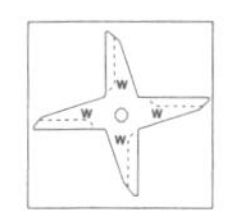

Wet Blade Container: Designed for processing liquids including juice, frozen mixtures, sauces, soups, purées, batters and for wet chopping. The wet blades can also grind grain and knead dough, but they are not quite as efficient as the dry blades in this application.

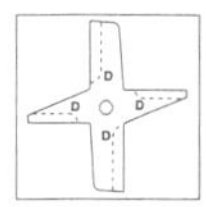

Dry Blade Container: These blades are clearly marked "D" and are designed specifically for grinding dry materials such as grains, cereal and coffee and are also used for kneading bread dough. The dry blades cannot process liquids efficiently.

CAUTION: Grinding dry material for more than 2 minutes could damage your machine. Regular use may result in cosmetic marring of the container and cause the blades to become dull over time.

⚠CAUTION		
	Moving Parts May Become Hot with Extended Use. **DO NOT** touch.	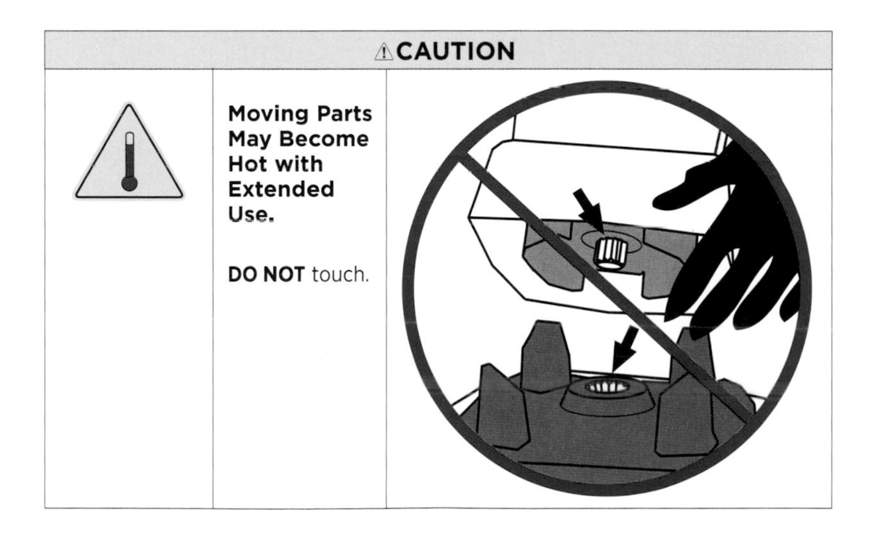

About Herb and Spice Grinding

Grinding some herbs may release volatile oils, causing the container to discolour permanently. Others have strong odours that may linger in the container, affecting the flavour of other foods. The grinding of some herbs and spices may also cause the blade to dull over time, or the container to crack. If you grind herbs on a regular basis, you may wish to purchase a separate dry blade container and replace the blades as needed.

GRINDING COFFEE BEANS

Watch the grinding process carefully, there are 6 levels of fineness. With this machine you can create your own style of gourmet coffee (see the list below).

speed: variable • processing: 10 seconds

2 cups (400 g) coffee beans	Place 2 cups (400 g) coffee beans into the container and secure the lid. Select Variable 1. Turn the machine on and slowly increase the speed to Variable 8. Grind for 10 seconds for "drip" style coffee.

Levels of fineness:

1. Percolator (very coarse). Grind on Variable 8 for 7-8 seconds.
2. Drip (coarse). Grind on Variable 8 for 10 seconds.
3. Cone Shaped (less coarse like cornmeal). Grind on Variable 8 for 12-13 seconds.
4. Hob/Flat (fairly fine). Grind on Variable 8 for 15-16 seconds.
5. Espresso (finer, like sugar, but not powdery). Grind on Variable 8 for 20 seconds.
6. Turkish grind (fine like flour). Grind on Variable 8 for 25 seconds.

The longer coffee beans are ground, the finer it gets. Ground coffee that will be brewed within two weeks should be stored in an airtight container and kept in a cool, dark place. Keep in the freezer in an airtight container if storing for longer than two weeks.

Troubleshooting for espresso makers: If your espresso pours slowly (from the espresso maker) and it is bitter, try a coarser grind. If it is thin and watery, try using a finer grind.

Baking Made Simple

The art of baking is a therapeutic escape, capturing every baker with its tantalising aromas, artistic expression and admiring praise. There is tremendous satisfaction in creating something entirely from scratch, in knowing exactly what went into the food you place on your table. And with the ability to grind your own whole-grain flour, Vitamix lets you take your baking to an entirely new level of freshness.

Your Vitamix machine effortlessly mixes batter and prepares dough, creating fluffy muffins, soft breads, light pizza crusts and more. Enjoy the recipes throughout this cookbook, as well as the helpful tips written by our own chef to help to ensure that every recipe comes out of the oven just the way you expected. And since the Vitamix container pours directly into your pan or griddle, cleaning up is simple, too.

Let's begin baking with the Vitamix - because there's nothing like the aroma of fresh-baked goods filling the house to bring everyone together.

About Bread Making

The Magic of Three Ingredients

Wheat

The majority of breads that you eat are really wheat breads. Rye bread is wheat bread with rye in it. Multi-grain bread is wheat bread containing smaller amounts of barley, oats, rye, corn, buckwheat or other grains. Bran bread is wheat bread with bran. Banana or courgette bread is wheat bread with banana or courgette. Regardless of the type of bread you like, most breads have a few things in common, wheat being one of them. Wheat has the best source of the protein component of grain, known as gluten. When wheat dough is "kneaded", the gluten develops a spongy network. This network traps the bubbles of carbon dioxide that are produced as the yeast digests the starches in the dough, causing the dough to rise. Without gluten, a dense, flat bread results.

In a kernel of wheat, the bran and germ have a tendency to make baked goods heavy and unresponsive to yeast and other leavening agents. Therefore, a high-protein wheat is necessary to counteract this situation. We recommend either hard red or the new hard white wheat. (Don't confuse hard white with soft white wheat, which is commonly used for pastry. Durum wheat is mainly used for pasta.) Bread made with hard white wheat combines the healthy goodness of whole wheat with a mild, sweet flavour. Hard white wheat does not contain strongly flavoured compounds that are part of red wheat. They are golden amber in colour and offer milder-flavoured, lighter-coloured baked goods. The protein content of hard white wheat rivals that of hard red wheat. If hard white wheat is not available in your area, you can contact the American White Wheat Producers Association on +1 (913) 367-4422 or +1 (800) 372-4422 or visit them on the web at www.farmerdirectfoods.com. High-altitude, hard red winter wheat with a protein content of at least 14 % and a moisture content of 9 % or below is also recommended.

Yeast

Leavening is essential in raised bread, and yeast is the most common bread leavening. Yeast is a living organism and becomes "active" with the addition of warm water and real sugar, such as honey, molasses, maple syrup and refined sugars. Artificial sweeteners are not real sugars and will not provide food for a yeast culture. However, flour, especially whole-wheat flour, contains enough natural sugar to feed the yeast.

Use caution when adding the yeast/water mixture to freshly ground flour. If the flour is too hot, it will raise the overall temperature of the mixture and will kill the yeast. For this reason, we suggest starting with frozen grains to avoid overheating the flour.

Liquid

Water, milk, potato water or juice can provide the liquid necessary for bread dough. You can even use eggs by placing the eggs in a measuring cup first, then adding the rest of the liquid to equal the amount listed in the recipe. When using flour at room temperature, the temperature of the liquid should be 105 °F to 115 °F (40 °C to 46 °C). When making bread in your Vitamix machine, take special note of the temperature of the flour. If you are using freshly ground whole-grain flour, the flour will already be warm. Removing ground flour from the container and then measuring the quantity desired will facilitate cooling.

Other Ingredients

Bread lends itself to all kinds of embellishments.

- Oil, when listed as an ingredient in bread making, helps to keep the bread moist and fresh longer.
- Eggs give bread a richer taste and supply protein that helps the loaf to rise higher; they also help the loaf to stay moist.
- Salt serves two purposes: 1) it's an inhibitor to the yeast as salt slows down the rising process; 2) it enhances the flavour. Without salt, bread tastes a little flat.

Good News for Bread Machine Owners

You won't find a better grain grinder on the market than the Vitamix machine. Use your freshly ground flour in whole-grain bread machine recipes. We know you'll like the results.

The Challenges Of Whole Wheat Bread Making

Yes, successful whole wheat bread making can be a challenge. Take heart, it can be done. The following will coach you in what to expect and how to avoid some possible pitfalls.

Used alone, whole wheat flour produces a heavier, more compact, dark bread. You should expect whole wheat loaves to be smaller in volume compared with white loaves of the same weight. The bran and germ make up 15 % of the grain and do not contain gluten. Remember, gluten is a protein substance that gives structure and strength to baked goods. In other words, whole wheat flour contains less gluten than the same weight of white flour. Though freshly baked whole wheat bread is heavier, it is delicious and satisfying.

Whole wheat bread will go stale quicker than white bread. It's best to make only what you can consume in one day. Use yesterday's bread for toast, stuffing, bread and milk, croutons, breadcrumbs or bread puddings.

How To Get A Smoother Loaf

Transfer the dough to a lightly floured board and knead for one to two minutes. Shape into a loaf and fit into a greased tin. Proceed to rise and bake as directed.

How To Adapt Your Bread Recipes

You can easily adapt your own bread recipes to the Vitamix. In the test kitchen, we divide most recipes in half (since bread recipes traditionally make two loaves). For the best results, make one loaf at a time, and reduce the ingredients to the following:

Flour: Use up to 2 1/2 cups (280 g) flour. This can be a mixture of grains, but keep in mind the ratio of 1:3 (one part other grains to 3 parts wheat or wheat flour).
Water: 1 to 1 1/4 cups (240 ml-300 ml).
Yeast: 1 packet per loaf (1 tablespoon).

High-Altitude Baking

Since atmospheric pressure decreases at high altitudes, leavened batters and doughs rise faster than they do at sea level. Decrease the proofing times for yeast breads by as much as half. High altitudes also cause greater moisture loss. Use flour sparingly when hand kneading. Add only enough flour to make the dough workable. Grease your hands to make the dough easier to handle.

If the bread is heavy and crumbly:

- Try substituting unbleached flour for some of the whole wheat flour.
- Try adding one teaspoon of gluten flour (found in health food shops) to each cup of whole wheat flour to get the loaf to rise better.
- If you are using other grains with wheat, be sure that the ratio is 1:3 (one part other grains to three parts wheat).
- What type of wheat are you using? The new hard white wheat is sweeter and it makes a lighter loaf.
- Try letting the dough rise twice: once in the machine container and once in the bread tin.
- Was the flour too coarse? Watch your time carefully when grinding grain. One minute is the recommended grinding time.
- Was the loaf kneaded until it was stretchy and elastic? It may have been under-kneaded.

If the loaf has a poor shape or a split crust:

- Did you add too much liquid? Was the dough too wet overall?
- Was the dough too dry? Did you add too much flour?
- How well was the dough kneaded? Was there a poor distribution of yeast?
- Was the tin in the centre of the oven? Is it possible that the heat was uneven?
- Was the loaf under-proofed when put in the oven to bake?

If the loaf is low and the texture too dense or close-grained:

- Was the loaf dense and difficult to knead? Maybe there was not enough liquid.
- Is the yeast too old? Check the expiry date. If in doubt, dissolve a packet of yeast and 1 teaspoon of sugar in 1/4 cup (60 ml) of warm (105 °F to 11 5°F/40 °C-46 °C) water. Stir and set aside for 5-10 minutes. If it produces a distinct foamy layer, it is okay to use. Yeast should be stored in the refrigerator or freezer. Never store it at room temperature.
- The yeast is inactive due to heat or cold. Yeast is very fragile. The high temperature of freshly ground flour will kill the yeast.
- The yeast is not active because the dough is not warm enough. Set the dough in a warm place to rise.
- Did the loaf rise high enough before baking? Maybe it was baked before it had finished proofing.
- Did you add too much salt? Salt can inhibit the growth of yeast.

If the texture is too coarse or open:

- Did you add too much yeast?
- Was the dough too wet?
- Did the loaf rise above the top of the tin? It may have risen for too long.
- Was the tin the correct size?

Custom-Made Crusts

How do you like your crust - tender to the bite, or thick, chewy and challenging? Using different glazes and a few baker's tricks, you can achieve a wide spectrum of textures, tastes and tones in your crust.

For a chewy, crispy crust like that of French bread, place a pan of water on the oven rack below the bread as it bakes. The steam encircling the bread in the hot oven does the trick. Another technique is to spray the bread with a fine mist of water at 10-minute intervals as it bakes.

For a chewy, glossy crust, brush the dough with a simple corn flour and water mixture. Dissolve 1 teaspoon of corn flour in 2/3 cup (160 ml) of water, and then heat the mixture in a saucepan until boiling. Let the mixture cool slightly and, with a soft brush, paint all exposed surfaces of the loaf just before baking. After baking for 10 minutes, remove the bread, paint it again and finish baking.

For a lustrous crust, try egg glazes. Because they're sticky, they come in handy for keeping poppy or sesame seeds in place. Just before baking, paint the bread with one lightly beaten whole egg - or use either one yolk or one white beaten with 1 tablespoon of cold water. If you use yolk, you'll get a deep golden colour; the white contributes sheen, but no extra colour. A whole egg gives you a little bit of each.

For a tender crust, brush loaves with melted butter just before baking or as soon as you remove them from the oven. Or, you can brush the loaves with milk or cream before baking.

About Grinding Whole Grain Flours

Grain increases in volume by about 25 % when ground into flour. Corn, soy beans and other high-moisture grains have a tendency to cake and stop circulating during grinding. To keep the flour moving, insert the tamper through the lid plug opening and, while the machine is running on high speed, gently nudge the flour back into the blades. This will ensure that all the grain is ground uniformly.

Important Note:
For best results, store grain in the freezer. Do not grind more than 2 cups (400 g) at a time.

WHOLE GRAIN FLOUR

speed: variable to high • processing: 1 minute • yield: up to 3 1/4 cups (390 g)

1/4-2 cups (50-400 g) whole kernel grain

Cook's Note: *At room temperature, flour will stay fresh for a month. In the refrigerator, two months. For longer storage, flour can be frozen for 6 months to a year. Bring to room temperature the amount you will need for baking.*

Place up to 2 cups (400 g) whole kernel grain into the Vitamix container and secure the lid.

Select Variable 1.

Turn the machine on and slowly increase the speed to Variable 10, then to High.

Grind to the desired degree of fineness (refer to the chart for recommended grinding times). The longer the machine runs, the finer the consistency of the flour, up to 1 minute.

Whole Kernel Wheat Measurement	Grinding Time	Speed	Approximate Flour Yield	Degree of Fineness
3/4 cup (144 g)	1 minute	VAR - HIGH	1 cup (120 g) + 2 1/2 teaspoons	very fine
1 cup (192 g)	1 minute	VAR - HIGH	1 1/2 cups (180 g)	very fine
1 1/4 cups (240 g)	1 minute	VAR - HIGH	1 3/4 cups (210 g) + 2 tablespoons (15 g)	very fine
1 1/2 cups (288 g)	1 minute	VAR - HIGH	2 1/3 cups (280 g) + 1 tablespoon (8 g)	very fine
1 3/4 cups (336 g)	1 minute	VAR - HIGH	2 1/2 cups (300 g) + 3 tablespoons (22 g)	very fine
2 cups (384 g)	1 minute	VAR - HIGH	3 1/4 cups (390 g)	very fine

Note: For the best results use special dry grinding blades when making flours. Select Variable 1. Turn the machine on and slowly increase the speed to Variable 10, then to High.

About Grinding Whole Grain Flours *(continued)*

Caution on Grinding Flour:

Please follow the recommended grinding times. Grinding dry materials, such as whole wheat, for more than two minutes can cause the flour to pack and overheat the container. Permanent damage to the container and bearing seals may result. Follow the recommended grinding times carefully.

Cooking Guide for Cracked Grains

Cracked Grain	Amount	Speed: Low Variable 7 or 8	Water	Cooking Time	Cereal Yield
Barley	1/2 cup (90 g)	10 seconds	2 cups (480 ml)	20 minutes	1 1/2 cups (360 g)
Buckwheat	1/2 cup (80 g)	5 seconds	2 cups (480 ml)	10 minutes	1 2/3 cups (400 g)
Corn	1/2 cup (80 g)	10 seconds	2 cups (480 ml)	20 minutes	1 1/2 cups (360 g)
Oats	1/2 cup (80 g)	10 seconds	2 cups (480 ml)	20 minutes	1 1/2 cups (360 g)
Rice (white)	1/2 cup (90 g)	10 seconds	2 cups (480 ml)	8-10 minutes	1 3/4 cups (420 g)
Rice (brown)	1/2 cup (90 g)	10 seconds	2 cups (480 ml)	20 minutes	1 3/4 cups (420 g)
Rye	1/2 cup (90 g)	10 seconds	1 1/2 cups (360 ml)	20 minutes	1 1/2 cups (360 g)
Wheat	1/2 cup (100 g)	10 seconds	1 1/2 cups (360 ml)	20 minutes	1 1/2 cups (360 g)
Wild Rice	1/2 cup (90 g)	10 seconds	1 1/2 cups (360 ml)	20 minutes	1 1/2 cups (360 g)

Helpful Hints

1. Grinding 2 cups (400 g) of grain at a time results in a more uniformly ground cereal.

2. 1/4-1/2 teaspoon salt may be added to the boiling water. It is for flavour only and not necessary if you are trying to restrict salt intake.

3. One way to enjoy the nutrition of whole grain cereals and the convenience of prepared cereals is to add the appropriate amount of cracked grain to a saucepan of boiling water at night before you go to bed. Turn the stove off, place a tightly fitting lid on the pan, and allow the cereal to soak overnight. By morning it will be ready to eat as a cold cereal. If you like it hot, just reheat on the hob or in the microwave.

4. Another convenient method requires the use of a Thermos. Place 1 cup (200 g) of grain in a 0.95 litre Thermos bottle (a wide mouth is most convenient), then add boiling water to just below 2.5 cm from the top. Use a wooden spoon handle to stir the grain and water. Close the Thermos and it will slow-cook in 8-12 hours.
5. For variety, combine grains. For example, oats and buckwheat, wild rice with brown rice, etc.
6. Spice up your cereal with nutmeg or cinnamon. Add your favourite fruits for a change in flavour and added nutrition - peaches, strawberries, blueberries, raisins or coconut.

   Cook's Note: *If you add dehydrated fruit to your cereals, remember that dried fruits rehydrate by absorbing water. You should increase the water portion of your cereal recipe just slightly to compensate for the water that will be absorbed by the dried fruit.*
7. For use in casseroles, substitute broth for cooking water.

CRACKING GRAINS FOR CEREAL

speed: variable • processing: 10 seconds

1/4-2 cups (50-400 g) whole kernel grain (choice of wheat, barley, oats, corn, rice, etc.)

Salt to taste (about 1/4 teaspoon per 1/2 cup (100 g) cereal)

Place up to 2 cups (400 g) whole kernel grain into the container and secure the lid.

Select Variable 1.

Turn the machine on and slowly increase the speed to Variable 7 or 8.

Grind until the desired degree of fineness. The longer the machine runs, the finer the consistency of the cereal, up to the point that it becomes flour.

How to Cook Cracked Grains

In a heavy saucepan (or in a double boiler), bring salted water to a boil. Slowly add the cereal, stirring constantly to prevent lumping.

Tightly cover the pan and reduce the temperature to Low. Cook until tender (see the above chart for the length of time), stirring frequently.

APPLE RAISIN CRACKED WHEAT CEREAL

preparation: 15 minutes • processing: 15 seconds • cooking time: 15-20 minutes
yield: 3 cups (720 g) cooked cereal

1 cup (180 g) whole kernel wheat

1 1/2 cups (360 ml) water

1/4 teaspoon salt

1 tart apple (170 g), peeled, seeded and quartered

1/8 teaspoon cinnamon

1/2 cup (72 g) raisins

2 tablespoons (18 g) sunflower seeds

Place the whole kernel wheat into the Vitamix DRY BLADE container and secure the lid.

Select Variable 1.

Turn the machine on and slowly increase the speed to Variable 7 or 8.

Grind to the desired degree of fineness, about 15 seconds.

In a saucepan, heat the salted water to boiling. Slowly add the cracked wheat to the boiling water, stirring constantly with a wire whisk.

Reduce the temperature to low, cover and simmer for 15 to 20 minutes, stirring frequently.

While the cracked wheat is cooking, use the Vitamix WET BLADE container to chop the apples.

Secure the lid and remove the lid plug.

Select Variable 1.

Turn the machine on and slowly increase the speed to Variable 4. While the machine is running, drop the apple quarters through the lid plug opening, using the tamper as needed to chop the apples.

Remove the saucepan from the heat and add the chopped apple, cinnamon, raisins and sunflower seeds to the cooked wheat. Stir to combine.

Cover and let the mixture stand for an additional 5 minutes before serving.

Nutritional Information Per 1 Cup (240 g) Serving: 342 cal (6 % from fat, 9 % from protein, 85 % from carb)
9 g protein • 2 g total fat • 0 g saturated fat • 79 g carbohydrates • 10 g fibre • 22 g sugar • 204 mg sodium
0 mg cholesterol

If food bounces around on top of the blades with very little chopping, the speed is set too slow. If it is violently thrown to the container walls, and the resulting particles are too coarse or unevenly chopped, the speed is too fast.

APRICOT BROWN RICE CEREAL

preparation: 10 minutes • processing: 10 seconds • cooking time: 20 minutes
yield: 3 1/2 cups (840 g) cooked cereal

1 cup (185 g) uncooked brown rice

3 1/2 cups (840 ml) water

1/2 teaspoon salt

8 dried (unsweetened) apricots

2 tablespoons (18 g) sunflower seeds

1/4 teaspoon almond extract, optional

Place the brown rice into the Vitamix DRY BLADE container and secure the lid.

Select Variable 1.

Turn the machine on and slowly increase the speed to Variable 7 or 8.

Grind to the desired degree of fineness, about 10 seconds. If a finer cereal is desired, grind for longer.

In a saucepan, heat the salted water to boiling. Slowly add the cracked rice to boiling water, stirring constantly with a wire whisk.

Reduce the temperature to low, cover and simmer for 20 minutes until cooked, stirring frequently.

While the rice is cooking, use the Vitamix WET BLADE container to chop the apricots.

Secure the lid and remove the lid plug.

Select Variable 1.

Turn the machine on and slowly increase the speed to Variable 5. While the machine is running, drop the apricots through the lid plug opening. If necessary adjust the Variable Speed for a finer chop.

Remove the saucepan from the heat and add the chopped apricots, sunflower seeds and almond extract to the cooked cereal. Stir to combine.

Cover and let the mixture stand for an additional 5 minutes before serving.

Nutritional Information Per 1 Cup (240 g) Serving: 224 cal (10 % from fat, 9 % from protein, 82 % from carb)
5 g protein • 2 g total fat • 0 g saturated fat • 46 g carbohydrates • 3 g fibre • 5 g sugar • 346 mg sodium
0 mg cholesterol

If food bounces around on top of the blades with very little chopping, the speed is set too slow. If it is violently thrown to the container walls, and the resulting particles are too coarse or unevenly chopped, the speed is too fast.

BROWN RICE GRITS

preparation: 10 minutes • processing: 10 seconds • cooking time: 20 minutes
yield: 3 1/2 cups (840 g) cooked cereal

1 cup (185 g) uncooked brown rice

3 1/2 cups (840 ml) water

1/2 teaspoon salt

Place the brown rice into the Vitamix DRY BLADE container and secure the lid.

Select Variable 1.

Turn the machine on and slowly increase the speed to Variable 7 or 8.

Grind to the desired degree of fineness, about 10 seconds. If a finer cereal is desired, grind for longer.

In a saucepan, heat the salted water to boiling. Slowly add the cracked rice to boiling water, stirring constantly with a wire whisk.

Reduce the temperature to low, cover and simmer for 20 minutes until cooked, stirring frequently.

Nutritional Information Per 1 Cup (240 g) Serving: 197 cal (7 % from fat, 8 % from protein, 85 % from carb)
4 g protein • 1 g total fat • 0 g saturated fat • 41 g carbohydrates • 2 g fibre • 0 g sugar • 344 mg sodium
0 mg cholesterol

CRACKED WHEAT CEREAL

preparation: 10 minutes • processing: 15 seconds • cooking time: 15-20 minutes
yield: 3 cups (720 g) cooked cereal

1 cup (180 g) whole kernel wheat

3 cups (720 ml) water

1/2 teaspoon salt

Place the whole kernel wheat into the Vitamix DRY BLADE container and secure the lid.

Select Variable 1.

Turn the machine on and slowly increase the speed to Variable 7 or 8.

Grind to the desired degree of fineness, about 15 seconds.

In a saucepan, heat the salted water to boiling. Slowly add the cracked wheat to the boiling water, stirring constantly with a wire whisk.

Reduce the temperature to low, cover and simmer for 15 to 20 minutes until cooked.

Nutritional Information Per 1 Cup (240 g) Serving: 219 cal (4 % from fat, 12 % from protein, 83 % from carb)
7 g protein • 1 g total fat • 0 g saturated fat • 49 g carbohydrates • 8 g fibre • 0 g sugar • 399 mg sodium
0 mg cholesterol

CREAMY RICE CEREAL

preparation: 10 minutes • processing: 10 seconds • cooking time: 8-10 minutes
yield: 1 3/4 cups (420 g) cooked cereal

1/2 cup (93 g) uncooked rice

2 cups (480 ml) water

1/4 teaspoon salt

Place the rice in the Vitamix DRY BLADE container and secure the lid.

Select Variable 1.

Turn the machine on and slowly increase the speed to Variable 7 or 8.

Grind to the desired degree of fineness, about 10 seconds. If a finer cereal is desired, grind for longer.

In a saucepan, heat the salted water to boiling. Slowly add the cracked rice to boiling water. Stir constantly with a wire whisk.

Reduce the temperature to low, cover and simmer for 8 to 10 minutes (slightly longer for brown rice) until cooked, stirring frequently.

Nutritional Information Per 1 Cup (240 g) Serving: 199 cal (2 % from fat, 8 % from protein, 90 % from carb)
4 g protein • 0 g total fat • 0 g saturated fat • 44 g carbohydrates • 1 g fibre • 0 g sugar • 355 mg sodium
0 mg cholesterol

GRANOLA

preparation: 15 minutes • processing: 3 minutes • baking time: 15 minutes • yield: 10 cups (2.4 kg)

1/2 cup (120 ml) honey

3/4 cup (165 g) brown sugar, packed

1/2 cup (120 ml) hot water

1 teaspoon salt

2 teaspoons vanilla extract

1 1/2 teaspoons cinnamon

5 cups (400 g) rolled oats

1 cup (104 g) wheat germ

1/4 cup (35 g) sunflower seeds

1/2 cup (42 g) chopped or flaked coconut

1/2 cup (58 g) chopped walnuts

1 cup (145 g) raisins

Heat the oven to 350 °F (180 °C). Lightly grease two 13 x 9 inch (33 x 23 cm) baking trays or a large roasting tin with vegetable cooking spray.

Place the honey, brown sugar, water, salt, vanilla extract and cinnamon into the Vitamix WET BLADE container in the order listed and secure the lid.

Select Variable 1.

Turn the machine on and slowly increase the speed to Variable 10, then to High.

Blend for 3 minutes or until the mixture is steaming.

In a large-size mixing bowl, combine the oats, wheat germ, sunflower seeds, coconut and chopped walnuts.

Pour the hot mixture over the dry ingredients and stir, leaving only a few lumps. Spread in the prepared tins and bake for 15 minutes, stirring every 5 minutes.

Remove the tin(s) from the oven and stir in the raisins. Set the tins on a wire rack and allow to cool completely. Store in jars or a large plastic bag.

Nutritional Information Per 1/2 Cup (120 g) Serving: 287 cal (18 % from fat, 12 % from protein, 69 % from carb)
9 g protein • 6 g total fat • 1 g saturated fat • 52 g carbohydrates • 6 g fibre • 20 g sugar • 124 mg sodium
0 mg cholesterol

The mixture can also be baked at a lower temperature until dried.

This unique recipe calls for no added fat. For a moist granola, add 1/4 cup (60 ml) light olive oil or grape seed oil with the liquid ingredients.

Granola

To chop nuts, select (DRY BLADE container) Variable 1. Turn the machine on and slowly increase the speed to Variable 4. Drop the walnuts through the lid plug opening and chop for 5 seconds.

OAT PORRIDGE

preparation: 10 minutes • processing: 10 seconds • cooking time: 30 minutes
yield: 3 1/2 cups (840 g) cooked cereal

1 cup (160 g) oat groats (NOT oatmeal)

4 cups (960 ml) water

1/2 teaspoon salt

Place the whole kernel oat groats into the Vitamix DRY BLADE container and secure the lid.

Select Variable 1.

Turn the machine on and slowly increase the speed to Variable 7.

Grind to the desired degree of fineness, about 10 seconds. If a finer cereal is desired, grind for longer.

In a saucepan, heat the salted water to boiling. Slowly add the cracked groats to boiling water, stirring constantly with a wire whisk.

Reduce the temperature to low, cover and simmer for 30 minutes or until cooked, stirring frequently.

Nutritional Information Per 1 Cup (240 g) Serving: 126 cal (14 % from fat, 18 % from protein, 68 % from carb)
8 g protein • 3 g total fat • 1 g saturated fat • 31 g carbohydrates • 5 g fibre • 1 g sugar • 342 mg sodium
0 mg cholesterol

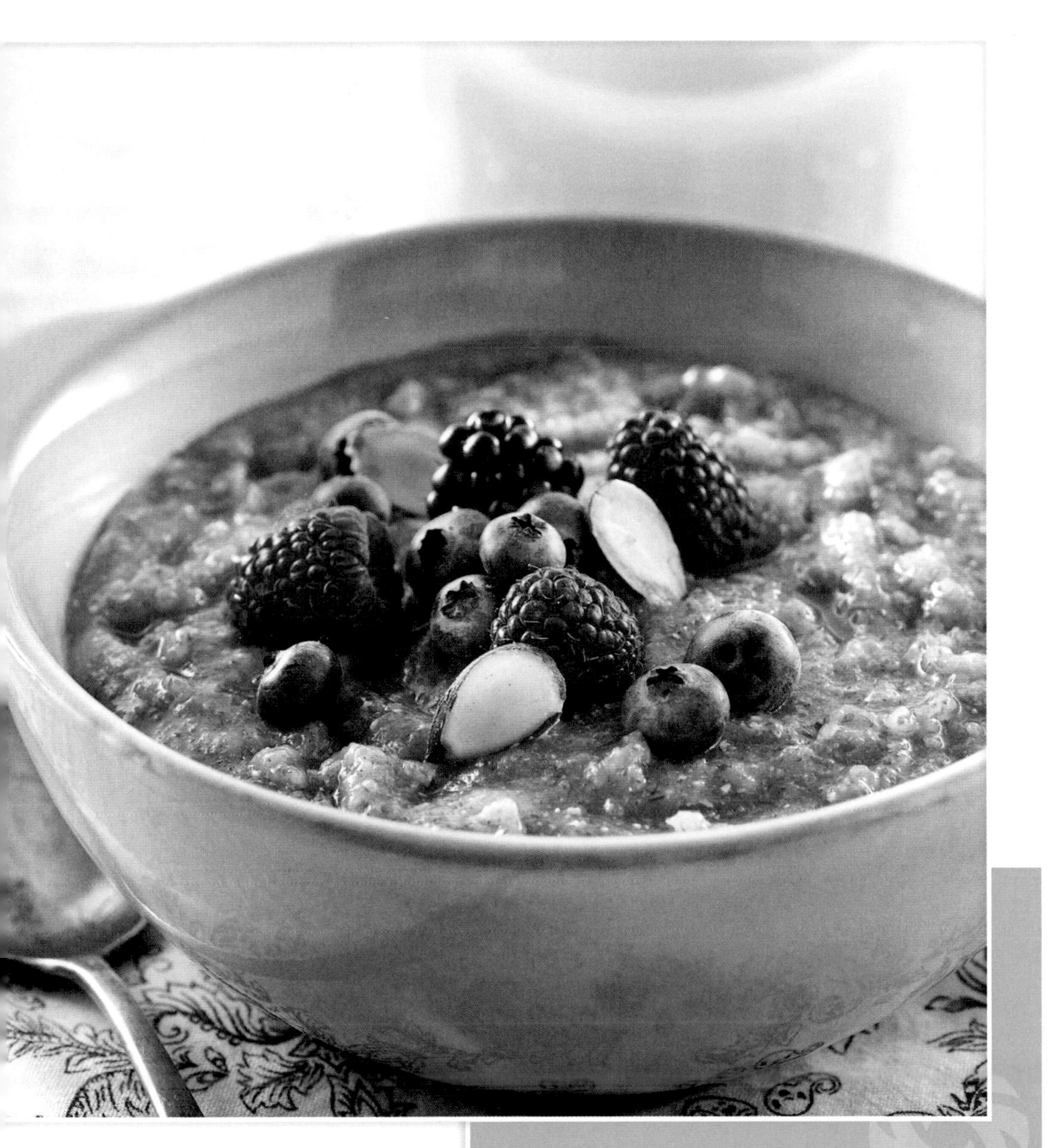

Oat Porridge

RICE WITH RAISIN CEREAL

preparation: 10 minutes • processing: 10 seconds • cooking time: 30 minutes
yield: 3 1/2 cups (840 g) cooked cereal

1/2 cup (93 g) uncooked rice

2 cups (480 ml) water

1/4 teaspoon salt

1/2 cup (72 g) raisins

A pinch of cinnamon

Place the rice in the Vitamix DRY BLADE container and secure the lid.

Select Variable 1.

Turn the machine on and slowly increase the speed to Variable 7 or 8.

Grind to the desired degree of fineness, about 10 seconds.

In a saucepan, heat the salted water to boiling. Slowly add the cracked rice to boiling water, stirring constantly with a wire whisk.

Reduce the temperature to low, cover and simmer for 8 to 10 minutes (slightly longer for brown rice) until cooked.

Remove the saucepan from the heat and add the raisins and cinnamon.

Cover and leave to stand for an additional 5 minutes before serving.

Nutritional Information Per 1 Cup (240 g) Serving: 292 cal (1 % from fat, 6 % from protein, 92 % from carb)
5 g protein • 0 g total fat • 0 g saturated fat • 70 g carbohydrates • 2 g fibre • 24 g sugar • 306 mg sodium
0 mg cholesterol

SUNRISE OAT CEREAL

preparation: 10 minutes • processing: 10 seconds • cooking time: 30 minutes
yield: 3 3/4 cups (900 g) cooked cereal

1 cup (184 g)
whole kernel oat groats
(NOT oatmeal)

4 cups (960 ml) water

1/2 teaspoon salt

6 to 7 pitted prunes

Place the whole kernel oat groats into the Vitamix DRY BLADE container and secure the lid.

Select Variable 1.

Turn the machine on and slowly increase the speed to Variable 7.

Grind to the desired degree of fineness, about 10 seconds. If a finer cereal is desired, grind for longer.

In a saucepan, heat the salted water to boiling. Slowly add the cracked groats to boiling water, stirring constantly with a wire whisk.

Reduce the temperature to low, cover and simmer for 30 minutes or until cooked, stirring frequently.

While the groats are cooking, use the Vitamix WET BLADE container to chop the prunes.

Secure the lid.

Select Variable 1.

Turn the machine on and slowly increase the speed to Variable 5 or 6. Remove the lid plug. While the machine is running, drop the prunes through the lid plug opening.

Remove the saucepan from the heat and add the chopped prunes. Stir to combine.

Cover and let the mixture stand for an additional 5 minutes before serving.

Nutritional Information Per 1 Cup (240 g) Serving: 209 cal (4 % from fat, 12 % from protein, 84 % from carb)
7 g protein • 1 g total fat • 0 g saturated fat • 47 g carbohydrates • 6 g fibre • 0 g sugar • 325 mg sodium
0 mg cholesterol

If food bounces around on top of the blades with very little chopping, the speed is set too slow. If it is violently thrown to the container walls, and the resulting particles are too coarse or unevenly chopped, the speed is too fast.

quick breads

Keys to Quick Bread Successes

- When a recipe calls for softened butter, let the butter stand at room temperature for about 20 minutes. Don't microwave the butter, as the high heat may cause melting rather than softening, and using melted butter instead of softened will unfavourably alter the outcome of your baked goods.
- If you over mix the batter for quick breads, the breads will be less tender when baked. Be sure to stir gently and minimally, just until the ingredients are mixed together.
- Let the oven preheat for at least 10 minutes before placing the quick bread on the middle rack. If you put quick bread into an oven that's not sufficiently heated, it won't rise as it should.
- Store quick breads by wrapping them in cling film or tin foil. Refrigerate for up to three days or freeze for up to three months.

Kids Cook - baking quick breads or muffins is a great way to get children excited about cooking. Encourage their participation by showing them how to grease pans or properly measure tasty ingredients, such as almonds, chocolate chips and dried cherries.

APPLE PECAN BREAD

preparation: 10 minutes • processing: 20 seconds • baking time: 40-50 minutes
yield: 1 loaf (12 slices)

1 cup (125 g) unbleached, all-purpose flour

1/2 cup (60 g) whole wheat flour

1 teaspoon baking powder

1/4 teaspoon baking soda

1/2 teaspoon salt

2 small apples, seeded, quartered, approximately 1 1/4 cups (156 g)

1 large egg

3 tablespoons (45 ml) light olive oil

2/3 cup (147 g) light brown sugar, packed

1/2 cup (54 g) chopped pecans

Lightly coat an 8 1/2 x 4 1/2-inch (22 x 11 cm) loaf tin with vegetable cooking spray or shortening. Heat the oven to 350 °F (180 °C).

In a large-size mixing bowl, combine the all-purpose flour, whole wheat flour, baking powder, baking soda and salt; stir well.

Place the apples, egg, oil and brown sugar into the Vitamix WET BLADE container in the order listed and secure the lid.

Select Variable 1.

Turn the machine on and slowly increase the speed to Variable 10, then to High.

Blend until the apples are chopped, about 20 seconds. If necessary, insert the tamper through the lid plug opening to help the mixture to circulate and chop.

Pour the apple mixture and pecans into a bowl containing the dry ingredients. Mix by hand until the dry ingredients are JUST moistened; do not over mix.

Spread the batter into the prepared tin. Bake for 40 to 50 minutes or until a toothpick inserted in the centre comes out clean.

Cool on a wire rack for 30 minutes, then carefully remove from the loaf tin and allow to cool completely before slicing.

Nutritional Information Per Slice: 175 cal (36 % from fat, 6 % from protein, 58 % from carb) • 3 g protein
7 g total fat • 1 g saturated fat • 26 g carbohydrates • 2 g fibre • 13 g sugar • 178 mg sodium • 18 mg cholesterol

"BROWNIE POINTS" BROWNIES

preparation: 20 minutes • processing: 20 seconds • baking time: 25-30 minutes • yield: 2 dozen

3/4 cup (64 g) unsweetened cocoa powder

1 teaspoon baking powder

1 teaspoon salt

1 teaspoon instant espresso powder

1 1/2 cups (180 g) whole wheat flour

2 cups (448 g) semi-sweet chocolate chips

1 cup (227 g) unsalted butter, softened and cut into pieces

2 cups (440 g) firmly packed light or dark brown sugar

1 tablespoon vanilla extract

4 large eggs

Lightly coat a 9 x 13-inch (23 x 33 cm) loaf tin with vegetable cooking spray or shortening. Heat the oven to 350 °F (180 °C).

When starting with whole kernel wheat: Place 1 1/2 cups (270 g) whole kernel wheat into the Vitamix DRY BLADE container and secure the lid.

Select Variable 1.

Turn the machine on and slowly increase the speed to Variable 10, then to High.

Grind the wheat for 1 minute. (Do not over process.)

Stop the machine to allow the flour to cool for a few minutes. Measure 1 1/2 cups (180 g) whole wheat flour for the recipe. Reserve and store the remaining flour for another time.

When starting with whole wheat flour: Place the cocoa powder, baking powder, salt, espresso powder and whole wheat flour in a large-size mixing bowl. Toss in the chocolate chips. Set aside.

Place the butter, sugar, vanilla extract and eggs into the Vitamix WET BLADE container and secure the lid. Select Variable 1.

Turn the machine on and slowly increase the speed to Variable 10, then to High.

Blend for 20 seconds until "creamy", using the tamper as needed.

Stir the butter mixture into the flour mixture and mix by hand to blend completely.

Use a nylon spatula to scrape the mixture into the prepared tin. Bake for 25 to 30 minutes or until a toothpick inserted in the centre comes out with a few moist crumbs attached. Do not over bake or the brownies will be dry.

Remove from the oven and let cool on a wire rack. Cut into pieces and serve.

Nutritional Information Per Brownie: 282 cal (44 % from fat, 5 % from protein, 51 % from carb) • 4 g protein
14 g total fat • 8 g saturated fat • 37 g carbohydrates • 3 g fibre • 28 g sugar • 144 mg sodium • 56 mg cholesterol

"Brownie Points" Brownies

CHOCOLATE COURGETTE CAKE

preparation: 20 minutes • processing: 35-40 seconds • baking time: 35-40 minutes • yield: 12 squares

1/2 cup (114 g) unsalted butter, cut into pieces, room temperature

1 1/2 cups (300 g) granulated sugar

2 large eggs

18 ounces (511 g) courgette, cut into chunks

1/2 cup (120 ml) light olive oil

1 teaspoon vanilla extract

1/2 cup (120 ml) buttermilk

1 1/2 cups (180 g) whole wheat flour

1 1/4 cups (156 g) unbleached, all-purpose flour

1/4 cup (21 g) unsweetened cocoa powder

1 1/4 teaspoons baking soda

1 teaspoon salt

1/4 cup (30 g) icing sugar, sifted

Heat the oven to 325 °F (160 °C). Lightly grease a 9-inch (23 cm) square cake tin.

Place the butter, sugar and eggs into the Vitamix WET BLADE container in the order listed and secure the lid.

Select Variable 1.

Turn the machine on and slowly increase the speed to Variable 10, then to High, using the tamper as needed to press the ingredients into the blades.

Blend for 25 seconds. Stop the machine, remove the lid and scrape down the sides.

Add the courgette chunks, oil, vanilla and buttermilk to the Vitamix WET BLADE container and secure the lid.

Select Variable 1.

Turn the machine on and slowly increase the speed to Variable 10, then to High.

Blend for 10 to 20 seconds or until the courgette is in small pieces.

In a large-size mixing bowl, combine the flours, cocoa powder, baking soda and salt.

Scrape the courgette mixture into the bowl of dry ingredients. Mix by hand until well combined.

With a spatula, scrape into the prepared tin.

Bake for 35 to 40 minutes or until a toothpick inserted in the centre comes out clean.

Chocolate Courgette Cake
(continued)

Cool on a wire rack for 30 minutes, then carefully run a knife along the inside edge of the cake to loosen. Invert onto a wire rack and allow to cool completely. Cut into squares and dust with sifted icing sugar when ready to serve.

To make Whole Wheat Flour with whole kernel wheat:
Place 1 1/2 cups (270 g) whole kernel wheat into the Vitamix DRY BLADE container and secure the lid.

Select Variable 1.

Turn the machine on and slowly increase the speed to Variable 10, then to High.

Grind the wheat for 1 minute. (Do not over process.)

Stop the machine to allow the flour to cool for a few minutes. Measure 1 1/2 cups (180 g) whole wheat flour for the recipe. Reserve and store the remaining flour for another time.

Nutritional Information Per Square: 386 cal (42 % from fat, 6 % from protein, 52 % from carb) • 6 g protein
19 g total fat • 7 g saturated fat • 52 g carbohydrates • 3 g fibre • 29 g sugar • 359 mg sodium • 56 mg cholesterol

CRANBERRY NUT BREAD

preparation: 15 minutes • processing: 30 seconds • baking time: 1 hour • yield: 1 loaf (12 slices)

1 cup (100 g) fresh or frozen cranberries

1 orange, peeled, seeded and quartered

1 to 2-inch (2.5 to 5 cm) strip of orange or lemon peel

1/4 cup (60 ml) light olive oil

1 cup (200 g) granulated sugar

1 large egg

1 teaspoon vanilla extract

1 1/2 teaspoons baking powder

1/2 teaspoon baking soda

1 teaspoon salt

2 cups (240 g) whole wheat flour

1/2 cup (46 g) chopped almonds

Lightly coat an 8 1/2 x 4 1/2-inch (22 x 11 cm) loaf tin with vegetable cooking spray or shortening. Heat the oven to 350 °F (180 °C).

Place the Vitamix WET BLADE container on the blender base and select Variable 1.

Turn the machine on and slowly increase the speed to Variable 3. Remove the lid plug and drop the cranberries through the lid plug opening just until chopped. Stop; scrape the sides and remove the chopped cranberries.

Place the orange quarters, peel, olive oil, sugar, egg and vanilla into the Vitamix WET BLADE container and secure the lid.

Select Variable 1.

Turn the machine on and slowly increase the speed to Variable 10, then to High.

Blend for 30 seconds, using the tamper as necessary to press the ingredients into the blades.

In a large-size mixing bowl, combine the baking powder, baking soda, salt and whole wheat flour; stir well.

Pour the orange mixture into the bowl of dry ingredients. Mix by hand until the dry ingredients are JUST moistened.

Stir the chopped nuts into the batter; do not over mix.

Spread the batter into the prepared tin. Bake for 1 hour or until a toothpick inserted in the centre comes out clean.

Cool on a wire rack for 30 minutes, then carefully remove from the loaf tin and allow to cool completely before slicing.

NOTE: To make Whole Wheat Flour with whole kernel wheat: Place 1 1/2 cups (270 g) whole kernel wheat into the Vitamix DRY BLADE container and secure the lid.

Cranberry Nut Bread *(continued)*

Select Variable 1.

Turn the machine on and slowly increase the speed to Variable 10, then to High.

Grind the wheat for 1 minute. (Do not over process.)

Stop the machine to allow the flour to cool for a few minutes. Measure 2 cups (240 g) whole wheat flour for the recipe. Reserve and store the remaining flour for another time.

Nutritional Information Per Slice: 224 cal (32 % from fat, 8 % from protein, 60 % from carb) • 4 g protein
8 g total fat • 1 g saturated fat • 35 g carbohydrates • 4 g fibre • 19 g sugar • 314 mg sodium • 17 mg cholesterol

Cranberry Nut Bread

CHICKPEA PANCAKES

preparation: 10 minutes • processing: 1 minute • yield: 4-5 pancakes

1 cup (172 g) dried chickpeas

1 teaspoon baking powder

1/2 teaspoon baking soda

1/4 teaspoon salt

3/4 cup (180 ml) cold water

2 tablespoons (30 ml) olive oil

1 large egg

When starting with dried chickpeas: Place the chickpeas into the Vitamix DRY BLADE container and secure the lid.

Select Variable 1.

Turn the machine on and slowly increase the speed to Variable 10, then to High.

Grind to the desired degree of fineness, about 1 minute. Measure 1 cup (120 g) chickpea flour from the ground mixture; reserve the remainder (about 1/3 cup (40 g)) for another use.

When starting with chickpea flour: Place 1 cup (120 g) flour, baking powder, baking soda and salt in a medium-size mixing bowl.

Place the water, oil and egg into the Vitamix DRY BLADE container in the order listed and secure the lid.

Select Variable 1.

Turn the machine on and slowly increase the speed to Variable 10, then to High.

Blend for 15 seconds.

Pour the water mixture into the bowl of dry ingredients. Mix by hand until the dry ingredients are JUST moistened.

Spray or oil a griddle or small frying pan. Heat the pan or griddle until hot.

Pour about 1/3 cup (80 ml) of batter into the pan and tilt slightly to form a pancake. Fry the pancake until bubbles appear on the surface. Flip over and fry until lightly browned. Serve immediately.

Nutritional Information Per Pancake: 193 cal (38 % from fat, 15 % from protein, 47 % from carb) • 10 g protein
11 g total fat • 1 g saturated fat • 29 g carbohydrates • 14 g fibre • 1 g sugar • 476 mg sodium • 53 mg cholesterol

WALNUT DATE BREAD

preparation: 30 minutes • processing: 25-30 seconds • baking time: 1 1/4-1 1/2 hours
yield: 1 loaf (12 slices)

1 cup (240 ml) boiling water

2 1/4 cups (340 g) pitted dried dates, coarsely chopped

4 tablespoons (56 g) unsalted butter, cut into pieces

1 1/4 cups (125 g) walnuts

1 cup (120 g) whole wheat flour

1 cup (125 g) unbleached, all-purpose flour

3/4 cup (150 g) granulated sugar

1 teaspoon baking powder

1/2 teaspoon baking soda

1/2 teaspoon sea salt

2 large eggs

1/2 teaspoon vanilla

Pour the boiling water over the dates and butter in a large-size mixing bowl. Let stand until cool, about 30 minutes.

Heat the oven to 325 °F (160 °C) with the rack in the middle. Lightly grease the loaf tin; set aside.

Place the walnuts into the Vitamix DRY BLADE container. Secure the lid.

Select Variable 1.

Turn the machine on and slowly increase the speed to Variable 3.

Blend for 10 to 15 seconds or until the walnuts are coarsely chopped. Do not over process.

Remove the chopped nuts to a small bowl and set aside.

Place the flours, sugar, baking powder, baking soda and salt into the Vitamix DRY BLADE container. Secure the lid.

Select Variable 1.

Turn the machine on and slowly increase the speed to Variable 6.

Blend for 15 seconds. Combine with chopped nuts.

Whisk the eggs and vanilla into the cooled date mixture, then stir into the flour/nut mixture until combined.

Spread evenly in the loaf tin and bake until a toothpick inserted into the centre comes out clean, about 1 1/4 to 1 1/2 hours.

Cool the bread in the tin on a wire rack for 25 minutes, then turn out onto the rack and cool completely.

Nutritional Information Per Slice: 346 cal (32 % from fat, 9 % from protein, 60 % from carb) • 8 g protein
13 g total fat • 3 g saturated fat • 55 g carbohydrates • 2 g fibre • 13 g sugar • 208 mg sodium • 51 mg cholesterol

Use kitchen scissors, dipped often in hot water, to coarsely chop the dates.

PEACH SPICE SCONES

preparation: 20 minutes • processing: 20 seconds • baking time: 30-35 minutes • yield: 8 scones

1 1/2 cups (180 g) whole wheat flour

1 cup (125 g) unbleached, all-purpose flour

1/3 cup (67 g) granulated sugar

2 1/4 teaspoons baking powder

1/2 teaspoon baking soda

1/4 teaspoon salt

1/2 cup (113 g) unsalted butter, softened and cut into pieces

1/2 cup (120 ml) milk

1 teaspoon vanilla extract

1 cup (186 g) frozen or fresh peach slices, (thawed and drained if using frozen) diced

Topping:

3 tablespoons (17 g) sliced almonds

1 tablespoon granulated sugar

1 teaspoon ground cinnamon

Additional milk or cream as needed for brushing the top of the dough

Combine the flours, sugar, baking powder, baking soda and salt in a large-size mixing bowl.

Place the butter, milk and vanilla extract into the Vitamix WET BLADE container and secure the lid.

Select Variable 1.

Turn the machine on and slowly increase the speed to Variable 6.

Blend until the butter is well mixed, about 20 seconds.

Gently stir the butter/milk mixture and peach pieces into the flour mixture, just into combine. Form the dough into a ball, then gently pat it to an 8-inch (20 cm) round on a baking parchment-lined baking sheet. Using a knife or pizza cutter, score into 8 wedges, cutting into but not through the dough.

Place the almonds, sugar and cinnamon into the Vitamix DRY BLADE container and secure the lid.

Select Variable 1.

Turn the machine on and slowly increase the speed to Variable 4.

Blend until the mixture is finely chopped and combined, about 10 seconds.

Brush the top of the dough with milk or cream and sprinkle with the almond mixture.

Bake in a pre-heated 400 °F (200 °C) oven for 30 to 35 minutes or until the scones are a light golden colour and no longer wet in the middle. Allow to cool for 10 minutes, then recut the wedges with a sharp knife or pizza cutter. Serve warm or at room temperature.

Peach Spice Scones
(continued)

NOTE: To make Whole Wheat Flour with whole kernel wheat: Place 1 1/2 cups (270 g) whole kernel wheat into the Vitamix DRY BLADE container and secure the lid.

Select Variable 1.

Turn the machine on and slowly increase the speed to Variable 10, then to High.

Grind the wheat for 1 minute. (Do not over process.) Stop the machine to allow the flour to cool for a few minutes. Measure 1 1/2 cups (180 g) whole wheat flour for the recipe. Reserve and store the remaining flour for another time.

Nutritional Information Per Scone: 311 cal (39 % from fat, 8 % from protein, 53 % from carb) • 6 g protein
14 g total fat • 8 g saturated fat • 42 g carbohydrates • 4 g fibre • 12 g sugar • 302 mg sodium • 31 mg cholesterol

WHOLE WHEAT BANANA BREAD

preparation: 10 minutes • processing: 30 seconds • baking time: 1 hour • yield: 1 loaf (12 slices)

1 large egg

1/4 cup (56 g) unsalted butter

1/3 cup (80 ml) milk

2 ripe bananas (284 to 310 g each), peeled and halved

1/2 teaspoon vanilla extract

2 teaspoons baking powder

2/3 cup (133 g) granulated sugar

1 2/3 cups (200 g) whole wheat flour

2/3 cup (77 g) walnuts, chopped (optional)

Lightly coat an 8 1/2 x 4 1/2-inch (22 x 11 cm) loaf tin with vegetable cooking spray or shortening. Heat the oven to 350 °F (180 °C).

Place the egg, butter, milk, bananas and vanilla extract into the Vitamix WET BLADE container in the order listed and secure the lid.

Select Variable 1.

Turn the machine on and slowly increase the speed to Variable 5.

Blend until well mixed, about 30 seconds.

In a large-size mixing bowl, combine the baking powder, sugar and whole wheat flour by hand; stir well.

Pour the banana mixture into the bowl of dry ingredients. Mix by hand until the dry ingredients are JUST moistened.

Stir the chopped nuts into the batter; do not over mix.

Spread the batter into the prepared tin. Bake for 1 hour or until a toothpick inserted in the centre comes out clean.

Cool on a wire rack for 30 minutes, then carefully remove from the loaf tin and allow to cool completely before slicing.

Nutritional Information Per Slice (with walnuts): 206 cal (38 % from fat, 9 % from protein, 53 % from carb)
5 g protein • 9 g total fat • 3 g saturated fat • 29 g carbohydrates • 3 g fibre • 14 g sugar • 93 mg sodium
28 mg cholesterol

Whole Wheat Banana Bread

WHOLE WHEAT MUFFINS WITH FRUIT AND CARROTS

preparation: 15 minutes • processing: 10-15 seconds • baking time: 20-25 minutes
yield: 6 muffins

1 cup (165 g) pineapple chunks

1/2 cup (64 g) rough chopped carrots

1 tablespoon light olive oil

1/4 cup (55 g) light brown sugar, packed

1 large egg

1 cup (120 g) whole wheat flour

1 teaspoon flax meal

1 teaspoon cinnamon

1 teaspoon baking powder

1/2 teaspoon baking soda

1/2 teaspoon salt

1/2 cup (72 g) raisins

Heat the oven to 375 °F (190 °C). Lightly coat a muffin tin with vegetable cooking spray or use cupcake cases.

Place the pineapple, carrots, oil, brown sugar and egg into the Vitamix WET BLADE container in the order listed and secure the lid.

Select Variable 1.

Turn the machine on and slowly increase the speed to Variable 4.

Blend for 10 to 15 seconds (the carrot and pineapple should still be chunky).

In a large-size mixing bowl, combine the flour, flax meal, cinnamon, baking powder, baking soda and salt.

Pour the pineapple mixture into the bowl of dry ingredients. Mix by hand until the dry ingredients are JUST moistened. Quickly but gently stir in the raisins.

Spoon into the prepared muffin tin, filling each cup full.

Bake for 20 to 25 minutes or until a toothpick inserted in the centre of one muffin comes out clean.

Cool on a wire rack for 5 minutes, then carefully remove each muffin from the muffin tin. Serve warm or at room temperature.

Nutritional Information Per Muffin: 203 cal (17 % from fat, 9 % from protein, 74 % from carb) • 5 g protein
4 g total fat • 1 g saturated fat • 40 g carbohydrates • 4 g fibre • 18 g sugar • 412 mg sodium • 35 mg cholesterol

Do not decrease the oil measurement. It is the minimum amount needed to produce a moist muffin. If you use honey or decrease the brown sugar the muffins will taste of soda.

Whole Wheat Muffins With Fruit And Carrots

COURGETTE BREAD

preparation: 15 minutes • processing: 15-20 seconds • baking time: 1 hour • yield: 1 loaf (12 slices)

1 large egg

2/3 cup (133 g) granulated sugar

1/4 cup (60 ml) light olive or grape seed oil

1 teaspoon vanilla extract

1 1/2 cups (200 g) courgette, cut into chunks

2 cups (250 g) unbleached, all-purpose flour

1 teaspoon baking soda

1/4 teaspoon baking powder

1/4 teaspoon salt

1/4 teaspoon ground nutmeg

1/2 teaspoon ground cinnamon

1/2 teaspoon ground allspice

Optional Ingredients:

1/2 cup (58 g) coarsely chopped walnuts

1/2 cup (72 g) raisins

Lightly coat an 8 1/2 x 4 1/2-inch (22 x 11 cm) loaf tin with vegetable cooking spray or shortening. Heat the oven to 350 °F (180 °C).

Place the egg, sugar, oil and vanilla extract into the Vitamix WET BLADE container in the order listed and secure the lid.

Select Variable 1.

Turn the machine on and slowly increase the speed to Variable 5.

Blend for 15 to 20 seconds or until the mixture is blended and the courgette is chopped.

In a large-size mixing bowl, combine the flour, baking soda, baking powder, salt, nutmeg, cinnamon and allspice; stir well.

Pour the courgette mixture into the bowl of dry ingredients. Mix by hand until the dry ingredients are JUST moistened; then quickly add and stir in the walnuts/and or raisins just to combine. Do not over mix.

Spread the batter into the prepared tin. Bake for 1 hour or until a toothpick inserted in the centre comes out clean.

Cool on a wire rack for 30 minutes, then carefully remove from the loaf tin and allow to cool completely before slicing.

Nutritional Information Per Slice (without optional ingredients): 171 cal (28 % from fat, 7 % from protein, 65 % from carb) • 3 g protein • 5 g total fat • 1 g saturated fat • 28 g carbohydrates • 1 g fibre • 12 g sugar • 174 mg sodium 18 mg cholesterol

PUMPKIN MUFFINS

preparation: 15 minutes • processing: 10 seconds • baking time: 20-25 minutes • yield: 12 muffins

2 large eggs

1/4 cup (60 ml) light olive oil

1 cup (245 g) pumpkin, freshly cooked or tinned

1/4 cup (60 ml) milk

3/4 cup (150 g) granulated sugar

1/2 teaspoon salt

2 teaspoons baking soda

1 teaspoon allspice

1 teaspoon cinnamon

1 3/4 cups (219 g) unbleached, all-purpose flour

1/2 cup (120 g) chocolate chips, mini or regular

Heat the oven to 350 °F (180 °C). Lightly coat a muffin tin with vegetable cooking spray or use cupcake cases.

Place the eggs, oil, pumpkin, milk and sugar into the Vitamix WET BLADE container in the order listed and secure the lid.

Select Variable 1.

Turn the machine on and slowly increase the speed to Variable 5.

Blend for 10 seconds.

In a medium-size mixing bowl, combine the salt, baking soda, allspice, cinnamon, flour and chocolate chips in the order listed.

Pour the pumpkin mixture into the bowl of dry ingredients. Mix by hand until the dry ingredients are JUST moistened.

Spoon into the prepared muffin tin, filling each cup 3/4 full.

Bake for 20 to 25 minutes or until a toothpick inserted in the centre of one muffin comes out clean.

Cool on a wire rack for 5 minutes, then carefully remove each muffin from the muffin tin. Serve warm or at room temperature.

Nutritional Information Per Muffin: 228 cal (32 % from fat, 7 % from protein, 61 % from carb) • 4 g protein
8 g total fat • 2 g saturated fat • 35 g carbohydrate • 2 g fibre • 18 g sugar • 326 mg sodium • 41 mg cholesterol

Yeast Bread Tutorial

Here are a few helpful tips for preparing yeast dough.

Measuring Flour

There's no need to sift flour before measuring, but for accuracy in measuring, lightly spoon flour into a dry measuring cup and then level with the straight edge of a spatula or a knife.

Temperature of Liquids

Proofing your yeast helps to ensure that it is alive and will work well in your recipe. Yeast is extremely sensitive to temperature - too much heat will kill the yeast; too little will retard its growth. Thus, it is important that the temperature of the liquid be at the correct temperature when added to the yeast.

The temperature range given most often when yeast is directly mixed with liquid, is 105 °F to 115 °F (40 °C-46 °C).

Let it Rise

Let dough rise, lightly covered, in a warm, draught-free place. For best results, let dough rise at room temperature. Higher temperatures can create a raw yeast flavour in the finished product; lower temperatures can cause dough to sour before it rises.

SOURDOUGH BLUEBERRY BREAD

preparation: 15 minutes • processing: 15 seconds • baking time: 35-40 minutes
yield: 1 round loaf (8-10 slices)

1 large egg

1/2 cup (120 ml) vegetable oil

1/2 cup (120 ml) milk

3/4 cup (180 ml) Potato Starter (recipe on page 75), at room temperature

1/2 cup (100 g) granulated sugar

1 1/2 cups (188 g) unbleached, all-purpose flour

1/2 cup (60 ml) whole wheat flour

1/2 teaspoon salt

3/4 teaspoon baking soda

1 cup (148 g) fresh or frozen (thaw and pat dry) blueberries

Sugar for topping, optional

Heat the oven to 375 °F (190 °C). Lightly grease a pan or cake tin.

Place the egg, oil, milk, Potato Starter and sugar into the Vitamix WET BLADE container in the order listed and secure the lid.

Select Variable 1.

Turn the machine on and slowly increase the speed to Variable 10, then to High.

Blend for 15 seconds.

In a medium-size mixing bowl, combine the flours, salt and baking soda.

Pour the Starter mixture into the bowl of dry ingredients. Mix by hand until the dry ingredients are JUST moistened. Quickly but gently stir in the blueberries.

Spoon into the prepared pan. Sprinkle the top with additional sugar if desired.

Bake for 35 to 40 minutes or until a toothpick inserted in the centre comes out clean. Serve warm or cool, cut into wedges.

Nutritional Information Per Slice: 249 cal (7 % from fat, 12 % from protein, 81 % from carb) • 8 g protein
2 g total fat • 0 g saturated fat • 51 g carbohydrates • 5 g fibre • 3 g sugar • 23 mg sodium • 0 mg cholesterol

CINNAMON ROLLS

preparation: 20 minutes • processing: 30 seconds • baking time: 30-35 minutes • yield: 9 rolls

1 packet (1 tablespoon) active dry yeast

4 tablespoons (60 ml) warm water, 105 °F-115 °F (40 °C-46 °C)

2 tablespoons (30 ml) honey

2 1/4 cups (281 g) unbleached, all-purpose flour plus extra for final mixing and rolling the dough

1/2 teaspoon salt

1/3 cup (80 ml) milk

1/4 cup (56 g) unsalted butter, softened and cut into pieces

1 large egg

Filling:

4 tablespoons (50 g) granulated sugar

1 tablespoon ground cinnamon

1/4 cup (56 g) unsalted butter, melted

1 large egg plus 2 tablespoons (30 ml) milk (to brush the tops of the rolls prior to baking)

Icing Sugar Icing (recipe on page 46)

To proof the yeast, combine the yeast, water and honey. Stir quickly to combine. Set aside for 5 minutes.

Place the flour and salt into the Vitamix DRY BLADE container and secure the lid.

Select Variable 1.

Turn the machine on and slowly increase the speed to Variable 6.

Blend until a hole forms in the centre of the mixture, about 5 seconds.

Select Variable 3. Turn the machine on and remove the lid plug. Add the yeast mixture, milk, butter and egg through the lid plug opening. Stop the machine and replace the lid plug.

Select High speed. Quickly turn the machine On and Off twice. Stop the machine and remove the lid.

While the dough rests, lightly grease an 8-inch (20 cm) square cake tin with vegetable cooking spray or shortening.

Use a wet nylon spatula to scrape the sides of the container, pulling the dough away from the container sides and into the centre of the mixture. Replace the lid.

Select High speed. Quickly turn the machine On and Off five times. Add additional water, 1 tablespoon at a time, only if the dough seems exceptionally dry. Repeat the process five times, scraping the sides of the container until the dough binds together into a soft, elastic mixture.

To remove the dough from the container, turn the machine On and Off five times (to assist in lifting the dough up and away from the blades). Invert the container over a greased bowl and allow the dough to fall into the bowl. Turn the dough once to coat the entire surface; cover with a clean, dry tea towel and let rise for 25 to 30 minutes.

Combine the sugar and cinnamon; set aside with the melted and cooled butter.

Cinnamon Rolls
(continued)

Transfer the dough to a floured work surface. Roll it into a large rectangle, turning and flouring often, about 8 x 16 inches (20 x 40 cm) in size. Spread with the melted butter, leaving about a 1/2-inch (1.3 cm) edge on all sides. Sprinkle the sugar/cinnamon mixture onto the butter.

Roll tightly, Swiss roll style. Cut into 9 pieces. Flip up and place into the tin.

Cover with a clean, dry tea towel and let rise for about 45 to 60 minutes.

Brush the tops of the rolls with the egg and milk mixture. Bake in a pre-heated 325 °F (160 °C) oven for 30 to 35 minutes or until light golden brown.

Cool on a wire rack for 10 minutes, then very carefully slide from the tin and allow to cool on a wire rack before slicing. Ice with Icing Sugar Icing and serve.

Nutritional Information Per Roll with Icing: 422 cal (37 % from fat, 5 % from protein, 58 % from carb)
6 g protein • 18 g total fat • 11 g saturated fat • 62 g carbohydrates • 2 g fibre • 35 g sugar • 162 mg sodium
88 mg cholesterol

Cinnamon Rolls

ICING SUGAR ICING

The perfect icing for Cinnamon Rolls.

preparation: 20 minutes • processing: 25 seconds • yield: 1 cup (240 g)

2 cups (240 g) icing sugar

1/4 cup (56 g) unsalted butter, softened

1 teaspoon vanilla extract

1 to 2 tablespoons hot water, plus more as needed

Place the icing sugar, butter, vanilla extract and hot water into the Vitamix WET BLADE container and secure the lid.

Select Variable 1.

Turn the machine on and slowly increase the speed to Variable 10, then to High.

Blend for 10 seconds. Stop the machine, remove the lid and scrape the sides of the container. Add additional water (by teaspoons) if needed at this point to make a spreadable (but not too thin) icing.

Select Variable 1 and secure the lid.

Turn the machine on and slowly increase the speed to Variable 10, then to High.

Blend until smooth and creamy, about 15 more seconds. Use immediately.

Nutritional Information Per 2 Tablespoon (30 g) Serving: 169 cal (30 % from fat, 0 % from protein, 70 % from carb)
0 g protein • 6 g total fat • 4 g saturated fat • 30 g carbohydrates • 0 g fibre • 29 g sugar • 1 mg sodium
15 mg cholesterol

POTATO STARTER

preparation: 10 minutes

1 packet (1 tablespoon) active dry yeast

2 teaspoons sugar

2 cups (480 ml) warm potato water, 110 °F (43 °C)

2 cups (480 ml) warm water, 110 °F (43 °C) or extra potato water, warmed

1 cup (125 g) unbleached, all-purpose flour

1 cup (120 g) whole wheat flour

Dissolve the yeast and sugar in the 2 cups (480 ml) potato water in a large-size mixing bowl.

Cover with a clean, dry tea towel and let sit in a warm place for 24 hours.

Add 2 cups (480 ml) warm water and stir into the flours.

Cover and let stand overnight or until the mixture is bubbly and smells sour. Refrigerate in a large covered jar.

Remove from the refrigerator and "feed". Use 1 cup (240 ml) for 1 loaf of bread in any recipe that requires a sponge or starter.

Nutritional Information Per 1 Cup (240 ml) Serving: 232 cal (4 % from fat, 14 % from protein, 82 % from carb)
8 g protein • 1 g total fat • 0 g saturated fat • 49 g carbohydrates • 5 g fibre • 2 g sugar • 6 mg sodium
0 mg cholesterol

Feeding the starter: In the morning, bring to room temperature and beat in 1 cup (240 ml) warm water, 110 °F (43 °C) and 1 cup (125 g) all-purpose flour. Let stand overnight. Use the amount needed for bread and refrigerate the rest. Renew every 2 to 3 weeks.

COLONIAL BREAD (FREE FORM)

preparation: 15 minutes • processing: 30 seconds • baking time: 25 minutes
yield: 1 oval loaf (8-10 slices)

1 1/4 cups (300 ml) warm water, 105 °F-115 °F (40 °C-46 °C)

3 tablespoons (41 g) brown sugar

1 packet (1 tablespoon) active dry yeast

1 1/2 cups (188 g) unbleached, all-purpose flour

1/2 cup (60 g) whole wheat flour

1/4 cup (26 g) light rye flour

1/4 cup (30 g) whole grain cornmeal

1/2 teaspoon salt

1 tablespoon light olive oil

1/4 cup (30 g) whole grain cornmeal for the baking sheet

1 egg mixed with 1 teaspoon water (for brushing the dough before baking)

To proof the yeast, combine the warm water, brown sugar and yeast. Stir quickly to combine. Set aside for 5 minutes.

Place the all-purpose flour, whole wheat flour, rye flour, cornmeal and salt into the Vitamix DRY BLADE container and secure the lid.

Select Variable 1.

Turn the machine on and slowly increase the speed to Variable 6.

Blend until a hole forms in the centre of the flour mixture, about 5 seconds.

Select Variable 3. Turn the machine on and remove the lid plug. Add the oil and yeast mixture through the lid plug opening. Stop the machine and replace the lid plug.

Select High speed. Quickly turn the machine On and Off twice. Stop the machine and remove the lid.

While the dough rests, sprinkle 1/4 cup (30 g) cornmeal on a baking sheet and set aside.

Use a wet nylon spatula to scrape the sides of the container, pulling the dough away from the container sides and into the centre of the mixture. Replace the lid.

Select High speed. Quickly turn the machine On and Off five times. Add additional water, 1 tablespoon at a time, only if the dough seems exceptionally dry. Repeat the process five times, scraping the sides of the container until the dough binds together into a soft, elastic mixture.

Place the lid on the container and allow the dough to rise for 15 minutes.

Deflate the dough with a nylon spatula, then turn out onto a piece of waxed paper lightly sprinkled with flour. (The dough will be sticky.) Quickly pull the dough off the waxed paper with lightly floured hands onto the baking sheet. Sprinkle the top of the dough with flour and shape into a large oval.

Cover the loaf with a clean, dry tea towel and allow the dough to rise until nearly doubled in size, about 15 to 20 minutes.

Colonial Bread (Free Form) *(continued)*	When ready to bake, quickly brush the dough with the egg mixture and make 3 quick angled slits with a serrated knife on top of the dough. Bake in a pre-heated 375 °F (190 °C) oven for 25 minutes or until the bread reaches an internal temperature of 190 °F (88 °C) when tested with an instant-read thermometer. Cool on a wire rack for 10 minutes, then carefully remove from the baking sheet and allow to cool completely before slicing.

Nutritional Information Per Slice: 160 cal (15 % from fat, 11 % from protein, 74 % from carb) • 5 g protein
3 g total fat • 0 g saturated fat • 30 g carbohydrates • 2 g fibre • 4 g sugar • 133 mg sodium • 21 mg cholesterol

Perfect as a flattish, artisan type loaf that can be used for slicing and dipping into olive oil.

COLONIAL BREAD (LOAF FORM)

preparation: 10 minutes • processing: 30 seconds • baking time: 25-30 minutes
yield: 1 loaf (12 slices)

1 1/4 cups (300 ml)
warm water, 105 °F-115 °F
(40 °C-46 °C)

3 tablespoons (41 g)
brown sugar

1 packet (1 tablespoon)
active dry yeast

1 1/2 cups (188 g)
unbleached,
all-purpose flour

1/2 cup (60 g)
whole wheat flour

1/4 cup (26 g)
light rye flour

1/4 cup (30 g)
whole grain cornmeal

1/2 teaspoon salt

1 tablespoon
light olive oil

1 large egg mixed with
1 teaspoon water
(for brushing the dough
before baking)

To proof the yeast, combine the warm water, brown sugar and yeast. Stir quickly to combine. Set aside for 5 minutes.

Place the all-purpose flour, whole wheat flour, rye flour, cornmeal and salt into the Vitamix DRY BLADE container and secure the lid.

Select Variable 1.

Turn the machine on and slowly increase the speed to Variable 6.

Blend until a hole forms in the centre of the flour mixture, about 5 seconds.

Select Variable 3. Turn the machine on and remove the lid plug. Add the oil and yeast mixture through the lid plug opening. Stop the machine and replace the lid plug.

Select High speed. Quickly turn the machine On and Off twice. Stop the machine and remove the lid.

While the dough rests, lightly coat an 8 1/2 x 4 1/2-inch (22 x 11 cm) loaf tin with vegetable cooking spray or shortening.

Use a wet nylon spatula to scrape the sides of the container, pulling the dough away from the container sides and into the centre of the mixture. Replace the lid.

Select High speed. Quickly turn the machine On and Off five times. Add additional water, 1 tablespoon at a time, only if the dough seems exceptionally dry. Repeat the process five times, scraping the sides of the container until the dough binds together into a soft, elastic mixture.

To aid in removing the dough from the container, turn the machine On and Off five times (this lifts the dough up and away from the blades) and quickly invert the container over the prepared tin. Let the dough fall into the tin, using a wet spatula to remove any remaining dough.

Use lightly floured fingers or an oiled spatula to shape the loaf into the tin, pressing gently to even the dough.

Colonial Bread (Loaf Form) *(continued)*	Cover the loaf with a clean, dry tea towel and allow the dough to rise until it reaches the top of the bread tin, about 18 to 20 minutes. When ready to bake, make 3 quick angled slits with a serrated knife on top of the dough. Bake in a pre-heated 375 °F (190 °C) oven for 25 to 30 minutes or until the bread reaches an internal temperature of 190 °F (88 °C) when tested with an instant-read thermometer. Cool on a wire rack for 10 minutes, then carefully remove from the loaf tin and allow to cool completely before slicing.

Nutritional Information Per Slice: 134 cal (15 % from fat, 11 % from protein, 74 % from carb) • 4 g protein
2 g total fat • 0 g saturated fat • 25 g carbohydrates • 2 g fibre • 3 g sugar • 111 mg sodium • 18 mg cholesterol

Slice into Colonial Bread after cooling...beautiful crumb and rise.

BUTTERMILK WHOLE WHEAT ROLLS

preparation: 20 minutes • processing: 15 seconds • baking time: 18-22 minutes • yield: 16 rolls

1/3 cup (80 ml)
warm water, 105 °F-115 °F
(40 °C-46 °C)

1 1/2 tablespoons honey

1 packet (1 tablespoon)
active dry yeast

2 1/2 cups (300 g)
finely ground
whole wheat flour

1 teaspoon salt

2 tablespoons (28 g)
unsalted butter,
room temperature

2/3 cup (160 ml)
buttermilk,
room temperature

1 large egg,
lightly beaten

To proof the yeast, combine the warm water, honey and yeast. Stir quickly to combine. Set aside for 5 minutes.

Place the whole wheat flour and salt into the Vitamix DRY BLADE container and secure the lid.

Select Variable 1.

Turn the machine on and slowly increase the speed to Variable 10, then to High.

Blend until a hole forms in the centre of the flour mixture, about 5 seconds.

Select Variable 3. Turn the machine on and remove the lid plug. Add the butter, buttermilk, egg and yeast mixture through the lid plug opening. Stop the machine and replace the lid plug.

Select High speed. Quickly turn the machine On and Off twice. Stop the machine and remove the lid.

While the dough rests, lightly coat an 8-inch (20 cm) square tin with vegetable cooking spray or shortening, or line a baking sheet with baking parchment (depending on the shape of your rolls).

Use a wet nylon spatula to scrape the sides of the container, pulling the dough away from the container sides and into the centre of the mixture. Replace the lid.

Select High speed. Quickly turn the machine On and Off five times. Add additional water, 1 tablespoon at a time, only if the dough seems exceptionally dry. Repeat the process five times or until the dough binds together into a soft, elastic mixture.

Place the lid on the container and allow the dough to rise until doubled in size, about 25 to 30 minutes.

Deflate the dough with a nylon spatula. Let it rise again, with the lid on, until the dough has once again doubled in size, about 20 minutes.

Turn out onto a lightly floured kneading surface and roll gently into a 16-inch (40 cm) log; cut the dough into 16 even pieces. Shape into rolls as desired; place into the tin or onto a baking sheet.

Buttermilk Whole Wheat Rolls *(continued)*

Cover the rolls with a clean, dry tea towel and allow the dough to rise until nearly doubled in size, about 35 to 45 minutes.

Bake in a pre-heated 375 °F (190 °C) oven for 18 to 22 minutes or until lightly browned. Cool on a wire rack.

Nutritional Information Per Roll: 95 cal (21 % from fat, 15 % from protein, 64 % from carb) • 4 g protein 2 g total fat • 1 g saturated fat • 16 g carbohydrates • 2 g fibre • 3 g sugar • 111 mg sodium • 18 mg cholesterol

For a delicious crust, combine 2 tablespoons (30 ml) melted butter with 3 tablespoons (45 ml) honey. When the rolls have finished baking, remove them from the oven and quickly brush the butter/honey glaze onto the hot rolls. Allow to cool before serving.

Buttermilk Whole Wheat Rolls

CINNAMON RAISIN BREAD

preparation: 30 minutes • processing: 40 seconds • baking time: 30-40 minutes
yield: 1 loaf (12 slices)

1/2 cup (120 ml)
warm water, 105 °F-115 °F (40-46 °C)

1/4 cup (50 g)
granulated sugar

1 packet (1 tablespoon)
active dry yeast

1/2 cup (112 g)
cream-style
cottage cheese

1 tablespoon (14 g)
unsalted butter,
room temperature

2 teaspoons
ground cinnamon

3/4 teaspoon salt

1 large egg

2 cups (275 g)
bread flour, divided use

1/2 cup (104 g)
toasted wheat germ

1/2 cup (72 g)
raisins, soaked in hot water for 30 minutes, then well drained, divided use

To proof the yeast, combine the warm water, sugar and yeast. Stir quickly to combine. Set aside for 5 minutes.

Place the cottage cheese, butter, cinnamon, salt and egg into the Vitamix WET BLADE container and secure the lid.

Select Variable 1.

Turn the machine on and slowly increase the speed to Variable 10, then to High.

Blend for 10 seconds. Stop and scrape the sides.

Select Variable 3. Turn the machine on and remove the lid plug. Add 1 cup (137 g) flour and the yeast mixture through the lid plug opening. Blend for 30 seconds. Stop the machine and remove the lid.

Add the remaining flour, wheat germ and 1/4 cup (72 g) pre-soaked/drained raisins to the Vitamix container and secure the lid.

Select High speed. Quickly turn the machine On and Off twice. Stop the machine and remove the lid.

While the dough rests, lightly coat an 8 1/2 x 4 1/2-inch (22 x 11 cm) loaf tin with vegetable cooking spray or shortening.

Use a wet nylon spatula to scrape the sides of the container, pulling the dough away from the container sides and into the centre of the mixture. Add the remaining raisins and secure the lid.

Select High speed. Quickly turn the machine On and Off five times. Add additional water, 1 tablespoon at a time, only if the dough seems exceptionally dry. Repeat the process five times, scraping the sides of the container until the dough binds together into a soft, elastic mixture.

To aid in removing the dough from the container, turn the machine On and Off five times (this lifts the dough up and away from the blades) and quickly invert the container over the prepared tin. Let the dough fall into the tin, using a wet spatula to remove any remaining dough.

Cinnamon Raisin Bread
(continued)

Use lightly floured fingers or an oiled spatula to shape the loaf into the tin, pressing gently to even the dough.

Cover the loaf with a clean, dry tea towel and allow the dough to rise until it reaches the top of the bread tin, about 25 to 35 minutes. When ready to bake, make 3 quick angled slits with a serrated knife on top of the dough.

Bake in a pre-heated 375 °F (190 °C) oven for 30 to 40 minutes or until the bread reaches an internal temperature of 190 °F (88 °C) when tested with an instant-read thermometer. Cool on a wire rack for 10 minutes, then carefully remove from the loaf tin and allow to cool completely before slicing.

Nutritional Information Per Slice: 162 cal (14 % from fat, 15 % from protein, 72 % from carb) • 6 g protein
3 g total fat • 1 g saturated fat • 30 g carbohydrates • 2 g fibre • 8 g sugar • 165 mg sodium • 20 mg cholesterol

It is hard to get an even distribution of raisins in the dough, so it is not perfect...which is what gives this bread its home-baked appeal.

FIVE GRAIN PIZZA

preparation: 20 minutes • processing: 35 seconds • baking time: 16-20 minutes • yield: 1 pizza (8 slices)

1 cup (240 ml) warm water, 105 °F-115 °F (40 °C-46 °C)

2 teaspoons brown sugar

1 packet (1 tablespoon) active dry yeast

3/4 cup (94 g) unbleached, all-purpose flour

3/4 cup (90 g) + 1 tablespoon whole wheat flour

1/4 cup (26 g) light rye flour

2 tablespoons (15 g) spelt flour

2 tablespoons (15 g) barley flour

2 tablespoons (21 g) flax seed or meal

2 tablespoons (15 g) whole grain cornmeal plus additional for sprinkling on the pizza tin

1/2 teaspoon salt

1 tablespoon olive oil

Topping:

2 tablespoons (30 ml) olive oil

1/3 cup (33 g) grated Parmesan cheese

1 1/3 cups (320 g) pizza sauce

Other toppings if desired

1 1/4 cups (141 g) grated mozzarella cheese

To proof the yeast, combine the warm water, brown sugar and yeast. Stir quickly to combine. Set aside for 5 minutes.

Place the flours (all-purpose, whole wheat, rye, spelt and barley), flax, cornmeal and salt into the Vitamix DRY BLADE container in the order listed and secure the lid.

Select Variable 1.

Turn the machine on and slowly increase the speed to Variable 10, then to High.

Blend until the mixture is blended and a hole forms in the centre of the ingredients, about 20 seconds. Stop the machine.

Select Variable 1 and remove the lid plug. Turn the machine on and slowly increase the speed to Variable 6. Add the yeast mixture and olive oil through the lid plug opening. Stop the machine and replace the lid plug.

Select High speed. Quickly turn the machine On and Off twice. Stop the machine and remove the lid.

While the dough rests, lightly coat the pizza tin with additional cornmeal.

Use a wet nylon spatula to scrape the sides of the container, pulling the dough away from the container sides and into the centre of the mixture. Replace the lid.

Select High speed. Quickly turn the machine On and Off five times. Add additional water, 1 tablespoon at a time, only if the dough seems exceptionally dry. Repeat the process five times, scraping the sides of the container until the dough binds together into a soft, elastic mixture.

To aid in removing the dough from the container, turn the machine On and Off five times (this lifts the dough up and away from the blades) and quickly invert the container over a clean work surface, lightly dusted with flour.

Cover the dough with a clean, dry tea towel or an inverted bowl and let rest for 15 minutes.

Five Grain Pizza
(continued)

Deflate with the heel of your hand, keeping it round. Using a rolling pin, roll lightly from the centre outwards using equal strokes in each direction, lifting and turning the dough 1/4 turn after each stroke. The final shape should be about 1-inch (2.5 cm) larger than your tin. Fit it into the tin. Pinch up a collar around the edge to hold the filling

Brush the dough lightly with olive oil, then sprinkle with Parmesan cheese. Spoon pizza sauce onto the dough, spreading with the back of a spoon. Top with any other of your favourite toppings, then sprinkle evenly with mozzarella cheese.

Bake on the bottom rack of a pre-heated 425 °F (220 °C) oven for 16 to 20 minutes until the bottom crust is lightly browned and the cheese is bubbly.

Remove the pizza tin from the oven, let stand for 5 minutes to allow the cheese to set, then cut into serving pieces.

Nutritional Information Per Slice (with toppings): 272 cal (39 % from fat, 17 % from protein, 44 % from carb)
12 g protein • 12 g total fat • 4 g saturated fat • 30 g carbohydrates • 4 g fibre • 5 g sugar • 551 mg sodium
15 mg cholesterol

Rolling from the centre outwards and turning the dough helps it to retain a round shape.

FRENCH BREAD

preparation: 10 minutes • processing: 15 seconds • baking time: 30-40 minutes
yield: 1 loaf (16-18 slices)

1 cup (240 ml)
warm water, divided use,
105 °F -115 °F
(40 °C-46 °C)

1 packet (1 tablespoon)
active dry yeast

2 1/2 cups (312 g)
unbleached,
all-purpose flour

1 teaspoon salt

1 tablespoon olive oil

2 tablespoons (15 g)
whole grain cornmeal

1 egg white beaten
with 1 tablespoon water
(for brushing the dough
before baking)

To proof the yeast, combine 1/2 cup (120 ml) warm water with the yeast. Stir quickly to combine. Set aside for 5 minutes.

Place the flour and salt into the Vitamix DRY BLADE container and secure the lid.

Select Variable 1.

Turn the machine on and slowly increase the speed to Variable 6.

Blend until a hole forms in the centre of the flour mixture, about 5 seconds.

Select Variable 3. Turn the machine on and remove the lid plug. Add the yeast mixture and remaining 1/2 cup (120 ml) warm water through the lid plug opening. Stop the machine and replace the lid plug.

Select High speed. Quickly turn the machine On and Off twice. Stop the machine and remove the lid.

While the dough rests, grease a medium-size mixing bowl with the olive oil and sprinkle the cornmeal on a baking sheet.

Use a wet nylon spatula to scrape the sides of the container, pulling the dough away from the container sides and into the centre of the mixture. Replace the lid.

Select High speed. Quickly turn the machine On and Off five times. Add additional water, 1 tablespoon at a time, only if the dough seems exceptionally dry. Repeat the process five times, scraping the sides of the container until the dough binds together into a soft, elastic mixture.

To aid in removing the dough from the container, turn the machine On and Off five times (this lifts the dough up and away from the blades) and quickly invert the container over the prepared bowl, using a wet spatula to remove any remaining dough. Turn the dough to coat well. Cover with cling film and allow to rise until almost triple in size, 45 minutes to 1 hour.

French Bread *(continued)*

Lightly knock back the dough and place on a floured work surface, adding additional flour as needed to make a workable, but still soft, dough. Roll into a 12 x 6-inch (30 x 15 cm) rectangle with a floured rolling pin. Roll from the long end down, pinching the seams together and using water to seal.

Place the dough, seam side down, on the prepared baking sheet. Cover with a clean, dry tea towel and allow the dough to rise until it doubles in size, about 45 minutes to 1 hour.

Brush the top of the loaf with egg mixture and make three to four diagonal slits about 1/4 inch deep on the top of the loaf using a sharp, serrated knife.

Bake in a pre-heated 425 °F (220 °C) oven for 30 to 40 minutes or until the bread is well browned and reaches an internal temperature of 190 °F (88 °C) when tested with an instant-read thermometer. Cool on a wire rack for 10 minutes, then carefully remove from the baking sheet and allow to cool completely before slicing.

Nutritional Information Per Slice: 86 cal (12 % from fat, 12 % from protein, 76 % from carb) • 3 g protein
1 g total fat • 0 g saturated fat • 16 g carbohydrates • 1 g fibre • 0 g sugar • 152 mg sodium • 0 mg cholesterol

A metal spatula helps in coaxing the bread off the baking sheet.

HAWAIIAN BREAD

preparation: 15 minutes • processing: 25 seconds • baking time: 35-40 minutes
yield: 1 loaf (8-10 slices)

2 tablespoons (30 ml) warm water, 105 °F -115 °F (40 °C-46 °C)

1/2 cup (120 ml) warm milk 105 °F -115 °F (40 °C-46 °C)

1 packet (1 tablespoon) active dry yeast

1/2 teaspoon plus 1/2 cup (100 g) sugar, divided use

2 1/2 cups (312 g) unbleached, all-purpose flour

1/4 teaspoon salt

1/4 cup (56 g) unsalted butter, melted

2 large eggs, beaten

1 large egg beaten with 1 teaspoon water (for brushing the dough before baking)

Additional sugar for dusting the loaf

To proof the yeast, combine the warm water, warm milk, yeast, and 1/2 teaspoon of the sugar. Stir quickly to combine. Set aside for 5 minutes.

Place the flour, 1/2 cup (100 g) sugar and salt into the Vitamix DRY BLADE container and secure the lid.

Select Variable 1.

Turn the machine on and slowly increase the speed to Variable 6.

Blend until a hole forms in the centre of the flour mixture, about 5 seconds.

Select Variable 3. Turn the machine on and remove the lid plug. Add the melted butter, eggs and yeast mixture through the lid plug opening. Stop the machine and replace the lid plug.

Select High speed. Quickly turn the machine On and Off twice. Stop the machine and remove the lid.

While the dough rests, lightly coat a 9-inch (23 cm) pie tin with vegetable cooking spray or shortening.

Use a wet nylon spatula to scrape the sides of the container, pulling the dough away from the container sides and into the centre of the mixture. Replace the lid.

Select High speed. Quickly turn the machine On and Off five times. Add additional water, 1 tablespoon at a time, only if the dough seems exceptionally dry. Repeat the process five times, scraping the sides of the container until the dough binds together into a soft, elastic mixture.

To aid in removing the dough from the container, turn the machine On and Off five times (this lifts the dough up and away from the blades) and quickly invert the container over a greased bowl (using a wet spatula to remove any remaining dough) and turn to coat the entire surface.

Cover the bowl with cling film that has been sprayed with vegetable cooking spray. Let the dough rise until doubled in size, about 40 to 45 minutes.

Hawaiian Bread
(continued)

Knock back and remove the dough to a floured work surface. Knead again for 1 to 2 minutes. Place in the prepared tin and use lightly floured fingers or an oiled spatula to shape the dough into the tin, pressing gently to even the dough.

Cover the dough with a clean, dry tea towel and allow it to rise until doubled in size, about 40 minutes. When ready to bake, brush the top with beaten egg mixture and sprinkle with sugar.

Bake in a pre-heated 350 °F (180 °C) oven for 35 to 40 minutes or until the bread is golden in colour and reaches an internal temperature of 190 °F (88 °C) when tested with an instant-read thermometer. Cool on a wire rack.

Nutritional Information Per Slice: 233 cal (29 % from fat, 10 % from protein, 61 % from carb) • 6 g protein
7 g total fat • 4 g saturated fat • 35 g carbohydrates • 1 g fibre • 11 g sugar • 126 mg sodium • 76 mg cholesterol

HEARTY MULTI-GRAIN BREAD

preparation: 20 minutes • processing: 25 seconds • baking time: 40-50 minutes
yield: 1 loaf (12 slices)

1 1/4 cups (300 ml) warm water, 105 °F-115 °F (40 °C-46 °C)

1 tablespoon honey

1 packet (1 tablespoon) active dry yeast

1 1/2 cups (156 g) unbleached, all-purpose flour

1/2 cup (60 g) whole wheat flour

1/4 cup (26 g) light rye flour

1 tablespoon wheat germ

1 tablespoon rolled oats

2 teaspoons whole grain cornmeal

2 teaspoons millet

2 teaspoons barley flour

2 teaspoons buckwheat flour

1/4 teaspoon flax meal

1/2 teaspoon salt

1 tablespoon light olive oil or grape seed oil

1 tablespoon sunflower seeds

1 tablespoon molasses

1/4 teaspoon sesame seeds, to sprinkle on top

To proof the yeast, combine the warm water, honey and yeast. Stir quickly to combine. Set aside for 5 minutes.

Place the all-purpose flour, whole wheat flour, rye flour, wheat germ, rolled oats, cornmeal, millet, barley flour, buckwheat flour, flax meal and salt into the Vitamix DRY BLADE container and secure the lid.

Select Variable 1.

Turn the machine on and slowly increase the speed to Variable 6.

Blend until a hole forms in the centre of the flour mixture, about 5 seconds.

Select Variable 3. Turn the machine on and remove the lid plug. Add the oil, sunflower seeds, molasses and yeast mixture through the lid plug opening. Stop the machine and replace the lid plug.

Select High speed. Quickly turn the machine On and Off twice. Stop the machine and remove the lid.

While the dough rests, lightly coat an 8 1/2 x 4 1/2-inch (22 x 11 cm) loaf tin with vegetable cooking spray or shortening.

Use a wet nylon spatula to scrape the sides of the container, pulling the dough away from the container sides and into the centre of the mixture. Replace the lid.

Select High speed. Quickly turn the machine On and Off five times. Add additional water, 1 tablespoon at a time, only if the dough seems exceptionally dry. Repeat the process five times, scraping the sides of the container until the dough binds together into a soft, elastic mixture.

To aid in removing the dough from the container, turn the machine On and Off five times (this lifts the dough up and away from the blades) and quickly invert the container over the prepared tin. Let the dough fall into the tin, using a wet spatula to remove any remaining dough.

Use lightly floured fingers or an oiled spatula to shape the loaf into the tin, pressing gently to even the dough.

Hearty Multi-Grain Bread *(continued)*	Cover the loaf with a clean, dry tea towel and allow the dough to rise until it reaches the top of the bread tin, about 25 to 30 minutes. When ready to bake, make 3 quick angled slits with a serrated knife on top of the dough. Sprinkle with 1/4 teaspoon sesame seeds. Bake in a pre-heated 350 °F (180 °C) oven for 40 to 50 minutes or until the bread reaches an internal temperature of 190 °F (88 °C) when tested with an instant-read thermometer. Cool on a wire rack for 10 minutes, then carefully remove from the loaf tin and allow to cool completely before slicing.

Nutritional Information Per Slice: 119 cal (13 % from fat, 11 % from protein, 75 % from carb) • 3 g protein
2 g total fat • 0 g saturated fat • 23 g carbohydrates • 2 g fibre • 3 g sugar • 101 mg sodium • 0 mg cholesterol

If you don't have some of the speciality grains or flours mentioned above, simply replace them with whole wheat flour or any other speciality flour that you have. (Remember, your machine can grind any of the above grains into flour.)

OAT BRAN BREAD

preparation: 10 minutes • processing: 30 seconds • baking time: 30-35 minutes
yield: 1 loaf (12 slices)

1 egg white and enough warm water, 105 °F-115 °F (40 °C-46 °C) to make 1 1/4 cups (300 ml)

2 tablespoons (30 ml) molasses

1 packet (1 tablespoon) active dry yeast

1-1 1/4 cups (80-100 g) oat bran (or rolled oats)

1 1/4 cups (150 g) whole wheat flour

1 cup (125 g) unbleached, all-purpose flour

1 teaspoon salt

1 tablespoon light olive oil or grape seed oil

To proof the yeast, combine the warm water, molasses and yeast. Stir quickly to combine. Set aside for 5 minutes.

Place the oat bran, flours and salt into the Vitamix DRY BLADE container and secure the lid.

Select Variable 1.

Turn the machine on and slowly increase the speed to Variable 6.

Blend until a hole forms in the centre of the flour mixture, about 10 seconds, using the tamper as needed to aid in mixing.

Select Variable 3. Turn the machine on and remove the lid plug. Add the yeast mixture and oil through the lid plug opening. Stop the machine and replace the lid plug.

Select High speed. Quickly turn the machine On and Off twice. Stop the machine and remove the lid.

While the dough rests, lightly coat an 8 1/2 x 4 1/2-inch (22 x 11 cm) loaf tin with vegetable cooking spray or shortening.

Use a wet nylon spatula to scrape the sides of the container, pulling the dough away from the container sides and into the centre of the mixture. Replace the lid.

Select High speed. Quickly turn the machine On and Off five times. Add additional water, 1 tablespoon at a time, only if the dough seems exceptionally dry. Repeat the process five times, scraping the sides of the container until the dough binds together into a soft, elastic mixture.

To aid in removing the dough from the container, turn the machine On and Off five times (this lifts the dough up and away from the blades) and quickly invert the container over the prepared tin. Let the dough fall into the tin, using a wet spatula to remove any remaining dough.

Use lightly floured fingers or an oiled spatula to shape the loaf into the tin, pressing gently to even the dough.

Oat Bran Bread
(continued)

Cover the loaf with a clean, dry tea towel and allow the dough to rise until it reaches the top of the bread tin, about 15 to 18 minutes. When ready to bake, make 3 quick angled slits with a serrated knife on top of the dough.

Bake in a pre-heated 350 °F (180 °C) oven for 30 to 35 minutes or until the bread reaches an internal temperature of 190 °F (88 °C) when tested with an instant-read thermometer. Cool on a wire rack for 10 minutes, then carefully remove from the loaf tin and allow to cool completely before slicing.

Nutritional Information Per Slice: 124 cal (13 % from fat, 14 % from protein, 73 % from carb) • 5 g protein
2 g total fat • 0 g saturated fat • 25 g carbohydrates • 3 g fibre • 2 g sugar • 8 mg sodium • 0 mg cholesterol

RYE FOCACCIA

preparation: 15 minutes • processing: 30 seconds • baking time: 35-40 minutes
yield: 1 loaf (8-10 slices)

3/4 cup (180 ml)
warm water, 105 °F-115 °F (40 °C-46 °C)

1 tablespoon
granulated sugar

1 packet (1 tablespoon)
active dry yeast

1 1/2 cups (188 g)
unbleached, all-purpose flour

1 cup (104 g)
light rye flour

1/2 cup (66 g)
coarsely chopped Swiss cheese

1 teaspoon salt

1 tablespoon dill

1 tablespoon
caraway seeds

3/4 cup (180 ml)
buttermilk, room temperature

Additional for topping:

2 tablespoons (30 ml)
extra virgin olive oil

1 1/2 teaspoons
Kosher salt

1/2 cup (66 g)
coarsely chopped Swiss cheese

1 teaspoon dill

To proof the yeast, combine the warm water, sugar and yeast. Stir quickly to combine. Set aside for 5 minutes.

Place the flours, cheese, salt, dill and caraway seeds into the Vitamix DRY BLADE container and secure the lid.

Select Variable 1.

Turn the machine on and slowly increase the speed to Variable 10, then to High.

Blend for 15 seconds. Reduce the speed to Variable 6 and blend until a hole forms in the centre of the flour mixture, about 5 seconds. Stop the machine.

Select Variable 1 and remove the lid plug. Turn the machine on and slowly increase the speed to Variable 6. Add the buttermilk and yeast mixture through the lid plug opening. Stop the machine and replace the lid plug.

Select High speed. Quickly turn the machine On and Off twice. Stop the machine and remove the lid.

While the dough rests, lightly coat a 9-inch (23 cm) round cake tin with vegetable cooking spray or shortening.

Use a wet nylon spatula to scrape the sides of the container, pulling the dough away from the container sides and into the centre of the mixture. Replace the lid.

Select High speed. Quickly turn the machine On and Off five times. Add additional water, 1 tablespoon at a time, only if the dough seems exceptionally dry. Repeat the process five times, scraping the sides of the container until the dough binds together into a soft, elastic mixture.

To aid in removing the dough from the container, turn the machine On and Off five times (this lifts the dough up and away from the blades) and quickly invert the container over the prepared tin. Let the dough fall into the tin, using a wet spatula to remove any remaining dough.

Use lightly floured fingers or an oiled spatula to shape the loaf into the tin, pressing gently to even the dough.

Rye Focaccia *(continued)*

Cover the tin with a clean, dry tea towel and allow the dough to rise until it reaches the top of the tin, about 30 minutes. When ready to bake, dimple the dough with your clean fingertips then brush the top of the dough with olive oil. Sprinkle with the Kosher salt, dill and remaining Swiss cheese.

Bake in a pre-heated 350 °F (180 °C) oven for 35 to 40 minutes or until the bread reaches an internal temperature of 190 °F (88 °C) when tested with an instant-read thermometer. Cool on a wire rack for 10 minutes, then carefully remove from the tin and allow to cool completely before slicing.

Nutritional Information Per Slice: 202 cal (32 % from fat, 15 % from protein, 52 % from carb) • 8 g protein
7 g total fat • 3 g saturated fat • 26 g carbohydrates • 3 g fibre • 3 g sugar • 448 mg sodium • 14 mg cholesterol

Rye doughs are always stickier and harder to work with than wheat doughs, so be patient and don't add too much flour simply to prevent sticking, or the bread will be too dense.

SOFT PRETZELS

preparation: 10 minutes • processing: 15 seconds • baking time: 8-10 minutes • yield: 12 pretzels

3/4 cup (180 ml)
warm water, 105 °F-115 °F
(40 °C-46 °C)

1/4 cup (55 g)
brown sugar, packed

1 packet (1 tablespoon)
active dry yeast

1/4 cup (30 g)
whole wheat flour

1/2 cup (62 g)
unbleached,
all-purpose flour

1 1/2 cups (205 g)
bread (high gluten) flour

Pinch of salt

1 large egg mixed with
2 tablespoons (30 ml)
water (for brushing the
dough before baking)

Kosher salt

To proof the yeast, combine the warm water, brown sugar and yeast. Stir quickly to combine. Set aside for 5 minutes.

Place the flours and salt into the Vitamix DRY BLADE container and secure the lid.

Select Variable 1.

Turn the machine on and slowly increase the speed to Variable 6.

Blend until a hole forms in the centre of the flour mixture, about 5 seconds.

Select Variable 3. Turn the machine on and remove the lid plug. Add the yeast mixture through the lid plug opening. Stop the machine and replace the lid plug.

Select High speed. Quickly turn the machine On and Off twice. Stop the machine and remove the lid.

While the dough rests, lightly coat a baking sheet with vegetable cooking spray or shortening.

Use a wet nylon spatula to scrape the sides of the container, pulling the dough away from the container sides and into the centre of the mixture. Replace the lid.

Select High speed. Quickly turn the machine On and Off five times. Add additional water, 1 tablespoon at a time, only if the dough seems exceptionally dry. Repeat the process five times, scraping the sides of the container until the dough binds together into a soft, elastic mixture.

With the lid on the container, let the dough rise until doubled in size, about 15 minutes.

Transfer the dough to a lightly floured surface and divide into 12 pieces. With your palms, roll each piece to form a rope about 12-inches to 18-inches (30 cm-46 cm) long. Loop into an oval, twist the ends together and gently press the ends to the top side of the oval.

Soft Pretzels *(continued)*	Whisk together the egg and water. Quickly and gently brush the egg mixture onto each pretzel shape and then sprinkle with kosher salt. Bake in a pre-heated 450 °F (230 °C) oven for 8 to 10 minutes or until crispy and lightly browned. Best when served warm

Nutritional Information Per Pretzel: 117 cal (8 % from fat, 13 % from protein, 79 % from carb) • 4 g protein
1 g total fat • 0 g saturated fat • 23 g carbohydrates • 1 g fibre • 5 g sugar • 11 mg sodium • 18 mg cholesterol

If you wish to top the pretzels with cinnamon and sugar, don't sprinkle with coarse salt before baking. Once they have been removed from the oven, brush with melted butter and sprinkle with a mixture of cinnamon and sugar.

PIZZA

preparation: 15 minutes • processing: 30 seconds • baking time: 15-18 minutes
yield: 1 large pizza (8 slices)

1 cup (240 ml) warm water, 105 °F-115 °F (40 °C-46 °C)

2 teaspoons granulated sugar

1 packet (1 tablespoon) active dry yeast

2 1/2 cups (312 g) unbleached, all-purpose flour

1/2 teaspoon salt

1 tablespoon light olive oil

2 tablespoons (15 g) whole grain cornmeal for sprinkling on the pizza tin

Topping:

2 tablespoons (30 ml) olive oil

1/3 cup (33 g) grated Parmesan cheese

1 1/3 cups (320 g) pizza sauce

1 1/4 cups (141 g) grated mozzarella cheese

To proof the yeast, combine the warm water, sugar and yeast. Stir quickly to combine. Set aside for 5 minutes.

Place the flour and salt into the Vitamix DRY BLADE container in the order listed and secure the lid.

Select Variable 1.

Turn the machine on and slowly increase the speed to Variable 6.

Blend until the mixture is blended and a hole forms in the centre of the ingredients, about 5 seconds.

Stop the machine and remove the lid plug. Select Variable 1. Turn the machine on and slowly increase the speed to Variable 6. Add the yeast mixture and olive oil through the lid plug opening. Stop the machine and replace the lid plug.

Select High speed. Quickly turn the machine On and Off twice. Stop the machine and remove the lid.

While the dough rests, lightly coat the pizza tin with the cornmeal.

Use a wet nylon spatula to scrape the sides of the container, pulling the dough away from the container sides and into the centre of the mixture. Replace the lid.

Select High speed. Quickly turn the machine On and Off five times. Add additional water, 1 tablespoon at a time, only if the dough seems exceptionally dry. Repeat the process five times, scraping the sides of the container until the dough binds together into a soft, elastic mixture.

To aid in removing the dough from the container, turn the machine On and Off five times (this lifts the dough up and away from the blades) and quickly invert the container over a clean work surface, lightly dusted with flour.

Cover the dough with a clean, dry tea towel or an inverted bowl and let rest for 15 minutes.

Deflate with the heel of your hand, keeping it round. Using a rolling pin, roll lightly from the centre outwards using equal strokes in each direction, lifting and turning the dough 1/4 turn after each stroke. The final shape should be about 1-inch (2.5 cm) larger than your tin. Fit it into the tin. Pinch up a collar around the edge to hold the filling.

Pizza *(continued)*

Brush the dough lightly with olive oil, then sprinkle with Parmesan cheese. Spoon pizza sauce onto the dough, spreading with the back of a spoon. Top with any other of your favourite toppings, then sprinkle evenly with mozzarella cheese.

Bake on the bottom rack of a pre-heated 425 °F (220 °C) oven for 15 to 18 minutes until the bottom crust is lightly browned and the cheese is bubbly.

Remove the pizza tin from the oven, let stand for 5 minutes to allow the cheese to set, then cut into serving pieces.

Nutritional Information Per Slice: 319 cal (35 % from fat, 15 % from protein, 51 % from carb) • 12 g protein
12 g total fat • 4 g saturated fat • 40 g carbohydrates • 3 g fibre • 6 g sugar • 320 mg sodium
13 mg cholesterol

Rolling from the centre outwards and turning the dough helps it to retain a round shape.

Pizza

POPPY SEED BRAID

preparation: 15 minutes • processing: 12 seconds • baking time: 35-40 minutes
yield: 1 loaf (12 slices)

4 tablespoons (60 ml) warm water, 105 °F-115 °F (40 °C-46 °C)

1 packet (1 tablespoon) active dry yeast

1/3 cup (80 ml) milk

1/4 cup (56 g) unsalted butter

1/3 cup (80 ml) honey

1/2 teaspoon salt

1 large egg

2 1/4 cups (281 g) unbleached, all-purpose flour plus extra for final mixing and rolling the dough

1 1/3 cups (320 g) Poppy Seed Filling (recipe on page 74)

1 large egg plus 2 tablespoons (30 ml) milk for brushing the braid

To proof the yeast, combine the warm water and yeast. Stir quickly to combine. Set aside for 5 minutes.

Scald the milk in a small saucepan, then add the butter and honey; cool to 110 °F to 115 °F (43 °C-46 °C).

Place the flour and salt into the Vitamix DRY BLADE container and secure the lid.

Select Variable 1.

Turn the machine on and slowly increase the speed to Variable 6.

Blend until a hole forms in the centre of the mixture, about 5 seconds.

Select Variable 3. Turn the machine on and remove the lid plug. Pour the egg, yeast mixture and milk mixture through the lid plug opening. Stop the machine and replace the lid plug.

Select High speed. Quickly turn the machine On and Off twice. Stop the machine and remove the lid.

While the dough rests, lightly grease a large bowl with vegetable cooking spray or shortening.

Use a wet nylon spatula to scrape the sides of the Vitamix container. Pull the dough away from the container sides and into the centre of the mixture. Replace the lid.

Select High speed. Quickly turn the machine On and Off five times. Add additional water, 1 tablespoon at a time, only if the dough seems exceptionally dry. Repeat the process five times, scraping the sides of the container until the dough binds together into a soft, elastic mixture.

To remove the dough from the container, turn the machine On and Off five times (to assist in lifting the dough up and away from the blades). Invert the container over the greased bowl and allow it to fall into the bowl. Turn the dough once to coat the entire surface; cover with a clean tea towel and leave to rise for 20 to 30 minutes.

Transfer the dough to a floured work surface. Roll it into a large rectangle, turning and flouring often, about 9 x 15 inches (23 x 38 cm) in size.

Poppy Seed Braid
(continued)

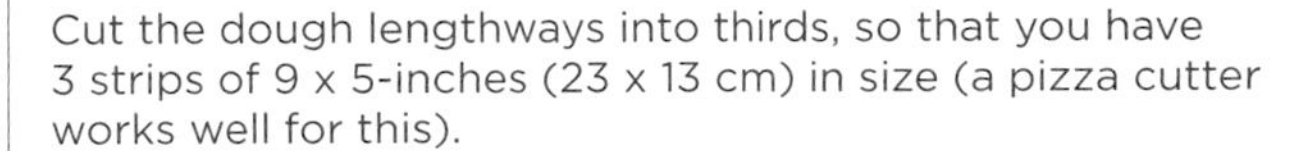

Cut the dough lengthways into thirds, so that you have 3 strips of 9 x 5-inches (23 x 13 cm) in size (a pizza cutter works well for this).

Spread the centre of each section with the Poppy Seed Filling. Dampen both ends of each strip and also dampen one long side with warm water.

Roll each third lengthways so that the poppy seeds are rolled inside Swiss-roll style. Seal the wet edges and then seal both ends of the strands.

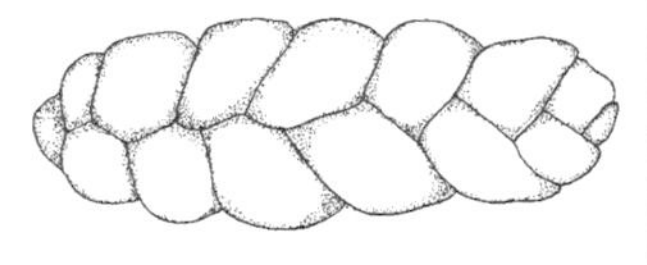

Line up the three strands on a baking parchment lined baking sheet (seam sides down). Braid the 3 strands loosely so the dough has room to expand. Seal the ends with your fingers and some additional water and tuck the sealed portion under the braid so the strands won't come apart during baking.

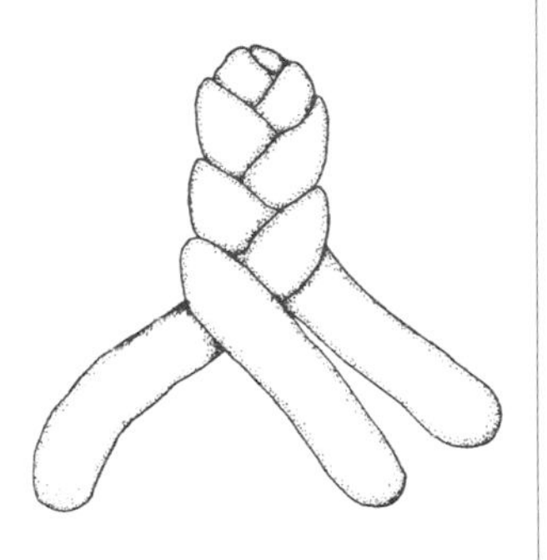

Cover with a clean, dry tea towel and leave to rise for about 20 to 25 minutes.

Brush the braid surface with the egg and milk mixture. Bake in a pre-heated 350 °F (180 °C) oven for 35 to 40 minutes or until golden brown and it reaches an internal temperature of 190 °F (88 °C) when tested with an instant-read thermometer.

Cool on a wire rack for 10 minutes, then very carefully slide from the tin and allow to cool completely on a wire rack before slicing.

Nutritional Information Per Slice (with Poppy Seed Filling): 282 cal (36 % from fat, 10 % from protein, 54 % from carb) • 7 g protein • 12 g total fat • 4 g saturated fat • 39 g carbohydrates • 2 g fibre • 18 g sugar 133 mg sodium • 48 mg cholesterol

POPPY SEED FILLING

preparation: 10 minutes • processing: 25 seconds • cooking time: 30-45 minutes
yield: 1 1/3 cups (320 g) filling, plus extra ground poppy seeds for later use

2 cups (282 g) poppy seeds

1 cup (240 ml) milk

1/2 cup (100 g) granulated sugar

2 teaspoons unsalted butter

2 teaspoons lemon zest

Place the poppy seeds into the Vitamix DRY BLADE container and secure the lid.

Select Variable 1.

Turn the machine on and slowly increase the speed to Variable 10, then to High.

Blend for 10 seconds.

Stop the machine and scrape the container sides with a spatula.

Replace the lid and grind for an additional 15 seconds, or until at the desired consistency. Measure 1 cup (142 g) ground poppy seeds. Freeze the remaining ground poppy seeds in a sealed container.

For the filling:

Combine 1 cup (142 g) ground poppy seeds, milk, sugar, butter and lemon zest in a medium saucepan.

Cook on a low heat, stirring often, for 30 to 45 minutes or until the desired thickness is reached. Remove from the heat to cool; stirring occasionally. When cool, cover and store in refrigerator until needed.

Nutritional Information Per 2 Tablespoons (30 g) Serving: 132 cal (48 % from fat, 10 % from protein, 42 % from carb) • 3 g protein • 7 g total fat • 1 g saturated fat • 15 g carbohydrates • 1 g fibre • 12 g sugar 16 mg sodium • 3 mg cholesterol

Poppy Seed Filling

SPELT BREAD

preparation: 10 minutes • processing: 1 minute 30 seconds • baking time: 35-40 minutes
yield: 1 loaf (12 slices)

1 cup (240 ml)
warm water, 105 °F-115 °F (40 °C-46 °C)

1 tablespoon honey

1 packet (1 tablespoon) active dry yeast

1 3/4 cups (315 g) whole kernel spelt or 2 1/2 cups (180 g) spelt flour

1/2 teaspoon salt

1 tablespoon light olive oil

To proof the yeast, combine the warm water, honey and yeast. Stir quickly to combine. Set aside for 5 minutes.

If starting with whole kernel spelt: place the spelt and salt into the Vitamix DRY BLADE container and secure the lid.

Select Variable 1.

Turn the machine on and slowly increase the speed to Variable 10, then to High.

Grind for 1 minute, using the tamper (inserted through the lid plug) to press the flour mixture into the blades. Remove the tamper during the last 5 seconds to allow a hole to form in the centre of the flour mixture.

If starting with spelt flour: place the spelt flour and salt into the Vitamix DRY BLADE container and secure the lid.

Select Variable 1.

Turn the machine on and slowly increase the speed to Variable 6.

Blend until a hole forms in the centre of the flour mixture, about 5 seconds.

Select Variable 3. Turn the machine on and remove the lid plug. Add the oil and yeast mixture through the lid plug opening. Stop the machine and replace the lid plug.

To mix the dough, select the High speed. Quickly turn the machine On and Off twice. Stop the machine and remove the lid.

While the dough rests, lightly coat an 8 1/2 x 4 1/2-inch (22 x 11 cm) loaf tin with vegetable cooking spray or shortening.

Use a wet nylon spatula to scrape the sides of the container, pulling the dough away from the container sides and into the centre of the mixture. Replace the lid.

Select High speed. Quickly turn the machine On and Off five times. Add additional water, 1 tablespoon at a time, only if the dough seems exceptionally dry. Repeat the process five times, scraping the sides of the container until the dough binds together into a soft, elastic mixture.

Spelt Bread *(continued)*

To aid in removing the dough from the container, turn the machine On and Off five times (this lifts the dough up and away from the blades) and quickly invert the container over the prepared tin. Let the dough fall into the tin, using a wet spatula to remove any remaining dough.

Use lightly floured fingers or an oiled spatula to shape the loaf into the tin, pressing gently to even the dough.

Cover the loaf with a clean, dry tea towel and allow the dough to rise until it reaches the top of the bread tin, about 15 to 20 minutes. When ready to bake, make 3 quick angled slits with a serrated knife on top of the dough.

Bake in a pre-heated 350 °F (180 °C) oven for 35 to 40 minutes or until the bread reaches an internal temperature of 190 °F (88 °C). Cool on a wire rack for 10 minutes, then carefully remove from the loaf tin and allow to cool completely before slicing.

Nutritional Information Per Slice: 106 cal (16 % from fat, 13 % from protein, 71 % from carb) • 4 g protein
2 g total fat • 0 g saturated fat • 21 g carbohydrates • 3 g fibre • 3 g sugar • 99 mg sodium • 0 mg cholesterol

Bread sliced while still warm, especially whole grain bread, is often wet inside; allow to cool completely before cutting.

SOURDOUGH BREAD (BASIC AND RICH)

preparation: 20 minutes • processing: 30 seconds • baking time: 30-40 minutes
yield: 1 loaf (12 slices)

Basic Recipe

1 cup (240 ml)
Potato Starter
(recipe on page 75)

1/2 teaspoon salt

1-1 1/2 cups (125-188 g)
unbleached,
all-purpose flour

Rich Recipe

1 cup (240 ml)
Potato Starter
(recipe on page 75)

1/4 cup (60 ml) honey

1 tablespoon
unsalted butter, softened

1/2 teaspoon salt

1 1/3 -1 2/3 cups
(166-208 g)
unbleached,
all-purpose flour

Choose either the Basic Recipe or the Rich Recipe.

Place all the ingredients in the Vitamix DRY BLADE container in the order listed and secure the lid.

To mix the dough, select the High speed. Quickly turn the machine On and Off twice. Stop the machine and remove the lid.

While the dough rests, lightly coat an 8 x 4-inch (20 x 10 cm) loaf tin with vegetable cooking spray or shortening.

Use a wet nylon spatula to scrape the sides of the container, pulling the dough away from the container sides and into the centre of the mixture. Replace the lid.

Select High speed. Quickly turn the machine On and Off five times. Add additional water, 1 tablespoon at a time, only if the dough seems exceptionally dry. Repeat the process five times, scraping the sides of the container until the dough binds together into a soft, elastic mixture.

To aid in removing the dough from the container, turn the machine On and Off five times (this lifts the dough up and away from the blades) and quickly invert the container over the prepared tin. Let the dough fall into the tin, using a wet spatula to remove any remaining dough.

Use lightly floured fingers or an oiled spatula to shape the loaf into the tin, pressing gently to even the dough.

Cover the tin with a clean, dry tea towel and allow the dough to rise until it reaches the top of the tin, about 30 minutes. When ready to bake, dimple the dough with your clean fingertips then brush the top of the dough with olive oil. Sprinkle with the Kosher salt, dill and remaining Swiss cheese.

Spelt Bread (*continued*)	Bake in a pre-heated 350 °F (180 °C) oven for 35 to 40 minutes or until the bread reaches an internal temperature of 190 °F (88 °C) when tested with an instant-read thermometer. Cool on a wire rack for 10 minutes, then carefully remove from the tin and allow to cool completely before slicing.

Basic Recipe: Nutritional Information Per Slice: 57 cal (3 % from fat, 12 % from protein, 85 % from carb) • 2 g protein
0 g total fat • 0 g saturated fat • 12 g carbohydrates • 1 g fibre • 0 g sugar • 99 mg sodium
0 mg cholesterol

Rich Recipe: Nutritional Information Per Slice: 106 cal (10 % from fat, 9 % from protein, 81 % from carb) • 2 g protein
1 g total fat • 1 g saturated fat • 22 g carbohydrates • 1 g fibre • 6 g sugar • 99 mg sodium • 3 mg cholesterol

SWEET POTATO ROLLS

preparation: 15 minutes • processing: 30 seconds • baking time: 20-25 minutes • yield: 12 rolls

1/2 pound (227 g) sweet potatoes, peeled and quartered

1 packet (1 tablespoon) active dry yeast

1 tablespoon granulated sugar

1 cup (125 g) unbleached, all-purpose flour

1 1/3 cups (160 g) whole wheat flour plus extra as needed

1/2 teaspoon salt

2 tablespoons (28 g) unsalted butter, melted

2 tablespoons (30 ml) honey

1 tablespoon vegetable oil

1 large egg, beaten to blend

Cook the potato in a saucepan of simmering water until tender, about 20 minutes. Drain, reserving 1/3 cup (80 ml) cooking liquid. Mash the potatoes lightly, then set aside. Cool the cooking liquid until it reaches 115 °F (46 °C).

To proof the yeast, combine 1/3 cup (80 ml) cooking liquid, yeast and sugar. Stir quickly to combine. Set aside for 5 minutes.

Place the flours and salt into the Vitamix DRY BLADE container and secure the lid.

Select Variable 1.

Turn the machine on and slowly increase the speed to Variable 10, then to High.

Blend until a hole forms in the centre of the flour mixture, about 5 seconds. Stop the machine.

Select Variable 3. Turn the machine on and remove the lid plug. Add the potato, butter, honey, oil, egg and yeast mixture through the lid plug opening. Stop the machine and replace the lid plug.

To mix the dough, select the High speed. Quickly turn the machine On and Off twice. Stop the machine and remove the lid.

Use a wet nylon spatula to scrape the sides of the container, pulling the dough away from the container sides and into the centre of the mixture. Replace the lid.

Select High speed. Quickly turn the machine On and Off five times. Add additional water, 1 tablespoon at a time, only if the dough seems exceptionally dry. Repeat the process five times, scraping the sides of the container until the dough binds together into a soft, elastic mixture.

Lightly grease a large bowl. Add the dough, turning to coat the entire surface. Cover the bowl with a clean tea towel or cling film. Let the dough rise in a warm, draught-free place until doubled in size, about 20 minutes.

Sweet Potato Rolls
(continued)

While the dough rises, lightly coat a 9-inch (23 cm) square cake tin with vegetable cooking spray or shortening. Knock back the dough. Turn it out onto a lightly floured surface and knead lightly until smooth. Cut the dough evenly into 12 pieces. Roll each piece into a ball and place into the prepared tin, arranging close together.

Cover the tin with a clean, dry tea towel or cling film and leave to rise for 20 minutes. Bake in a pre-heated 375 °F (190 °C) oven for 20 to 25 minutes or until lightly browned, turning the tin once for even browning. Cool on a wire rack.

Nutritional Information Per Roll: 150 cal (24 % from fat, 11 % from protein, 66 % from carb) • 4 g protein
4 g total fat • 2 g saturated fat • 25 g carbohydrates • 3 g fibre • 5 g sugar • 113 mg sodium • 23 mg cholesterol

WHOLE WHEAT BREAD

preparation: 10 minutes • processing: 35 seconds • baking time: 35 minutes
yield: 1 loaf (12 slices)

1 packet (1 tablespoon) active dry yeast

1 1/4 cups (300 ml) warm water, 105 °F-115 °F (40 °C-46 °C)

1 tablespoon honey

1 1/2 cups (270 g) whole kernel wheat or 2 1/4 cups (270 g) whole wheat flour

1 teaspoon salt

1 tablespoon light olive or grape seed oil

1 teaspoon lemon juice

1 egg white mixed with 1 tablespoon water, optional (for brushing the dough before baking)

To proof the yeast, combine the warm water, honey and yeast. Stir quickly to combine. Set aside for 5 minutes.

When starting with whole kernel wheat: Place the wheat and salt into the Vitamix DRY BLADE container and secure the lid.

Select Variable 1.

Turn the machine on and slowly increase the speed to Variable 10, then to High.

Grind the wheat for 1 minute. (Do not over process.) Stop the machine to allow the flour to cool for a few minutes.

When starting with whole wheat flour: Place the flour and salt into the Vitamix DRY BLADE container and secure the lid.

Select Variable 1.

Turn the machine on and slowly increase the speed to Variable 6.

Blend until a hole forms in the centre of the mixture, about 5 seconds.

Select Variable 3. Turn the machine on and remove the lid plug. Pour the oil, lemon juice and yeast mixture through the lid plug opening. Stop the machine and replace the lid plug.

Select High speed. Quickly turn the machine On and Off twice. Stop the machine and remove the lid.

While the dough rests, lightly coat an 8 1/2 x 4 1/2-inch (22 x 11 cm) loaf tin with vegetable cooking spray or shortening.

Use a nylon spatula to scrape the sides of the Vitamix container. Pull the dough away from the container sides and into the centre of the mixture. Replace the lid.

Select High speed. Quickly turn the machine On and Off five times. Add additional water, 1 tablespoon at a time, only if the dough seems exceptionally dry. Repeat the process five times, scraping the sides of the container until the dough binds together into a soft, elastic mixture.

Whole Wheat Bread
(continued)

To remove the dough from the container, turn the machine on and off five times (to assist in lifting the dough up and away from the blades). Invert the container over the prepared tin and let the dough fall into the tin. Use a wet nylon spatula to remove any remaining dough.

Use a wet or oiled nylon spatula (or lightly floured fingers) to shape the loaf. Allow the dough to rise, covered with a clean, dry tea towel, until the top of it reaches the top of the bread tin, about 20 to 25 minutes.

If desired, brush the loaf quickly and gently with the egg white wash and make three to four diagonal slits about 1/4-inch (0.6 cm) deep on the top of the loaf using a sharp, serrated knife.

Bake in a pre-heated 350 °F (180 °C) oven for 35 minutes or until the bread is well browned and reaches an internal temperature of 190 °F (88 °C) when tested with an instant-read thermometer.

Cool on a wire rack for 10 minutes, then carefully remove from the tin and allow to cool completely before slicing.

Nutritional Information Per Slice: 102 cal (13 % from fat, 13 % from protein, 74 % from carb) • 3 g protein
2 g total fat • 0 g saturated fat • 20 g carbohydrates • 3 g fibre • 2 g sugar • 203 mg sodium • 0 mg cholesterol

WHOLE GRAINS BAGUETTE

preparation: 15 minutes • processing: 35 seconds • baking time: 30-40 minutes
yield: 1 loaf (16-18 slices)

1 cup (240 ml)
warm water, divided use, 105 °F -115 °F
(40 °C-46 °C)

1 packet (1 tablespoon)
active dry yeast

1 1/4 cups (150 g)
whole wheat flour

3/4 cup (103 g)
bread flour

1 1/2 teaspoons salt

2 tablespoons (21 g)
flax seeds

2 tablespoons (18 g)
sunflower seeds

1 tablespoon
pumpkin seeds or
1 tablespoon millet

1 tablespoon wheat germ

1 tablespoon olive oil

2 tablespoons (15 g)
whole grain cornmeal

1 egg white mixed with
1 teaspoon water (for
brushing the dough
before baking)

To proof the yeast, combine 1/2 cup (120 ml) warm water with the yeast. Stir quickly to combine. Set aside for 5 minutes.

Place the whole wheat flour, bread flour, salt, flax seeds, sunflower seeds, pumpkin seeds OR millet and wheat germ into the Vitamix DRY BLADE container and secure the lid.

Select Variable 1.

Turn the machine on and slowly increase the speed to Variable 6.

Blend until a hole forms in the centre of the flour mixture, about 5 seconds. Stop the machine.

Select Variable 3. Turn the machine on and remove the lid plug. Add the yeast mixture and remaining 1/2 cup (120 ml) warm water through the lid plug opening. Stop the machine and replace the lid plug.

To mix the dough, select the High speed. Quickly turn the machine On and Off twice. Stop the machine and remove the lid.

While the dough rests, grease a medium-size mixing bowl with olive oil and sprinkle the cornmeal on a baking sheet.

Use a wet nylon spatula to scrape the sides of the container, pulling the dough away from the container sides and into the centre of the mixture. Replace the lid.

Select High speed. Quickly turn the machine On and Off five times. Add additional water, 1 tablespoon at a time, only if the dough seems exceptionally dry. Repeat the process five times, scraping the sides of the container until the dough binds together into a soft, elastic mixture.

To aid in removing the dough from the container, turn the machine On and Off five times (this lifts the dough up and away from the blades) and quickly invert the container over the prepared bowl, using a wet spatula to remove any remaining dough. Turn the dough to coat well. Cover with cling film and allow to rise until almost triple in size, about 1 hour.

Whole Grains Baguette *(continued)*

Lightly knock back the dough and place on a floured work surface. Roll into a 12 x 6-inch (30 x 15 cm) rectangle with a floured rolling pin. Roll from the long end down, pinching the seams together and using water to seal.

Place the dough, seam side down, on the prepared baking sheet. Cover with a clean, dry tea towel and allow the dough to rise until it doubles in size, about 45 minutes.

Brush the top with egg mixture and make three to four diagonal slits about 1/4-inch (0.6 cm) deep on the top of the loaf using a sharp, serrated knife.

Bake in a pre-heated 425 °F (220 °C) oven for 30 to 40 minutes or until the bread is well browned and reaches an internal temperature of 190 °F (88 °C) when tested with an instant-read thermometer. Cool on a wire rack for 10 minutes, then carefully remove from the baking sheet and allow to cool completely before slicing.

Nutritional Information Per Slice: 74 cal (23 % from fat, 16 % from protein, 62 % from carb) • 3 g protein
2 g total fat • 0 g saturated fat • 12 g carbohydrates • 2 g fibre • 0 g sugar • 202 mg sodium • 0 mg cholesterol

A metal spatula helps in coaxing the bread off the baking sheet.

WHOLE WHEAT, OAT AND FLAX SEED BREAD

preparation: 10 minutes • processing: 40 seconds • baking time: 30-35 minutes
yield: 1 loaf (12 slices)

1 cup (240 ml)
warm water, 105 °F-115 °F (40 °C-46 °C)

2 tablespoons (30 ml)
honey

1 packet (1 tablespoon)
active dry yeast

2 tablespoons (10 g)
rolled oats (not instant)

2 tablespoons (20 g)
flax seeds

3/4 cup (135 g)
whole kernel wheat
or 1 cup (120 g)
whole wheat flour

1 1/4 cups (171 g)
bread flour

1 teaspoon salt

1 tablespoon
light olive oil

To proof the yeast, combine the warm water, honey and yeast. Stir quickly to combine. Set aside for 5 minutes.

If starting with the whole kernel wheat, place the oats, flax seeds and whole kernel wheat into the Vitamix DRY BLADE container and secure the lid.

Select Variable 1.

Turn the machine on and slowly increase the speed to Variable 10, then to High.

Grind for 30 seconds.

Stop the machine. Add the bread flour and salt to the Vitamix container and secure the lid.

Select Variable 1.

Turn the machine on and slowly increase the speed to Variable 10, then to High.

Blend for 30 seconds, using the tamper (inserted through the lid plug) to press the flour mixture into the blades. Remove the tamper during the last 5 seconds to allow a hole to form in the centre of the flour mixture.

If starting with the whole wheat flour, place the oats, flax seeds, whole wheat flour, bread flour and salt into the Vitamix DRY BLADE container and secure the lid.

Select Variable 1.

Turn the machine on and slowly increase the speed to Variable 10, then to High.

Blend for 30 seconds, using the tamper (inserted through the lid plug) to press the flour mixture into the blades. Remove the tamper during the last 5 seconds to allow a hole to form in the centre of the flour mixture.

Select Variable 3. Turn the machine on and remove the lid plug. Add the oil and yeast mixture through the lid plug opening. Stop the machine and replace the lid plug.

Whole Wheat, Oat and Flax Seed Bread *(continued)*

Select High speed. Quickly turn the machine On and Off twice. Stop the machine and remove the lid.

While the dough rests, lightly coat an 8 x 4-inch (20 x 10 cm) loaf tin with vegetable cooking spray or shortening.

Use a wet nylon spatula to scrape the sides of the container, pulling the dough away from the container sides and into the centre of the mixture. Replace the lid.

Select High speed. Quickly turn the machine On and Off five times. Add additional water, 1 tablespoon at a time, only if the dough seems exceptionally dry. Repeat the process five times, scraping the sides of the container until the dough binds together into a soft, elastic mixture.

To aid in removing the dough from the container, turn the machine On and Off five times (this lifts the dough up and away from the blades) and quickly invert the container over the prepared tin. Let the dough fall into the tin, using a wet spatula to remove any remaining dough.

Use lightly floured fingers or an oiled spatula to shape the loaf into the tin, pressing gently to even the dough.

Cover the loaf with a clean, dry tea towel and allow the dough to rise until it reaches the top of the bread tin, about 20 to 25 minutes. When ready to bake, make 3 quick angled slits with a serrated knife on top of the dough.

Bake in a pre-heated 375 °F (190 °C) oven for 30 to 35 minutes or until the bread reaches an internal temperature of 190 °F (88 °C). Cool on a wire rack for 10 minutes, then carefully remove from the loaf tin and allow to cool completely before slicing.

Nutritional Information Per Slice: 130 cal (15 % from fat, 12 % from protein, 73 % from carb) • 4 g protein
2 g total fat • 0 g saturated fat • 24 g carbohydrates • 3 g fibre • 3 g sugar • 199 mg sodium • 0 mg cholesterol

Bread sliced while still warm, especially whole grain bread, is often wet inside; allow to cool completely before cutting.

Butters for Your Bread

What better way to enhance freshly baked bread than with fresh, home-made butter spreads? Making your own butter spreads with delicate flavours and unique combinations is so quick and easy with the Vitamix. Here are five flavour profiles to get you started on creating butter spreads. Each one starts with 1/2 cup (113 g) of unsalted butter - either purchased or home-made in your Vitamix. Be sure to serve them at room temperature as flavoured butters spread more easily and melt faster when they're not ice cold.

For a Cinnamon Butter: To the butter, add 1 teaspoon of ground cinnamon and 3 tablespoons (24 g) of icing sugar. Blend on Variable Speed 5 for 15-30 seconds, using the tamper to press the ingredients into the blades. The mixture should be fluffy.

For a Date-Nut Butter: To the butter, add 1/4 cup (60 ml) honey and 1/2 to 1 cup (80-160 g) of chopped dates. Blend on Variable Speed 5 for 15-30 seconds, using the tamper to press the ingredients into the blades. The mixture should be fluffy.

For an Orange Butter: To the butter, add 1 1/2 teaspoons of grated orange peel and 3 tablespoons (24 g) of icing sugar. Blend on Variable Speed 5 for 15-30 seconds, using the tamper to press the ingredients into the blades. The mixture should be fluffy.

For a Spice Butter: To the butter, add 3 tablespoons (41 g) of firmly packed light brown sugar, 1/4 teaspoon of ground cinnamon, 1/4 teaspoon of ground allspice and 1/8 teaspoon of ground nutmeg. Blend on Variable Speed 5 for 15-30 seconds, using the tamper to press the ingredients into the blades. The mixture should be fluffy.

For a Peach Butter: Peel, pit and chop 1 medium-size peach or nectarine. Purée in the Vitamix container on Variable Speed 10 with 1 teaspoon of lemon juice for 20 seconds. Add butter, 2 tablespoons (28 g) of firmly packed light brown sugar or honey and 1/4 teaspoon of ground nutmeg. Blend on Variable Speed 5 for 15-30 seconds, using the tamper to press the ingredients into the blades. The mixture should be fluffy.

Butter

dry rubs

Using Dry Rubs

Dry rubs add depth of flavour to your favourite grilled foods. Explore our combinations and follow a few guidelines for the best results.

- Dry rubs add a burst of flavour and work best when pan frying, grilling or baking. They are great for tofu, fish, pork chops, chicken breasts and veggies.
- Store your rubs in an airtight glass jar in a cool place, using as desired.
- Three or four tablespoons of dry rub seasoning should be enough for just under a kilo of food.
- To apply a rub, sprinkle it over your choice of meat, poultry, fish or veggies and lightly rub into the surface with your hands. Or, place the rub in a large plastic bag, add your ingredients and shake to coat. Then let the food sit in the refrigerator for several hours or overnight before cooking.
- For an extra flavour boost on the grill, generously coat meat, fish or any other protein of your choice on both sides with a rub. Cover with cling film and refrigerate for 30 minutes. Proceed to grill.

Important Notes:

Grinding dry material for more than two minutes could damage your machine. Regular use may result in cosmetic marring of the container and cause the blades to become dull over time.

Grinding some herbs may release volatile oils, causing the container to discolour permanently. Others have strong odours that may linger in the container, affecting the flavour of other foods. The grinding of some herbs and spices may also cause the blade to dull over time, or the container to crack.

ALL PURPOSE BARBECUE RUB

preparation: 10 minutes • processing: 45 seconds • yield: 1 cup (240 g)

1 tablespoon sea salt

1/4 cup (55 g)
dark brown sugar

1/4 cup (28 g)
sweet Hungarian paprika

2 tablespoons (24 g)
black peppercorns

1 tablespoon
dried garlic flakes

1 tablespoon
dried onion flakes

1 whole dried Pasilla chilli,
seeded and halved

1/2 teaspoon
celery seeds

Place all the ingredients in the Vitamix DRY BLADE container in the order listed and secure the lid.

Select Variable 1.

Turn the machine on and slowly increase the speed to Variable 10, then to High.

Blend for 45 seconds. Use immediately or store in an airtight container with your spices until ready to use.

NOTE: Adds spice and kick to anything from ribs to salmon!

Nutritional Information Per 1 Teaspoon Serving: 8 cal (11 % from fat, 7 % from protein, 82 % from carb)
0 g protein • 0 g total fat • 0 g saturated fat • 2 g carbohydrates • 0 g fibre • 1 g sugar • 71 mg sodium
0 mg cholesterol

All Purpose Barbecue Rub

CAJUN RUB

preparation: 10 minutes • processing: 30 seconds • yield: 1 cup (240 g)

1/4 cup (67 g) coarse sea salt

3 tablespoons (21 g) sweet Hungarian paprika

2 tablespoons (17 g) garlic powder

2 tablespoons (14 g) onion powder

2 tablespoons (5 g) dried thyme

2 tablespoons (6 g) dried oregano

1 tablespoon ground black pepper or 1 teaspoon black peppercorns

1 tablespoon ground white pepper or 1 teaspoon white peppercorns

2 teaspoons dried sage leaves

2 teaspoons cayenne pepper or 1 dried Thai chilli

Place all the ingredients in the Vitamix DRY BLADE container in the order listed and secure the lid.

Select Variable 1.

Turn the machine on and slowly increase the speed to Variable 10, then to High.

Blend for 30 seconds, using the tamper as needed to keep the mixture flowing into the blades. Use immediately or store in an airtight container with your spices until ready to use.

Nutritional Information Per 2 Tablespoon (30 g) Serving: 31 cal (15 % from fat, 14 % from protein, 71 % from carb) 1 g protein • 1 g total fat • 0 g saturated fat • 7 g carbohydrates • 3 g fibre • 1 g sugar • 1683 mg sodium 0 mg cholesterol

COFFEE DRY RUB

preparation: 15 minutes • processing: 45 seconds • yield: 1/2 cup (120 g)

1 1/2 teaspoons sea salt

4 teaspoons ground coffee or 1 tablespoon whole coffee beans

1 whole dried Pasilla chilli, seeded

2 tablespoons (28 g) dark brown sugar

1/2 teaspoon ground black pepper or 1/4 teaspoon whole black peppercorns

1/2 teaspoon onion powder

1/2 teaspoon garlic powder

1/4 teaspoon cayenne pepper

1/4 teaspoon whole coriander seeds

1/4 teaspoon turmeric

Place all the ingredients in the Vitamix DRY BLADE container in the order listed and secure the lid.

Select Variable 1.

Turn the machine on and slowly increase the speed to Variable 10, then to High.

Blend for 45 seconds. Use immediately or store in an airtight container with your spices until ready to use.

Nutritional Information Per 1 Teaspoon Serving: 7 cal (8 % from fat, 6 % from protein, 86 % from carb)
0 g protein • 0 g total fat • 0 g saturated fat • 2 g carbohydrates • 0 g fibre • 1 g sugar • 71 mg sodium
0 mg cholesterol

The coffee in this rub gives food a rich, earthy flavour. It is delicious with beef.

DRY JERK SEASONING

preparation: 10 minutes • processing: 45 seconds • yield: 1/2 cup (67 g)

3 tablespoons (41 g) dark brown sugar

1 1/2 tablespoons coarse sea salt

1 tablespoon whole coriander seeds

1 teaspoon whole black peppercorns

1 1/2 teaspoons garlic powder

1 1/2 teaspoons onion powder

1 1/2 teaspoons dried thyme

1 teaspoon whole allspice or 1 1/2 teaspoons ground allspice

1 teaspoon ground cinnamon

1/2 to 1 teaspoon cayenne pepper or 1 dried Thai chilli

Place all the ingredients in the Vitamix DRY BLADE container in the order listed and secure the lid.

Select Variable 1.

Turn the machine on and slowly increase the speed to Variable 10, then to High.

Blend for 45 seconds. Use immediately or store in an airtight container with your spices until ready to use.

Nutritional Information Per 1 Teaspoon Serving: 9 cal (6 % from fat, 4 % from protein, 90 % from carb)
0 g protein • 0 g total fat • 0 g saturated fat • 2 g carbohydrates • 0 g fibre • 2 g sugar • 443 mg sodium
0 mg cholesterol

"NEW" BAY SEASONING

preparation: 10 minutes • processing: 1 minute • yield: 1 1/4 cups (300 g)

1/2 cup (134 g)
coarse sea salt

1/2 cup (56 g)
sweet Hungarian paprika

2 tablespoons (13 g)
celery seeds

1 tablespoon
allspice berries

1 tablespoon
black peppercorns

1 tablespoon
dried ground mustard

1 tablespoon
ground ginger

1 tablespoon
ground cinnamon

1 tablespoon
ground cayenne

1/2 tablespoon
cardamom seeds

1/2 tablespoon
whole cloves

10 bay leaves

Place all the ingredients in the Vitamix DRY BLADE container in the order listed and secure the lid.

Select Variable 1.

Turn the machine on and slowly increase the speed to Variable 10, then to High.

Blend for 1 minute using the tamper as needed to keep the mixture flowing into the blades. Use immediately or store in an airtight container with your spices until ready to use.

Nutritional Information Per 1 Teaspoon Serving: 6 cal (31 % from fat, 14 % from protein, 55 % from carb)
0 g protein • 0 g total fat • 0 g saturated fat • 1 g carbohydrates • 1 g fibre • 0 g sugar • 449 mg sodium
0 mg cholesterol

This seasoning blend is flexible enough to use as a boiling spice for prawns and crabs, for a rub on fish or even for infusing into dipping butters for lobster and prawns.

PAPRIKA POULTRY RUB

preparation: 15 minutes • processing: 1 seconds • yield: 3/4 cup (180 g)

1/3 cup (9 g)
dried marjoram

1/4 cup (28 g)
sweet Hungarian paprika

1 dried Pasilla
chilli, seeded

2 tablespoons (14 g)
onion powder

2 tablespoons (36 g)
dried lemon peel

1/4 cup (24 g)
dried sage leaves

1 tablespoon
coarse sea salt or
Kosher salt

1 tablespoon
black peppercorns

1/2 tablespoon
celery seeds

Place all the ingredients in the Vitamix DRY BLADE container in the order listed and secure the lid.

Select Variable 1.

Turn the machine on and slowly increase the speed to Variable 10, then to High.

Blend for 1 minute. Use immediately or store in an airtight container with your spices until ready to use.

Nutritional Information Per 1 Teaspoon Serving: 7 cal (22 % from fat, 13 % from protein, 65 % from carb)
0 g protein • 0 g total fat • 0 g saturated fat • 1 g carbohydrates • 1 g fibre • 0 g sugar • 94 mg sodium
0 mg cholesterol

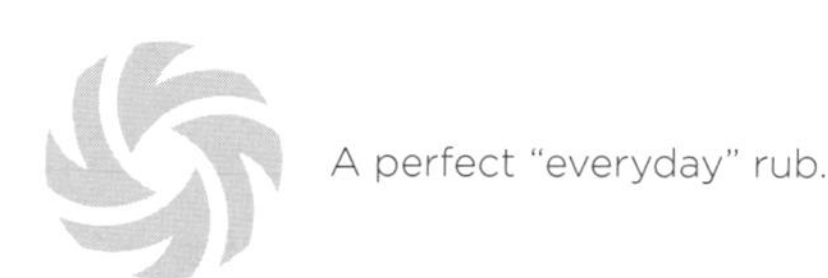

A perfect "everyday" rub.

PUMPKIN PIE SPICE BLEND

preparation: 10 minutes • processing: 45 seconds • yield: 2 tablespoons (30 g)

1 tablespoon ground cinnamon

1 teaspoon ground ginger

6 cloves

3 whole allspice berries

1/2 teaspoon ground mace

1/2 teaspoon freshly grated nutmeg

Place all the ingredients in the Vitamix DRY BLADE container in the order listed and secure the lid.

Select Variable 1.

Turn the machine on and slowly increase the speed to Variable 10, then to High.

Blend for 45 seconds. Use immediately or store in an airtight container with your spices until ready to use.

NOTE: This mixture may leave a slight stain in your container.

Nutritional Information Per 1 Teaspoon Serving: 6 cal (22 % from fat, 5 % from protein, 73 % from carb)
0 g protein • 0 g total fat • 0 g saturated fat • 1 g carbohydrates • 1 g fibre • 0 g sugar • 1 mg sodium
0 mg cholesterol

This blend is popular that you'll see it called for in everything from apple tarts to mashed potatoes and to, of course, a classic pumpkin pie. Your Vitamix makes it easy to take advantage of the freshness of the aromatic components so you can make small batches to maximize flavour.

SWEET & SAVOURY DRY RUB

preparation: 10 minutes • processing: 30 seconds • yield: 1/4 cup (60 g)

2 teaspoons light brown sugar

2 teaspoons dry mustard

1 teaspoon onion powder

1/2 teaspoon Kosher salt

6 white peppercorns or 1/4 teaspoon ground white pepper

Place all the ingredients into the Vitamix DRY BLADE container and secure the lid.

Select Variable 1.

Turn the machine on and slowly increase the speed to Variable 10, then to High.

Blend for 30 seconds. Use immediately or store in an airtight container with your spices until ready to use.

Nutritional Information Per 1 Teaspoon Serving: 7 cal (24 % from fat, 10 % from protein, 66 % from carb)
0 g protein • 0 g total fat • 0 g saturated fat • 1 g carbohydrates • 0 g fibre • 1 g sugar • 47 mg sodium
0 mg cholesterol

TRINIDAD CURRY DRY RUB

preparation: 10 minutes • processing: 45 seconds • yield: 1/2 cup (120 g)

3 tablespoons (15 g) whole coriander seeds

3 tablespoons (20 g) ground turmeric

2 tablespoons (24 g) black peppercorns

1 tablespoon Kosher salt

1 tablespoon cumin seeds

1 teaspoon allspice berries

1 teaspoon cardamom seeds

1 teaspoon freshly grated nutmeg

1 teaspoon ground cinnamon

3/4 teaspoon ground ginger

2 dried Thai chilis, seeded

Place all the ingredients in the Vitamix DRY BLADE container in the order listed and secure the lid.

Select Variable 1.

Turn the machine on and slowly increase the speed to Variable 10, then to High.

Blend for 45 seconds. Use immediately or store in an airtight container with your spices until ready to use.

NOTE: This mixture may leave a slight stain in your container.

Nutritional Information Per 1 Teaspoon Serving: 21 cal (29 % from fat, 11 % from protein, 60 % from carb)
1 g protein • 1 g total fat • 0 g saturated fat • 4 g carbohydrates • 2 g fibre • 0 g sugar • 284 mg sodium
0 mg cholesterol

ADOBO DRY RUB

preparation: 10 minutes • processing: 1 minute • yield: 1 cup (240 g)

1/4 cup (34 g) garlic powder

1/4 cup (28 g) onion powder

3 tablespoons (9 g) dried oregano

2 tablespoons (12 g) cumin seeds

2 tablespoons (29 g) Kosher salt

2 tablespoons (24 g) black peppercorns

1 tablespoon dried lemon peel

Place all the ingredients in the Vitamix DRY BLADE container in the order listed and secure the lid.

Select Variable 1.

Turn the machine on and slowly increase the speed to Variable 10, then to High.

Blend for 1 minute. Use immediately or store in an airtight container with your spices until ready to use.

Nutritional Information Per 1 Teaspoon Serving: 7 cal (11 % from fat, 14 % from protein, 74 % from carb)
0 g protein • 0 g total fat • 0 g saturated fat • 1 g carbohydrates • 0 g fibre • 0 g sugar • 141 mg sodium
0 mg cholesterol

A Latin American all-purpose spice mix, perfect with meat and tossed on beans or roasted veggies.

Troubleshooting Guide

If you're a novice baker, then all the variables in making yeast bread may seem daunting, and you might wonder what to do if things don't go just as the recipe says. It's true that yeast baking is not an exact science — but it's also true that it's a forgiving one. Here are answers to some questions you may have.

How can I tell if the yeast is active?

Envelopes of active dry yeast are dated to tell you how long the yeast will be active. But if you buy bulk yeast, it's not always easy to tell. You can test your yeast by proofing it, a simple step that's built into many bread recipes. When dissolving the yeast in the warm water, add 1 to 3 teaspoons of the sugar or honey called for in the recipe. (If none is called for, you can add 1 teaspoon without affecting the flavour of the bread.) Let the mixture stand for five to 15 minutes or until bubbly; the bubbling tells you that the yeast is still fresh and active.

How do I handle interruptions during the bread-making process?

Don't worry about short interruptions — up to half an hour. If you've just dissolved the yeast, cover it and leave it at room temperature — it won't hurt it to ferment for a while. If you're mixing or kneading the dough, cover it with cling film to keep it from drying out.

Should it be inconvenient to shape the loaves when the dough has doubled, just knock it back and let it rise again — this time at room temperature. You can knock it back two or three times and still bake excellent bread.

You can postpone the last steps — shaping, second rising and baking — by placing the dough, covered with cling film, in the refrigerator during the first rising. You can leave it there for several hours; the rising action will continue, but at a much slower pace. When you're ready, let the dough finish rising, covered, in a warm place.

How can I tell if I've kneaded in enough flour?

If you're not sure if there's enough flour in your dough (remember, too much will make for a very dry loaf), invert a bowl over your dough and let it rest for about 15 minutes. When you return, if the dough is very sticky and has spread out sideways rather than starting to rise, knead in more flour.

What if the dough rises too long?

If you happen to leave the dough too long so that it rises too high (becomes "over-proofed"), the solution is to knock it back, knead it a bit to release air and then let it rise again. Over-proofed dough looks as though it has ballooned beyond double its original size. Its "skin" is thin and transparent, with bubbles just below the surface.

If left long enough, it may deflate itself, in which case you would knock it back and let it rise again. You can use the same technique if you've let your shaped loaves rise too long. Knead the dough lightly to release air, then reshape and let rise again, but watch carefully as the loaves will rise faster.

What if the bottoms of the loaves aren't browned enough when I turn them out of the pans?

If you prefer a browner crust, you can return your loaves to the oven — either in the baking pans or directly on the oven rack. A few extra minutes will give you a darker, crisper crust.

Notes

Français

table des matières

aide spéciale

recettes vitamix

céréales

pains minute

pâtes levées

(suite à la page suivante)

table des matières

pâtes levées

marinades sèches

À propos des lames et du récipient

L'appareil Vitamix est livré standard avec le récipient à lames pour **ingrédients humides**. Bien que les recettes de ce livre puissent être réalisées dans le récipient à ingrédients humides, pour obtenir les meilleurs résultats, Vitamix recommande l'utilisation du récipient à ingrédients secs. D'autres récipients comportant des lames pour ingrédients humides ou secs sont vendus séparément.

⚠AVERTISSEMENT

Les lames en mouvement peuvent occasionner de graves blessures.

N'INTRODUISEZ NI la main ni aucun ustensile dans le récipient lorsque l'appareil fonctionne.

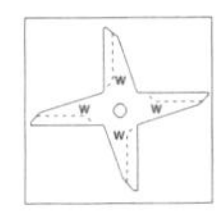

Récipient à ingrédients humides : Conçu pour les liquides, notamment les jus, les mélanges congelés, les sauces, les soupes, les purées, la pâte à frire, et le broyage liquide. Les lames pour ingrédients humides peuvent également moudre les grains et pétrir la pâte, mais ne sont pas aussi efficaces que les lames spéciales ingrédients secs pour cette application.

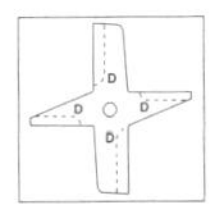

Récipient à ingrédients secs : Ces lames sont clairement identifiées « D » (ingrédients secs) et sont conçues spécialement pour moudre les ingrédients secs tels que les grains, les céréales et le café. Elles servent également à pétrir la pâte à pain. Les lames pour ingrédients secs ne sont PAS conçues pour le mixage des liquides.

ATTENTION : La mouture d'ingrédients secs pendant plus de 2 minutes risque d'endommager votre appareil. L'utilisation régulière peut causer des rayures du récipient et entraîner l'usure prématurée des lames.

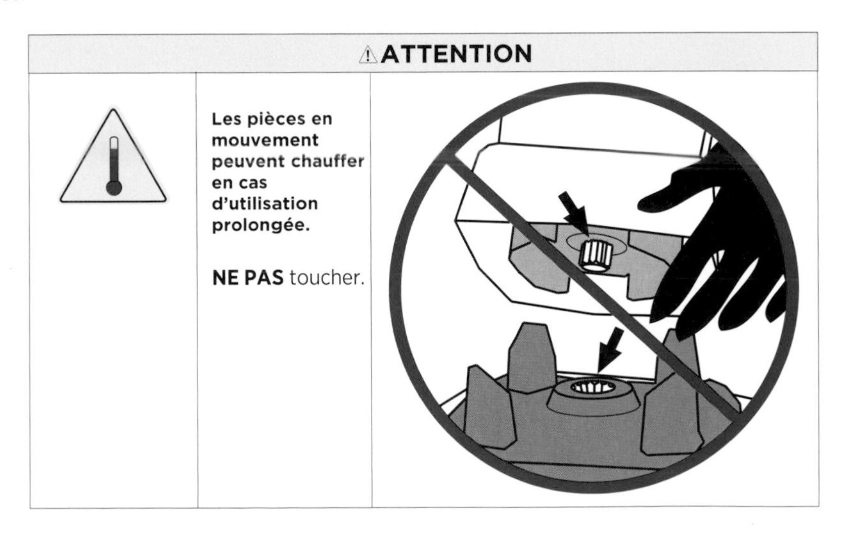

À propos du broyage des herbes et des épices
Certaines herbes et épices peuvent libérer des huiles volatiles et décolorer le récipient de façon permanente. D'autres, fortement odorantes, peuvent laisser leur empreinte olfactive sur les parois du récipient, et affecter du même coup la saveur des autres aliments qui y sont préparés. Le broyage de certaines herbes et épices peut également entraîner l'usure prématurée de la lame ou fissurer le récipient. Si vous broyez régulièrement des herbes, vous devriez peut-être acheter un récipient distinct pour ingrédients secs et remplacer les lames si nécessaire.

MOUDRE DES GRAINS DE CAFÉ

Surveillez le processus de mouture de près, il existe 6 niveaux de finesse. Avec votre appareil, vous pouvez créer votre propre style de café sophistiqué (voir la liste ci-dessous).
vitesse : position Variable • mixage : 10 secondes

Ingrédients	Instructions
2 tasses (400 g) de grains de café	Versez 2 tasses (400 g) de grains de café dans le récipient Vitamix, et verrouillez le couvercle. Réglez le commutateur sur la position Variable et la vitesse sur 1. Mettez l'appareil en marche et augmentez progressivement la vitesse jusqu'à la position Variable 8. Moulez pendant 10 secondes pour obtenir du café pour cafetière.

Niveaux de finesse :

1. Percolateur (très grossier). Moulez en réglant la vitesse sur la position Variable 8 pendant 7 à 8 secondes.
2. Cafetière (grossier). Moulez en réglant la vitesse sur la position Variable 8 pendant 10 secondes.
3. Filtre conique (moins grossier, comme la farine de maïs). Moulez en réglant la vitesse sur la position Variable 8 pendant 12 à 13 secondes.
4. Cuisinière (relativement fin). Moulez en réglant la vitesse sur la position Variable 8 pendant 15 à 16 secondes.
5. Espresso (plus fin, comme du sucre, mais non poudreux). Moulez en réglant la vitesse sur la position Variable 8 pendant 20 secondes.
6. À la turque (fin comme de la farine). Moulez en réglant la vitesse sur la position Variable 8 pendant 25 secondes.

Plus vous moulez les grains longtemps, plus le café obtenu est fin. Conservez le café moulu destiné à être consommé dans un délai de deux semaines, dans un récipient hermétique, au frais et à l'abri de la lumière. Si vous souhaitez le conserver au-delà de deux semaines, mettez-le au réfrigérateur dans un récipient hermétique.

Dépannage pour les machines à espresso : Si le café coule lentement (de la machine à espresso) et s'il est amer, essayez de le moudre moins pour obtenir une texture plus grossière. Si, au contraire, il est trop léger et aqueux, essayez de le moudre davantage pour obtenir une texture plus fine.

Préparer du pain et des gâteaux en toute simplicité

L'art de la fabrication du pain est une évasion thérapeutique, avec ses arômes délicieux, l'expression artistique qu'il favorise et les compliments qu'il génère. Créer quelque chose de toutes pièces est extrêmement satisfaisant, sans parler du plaisir de connaître parfaitement la nourriture offerte à votre table. Et grâce à la possibilité de moudre votre propre farine, Vitamix vous apporte un niveau de fraîcheur encore supérieur.

Votre appareil Vitamix mixe facilement toutes les pâtes, vous permettant de créer des muffins moelleux, des pains tendres, des pizzas à la croûte légère, et bien davantage. Nous espérons que les recettes de ce livre de cuisine vous plairont et que les conseils écrits par notre propre chef pour permettront de prendre plaisir à chacune de vos réussites. Et puisqu'il vous suffit de verser le contenu du récipient Vitamix directement dans le moule ou la poêle, même le nettoyage est un jeu d'enfant.

Alors, aux fourneaux avec l'appareil Vitamix, car rien ne vaut l'odeur du pain et des gâteaux frais.

À propos de la préparation du pain

Trois ingrédients magiques

Le blé

La plupart des pains que nous mangeons sont à base de blé. Le pain de seigle est en fait un pain de blé contenant du seigle. Le pain multicéréale est un pain de blé contenant de petites quantités d'avoine, d'orge, de seigle, de maïs, de sarrasin ou autres céréales. Le pain de son est un pain de blé contenant du son. Le pain aux bananes ou aux courgettes est un pain de blé contenant de la banane ou de la courgette. La plupart des pains ont des ingrédients communs, dont le blé. Le blé est la meilleure source du composant des céréales contenant des protéines, le gluten. Quand une pâte à base de blé est pétrie, le gluten développe un réseau spongieux. Ce réseau piège les bulles de dioxyde de carbone produites lors de la digestion des amidons contenus dans la pâte par la levure, et ainsi la pâte lève. Sans gluten, le pain est compact et ne lève pas.

Dans un grain de blé, le son et le germe tendent à rendre les pains et autres produits de boulangerie lourds. Ils réagissent donc peu à la levure et autres agents de levage. Ainsi, un blé à haute teneur en protéines est nécessaire pour compenser ce problème. Nous vous conseillons du blé roux dur ou du blé blanc dur nouveau. (Ne confondez pas le blé blanc dur avec le blé blanc tendre, couramment utilisé en pâtisserie. Le blé dur est essentiellement utilisé pour les pâtes.) Le pain fait à base de blé blanc dur allie les bienfaits du blé complet et un goût doux, légèrement sucré. Le blé blanc dur ne contient pas les composants au goût prononcé caractéristiques du blé roux. Il présente une couleur ambre dorée et produit des pains au goût plus discret et plus clairs. Le blé blanc dur contient quasiment autant de protéines que le blé roux dur. Si vous ne pouvez pas vous procurer de blé blanc dur près de chez vous, contactez l'American White Wheat Producers Association au (913) 367-4422 ou (800) 372-4422, ou consultez son site Web sur www.farmerdirectfoods.com. Le blé roux dur d'hiver, qui pousse à des altitudes élevées et qui offre une teneur en protéines de 14 % et une teneur en eau de 9 % ou moins, est également recommandé.

La levure

Les agents de levage sont un composant essentiel des pains levés et la levure est le plus courant de ces agents. La levure est un organisme vivant qui devient « actif » dès lors qu'on y ajoute de l'eau tiède et du vrai sucre, comme du miel, de la mélasse, du sirop d'érable ou du sucre raffiné. Les édulcorants ne sont pas de vrais sucres et ne permettent pas d'activer la levure. Cependant, la farine, en particulier la farine de blé complet, contient suffisamment de sucre naturel pour nourrir la levure.

Faites attention quand vous ajoutez le mélange levure/eau à de la farine fraîchement moulue. Si la farine est trop chaude, la température globale du mélange montera et tuera la levure. Pour cette raison, nous suggérons de commencer avec des céréales congelées, ce qui évite une surchauffe de la farine.

Un liquide

Eau, lait, eau de pomme de terre ou jus peuvent tous fournir le liquide nécessaire à la pâte à pain. Vous pouvez même ajouter des œufs en les plaçant dans un verre gradué, puis en y ajoutant le reste du liquide jusqu'à obtenir la quantité indiquée dans la recette. Si vous utilisez de la farine à température ambiante, la température du liquide doit être comprise entre 40 °C et 46 °C (105 °F et 115 °F). Quand vous faites du pain dans votre appareil Vitamix, faites particulièrement attention à la température de la farine. Si vous utilisez de la farine complète fraîchement moulue, elle sera déjà tiède. Enlevez la farine moulue du récipient et mesurez-en la quantité souhaitée pour la refroidir.

Les autres ingrédients

Il est possible d'ajouter de nombreux ingrédients au pain.

- L'huile aide à conserver le pain tendre et frais plus longtemps.
- Les œufs donnent au pain une saveur plus prononcée et fournissent des protéines pour un pain plus levé. Ils aident aussi à conserver le pain plus tendre.
- Le sel joue deux rôles distincts : 1) C'est un agent modérateur ou inhibiteur de la levure, car il ralentit le processus de levage ; 2) C'est un exhausteur de goût. Sans sel, le pain est un peu fade.

De bonnes nouvelles pour les propriétaires de machines à pain

Vous ne trouverez pas de meilleure machine à moudre le grain que l'appareil Vitamix. Utilisez de la farine fraîchement moulue dans les recettes réalisées dans une machine à pain et utilisant des céréales complètes. Nous sommes convaincus que vous serez satisfait des résultats.

Les difficultés liées à la fabrication du pain au blé complet

Oui, il peut être difficile de réaliser du pain de blé complet. Mais ne vous découragez pas, ce n'est pas une tâche impossible. Vous trouverez ci-dessous quelques trucs et astuces utiles.

Utilisée seule, la farine de blé complet produit un pain plus lourd et plus compact, de couleur sombre. Les pains au blé complet sont plus petits que les pains blancs du même poids. Le son et le germe représentent 15 % du blé entier et ne contiennent pas de gluten. N'oublions pas que le gluten est une protéine qui donne structure et force au pain. Donc, la farine de blé complet contient moins de gluten que la farine blanche. Si le pain au blé complet frais est plus lourd, il n'en est pas moins délicieux et satisfaisant.

Le pain au blé complet rancit plus vite que le pain blanc. Il vaut donc mieux ne pas en préparer plus que ce que vous pouvez consommer en une journée. Utilisez le pain de la veille pour faire du pain grillé, de la farce, du pain perdu, des croûtons, de la panure ou du pudding au pain.

Comment obtenir un pain plus homogène

Transférez la pâte sur une planche légèrement farinée et pétrissez pendant 1 à 2 minutes. Formez un pain et placez-le dans un moule huilé. Laissez lever et cuisez selon la recette.

Comment adapter vos recettes de pain

Vous pouvez facilement adapter vos recettes de pain pour l'appareil Vitamix. Dans la cuisine test, nous divisons la plupart des recettes par deux (car les recettes de pain produisent généralement deux pains). Pour obtenir de meilleurs résultats, faites un pain à la fois et réduisez les ingrédients comme suit :

Farine : Utilisez 2 1/2 tasses (280 g) de farine. Il peut s'agir d'un mélange de céréales, mais n'oubliez pas le rapport 1:3 (une part d'autres céréales pour 3 parts de blé ou farine de blé).

Eau : 1 à 1 1/4 tasse (240 à 300 ml).

Levure : 1 sachet par pain (1 cuillerée à soupe).

Fabrication de pain en altitude

Comme la pression atmosphérique diminue à haute altitude, les pâtes levées montent plus rapidement qu'au niveau de la mer. Divisez par deux le temps d'activation des pains au levain. Une altitude élevée provoque également une perte d'humidité. Utilisez des quantités de farine modérées lorsque vous pétrissez à la main. Ajoutez juste ce qu'il faut de farine pour pouvoir travailler la pâte. Huilez vos mains pour pouvoir manipuler la pâte plus facilement.

Si le pain est lourd et friable :

- Essayez de remplacer une partie de la farine de blé complet par de la farine non blanchie.
- Essayez d'ajouter une cuillerée à café de farine de gluten (que vous trouverez dans les magasins bio) pour chaque tasse de farine de blé complet afin que le pain lève mieux.
- Si vous utilisez d'autres céréales en plus du blé, le rapport doit être 1:3 (une part d'autres céréales pour trois parts de blé).
- Quel type de blé utilisez-vous ? Le blé blanc dur nouveau est plus doux et produit un pain plus léger.
- Essayez de laisser la pâte lever deux fois : une fois dans le récipient de l'appareil et une fois dans le moule.
- La farine n'était-elle pas assez fine ? Quand vous moulez des céréales, gardez l'œil sur votre montre. Il est recommandé de les moudre pendant une minute.
- Avez-vous pétri le pain jusqu'à ce qu'il soit souple et élastique ? Il est possible que vous n'ayez pas suffisamment pétri votre pain.

Si le pain est déformé ou si la croûte est fendue :

- Avez-vous ajouté trop de liquide ? La pâte était-elle trop humide ?
- La pâte était-elle trop sèche ? Avez-vous ajouté trop de farine ?
- Avez-vous bien pétri la pâte ? Avez-vous mal distribué la levure ?
- Avez-vous placé le moule au centre du four ? Est-il possible que la chaleur n'ait pas été régulière ?
- Avez-vous mis le pain au four avant qu'il n'ait fini de lever ?

Si le pain a mal levé et présente une texture trop dense ou trop serrée :

- La pâte était-elle dense et difficile à pétrir ? Il n'y avait peut-être pas suffisamment de liquide.
- Votre levure est-elle trop vieille ? Vérifiez la date de péremption. En cas de doute, dissolvez un sachet de levure et 1 cuillerée à café de sucre dans 1/4 tasse (60 ml) d'eau tiède (40 °C à 46 °C, 105 °F à 115 °F). Mélangez et mettez de côté pendant 5 à 10 minutes. Si une couche mousseuse se forme, votre levure est encore bonne. La levure doit être conservée au réfrigérateur ou au congélateur. Ne la conservez jamais à température ambiante.
- La levure est inactive à cause du froid ou de la chaleur. La levure est très fragile. La température élevée de la farine fraîchement moulue tue la levure.
- La levure est inactive, car la pâte n'est pas assez chaude. Placez la pâte à un endroit suffisamment chaud pour qu'elle lève.
- Le pain a-t-il levé suffisamment avant de l'enfourner ? Vous l'avez peut-être cuit avant qu'il n'ait fini de lever.
- Avez-vous ajouté trop de sel ? Le sel peut inhiber la levure.

Si la texture est trop grossière ou ouverte :

- Avez-vous ajouté trop de levure ?
- La pâte était-elle trop humide ?
- Le pain a-t-il levé au-dessus du bord du moule ? Vous avez peut-être laissé le pain lever trop longtemps.
- Le moule était-il de la bonne taille ?

Croûtes personnalisées

Quel genre de croûte aimez-vous ? Tendre, épaisse, élastique... ? En utilisant différents glaçages et quelques astuces de boulanger, vous pouvez obtenir un vaste éventail de textures, de goûts et de couleurs.

Pour une croûte élastique et croustillante comme celle d'une baguette, placez un récipient d'eau sur la grille du four en dessous du pain pendant la cuisson. La vapeur s'élevant autour du pain dans le four chaud fera le travail. Vous pouvez aussi vaporiser le pain d'une fine vapeur d'eau toutes les 10 minutes pendant la cuisson.

Pour une croûte élastique et brillante, enduisez la pâte d'un mélange de fécule de maïs et d'eau, à l'aide d'un pinceau. Dissolvez 1 cuillerée à café de fécule de maïs dans 2/3 tasse (160 ml) d'eau, puis portez ce mélange à ébullition dans une casserole. Laissez le mélange refroidir légèrement et, avec un pinceau souple, enduisez toutes les surfaces exposées juste avant la cuisson. Après 10 minutes de cuisson, sortez le pain du four, enduisez-le à nouveau puis terminez la cuisson.

Pour une croûte très brillante, essayez les glaçages à base d'œuf. Comme ils sont collants, ils sont pratiques pour maintenir les graines de pavot ou de sésame en place. Juste avant la cuisson, enduisez le pain avec un œuf entier légèrement battu ou avec un jaune ou un blanc d'œuf battus avec 1 cuillerée à soupe d'eau froide. Si vous choisissez d'utiliser un jaune d'œuf, votre pain aura une couleur dorée. Le blanc d'œuf ajoute du brillant, mais pas de couleur. Un œuf entier vous donne un peu des deux.

Pour une croûte tendre, enduisez le pain de beurre fondu à l'aide d'un pinceau juste avant ou juste après la cuisson. Vous pouvez aussi l'enduire de lait ou de crème avant la cuisson.

Moudre des farines à base de céréales complètes

Les céréales augmentent d'environ 25 % de volume quand elles sont moulues pour faire de la farine. Le maïs, le soja et autres céréales à haute teneur en humidité ont tendance à coller et à arrêter de circuler quand vous les moulez. Pour éviter ce problème, insérez le poussoir dans l'orifice du bouchon du couvercle et, alors que l'appareil tourne en vitesse rapide, repoussez délicatement la farine vers les lames. Ainsi, les céréales sont moulues uniformément.

Remarque importante :
Pour obtenir les meilleurs résultats, conservez les céréales au congélateur. Ne moulez pas plus de 2 tasses (400 g) à la fois.

FARINE À BASE DE CÉRÉALES COMPLÈTES

vitesse : position Variable à High (rapide)• mixage : 1 minute
quantité obtenue : jusqu'à 3 1/4 tasses (390 g)

1/4 à 2 tasses (50 à 400 g) de céréales complètes

Remarque du cuisinier :
À température ambiante, la farine reste fraîche pendant un mois. Au réfrigérateur, pendant deux mois. Elle peut aussi être congelée et ainsi conservée de 6 mois à 1 an. Amenez à température ambiante la quantité dont vous avez besoin pour votre recette.

Versez 2 tasses (400 g) maximum de céréales complètes dans le récipient Vitamix, et verrouillez le couvercle.

Réglez le commutateur sur la position Variable et la vitesse sur 1.

Mettez l'appareil en marche et augmentez lentement la vitesse jusqu'à la position Variable 10, puis High (Rapide).

Moulez jusqu'à obtenir la finesse désirée (consultez le tableau pour les temps de mouture recommandés). Plus vous mixez longtemps, plus la farine est fine (ne dépassez pas 1 minute).

Mesure de blé complet	Temps de mouture	Vitesse	Volume approximatif de farine obtenu	Degré de finesse
3/4 tasse (144 g)	1 minute	VAR - HIGH (RAPIDE)	1 tasse (120 g) + 2 1/2 cuillerées à café	très fine
1 tasse (192 g)	1 minute	VAR - HIGH (RAPIDE)	1 1/2 tasse (180 g)	très fine
1 1/4 tasse (240 g)	1 minute	VAR - HIGH (RAPIDE)	1 3/4 tasse (210 g) + 2 cuillerées à soupe (15 g)	très fine
1 1/2 tasse (288 g)	1 minute	VAR - HIGH (RAPIDE)	2 1/3 tasses (280 g) + 1 cuillerée à soupe (8 g)	très fine
1 3/4 tasse (336 g)	1 minute	VAR - HIGH (RAPIDE)	2 1/2 tasses (300 g) + 3 cuillerées à soupe (22 g)	très fine
2 tasses (384 g)	1 minute	VAR - HIGH (RAPIDE)	3 1/4 tasses (390 g)	très fine

Remarque : Pour obtenir les meilleurs résultats, utilisez des lames spéciales pour moudre la farine. Réglez le commutateur sur la position Variable et la vitesse sur 1. Mettez l'appareil en marche et augmentez lentement la vitesse jusqu'à la position Variable 10, puis High (Rapide).

Moudre des farines à base de céréales complètes *(suite)*

Attention :
Respectez les temps de mouture recommandés. Si vous moulez des ingrédients secs, comme le blé complet, pendant plus de deux minutes, la farine risque de se tasser et de surchauffer le récipient. Cela peut causer des dommages irréversibles au récipient et aux joints. Suivez scrupuleusement les temps de mouture recommandés.

Guide de cuisson des céréales concassées

Céréales concassées	Quantité	Vitesse: (Low) Lente Variable 7 ou 8	Eau	Temps de cuisson	Quantité obtenue
Orge	1/2 tasse (90 g)	10 secondes	2 tasses (480 ml)	20 minutes	1 1/2 tasse (360 g)
Sarrasin	1/2 tasse (80 g)	5 secondes	2 tasses (480 ml)	10 minutes	1 2/3 tasse (400 g)
Maïs	1/2 tasse (80 g)	10 secondes	2 tasses (480 ml)	20 minutes	1 1/2 tasse (360 g)
Avoine	1/2 tasse (80 g)	10 secondes	2 tasses (480 ml)	20 minutes	1 1/2 tasse (360 g)
Riz (blanc)	1/2 tasse (90 g)	10 secondes	2 tasses (480 ml)	8 à 10 minutes	1 3/4 tasse (420 g)
Riz (brun)	1/2 tasse (90 g)	10 secondes	2 tasses (480 ml)	20 minutes	1 3/4 tasse (420 g)
Seigle	1/2 tasse (90 g)	10 secondes	1 1/2 tasse (360 ml)	20 minutes	1 1/2 tasse (360 g)
Blé	1/2 tasse (100 g)	10 secondes	1 1/2 tasse (360 ml)	20 minutes	1 1/2 tasse (360 g)
Riz sauvage	1/2 tasse (90 g)	10 secondes	1 1/2 tasse (360 ml)	20 minutes	1 1/2 tasse (360 g)

Astuces utiles

1. Si vous moulez 2 tasses (400 g) de céréales en même temps, vous obtenez des céréales moulues plus uniformément.

2. Vous pouvez ajouter 1/4 à 1/2 cuillerée à café de sel à l'eau bouillante. Cela ne sert qu'à relever le goût et n'est pas nécessaire si vous essayez de limiter votre consommation de sel.

3. Pour profiter des qualités nutritionnelles des céréales complètes sans sacrifier la commodité des céréales préparées, versez la quantité désirée de céréales concassées dans une casserole d'eau bouillante le soir, avant de vous coucher. Éteignez le feu, placez un couvercle hermétique sur la casserole et laissez tremper les céréales toute la nuit. Le matin, elles seront prêtes et vous pourrez les savourer froides. Si vous les préférez chaudes, réchauffez-les sur la cuisinière ou au micro-ondes.

4. Une autre méthode pratique nécessite l'utilisation d'un thermos. Versez une tasse (200 g) de céréales dans un thermos de 0,95 l (1 quart) (un col large est plus pratique), puis ajoutez de l'eau bouillante jusqu'à 2,5 cm (1 pouce) du haut du thermos. Mélangez les céréales et l'eau avec la queue d'une cuillère en bois. Fermez le thermos et laissez les céréales cuire lentement pendant 8 à 12 heures.

5. Vous pouvez mélanger diverses céréales pour une plus grande variété. Par exemple, avoine et sarrasin, riz sauvage et riz brun, etc.

6. Relevez vos céréales en ajoutant de la noix de muscade ou de la cannelle. Ajoutez vos fruits préférés pour plus de goût et des apports nutritionnels accrus : pêches, fraises, myrtilles, raisins secs ou noix de coco.

   Remarque du cuisinier : *Si vous avez ajouté des fruits secs, n'oubliez pas que les fruits secs se réhydratent en absorbant de l'eau. Augmentez légèrement la quantité d'eau de vos céréales pour compenser l'eau qui sera absorbée par les fruits secs.*

7. Si vous voulez utiliser vos céréales dans un ragoût, remplacez l'eau de cuisson par du bouillon.

CONCASSAGE DES CÉRÉALES

vitesse : position Variable • mixage : 10 secondes

1/4 à 2 tasses (50 à 400 g) de grains entiers (au choix, blé, orge, avoine, maïs, riz, etc.)

Sel à discrétion (environ 1/4 cuillerée à café par 1/2 tasse (100 g) de céréales)

Versez 2 tasses (400 g) maximum de grains entiers dans le récipient, et verrouillez le couvercle.

Réglez le commutateur sur la position Variable et la vitesse sur 1.

Mettez l'appareil en marche et augmentez lentement la vitesse jusqu'à la position Variable 7 ou 8.

Moulez jusqu'au degré désiré de finesse. Plus vous mixez longtemps, plus la céréale se transforme, jusqu'à devenir de la farine.

Comment cuire les céréales concassées

Dans une casserole lourde ou au bain-marie, portez l'eau salée à ébullition. Ajoutez lentement les céréales, en mélangeant constamment pour éviter les grumeaux.

Couvrez la casserole hermétiquement et réduisez la température à feu doux. Laissez cuire jusqu'à ce que les céréales soient tendres (consultez le tableau ci-dessus pour les temps de cuisson), en mélangeant fréquemment.

GRUAU DE BLÉ AUX POMMES ET AUX RAISINS SECS

préparation : 15 minutes • mixage : 15 secondes • cuisson : 15 à 20 minutes
quantité obtenue : 3 tasses (720 g) de céréales cuites

1 tasse (180 g) de grains de blé entier

1 1/2 tasses (360 ml) d'eau

1/4 cuillerée à café de sel

1 pomme à tarte (170 g), pelée, épépinée et coupée en quartiers

1/8 cuillerée à café de cannelle

1/2 tasse (72 g) de raisins secs

2 cuillerées à soupe (18 g) de graines de tournesol

Versez le blé entier dans le récipient à INGRÉDIENTS SECS Vitamix, et verrouillez le couvercle.

Réglez le commutateur sur la position Variable et la vitesse sur 1.

Mettez l'appareil en marche et augmentez lentement la vitesse jusqu'à la position Variable 7 ou 8.

Moulez pendant 15 secondes environ jusqu'à obtention du degré de finesse désiré.

Dans une casserole, faites bouillir de l'eau salée. Ajoutez lentement le blé concassé à l'eau bouillante, en remuant sans cesse avec un fouet en métal.

Réduisez la température, couvrez et laissez mijoter pendant 15 à 20 minutes en remuant fréquemment.

Pendant que le blé cuit, émincez la pomme dans le récipient à INGRÉDIENTS HUMIDES Vitamix.

Verrouillez le couvercle et ôtez le bouchon du couvercle.

Réglez le commutateur sur la position Variable et la vitesse sur 1.

Mettez l'appareil en marche et augmentez lentement la vitesse jusqu'à la position Variable 4. Insérez les quartiers de pomme dans l'appareil en marche à travers l'orifice du bouchon du couvercle, en utilisant le poussoir au besoin pour les émincer.

Enlevez la casserole du feu et ajoutez les morceaux de pomme, la cannelle, les raisins secs et les graines de tournesol au blé cuit. Mélangez le tout.

Couvrez et attendez 5 minutes avant de servir.

Informations nutritionnelles (par tasse, soit 240 g) : 342 kcal (lipides 6 %, protéines 9 %, glucides 85 %)
protéines 9 g • lipides totaux 2 g • acides gras saturés 0 g • glucides 79 g • fibres alimentaires 10 g • sucre 22 g
sodium 204 mg • cholestérol 0 mg

Si les aliments sont projetés sur les lames de l'appareil sans être émincés, la vitesse est trop faible. S'ils sont projetés violemment contre les parois du récipient et si les particules résultantes sont trop grossières ou inégales, la vitesse est trop élevée.

CÉRÉALES AU RIZ BRUN ET AUX ABRICOTS

préparation : 10 minutes • mixage : 10 secondes • cuisson : 20 minutes
quantité obtenue : 3 1/2 tasses (840 g) de céréales cuites

1 tasse (185 g) de riz brun cru

3 1/2 tasses (840 ml) d'eau

1/2 cuillerée à café de sel

8 abricots secs (non sucrés)

2 cuillerées à soupe (18 g) de graines de tournesol

1/4 cuillerée à café d'extrait d'amande, facultatif

Versez le riz brun dans le récipient à INGRÉDIENTS SECS Vitamix, et verrouillez le couvercle.

Réglez le commutateur sur la position Variable et la vitesse sur 1.

Mettez l'appareil en marche et augmentez lentement la vitesse jusqu'à la position Variable 7 ou 8.

Moulez jusqu'à obtention du degré de finesse désiré, pendant 10 secondes environ. Si vous souhaitez obtenir des céréales plus fines, moulez-les pendant plus longtemps.

Dans une casserole, faites bouillir de l'eau salée. Ajoutez lentement le riz concassé à l'eau bouillante, en remuant sans cesse avec un fouet en métal.

Réduisez la température sur feu doux, couvrez et laissez mijoter pendant 20 minutes, ou jusqu'à ce que le riz soit cuit, en remuant fréquemment.

Pendant que le riz cuit, émincez les abricots dans le récipient à INGRÉDIENTS HUMIDES Vitamix.

Verrouillez le couvercle et ôtez le bouchon du couvercle.

Réglez le commutateur sur la position Variable et la vitesse sur 1.

Mettez l'appareil en marche et augmentez lentement la vitesse jusqu'à la position Variable 5. Pendant que l'appareil est en fonctionnement, insérez les abricots à travers l'orifice du bouchon du couvercle. Si nécessaire, réglez la vitesse sur la position Variable pour obtenir des morceaux plus petits.

Enlevez la casserole du feu et ajoutez les morceaux d'abricot, les graines de tournesol et l'extrait d'amande aux céréales cuites. Mélangez le tout.

Couvrez et attendez 5 minutes avant de servir.

Informations nutritionnelles (par tasse, soit 240 g) : 224 kcal (lipides 10 %, protéines 9 %, glucides 82 %)
protéines 5 g • lipides totaux 2 g • acides gras saturés 0 g • glucides 46 g • fibres alimentaires 3 g • sucre 5 g
sodium 346 mg • cholestérol 0 mg

Si les aliments sont projetés sur les lames de l'appareil sans être émincés, la vitesse est trop faible. S'ils sont projetés violemment contre les parois du récipient et si les particules résultantes sont trop grossières ou inégales, la vitesse est trop élevée.

GRUAU DE RIZ BRUN

préparation : 10 minutes • mixage : 10 secondes • cuisson : 20 minutes
quantité obtenue : 3 1/2 tasses (840 g) de céréales cuites

1 tasse (185 g) de riz brun cru

3 1/2 tasses (840 ml) d'eau

1/2 cuillerée à café de sel

Versez le riz brun dans le récipient à INGRÉDIENTS SECS Vitamix, et verrouillez le couvercle.

Réglez le commutateur sur la position Variable et la vitesse sur 1.

Mettez l'appareil en marche et augmentez lentement la vitesse jusqu'à la position Variable 7 ou 8.

Moulez jusqu'à obtention du degré de finesse désiré, pendant 10 secondes environ. Si vous souhaitez obtenir des céréales plus fines, moulez-les pendant plus longtemps.

Dans une casserole, faites bouillir de l'eau salée. Ajoutez lentement le riz concassé à l'eau bouillante, en remuant sans cesse avec un fouet en métal.

Réduisez la température sur feu doux, couvrez et laissez mijoter pendant 20 minutes jusqu'à ce que le riz soit cuit, en remuant fréquemment.

Informations nutritionnelles (par tasse, soit 240 g) : 197 kcal (lipides 7 %, protéines 8 %, glucides 85 %)
protéines 4 g • lipides totaux 1 g • acides gras saturés 0 g • glucides 41 g • fibres alimentaires 2 g • sucre 0 g
sodium 344 mg • cholestérol 0 mg

CÉRÉALES AU BLÉ CONCASSÉ

préparation : 10 minutes • mixage : 15 secondes • cuisson : 15 à 20 minutes
quantité obtenue : 3 tasses (720 g) de céréales cuites

1 tasse (180 g) de grains de blé entier

3 tasses (720 ml) d'eau

1/2 cuillerée à café de sel

Versez le blé entier dans le récipient à INGRÉDIENTS SECS Vitamix, et verrouillez le couvercle.

Réglez le commutateur sur la position Variable et la vitesse sur 1.

Mettez l'appareil en marche et augmentez lentement la vitesse jusqu'à la position Variable 7 ou 8.

Moulez jusqu'à obtention du degré de finesse désiré.

Dans une casserole, faites bouillir de l'eau salée. Ajoutez lentement le blé concassé à l'eau bouillante, en touillant sans cesse avec un fouet en métal.

Réduisez la température sur feu doux, couvrez et laissez mijoter pendant 15 à 20 minutes, ou jusqu'à ce que le riz soit cuit.

Informations nutritionnelles (par tasse, soit 240 g) : 219 kcal (lipides 4 %, protéines 12 %, glucides 83 %)
protéines 7 g • lipides totaux 1 g • acides gras saturés 0 g • glucides 49 g • fibres alimentaires 8 g • sucre 0 g
sodium 399 mg • cholestérol 0 mg

CÉRÉALES CRÉMEUSES AU RIZ

préparation : 10 minutes • mixage : 10 secondes • cuisson : 8 à 10 minutes
quantité obtenue : 1 3/4 tasse (420 g) de céréales cuites

1/2 tasse (93 g) de riz cru

2 tasses (480 ml) d'eau

1/4 cuillerée à café de sel

Versez le riz dans le récipient à INGRÉDIENTS SECS Vitamix, et verrouillez le couvercle.

Réglez le commutateur sur la position Variable et la vitesse sur 1.

Mettez l'appareil en marche et augmentez lentement la vitesse jusqu'à la position Variable 7 ou 8.

Moulez jusqu'à obtention du degré de finesse désiré, pendant 10 secondes environ. Si vous souhaitez obtenir des céréales plus fines, moulez-les pendant plus longtemps.

Dans une casserole, faites bouillir de l'eau salée. Versez doucement le riz concassé dans l'eau bouillante. Remuez constamment avec un fouet en métal.

Réduisez la température sur feu doux et laissez mijoter pendant 8 à 10 minutes (un peu plus longtemps pour le riz brun) jusqu'à ce que le riz soit cuit, en remuant fréquemment.

Informations nutritionnelles (par tasse, soit 240 g) : 199 kcal (lipides 2 %, protéines 8 %, glucides 90 %)
protéines 4 g • lipides totaux 0 g • acides gras saturés 0 g • glucides 44 g • fibres alimentaires 1 g • sucre 0 g
sodium 355 mg • cholestérol 0 mg

MUESLI

préparation : 15 minutes • mixage : 3 minutes • cuisson : 15 minutes
quantité obtenue : 10 tasses (2,4 kg)

- 1/2 tasse (120 ml) de miel
- 3/4 tasse (165 g) de sucre roux, bien tassé
- 1/2 tasse (120 ml) d'eau chaude
- 1 cuillerée à café de sel
- 2 cuillerées à café d'extrait de vanille
- 1 1/2 cuillerée à café de cannelle
- 5 tasses (400 g) de flocons d'avoine
- 1 tasse (104 g) de germe de blé
- 1/4 tasse (35 g) de graines de tournesol
- 1/2 tasse (42 g) de noix de coco hachée ou en poudre
- 1/2 tasse (58 g) de noix broyées
- 1 tasse (145 g) de raisins secs

Préchauffez le four à 180 °C (350 °F). Huilez légèrement en vaporisant d'huile végétale deux moules de 33 cm x 23 cm (13 pouces x 9 pouces) ou un grand plat à four.

Versez le miel, le sucre roux, l'eau, le sel, l'extrait de vanille et la cannelle dans le récipient à INGRÉDIENTS HUMIDES Vitamix dans l'ordre indiqué, et verrouillez le couvercle.

Réglez le commutateur sur la position Variable et la vitesse sur 1.

Mettez l'appareil en marche et augmentez lentement la vitesse jusqu'à la position Variable 10, puis High (Rapide).

Mixez 3 minutes ou jusqu'à ce que la préparation soit fumante.

Dans un grand saladier, mélangez l'avoine, le germe de blé, les graines de tournesol, la noix de coco et les noix broyées.

Versez le mélange chaud sur les ingrédients secs et mélangez, en ne laissant que quelques grumeaux. Étalez dans les moules et enfournez pendant 15 minutes. Mélangez toutes les 5 minutes.

Retirez les moules du four et ajoutez les raisins secs. Mélangez. Placez les moules sur une grille à pâtisserie et laissez refroidir complètement. Conservez dans des bocaux ou dans un grand sac en plastique.

Informations nutritionnelles (par 1/2 tasse, soit 120 g) : 287 kcal (lipides 18 %, protéines 12 %, glucides 69 %)
protéines 9 g • lipides totaux 6 g • acides gras saturés 1 g • glucides 52 g • fibres alimentaires 6 g • sucre 20 g
sodium 124 mg • cholestérol 0 mg

Vous pouvez aussi faire cuire le mélange à une température plus basse jusqu'à ce qu'il soit sec.

Cette recette unique ne requiert pas de graisses ajoutées. Pour un muesli moelleux, ajoutez 1/4 tasse (60 ml) d'huile de pépin de raisin ou d'huile d'olive légère aux ingrédients liquides.

Muesli

Pour broyer les noix, sélectionnez la position Variable 1 (récipient à INGRÉDIENTS SECS). Mettez l'appareil en marche et augmentez lentement la vitesse jusqu'à la position Variable 4. Insérez les noix à travers l'orifice du bouchon du couvercle et broyez pendant 5 secondes.

PORRIDGE

préparation : 10 minutes • mixage : 10 secondes • cuisson : 30 minutes
quantité obtenue : 3 1/2 tasses (840 g) de céréales cuites

1 tasse (160 g) de grains d'avoine (PAS de flocons)

4 tasses (960 ml) d'eau

1/2 cuillerée à café de sel

Versez l'avoine complète dans le récipient à INGRÉDIENTS SECS Vitamix, et verrouillez le couvercle.

Réglez le commutateur sur la position Variable et la vitesse sur 1.

Mettez l'appareil en marche et augmentez lentement la vitesse jusqu'à la position Variable 7.

Moulez jusqu'à obtention du degré de finesse désiré, pendant 10 secondes environ. Si vous souhaitez obtenir des céréales plus fines, moulez-les pendant plus longtemps.

Dans une casserole, faites bouillir de l'eau salée. Ajoutez lentement l'avoine concassée à l'eau bouillante, en remuant sans cesse avec un fouet en métal.

Réduisez la température sur feu doux, couvrez et laissez mijoter pendant 30 minutes, ou jusqu'à ce que l'avoine soit cuite, en remuant fréquemment.

Informations nutritionnelles (par tasse, soit 240 g) : 126 kcal (lipides 14 %, protéines 18 %, glucides 68 %)
protéines 8 g • lipides totaux 3 g • acides gras saturés 1 g • glucides 31 g • fibres alimentaires 5 g • sucre 1 g
sodium 342 mg • cholestérol 0 mg

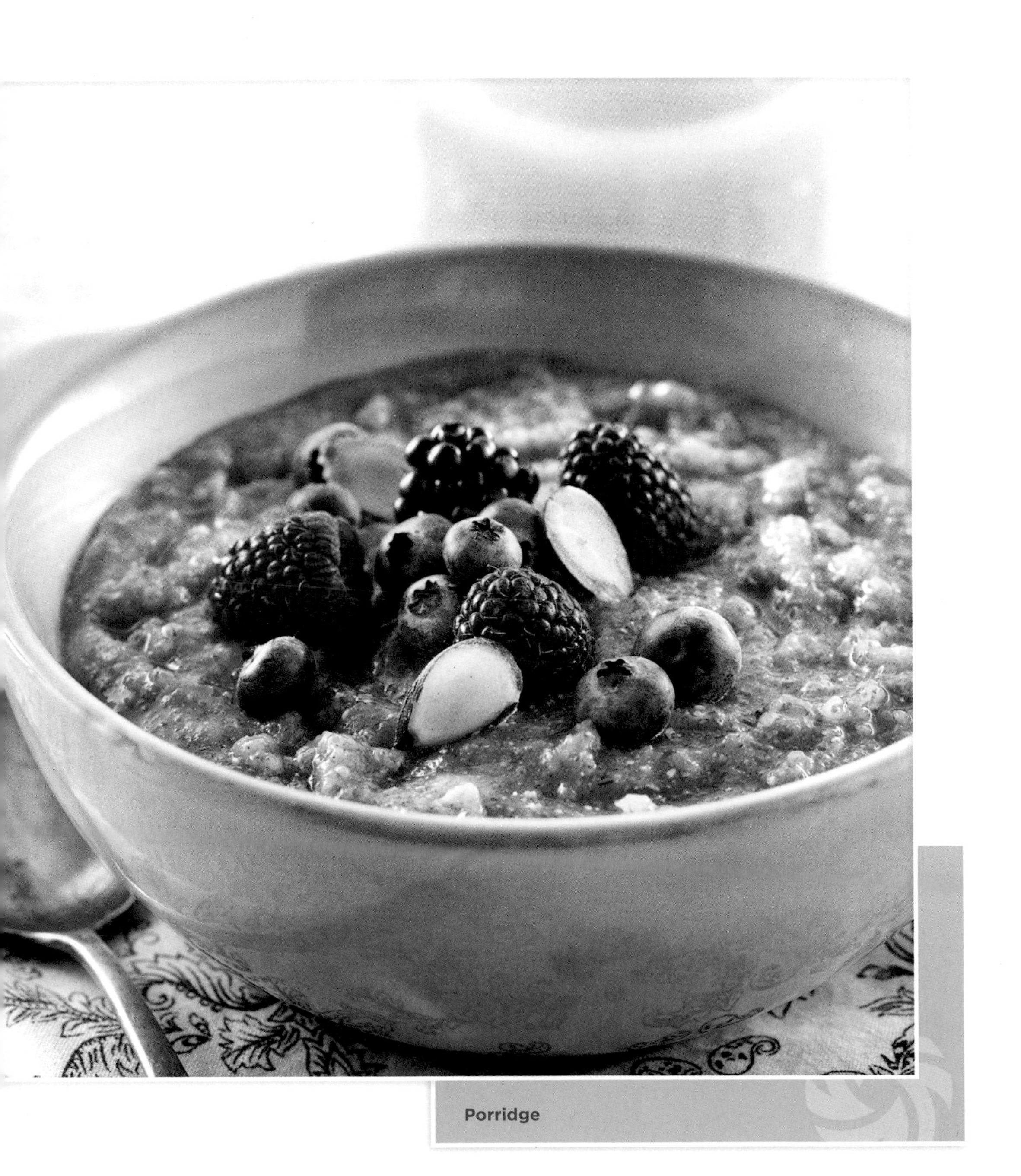

Porridge

RIZ AUX CÉRÉALES ET RAISINS SECS

préparation : 10 minutes • mixage : 10 secondes • cuisson : 30 minutes
quantité obtenue : 3 1/2 tasses (840 g) de céréales cuites

1/2 tasse (93 g) de riz non cuit

2 tasses (480 ml) d'eau

1/4 cuillerée à café de sel

1/2 tasse (72 g) de raisins secs

Une pincée de cannelle

Versez le riz dans le récipient à INGRÉDIENTS SECS Vitamix, et verrouillez le couvercle.

Réglez le commutateur sur la position Variable et la vitesse sur 1.

Mettez l'appareil en marche et augmentez lentement la vitesse jusqu'à la position Variable 7 ou 8.

Moulez jusqu'à obtention du degré de finesse désiré, pendant 10 secondes environ.

Dans une casserole, faites bouillir de l'eau salée. Ajoutez lentement le riz concassé à l'eau bouillante, en remuant sans cesse avec un fouet en métal.

Reduisez la température sur feu doux, et laissez mijoter pendant 8 à 10 minutes (un peu plus longtemps pour le riz brun) jusqu'à ce que le riz soit cuit.

Retirez la casserole du feu, puis ajoutez les raisins secs et la cannelle.

Couvrez et attendez 5 minutes avant de servir.

Informations nutritionnelles (par tasse, soit 240 g) : 292 kcal (lipides 1 %, protéines 6 %, glucides 92 %)
protéines 5 g • lipides totaux 0 g • acides gras saturés 0 g • glucides 70 g • fibres alimentaires 2 g • sucre 24 g
sodium 306 mg • cholestérol 0 mg

AVOINE SOLEIL LEVANT

préparation : 10 minutes • mixage : 10 secondes • cuisson : 30 minutes
quantité obtenue : 3 3/4 tasses (900 g) de céréales cuites

1 tasse (184 g) de grains d'avoine complète (PAS en flocons)

4 tasses (960 ml) d'eau

1/2 cuillerée à café de sel

6 ou 7 pruneaux dénoyautés

Versez l'avoine complète dans le récipient à INGRÉDIENTS SECS Vitamix, et verrouillez le couvercle.

Réglez le commutateur sur la position Variable et la vitesse sur 1.

Mettez l'appareil en marche et augmentez lentement la vitesse jusqu'à la position Variable 7.

Moulez jusqu'à obtention du degré de finesse désiré, pendant 10 secondes environ. Si vous souhaitez obtenir des céréales plus fines, moulez-les pendant plus longtemps.

Dans une casserole, faites bouillir de l'eau salée. Ajoutez lentement l'avoine concassée à l'eau bouillante, en remuant sans cesse avec un fouet en métal.

Reduisez la température sur feu doux, couvrez et laissez mijoter pendant 30 minutes, ou jusqu'à ce que l'avoine soit cuite, en remuant fréquemment.

Pendant que l'avoine cuit, émincez les pruneaux dans le récipient à INGRÉDIENTS HUMIDES Vitamix.

Verrouillez le couvercle.

Réglez le commutateur sur la position Variable et la vitesse sur 1.

Mettez l'appareil en marche et augmentez lentement la vitesse jusqu'à la position Variable 5 ou 6. Ôtez le bouchon du couvercle. Pendant que l'appareil est en fonctionnement, insérez les pruneaux à travers l'orifice du bouchon du couvercle.

Retirez la casserole du feu et ajoutez les pruneaux émincés. Mélangez le tout.

Couvrez et attendez 5 minutes avant de servir.

Informations nutritionnelles (par tasse, soit 240 g) : 209 kcal (lipides 4 %, protéines 12 %, glucides 84 %)
protéines 7 g • lipides totaux 1 g • acides gras saturés 0 g • glucides 47 g • fibres alimentaires 6 g • sucre 0 g
sodium 325 mg • cholestérol 0 mg

Si les aliments sont projetés sur les lames de l'appareil sans être émincés, la vitesse est trop faible. S'ils sont projetés violemment contre les parois du récipient et si les particules résultantes sont trop grossières ou inégales, la vitesse est trop élevée.

pains minute

Comment réussir les pains minute

- Quand une recette spécifie du beurre ramolli, laissez le beurre à température ambiante pendant 20 minutes environ. Ne passez pas le beurre au micro-ondes, car la température élevée risque de faire fondre le beurre au lieu de le ramollir, et l'utilisation de beurre fondu au lieu de beurre ramolli a un impact négatif sur les produits finis.
- Si vous mixez trop la pâte des pains minute, ils seront moins tendres une fois cuits. Tournez délicatement et au minimum, juste assez pour mélanger les ingrédients.
- Préchauffez le four pendant 10 minutes au moins avant de placer le pain minute sur la grille du milieu. Si vous cuisez un pain minute dans un four insuffisamment chaud, il ne lèvera pas comme il faut.
- Conservez les pains minute dans du film alimentaire ou du papier d'aluminium. Vous pouvez ainsi les conserver trois jours au réfrigérateur et trois mois au congélateur.

Cuisiner avec les enfants – Les enfants adorent généralement préparer des pains minute ou des muffins. Encouragez-les à participer en leur montrant comment huiler le moule ou mesurer les ingrédients qu'ils aiment, comme les amandes, le chocolat ou les cerises sèches.

PAIN AUX POMMES ET NOIX DE PÉCAN

préparation : 10 minutes • mixage : 20 secondes • cuisson : 40 à 50 minutes
quantité obtenue : 1 pain (12 tranches)

1 tasse (125 g) de farine non blanchie

1/2 tasse (60 g) de farine de blé complet

1 cuillerée à café de levure chimique

1/4 cuillerée à café de bicarbonate de soude

1/2 cuillerée à café de sel

2 petites pommes, épépinées et coupées en quartier, 1 1/4 tasse (156 g) environ

1 gros œuf

3 cuillerées à soupe (45 ml) d'huile d'olive légère

2/3 tasse (147 g) de sucre roux léger, bien tassé

1/2 tasse (54 g) de noix de pécan hachées

Huilez légèrement en vaporisant avec une huile végétale ou en enduisant de matière grasse un moule à cake de 22 cm x 11 cm (8 1/2 pouces x 4 1/2 pouces). Préchauffez le four à 180 °C (350 °F).

Dans un grand saladier, mélangez bien la farine, la farine de blé complet, la levure chimique, le bicarbonate de soude et le sel.

Mettez les pommes, l'œuf, l'huile et le sucre roux dans le récipient à INGRÉDIENTS SECS Vitamix dans l'ordre indiqué, et verrouillez le couvercle.

Réglez le commutateur sur la position Variable et la vitesse sur 1.

Mettez l'appareil en marche et augmentez lentement la vitesse jusqu'à la position Variable 10, puis High (Rapide).

Mixez jusqu'à ce que les pommes soient émincées, pendant 20 secondes environ. Si nécessaire, insérez le poussoir à travers l'orifice du bouchon du couvercle pour que le mélange se déplace et que les pommes soient émincées.

Versez le mélange à base de pommes et les noix de pécan dans le saladier contenant les ingrédients secs. Mélangez à la main SUFFISAMMENT pour humidifier les ingrédients secs, pas plus.

Répartissez la pâte dans le moule. Enfournez 40 à 50 minutes. Surveillez la fin de la cuisson en piquant le pain avec la lame d'un couteau ; il est cuit quand elle ressort sèche.

Laissez le pain reposer sur une grille à pâtisserie pendant 30 minutes, puis retirez-le avec précaution du moule et laissez-le refroidir complètement avant de découper.

Informations nutritionnelles (par tranche) : 175 kcal (lipides 36 %, protéines 6 %, glucides 58 %) • protéines 3 g
lipides totaux 7 g • acides gras saturés 1 g • glucides 26 g • fibres alimentaires 2 g • sucre 13 g • sodium 178 mg
cholestérol 18 mg

BROWNIES « EXTRA »

préparation : 20 minutes • mixage : 20 secondes • cuisson : 25 à 30 minutes
quantité obtenue : 2 douzaines

3/4 tasse (64 g) de poudre de cacao non sucrée

1 cuillerée à café de levure chimique

1 cuillerée à café de sel

1 cuillerée à café de poudre de café soluble

1 1/2 tasse (180 g) de farine de blé complet

2 tasses (448 g) de grains de chocolat mi-sucré

1 tasse (227 g) de beurre doux, ramolli et coupé en morceaux

2 tasses (440 g) de sucre roux clair ou foncé, bien tassé

1 cuillerée à soupe d'extrait de vanille

4 gros œufs

Huilez légèrement en vaporisant une huile végétale ou en enduisant de matière grasse un moule à cake de 23 cm x 33 cm (9 pouces x 13 pouces). Préchauffez le four à 180 °C (350 °F).

Si vous utilisez des grains de blé complet : Placez 1 1/2 tasse (270 g) de grains de blé entier dans le récipient à INGRÉDIENTS SECS Vitamix, et verrouillez le couvercle.

Réglez le commutateur sur la position Variable et la vitesse sur 1.

Mettez l'appareil en marche et augmentez lentement la vitesse jusqu'à la position Variable 10, puis High (Rapide).

Moulez pendant 1 minute (pas plus longtemps).

Arrêtez l'appareil pour permettre à la farine de refroidir pendant quelques minutes. Mesurez 1 1/2 tasse (180 g) de farine de blé complet pour la recette. Réservez le surplus de farine pour un autre usage.

Si vous utilisez de la farine de blé complet : Versez la poudre de cacao, la levure, le sel, la poudre de café soluble et la farine de blé complet dans un grand saladier. Ajoutez les grains de chocolat. Réservez.

Mettez le beurre, le sucre, l'extrait de vanille et les œufs dans le récipient à INGRÉDIENTS HUMIDES Vitamix, et verrouillez le couvercle. Réglez le commutateur sur la position Variable et la vitesse sur 1.

Mettez l'appareil en marche et augmentez lentement la vitesse jusqu'à la position Variable 10, puis High (Rapide).

Mixez pendant 20 secondes jusqu'à obtention d'une texture crémeuse, en utilisant le poussoir si nécessaire.

Versez le mélange à base de beurre dans le mélange à base de farine et malaxez soigneusement à la main.

Versez le tout dans le moule en vous aidant d'une spatule en caoutchouc. Enfournez 25 à 30 minutes. Surveillez la fin de la cuisson en piquant le centre avec la lame d'un couteau ; les brownies sont cuits quand la lame ressort couverte de quelques miettes humides. Ne laissez pas cuire trop longtemps, sinon les brownies seront secs.

Retirez du four et laissez refroidir sur une grille à pâtisserie. Coupez en morceaux et servez.

Informations nutritionnelles (par brownie) : 282 kcal (lipides 44 %, protéines 5 %, glucides 51 %) • protéines 4 g lipides totaux 14 g • acides gras saturés 8 g • glucides 37 g • fibres alimentaires 3 g • sucre 28 g • sodium 144 mg cholestérol 56 mg

Brownies « extra »

GÂTEAU AUX COURGETTES ET AU CHOCOLAT

préparation : 20 minutes • mixage : 35 à 40 secondes • cuisson : 35 à 40 minutes
quantité obtenue : 12 carrés

1/2 tasse (114 g) de beurre doux coupé en morceaux, à température ambiante

1 1/2 tasse (300 g) de sucre cristallisé

2 gros œufs

511 g (18 onces) de courgettes coupées en morceaux

1/2 tasse (120 ml) d'huile d'olive légère

1 cuillerée à café d'extrait de vanille

1/2 tasse (120 ml) de babeurre

1 1/2 tasse (180 g) de farine de blé complet

1 1/4 tasse (156 g) de farine non blanchie

1/4 tasse (21 g) de poudre de cacao non sucrée

1 1/4 cuillerée à café de bicarbonate de sodium

1 cuillerée à café de sel

1/4 tasse (30 g) de sucre glace tamisé

Préchauffez le four à 160 °C (325 °F). Huilez légèrement un moule à gâteau carré de 23 cm (9 pouces) de côté.

Mettez le beurre, le sucre et les œufs dans le récipient à INGRÉDIENTS HUMIDES Vitamix dans l'ordre indiqué, et verrouillez le couvercle.

Réglez le commutateur sur la position Variable et la vitesse sur 1.

Mettez l'appareil en marche et augmentez progressivement la vitesse jusqu'à la position Variable 10, puis High (Rapide), en utilisant le poussoir au besoin pour diriger les ingrédients sur les lames.

Mixer pendant 25 secondes. Arrêtez l'appareil, ôtez le couvercle et raclez les parois.

Ajoutez les morceaux de courgette, l'huile, l'extrait de vanille et le babeurre dans le récipient à INGRÉDIENTS HUMIDES Vitamix, et verrouillez le couvercle.

Réglez le commutateur sur la position Variable et la vitesse sur 1.

Mettez l'appareil en marche et augmentez lentement la vitesse jusqu'à la position Variable 10, puis High (Rapide).

Mélangez pendant 10 à 20 secondes ou jusqu'à ce que les courgettes soient émincées.

Dans un grand saladier, mélangez les farines, la poudre de cacao, le bicarbonate de soude et le sel.

Ajoutez le mélange à base de courgettes. Mélangez bien à la main.

Versez le mélange dans le moule en vous aidant d'une spatule.

Enfournez 35 à 40 minutes. Surveillez la fin de la cuisson en piquant avec la lame d'un couteau ; le gâteau est cuit quand elle ressort sèche.

Gâteau aux courgettes et au chocolat *(suite)*

Laissez refroidir sur une grille à pâtisserie pendant 30 minutes, puis passez la lame d'un couteau le long du bord pour décoller le gâteau. Renversez-le sur une grille à pâtisserie et laissez-le refroidir complètement. Coupez en carrés et saupoudrez de sucre glace tamisé au moment de servir.

Pour faire de la farine de blé complet à partir de grains de blé complet : Versez 1 1/2 tasse (270 g) de grains de blé entier dans le récipient à INGRÉDIENTS SECS Vitamix, et verrouillez le couvercle.

Réglez le commutateur sur la position Variable et la vitesse sur 1.

Mettez l'appareil en marche et augmentez lentement la vitesse jusqu'à la position Variable 10, puis High (Rapide).

Moulez pendant 1 minute (pas plus longtemps).

Arrêtez l'appareil pour permettre à la farine de refroidir pendant quelques minutes. Mesurez 1 1/2 tasse (180 g) de farine de blé complet pour la recette. Réservez le surplus de farine pour un autre usage.

Informations nutritionnelles (par carré) : 386 kcal (lipides 42 %, protéines 6 %, glucides 52 %) • protéines 6 g lipides totaux 19 g • acides gras saturés 7 g • glucides 52 g • fibres alimentaires 3 g • sucre 29 g • sodium 359 mg cholestérol 56 mg

PAIN AUX AMANDES ET CRANBERRIES

préparation : 15 minutes • mixage : 30 secondes • cuisson : 1 heure
quantité obtenue : 1 pain (12 tranches)

1 tasse (100 g) de cranberries (canneberges) fraîches ou surgelées

1 orange pelée, épépinée et coupée en quartiers

1 bande de zeste d'orange ou de citron de 2,5 à 5 cm (1 à 2 pouces)

1/4 tasse (60 ml) d'huile d'olive légère

1 tasse (200 g) de sucre cristallisé

1 gros œuf

1 cuillerée à café d'extrait de vanille

1 1/2 cuillerée à café de levure chimique

1/2 cuillerée à café de bicarbonate de soude

1 cuillerée à café de sel

2 tasses (240 g) de farine de blé complet

1/2 tasse (46 g) d'amandes broyées

Huilez légèrement en vaporisant avec une huile végétale ou en enduisant de matière grasse un moule à cake de 22 cm x 11 cm (8 1/2 pouces x 4 1/2 pouces). Préchauffez le four à 180 °C (350 °F).

Placez le récipient à INGRÉDIENTS HUMIDES sur la base du mixeur, réglez le commutateur sur la position Variable et la vitesse sur 1.

Mettez l'appareil en marche et augmentez lentement la vitesse jusqu'à la position Variable 3. Otez le bouchon du couvercle et insérez les cranberries à travers l'orifice. Mixez jusqu'à ce qu'elles soient hachées. Arrêtez l'appareil, raclez les parois et retirez les cranberries hachées.

Mettez les quartiers d'orange, le zeste, l'huile d'olive, le sucre, l'œuf et la vanille dans le récipient à INGRÉDIENTS HUMIDES Vitamix, et verrouillez le couvercle.

Réglez le commutateur sur la position Variable et la vitesse sur 1.

Mettez l'appareil en marche et augmentez lentement la vitesse jusqu'à la position Variable 10, puis High (Rapide).

Mixez 30 secondes en utilisant le poussoir pour diriger les ingrédients vers les lames.

Dans un grand saladier, mélangez bien la farine de blé complet, la levure, le bicarbonate de soude et le sel.

Ajoutez le mélange à base d'orange. Mélangez à la main SUFFISAMMENT pour humidifier les ingrédients secs, pas plus.

Ajoutez les amandes hachées à la pâte. Mélangez légèrement.

Répartissez la pâte dans le moule. Enfournez 1 heure. Surveillez la fin de la cuisson en piquant avec la lame d'un couteau ; le pain est cuit quand elle ressort sèche.

Laissez le pain reposer sur une grille à pâtisserie pendant 30 minutes, puis retirez-le avec précaution du moule et laissez-le refroidir complètement avant de découper.

REMARQUE : Pour faire de la farine de blé complet à partir de grains de blé complet : Placez 1 1/2 tasse (270 g) de grains de blé entier dans le récipient à INGRÉDIENTS SECS Vitamix, et verrouillez le couvercle.

Pain aux amandes et cranberries *(suite)*	Réglez le commutateur sur la position Variable et la vitesse sur 1. Mettez l'appareil en marche et augmentez lentement la vitesse jusqu'à la position Variable 10, puis High (Rapide). Moulez pendant 1 minute (pas plus longtemps). Arrêtez l'appareil pour permettre à la farine de refroidir pendant quelques minutes. Mesurez 2 tasses (240 g) de farine de blé complet pour la recette. Réservez le surplus de farine pour un autre usage.

Informations nutritionnelles (par tranche) : 224 kcal (lipides 32 %, protéines 8 %, glucides 60 %) • protéines 4 g lipides totaux 8 g • acides gras saturés 1 g • glucides 35 g • fibres alimentaires 4 g • sucre 19 g • sodium 314 mg cholestérol 17 mg

Pain aux amandes et cranberries

CRÊPES AUX POIS CHICHES

préparation : 10 minutes • mixage : 1 minute • quantité obtenue : 4 à 5 crêpes

1 tasse (172 g) de pois chiches secs

1 cuillerée à café de levure chimique

1/2 cuillerée à café de bicarbonate de soude

1/4 cuillerée à café de sel

3/4 tasse (180 ml) d'eau froide

2 cuillerées à soupe (30 ml) d'huile d'olive

1 gros œuf

Si vous utilisez des pois chiches secs : Versez les pois chiches dans le récipient à INGRÉDIENTS SECS Vitamix, et verrouillez le couvercle.

Réglez le commutateur sur la position Variable et la vitesse sur 1.

Mettez l'appareil en marche et augmentez lentement la vitesse jusqu'à la position Variable 10, puis High (Rapide).

Moulez jusqu'à obtention du degré de finesse désiré, pendant 1 minute environ. Mesurez 1 tasse (120 g) de farine de pois chiche. Réservez le surplus (1/3 tasse ou 40 g environ) pour un autre usage.

Si vous utilisez de la farine de pois chiche : Versez 1 tasse (120 g) de farine, la levure, le bicarbonate de soude et le sel dans un saladier de taille moyenne.

Versez l'eau, l'huile et l'œuf dans le récipient à INGRÉDIENTS SECS Vitamix dans l'ordre indiqué, et verrouillez le couvercle.

Réglez le commutateur sur la position Variable et la vitesse sur 1.

Mettez l'appareil en marche et augmentez lentement la vitesse jusqu'à la position Variable 10, puis High (Rapide).

Mixer pendant 15 secondes.

Versez le mélange à base d'eau dans le saladier contenant les ingrédients secs. Mélangez à la main SUFFISAMMENT pour humidifier les ingrédients secs, pas plus.

Enduisez ou vaporisez d'huile une crêpière ou une petite poêle. Faites-la chauffer.

Versez-y 1/3 tasse (80 ml) de pâte et inclinez légèrement pour former une crêpe. Faites frire jusqu'à ce que des bulles se forment à la surface de la crêpe. Retournez-la et faites frire jusqu'à ce qu'elle soit légèrement dorée. Servez immédiatement.

Informations nutritionnelles (par crêpe) : 193 kcal (lipides 38 %, protéines 15 %, glucides 47 %) • protéines 10 g lipides totaux 11 g • acides gras saturés 1 g • glucides 29 g • fibres alimentaires 14 g • sucre 1 g • sodium 476 mg cholestérol 53 mg

PAIN AUX NOIX ET AUX DATTES

préparation : 30 minutes • mixage : 25 à 30 secondes • cuisson : 1 1/4 à 1 1/2 heure
quantité obtenue : 1 pain (12 tranches)

- 1 tasse (240 ml) d'eau bouillante
- 2 1/4 tasses (340 g) de dattes séchées dénoyautées, hachées grossièrement
- 4 cuillerées à soupe (56 g) de beurre doux, coupé en morceaux
- 1 1/4 tasse (125 g) de noix
- 1 tasse (120 g) de farine de blé complet
- 1 tasse (125 g) de farine non blanchie
- 3/4 tasse (150 g) de sucre cristallisé
- 1 cuillerée à café de levure chimique
- 1/2 cuillerée à café de bicarbonate de soude
- 1/2 cuillerée à café de sel de mer
- 2 gros œufs
- 1/2 cuillerée à café d'extrait de vanille

Dans un grand saladier, versez l'eau bouillante sur les dattes et le beurre. Laissez refroidir, pendant environ 30 minutes.

Préchauffez le four sur 160 °C (325 °F), en plaçant la grille à mi-hauteur. Huilez légèrement le moule à cake et réservez.

Mettez les noix dans le récipient à INGRÉDIENTS SECS Vitamix. Verrouillez le couvercle.

Réglez le commutateur sur la position Variable et la vitesse sur 1.

Mettez l'appareil en marche et augmentez lentement la vitesse jusqu'à la position Variable 3.

Mixez pendant 10 à 15 secondes ou jusqu'à ce que les noix soient grossièrement hachées (pas plus longtemps).

Mettez les noix hachées dans un bol et réservez.

Versez les farines, le sucre, la levure, le bicarbonate de soude et le sel dans le récipient à INGRÉDIENTS SECS Vitamix. Verrouillez le couvercle.

Réglez le commutateur sur la position Variable et la vitesse sur 1.

Mettez l'appareil en marche et augmentez lentement la vitesse jusqu'à la position Variable 6.

Mixer pendant 15 secondes. Mélangez aux noix hachées.

Battez les œufs et l'extrait de vanille dans le mélange à base de dattes refroidi, puis ajoutez le mélange à base de farine/noix, et mélangez.

Versez la pâte uniformément dans le moule à cake. Enfournez pendant 1 1/4 à 1 1/2 heure et surveillez la fin de la cuisson en piquant le centre avec la lame d'un couteau ; le pain est cuit quand la lame ressort sèche.

Laissez le pain refroidir dans le moule placé sur une grille à pâtisserie pendant 25 minutes, puis démoulez-le sur la grille et laissez-le refroidir complètement.

Informations nutritionnelles (par tranche) : 346 kcal (lipides 32 %, protéines 9 %, glucides 60 %) • protéines 8 g lipides totaux 13 g • acides gras saturés 3 g • glucides 55 g • fibres alimentaires 2 g • sucre 13 g • sodium 208 mg cholestérol 51 mg

Servez-vous de ciseaux de cuisine, plongés fréquemment dans de l'eau chaude, pour couper les dattes grossièrement.

SCONES ÉPICÉS AUX PÊCHES

préparation : 20 minutes • mixage : 20 secondes • cuisson : 30 à 35 minutes
quantité obtenue : 8 scones

1 1/2 tasse (180 g) de farine de blé complet

1 tasse (125 g) de farine non blanchie

1/3 tasse (67 g) de sucre cristallisé

2 1/4 cuillerées à café de levure chimique

1/2 cuillerée à café de bicarbonate de soude

1/4 cuillerée à café de sel

1/2 tasse (113 g) de beurre doux, ramolli et coupé en morceaux

1/2 tasse (120 ml) de lait

1 cuillerée à café d'extrait de vanille

1 tasse (186 g) de tranches de pêches fraîches ou surgelées (décongelées et égouttées), coupées en cubes

Garniture :

3 cuillerées à soupe (17 g) d'amandes émincées

1 cuillerée à soupe de sucre cristallisé

1 cuillerée à café de cannelle moulue

Lait ou crème supplémentaire pour enduire le dessus des scones

Mélangez les farines, le sucre, la levure, le bicarbonate de soude et le sel dans un grand saladier.

Mettez le beurre, le lait et l'extrait de vanille dans le récipient à INGRÉDIENTS HUMIDES Vitamix, et verrouillez le couvercle.

Réglez le commutateur sur la position Variable et la vitesse sur 1.

Mettez l'appareil en marche et augmentez lentement la vitesse jusqu'à la position Variable 6.

Mélangez jusqu'à incorporation du beurre, pendant 20 secondes environ.

Mélangez doucement le mélange à base de beurre/lait et les morceaux de pêche avec le mélange à base de farine. Formez une boule, puis aplatissez-la doucement pour former un cercle de 20 cm (8 pouces) de diamètre sur une plaque à pâtisserie recouverte de papier parcheminé. Avec un couteau ou un découpe-pizza, tracez 8 segments sans couper entièrement la pâte.

Versez les amandes, le sucre et la cannelle dans le récipient à INGRÉDIENTS SECS Vitamix, et verrouillez le couvercle.

Réglez le commutateur sur la position Variable et la vitesse sur 1.

Mettez l'appareil en marche et augmentez lentement la vitesse jusqu'à la position Variable 4.

Mixez jusqu'à ce que le mélange soit finement émincé et bien mélangé, pendant 10 secondes environ.

Avec un pinceau, enduisez le dessus de la pâte de lait ou de crème, puis saupoudrez avec le mélange à base d'amandes.

Enfournez à 200 °C (400 °F) pendant 30 à 35 minutes ou jusqu'à ce que les scones soient légèrement dorés et ne soient plus humides au centre. Laissez refroidir pendant 10 minutes, puis recoupez les segments avec un découpe-pizza ou un couteau aiguisé. Servez tièdes ou à température ambiante.

Scones épicés aux pêches
(suite)

REMARQUE : Pour faire de la farine de blé complet à partir de grains de blé complet : Versez 1 1/2 tasse (270 g) de grains de blé entier dans le récipient à INGRÉDIENTS SECS Vitamix, et verrouillez le couvercle.

Réglez le commutateur sur la position Variable et la vitesse sur 1.

Mettez l'appareil en marche et augmentez lentement la vitesse jusqu'à la position Variable 10, puis High (Rapide).

Moulez pendant 1 minute (pas plus longtemps). Arrêtez l'appareil pour permettre à la farine de refroidir pendant quelques minutes. Mesurez 1 1/2 tasse (180 g) de farine de blé complet pour la recette. Réservez le surplus de farine pour un autre usage.

Informations nutritionnelles (par scone) : 311 kcal (lipides 39 %, protéines 8 %, glucides 53 %) • protéines 6 g lipides totaux 14 g • acides gras saturés 8 g • glucides 42 g • fibres alimentaires 4 g • sucre 12 g • sodium 302 mg cholestérol 31 mg

PAIN À LA BANANE ET AU BLÉ COMPLET

préparation : 10 minutes • mixage : 30 secondes • cuisson : 1 heure
quantité obtenue : 1 pain (12 tranches)

1 gros œuf

1/4 tasse (56 g) de beurre doux

1/3 tasse (80 ml) de lait

2 bananes mûres (283 à 312 g chacune / 10 à 11 onces), pelées et coupées en deux

1/2 cuillerée à café d'extrait de vanille

2 cuillerées à café de levure

2/3 tasse (133 g) de sucre cristallisé

1 2/3 tasse (200 g) de farine de blé complet

2/3 tasse (77 g) de noix broyées (facultatif)

Huilez légèrement en vaporisant avec une huile végétale ou en enduisant de matière grasse un moule à cake de 22 cm x 11 cm (8 1/2 pouces x 4 1/2 pouces). Préchauffez le four à 180 °C (350 °F).

Mettez l'œuf, le beurre, le lait, les bananes et l'extrait de vanille dans le récipient à INGRÉDIENTS HUMIDES Vitamix dans l'ordre indiqué, et verrouillez le couvercle.

Réglez le commutateur sur la position Variable et la vitesse sur 1.

Mettez l'appareil en marche et augmentez lentement la vitesse jusqu'à la position Variable 5.

Mélangez bien, pendant 30 secondes environ.

Dans un grand saladier, mélangez à la main la farine de blé complet, la levure et le sucre de sorte à former un ensemble homogène.

Ajoutez le mélange à base de banane. Mélangez à la main SUFFISAMMENT pour humidifier les ingrédients secs, pas plus.

Ajoutez les amandes hachées à la pâte. Mélangez légèrement.

Répartissez la pâte dans le moule. Enfournez 1 heure. Surveillez la fin de la cuisson en piquant avec la lame d'un couteau ; le pain est cuit quand elle ressort sèche.

Laissez le pain reposer sur une grille à pâtisserie pendant 30 minutes, puis retirez-le avec précaution du moule et laissez-le refroidir complètement avant de découper.

Informations nutritionnelles (par tranche, avec noix) : 206 kcal (lipides 38 %, protéines 9 %, glucides 53 %)
protéines 5 g • lipides totaux 9 g • acides gras saturés 3 g • glucides 29 g • fibres alimentaires 3 g • sucre 14 g
sodium 93 mg • cholestérol 28 mg

Pain à la banane et au blé complet

MUFFINS AU BLÉ COMPLET, AUX FRUITS ET AUX CAROTTES

préparation : 15 minutes • mixage : 10 à 15 secondes • cuisson : 20 à 25 minutes
quantité obtenue : 6 muffins

1 tasse (165 g) de morceaux d'ananas

1/2 tasse (64 g) de carottes grossièrement émincées

1 cuillerée à soupe d'huile d'olive

1/4 tasse (55 g) de sucre roux léger, bien tassé

1 gros œuf

1 tasse (120 g) de farine de blé complet

1 cuillerée à café de farine de lin

1 cuillerée à café de cannelle

1 cuillerée à café de levure chimique

1/2 cuillerée à café de bicarbonate de soude

1/2 cuillerée à café de sel

1/2 tasse (72 g) de raisins secs

Préchauffez le four à 190 °C (375 °F). Huilez légèrement en vaporisant avec une huile végétale un plat à muffins, ou utilisez des moules en papier.

Mettez l'ananas, les carottes, l'huile, le sucre roux et l'œuf dans le récipient à INGRÉDIENTS HUMIDES Vitamix dans l'ordre indiqué, et verrouillez le couvercle.

Réglez le commutateur sur la position Variable et la vitesse sur 1.

Mettez l'appareil en marche et augmentez lentement la vitesse jusqu'à la position Variable 4.

Mélangez pendant 10 à 15 secondes (l'ananas et les carottes ne doivent pas être trop finement émincés).

Dans un grand saladier, mélangez la farine, la farine de lin, la cannelle, la levure, le bicarbonate de soude et le sel.

Ajoutez le mélange à base d'ananas. Mélangez à la main SUFFISAMMENT pour humidifier les ingrédients secs, pas plus. Ajoutez les raisins secs rapidement mais avec soin.

Remplissez chaque récipient du moule à muffins.

Enfournez 20 à 25 minutes. Surveillez la fin de la cuisson en piquant un muffin avec la lame d'un couteau ; ils sont cuits quand elle ressort sèche.

Laissez refroidir sur une grille à pâtisserie pendant 5 minutes, puis démoulez délicatement chaque muffin. Servez tièdes ou à température ambiante.

Informations nutritionnelles (par muffin) : 203 kcal (lipides 17 %, protéines 9 %, glucides 74 %) • protéines 5 g
lipides totaux 4 g • acides gras saturés 1 g • glucides 40 g • fibres alimentaires 4 g • sucre 18 g • sodium 412 mg
cholestérol 35 mg

Ne réduisez pas la quantité d'huile. Il s'agit de la quantité minimum nécessaire pour obtenir des muffins moelleux. Si vous utilisez du miel ou réduisez la quantité de sucre roux, les muffins auront goût de bicarbonate de soude.

Muffins au blé complet, aux fruits et aux carottes

PAIN AUX COURGETTES

préparation : 15 minutes • mixage : 15 à 20 secondes • cuisson : 1 heure
quantité obtenue : 1 pain (12 tranches)

1 gros œuf

2/3 tasse (133 g) de sucre cristallisé

1/4 tasse (60 ml) d'huile de pépin de raisin ou d'olive légère

1 cuillerée à café d'extrait de vanille

200 g (7 onces) de courgettes coupées en morceaux (1 1/2 tasse environ)

2 tasses (250 g) de farine non blanchie

1 cuillerée à café de bicarbonate de soude

1/4 cuillerée à café de levure chimique

1/4 cuillerée à café de sel

1/4 cuillerée à café de noix de muscade moulue

1/2 cuillerée à café de cannelle moulue

1/2 cuillerée à café de piment de la Jamaïque

Ingrédients facultatifs :

1/2 tasse (58 g) de noix hachées grossièrement

1/2 tasse (72 g) de raisins secs

Huilez légèrement en vaporisant avec une huile végétale ou en enduisant de matière grasse un moule à cake de 22 cm x 11 cm (8 1/2 pouces x 4 1/2 pouces). Préchauffez le four à 180 °C (350 °F).

Mettez l'œuf, le sucre, l'huile et l'extrait de vanille dans le récipient à INGRÉDIENTS HUMIDES Vitamix dans l'ordre indiqué, et verrouillez le couvercle.

Réglez le commutateur sur la position Variable et la vitesse sur 1.

Mettez l'appareil en marche et augmentez lentement la vitesse jusqu'à la position Variable 5.

Mixez pendant 15 à 20 secondes ou jusqu'à ce que le tout soit bien mélangé et que les courgettes soient émincées.

Dans un grand saladier, mélangez bien la farine, le bicarbonate de soude, la levure, le sel, la noix de muscade, la cannelle et le piment de la Jamaïque.

Ajoutez le mélange à base de courgettes. Mélangez à la main SUFFISAMMENT pour humidifier les ingrédients secs, pas plus, puis ajoutez rapidement les noix et/ou les raisins secs. Mélangez le tout, mais pas trop.

Répartissez la pâte dans le moule. Enfournez 1 heure. Surveillez la fin de la cuisson en piquant avec la lame d'un couteau ; le pain est cuit quand elle ressort sèche.

Laissez le pain reposer sur une grille à pâtisserie pendant 30 minutes, puis retirez-le avec précaution du moule et laissez-le refroidir complètement avant de découper.

Informations nutritionnelles (par tranche, sans les ingrédients facultatifs) : 171 kcal (lipides 28 %, protéines 7 %, glucides 65 %) • protéines 3 g • lipides totaux 5 g • acides gras saturés 1 g • glucides 28 g • fibres alimentaires 1 g sucre 12 g • sodium 174 mg • cholestérol 18 mg

MUFFINS À LA CITROUILLE

préparation : 15 minutes • mixage : 10 secondes • cuisson : 20 à 25 minutes
quantité obtenue : 12 muffins

2 gros œufs

1/4 tasse (60 ml) d'huile d'olive légère

1 tasse (245 g) de citrouille, fraîchement cuite ou en conserve

1/4 tasse (60 ml) de lait

3/4 tasse (150 g) de sucre cristallisé

1/2 cuillerée à café de sel

2 cuillerées à café de bicarbonate de soude

1 cuillerée à café de piment de la Jamaïque

1 cuillerée à café de cannelle

1 3/4 tasse (219 g) de farine non blanchie

1/2 tasse (120 g) de grains de chocolat (mini ou normaux)

Préchauffez le four à 180 °C (350 °F). Huilez légèrement en vaporisant avec une huile végétale un plat à muffins, ou utilisez des moules en papier.

Mettez les œufs, l'huile, la citrouille, le lait et le sucre dans le récipient à INGRÉDIENTS HUMIDES Vitamix dans l'ordre indiqué, et verrouillez le couvercle.

Réglez le commutateur sur la position Variable et la vitesse sur 1.

Mettez l'appareil en marche et augmentez lentement la vitesse jusqu'à la position Variable 5.

Mixer pendant 10 secondes.

Dans un saladier de taille moyenne, mélangez le sel, le bicarbonate de soude, le piment de la Jamaïque, la cannelle, la farine et les grains de chocolat, dans l'ordre indiqué.

Ajoutez le mélange à base de citrouille. Mélangez à la main SUFFISAMMENT pour humidifier les ingrédients secs, pas plus.

Remplissez chaque récipient du moule à muffins au 3/4.

Enfournez 20 à 25 minutes. Surveillez la fin de la cuisson en piquant un muffin avec la lame d'un couteau ; ils sont cuits quand elle ressort sèche.

Laissez refroidir sur une grille à pâtisserie pendant 5 minutes, puis démoulez délicatement chaque muffin. Servez tièdes ou à température ambiante.

Informations nutritionnelles (par muffin) : 228 kcal (lipides 32 %, protéines 7 %, glucides 61 %) • protéines 4 g
lipides totaux 8 g • acides gras saturés 2 g • glucides 35 g • fibres alimentaires 2 g • sucre 18 g • sodium 326 mg
cholestérol 41 mg

pâtes levées

Pains au levain - Guide pratique

Voici quelques conseils utiles pour préparer une pâte levée.

Mesurer la farine

Il est inutile de tamiser la farine avant de la mesurer, mais pour une mesure précise, versez délicatement la farine dans un verre gradué sec, puis égalisez le sommet avec le bord droit d'une spatule ou un couteau.

Température des liquides

L'activation de la levure permet de s'assurer qu'elle est vivante et remplira son rôle dans la recette. La levure est extrêmement sensible à la température : trop chaude, elle tue la levure, trop froide, elle retarde son développement. Il est donc crucial que le liquide soit à la bonne température quand il est ajouté à la levure.

La plage de températures quand la levure est mélangée directement au liquide est généralement comprise entre 40 °C et 46 °C (105 °F et 115 °F).

Laissez-la lever

Laissez la pâte lever, légèrement couverte, dans un endroit tiède à l'abri des courants d'air. Pour les meilleurs résultats, laissez-la lever à température ambiante. Une température plus élevée risque de produire un goût de levure crue dans le produit fini, alors qu'une température plus basse risque de faire tourner la pâte avant qu'elle ne lève.

PAIN AU LEVAIN ET AUX MYRTILLES

préparation : 15 minutes • mixage : 15 secondes • cuisson : 35 à 40 minutes
quantité obtenue : 1 pain rond (8 à 10 tranches)

1 gros œuf

1/2 tasse (120 ml) d'huile végétale

1/2 tasse (120 ml) de lait

3/4 tasse (180 ml) de levain chef à la pomme de terre (recette à la page 75), à température ambiante

1/2 tasse (100 g) de sucre cristallisé

1 1/2 tasse (188 g) de farine non blanchie

1/2 tasse (60 ml) de farine de blé complet

1/2 cuillerée à café de sel

3/4 cuillerée à café de bicarbonate de soude

1 tasse (148 g) de myrtilles fraîches ou surgelées (décongelées et égouttées)

Sucre à saupoudrer sur le dessus, facultatif

Préchauffez le four à 190 °C (375 °F). Huilez légèrement une poêle ou un moule à cake.

Versez l'œuf, l'huile, le lait, le levain chef à la pomme de terre et le sucre dans le récipient à INGRÉDIENTS HUMIDES Vitamix dans l'ordre indiqué, et verrouillez le couvercle.

Réglez le commutateur sur la position Variable et la vitesse sur 1.

Mettez l'appareil en marche et augmentez lentement la vitesse jusqu'à la position Variable 10, puis High (Rapide).

Mixer pendant 15 secondes.

Dans un saladier de taille moyenne, mélangez les farines, le sel et le bicarbonate de soude.

Ajoutez le mélange à base de levain chef. Mélangez à la main SUFFISAMMENT pour humidifier les ingrédients secs, pas plus. Ajoutez les myrtilles et mélangez rapidement, mais délicatement.

Versez dans le moule. Saupoudrez de sucre si vous le désirez.

Enfournez 35 à 40 minutes. Surveillez la fin de la cuisson en piquant avec la lame d'un couteau ; le gâteau est cuit quand elle ressort sèche. Servez tiède ou froid, coupé en tranches.

Informations nutritionnelles (par tranche) : 249 kcal (lipides 7 %, protéines 12 %, glucides 81 %) •protéines 8 g
lipides totaux 2 g • acides gras saturés 0 g • glucides 51 g • fibres alimentaires 5 g • sucre 3 g • sodium 23 mg
cholestérol 0 mg

PETITS PAINS À LA CANNELLE

préparation : 20 minutes • mixage : 30 secondes • cuisson : 30 à 35 minutes
quantité obtenue : 9 petits pains

1 sachet (1 cuillerée à soupe) de levure de boulanger sèche

4 cuillerées à soupe (60 ml) d'eau tiède, 40 °C à 46 °C (105 °F à 115 °F)

2 cuillerées à soupe (30 ml) de miel

2 1/4 tasses (281 g) de farine non blanchie, plus quantité nécessaire pour mélanger et étaler la pâte

1/2 cuillerée à café de sel

1/3 tasse (80 ml) de lait

1/4 tasse (56 g) de beurre doux, ramolli et coupé en morceaux

1 gros œuf

Garniture :

4 cuillerées à soupe (50 g) de sucre cristallisé

1 cuillerée à soupe de cannelle moulue

1/4 tasse (56 g) de beurre doux fondu

1 gros œuf plus 2 cuillerées à soupe (30 ml) de lait (pour enduire le dessus des petits pains avant la cuisson)

Glaçage au sucre glace (recette à la page 46)

Pour activer la levure, mélangez-la avec l'eau et le miel. Mélangez le tout rapidement. Laissez reposer pendant 5 minutes.

Versez la farine et le sel dans le récipient à INGRÉDIENTS SECS Vitamix, et verrouillez le couvercle.

Réglez le commutateur sur la position Variable et la vitesse sur 1.

Mettez l'appareil en marche et augmentez lentement la vitesse jusqu'à la position Variable 6.

Mixez 5 secondes environ, jusqu'à ce qu'une dépression se forme au centre de la préparation.

Réglez le commutateur sur la position Variable et la vitesse sur 3. Mettez l'appareil en marche, puis ôtez le bouchon du couvercle. Ajoutez le lait, le beurre, l'œuf et le mélange à base de levure à travers l'orifice du bouchon du couvercle. Arrêtez l'appareil et remettez le bouchon du couvercle en place.

Sélectionnez la vitesse High (Rapide). Démarrez et arrêtez l'appareil par à-coups deux fois de suite. Arrêtez l'appareil et ôtez le couvercle.

Pendant que la pâte repose, huilez légèrement en vaporisant une huile végétale ou en enduisant de matière grasse un moule carré de 20 cm (8 pouces) de côté.

Avec une spatule en caoutchouc humide, raclez les parois du récipient pour ramener la pâte vers le centre du mélange. Remettez le couvercle en place.

Sélectionnez la vitesse High (Rapide). Démarrez et arrêtez l'appareil par à-coups cinq fois de suite. Ajoutez l'eau supplémentaire, 1 cuillerée à la fois, si la pâte semble particulièrement sèche uniquement. Répétez le processus cinq fois, en raclant les parois du récipient jusqu'à ce que la pâte devienne élastique et compacte.

Pour retirer la pâte du récipient, démarrez et arrêtez l'appareil par à-coups cinq fois (ce qui va soulever la pâte et la décoller des lames). Renversez le récipient au-dessus d'un saladier huilé et laissez la pâte s'y déposer. Retournez la pâte une fois pour enduire toute la surface. Couvrez avec un torchon propre et sec, puis laissez lever pendant 25 à 30 minutes.

Mélangez le sucre et la cannelle. Réservez avec le beurre fondu et refroidi.

Petits pains à la cannelle *(suite)*

Transférez la pâte sur un plan de travail fariné. En la retournant et la farinant fréquemment, étalez la pâte de façon à former un grand rectangle de 20 cm x 40 cm (8 pouces x 16 pouces). Enduisez la totalité de ce rectangle avec le beurre fondu, sauf un bord de 1,3 cm (1/2 pouce). Saupoudrez du mélange sucre/cannelle.

Enroulez la pâte sur elle-même, comme pour un gâteau roulé. Découpez en 9 morceaux. Placez-les verticalement dans le moule.

Couvrez d'un torchon propre et sec, puis laissez lever pendant 45 à 60 minutes.

À l'aide d'un pinceau, enduisez le dessus des petits pains avec le mélange œuf/lait. Faites cuire au four à 160 °C (325 °F) pendant 30 à 35 minutes ou jusqu'à ce que les petits pains soient légèrement dorés.

Laissez reposer sur une grille à pâtisserie pendant 10 minutes, puis retirez-les délicatement du moule et laissez refroidir complètement avant de découper. Enduisez les petits pains de glaçage au sucre glace avant de servir.

Informations nutritionnelles (par petit pain avec glaçage) : 422 kcal (lipides 37 %, protéines 5 %, glucides 58 %)
protéines 6 g • lipides totaux 18 g • acides gras saturés 11 g • glucides 62 g • fibres alimentaires 2 g • sucre 35 g
sodium 162 mg • cholestérol 88 mg

Petits pains à la cannelle

GLAÇAGE AU SUCRE GLACE

Le glaçage idéal pour les petits pains à la cannelle.
préparation : 20 minutes • mixage : 25 secondes • quantité obtenue : 1 tasse (240 g)

2 tasses (240 g) de sucre glace

1/4 tasse (56 g) de beurre doux, ramolli

1 cuillerée à café d'extrait de vanille

1 ou 2 cuillerées à soupe d'eau chaude, plus selon les besoins

Versez le sucre glace, le beurre, l'extrait de vanille et l'eau chaude dans le récipient à INGRÉDIENTS HUMIDES Vitamix, et verrouillez le couvercle.

Réglez le commutateur sur la position Variable et la vitesse sur 1.

Mettez l'appareil en marche et augmentez lentement la vitesse jusqu'à la position Variable 10, puis High (Rapide).

Mixer pendant 10 secondes. Arrêtez l'appareil, ôtez le couvercle et raclez les parois du récipient. Ajoutez de l'eau (une cuillerée à café à la fois) si nécessaire pour que le glaçage soit facile à étaler, mais pas trop liquide.

Réglez le commutateur sur la position Variable et la vitesse sur 1, puis verrouillez le couvercle.

Mettez l'appareil en marche et augmentez lentement la vitesse jusqu'à la position Variable 10, puis High (Rapide).

Mélangez jusqu'à obtention d'une texture lisse et crémeuse, pendant 15 secondes environ. Utilisez immédiatement.

Informations nutritionnelles (pour 2 cuillerées à soupe, soit 30 g) : 169 kcal (lipides 30 %, protéines 0 %, glucides 70 %) • protéines 0 g • lipides totaux 6 g • acides gras saturés 4 g • glucides 30 g • fibres alimentaires 0 g sucre 29 g • sodium 1 mg • cholestérol 15 mg

LEVAIN CHEF À LA POMME DE TERRE

préparation : 10 minutes

- 1 sachet (1 cuillerée à soupe) de levure de boulanger sèche
- 2 cuillerées à café de sucre
- 2 tasses (480 ml) d'eau de pomme de terre tiède, 43 °C (110 °F)
- 2 tasses (480 ml) d'eau tiède, 43 °C (110 °F) ou d'eau de pomme de terre supplémentaire, tiède
- 1 tasse (125 g) de farine non blanchie
- 1 tasse (120 g) de farine de blé complet

Dans un grand saladier, dissolvez la levure et le sucre dans 2 tasses (480 ml) d'eau de pomme de terre.

Couvrez avec un torchon propre et sec, puis laissez reposer dans un endroit tiède pendant 24 heures.

Ajoutez 2 tasses (480 ml) d'eau tiède, puis les farines.

Couvrez et laissez reposer toute une nuit ou jusqu'à ce que des bulles se forment et que le mélange dégage une odeur aigre. Réfrigérez dans un grand bocal couvert.

Sortez le mélange du réfrigérateur pour le « nourrir ». Utilisez 1 tasse (240 ml) pour un pain dans toute recette nécessitant une mère ou un levain chef.

Informations nutritionnelles (par tasse, soit 240 ml) : 232 kcal (lipides 4 %, protéines 14 %, glucides 82 %)
protéines 8 g • lipides totaux 1 g • acides gras saturés 0 g • glucides 49 g • fibres alimentaires 5 g • sucre 2 g
sodium 6 mg • cholestérol 0 mg

Nourrir le levain chef : Le matin, portez-le à température ambiante et mélangez-y 1 tasse (240 ml) d'eau tiède à 43 °C (110 °F) et 1 tasse (125 g) de farine. Laissez reposer toute la nuit. Utilisez la quantité nécessaire pour votre pain et réfrigérez le surplus. Renouvelez toutes les 2 ou 3 semaines.

PAIN COLONIAL (FORME LIBRE)

préparation : 15 minutes • mixage : 30 secondes • cuisson : 25 minutes • quantité obtenue : 1 pain ovale (8 à 10 tranches)

1 1/4 tasse (300 ml) d'eau tiède, 40 °C à 46 °C (105 °F à 115 °F)

3 cuillerées à soupe (41 g) de sucre roux

1 sachet (1 cuillerée à soupe) de levure de boulanger sèche

1 1/2 tasse (188 g) de farine non blanchie

1/2 tasse (60 g) de farine de blé complet

1/4 tasse (26 g) de farine de seigle légère

1/4 tasse (30 g) de farine de maïs complet

1/2 cuillerée à café de sel

1 cuillerée à soupe d'huile d'olive

1/4 tasse (30 g) de farine de maïs complet pour la plaque à pâtisserie

1 œuf mélangé à 1 cuillerée à café d'eau (pour enduire la pâte avant la cuisson)

Pour activer la levure, mélangez-la avec l'eau tiède et le sucre roux. Mélangez le tout rapidement. Laissez reposer pendant 5 minutes.

Versez la farine non blanchie, la farine de blé complet, la farine de seigle, la farine de maïs et le sel dans le récipient à INGRÉDIENTS SECS Vitamix, et verrouillez le couvercle.

Réglez le commutateur sur la position Variable et la vitesse sur 1.

Mettez l'appareil en marche et augmentez lentement la vitesse jusqu'à la position Variable 6.

Mixez 5 secondes environ, jusqu'à ce qu'une dépression se forme au centre de la préparation.

Réglez le commutateur sur la position Variable et la vitesse sur 3. Remettez l'appareil en marche, puis ôtez le bouchon du couvercle. Ajoutez l'huile et le mélange à base de levure à travers l'orifice du bouchon du couvercle. Arrêtez l'appareil et remettez le bouchon du couvercle en place.

Sélectionnez la vitesse High (Rapide). Démarrez et arrêtez l'appareil par à-coups deux fois de suite. Arrêtez l'appareil et ôtez le couvercle.

Pendant que la pâte repose, saupoudrez la plaque à pâtisserie de 1/4 tasse (30 g) de farine de maïs. Mettez-la de côté.

Avec une spatule en caoutchouc humide, raclez les parois du récipient pour ramener la pâte vers le centre du mélange. Remettez le couvercle en place.

Sélectionnez la vitesse High (Rapide). Démarrez et arrêtez l'appareil par à-coups cinq fois de suite. Ajoutez l'eau supplémentaire, 1 cuillerée à la fois, si la pâte semble particulièrement sèche uniquement. Répétez le processus cinq fois, en raclant les parois du récipient jusqu'à ce que la pâte devienne élastique et compacte.

Replacez le couvercle sur le récipient et laissez la pâte lever pendant 15 minutes.

Aplatissez la pâte avec une spatule en caoutchouc, puis retournez-la sur un morceau de papier sulfurisé, légèrement saupoudré de farine. (La pâte sera collante.) Farinez légèrement vos mains et retirez rapidement la pâte du papier sulfurisé pour la transférer sur la plaque à pâtisserie. Saupoudrez la pâte de farine et formez un grand ovale.

Pain colonial (forme libre) *(suite)*	Couvrez le pain d'un torchon propre et sec, puis laissez la pâte lever jusqu'à ce qu'elle ait quasiment doublé de volume, pendant 15 à 20 minutes environ. Quand le pain est prêt à cuire, enduisez rapidement la pâte du mélange œuf/eau et avec un couteau à dents, faites trois entailles diagonales sur le dessus du pain. Faites cuire au four à 190 °C (375 °F) pendant 25 minutes, ou jusqu'à ce que le pain atteigne une température interne de 88 °C (190 °F), que vous pouvez vérifier avec un thermomètre à lecture rapide. Laissez le pain reposer sur une grille à pâtisserie pendant 10 minutes, puis retirez-le avec précaution de la plaque et laissez-le refroidir complètement avant de découper.

Informations nutritionnelles (par tranche) : 160 kcal (lipides 15 %, protéines 11 %, glucides 74 %) • protéines 5 g lipides totaux 3 g • acides gras saturés 0 g • glucides 30 g • fibres alimentaires 2 g • sucre 4 g • sodium 133 mg cholestérol 21 mg

Un pain plat artisanal, idéal à trancher et trempé dans de l'huile d'olive.

PAIN COLONIAL (EN MOULE)

préparation : 10 minutes • mixage : 30 secondes • cuisson : 25 à 30 minutes
quantité obtenue : 1 pain (12 tranches)

1 1/4 tasse (300 ml) d'eau tiède, 40 °C à 46 °C (105 °F à 115 °F)

3 cuillerées à soupe (41 g) de sucre roux

1 sachet (1 cuillerée à soupe) de levure de boulanger sèche

1 1/2 tasse (188 g) de farine non blanchie

1/2 tasse (60 g) de farine de blé complet

1/4 tasse (26 g) de farine de seigle légère

1/4 tasse (30 g) de farine de maïs complet

1/2 cuillerée à café de sel

1 cuillerée à soupe d'huile d'olive

1 gros œuf mélangé à 1 cuillerée à café d'eau (pour enduire la pâte avant la cuisson)

Pour activer la levure, mélangez-la avec l'eau tiède et le sucre roux. Mélangez le tout rapidement. Laissez reposer pendant 5 minutes.

Versez la farine non blanchie, la farine de blé complet, la farine de seigle, la farine de maïs et le sel dans le récipient à INGRÉDIENTS SECS Vitamix, et verrouillez le couvercle.

Réglez le commutateur sur la position Variable et la vitesse sur 1.

Mettez l'appareil en marche et augmentez lentement la vitesse jusqu'à la position Variable 6.

Mixez 5 secondes environ, jusqu'à ce qu'une dépression se forme au centre de la préparation.

Réglez le commutateur sur la position Variable et la vitesse sur 3. Remettez l'appareil en marche, puis ôtez le bouchon du couvercle. Ajoutez l'huile et le mélange à base de levure à travers l'orifice du bouchon du couvercle. Arrêtez l'appareil et remettez le bouchon du couvercle en place.

Sélectionnez la vitesse High (Rapide). Démarrez et arrêtez l'appareil par à-coups deux fois de suite. Arrêtez l'appareil et ôtez le couvercle.

Pendant que la pâte repose, huilez légèrement en vaporisant avec une huile végétale ou en enduisant de matière grasse un moule à pain de 22 cm x 11 cm (8 1/2 pouces x 4 1/2 pouces).

Avec une spatule en caoutchouc humide, raclez les parois du récipient pour ramener la pâte vers le centre du mélange. Remettez le couvercle en place.

Sélectionnez la vitesse High (Rapide). Démarrez et arrêtez l'appareil par à-coups cinq fois de suite. Ajoutez l'eau supplémentaire, 1 cuillerée à la fois, si la pâte semble particulièrement sèche uniquement. Répétez le processus cinq fois, en raclant les parois du récipient jusqu'à ce que la pâte devienne élastique et compacte.

Pour retirer plus facilement la pâte du récipient, démarrez et arrêtez l'appareil par à-coups cinq fois de suite (ce qui va soulever la pâte et la décoller des lames), puis renversez rapidement le récipient au-dessus du moule. Laissez la pâte se déposer dans le moule, en récupérant les restes de pâte avec une spatule humide.

Tassez la pâte dans le moule en vous servant d'une spatule huilée, ou de vos mains légèrement farinées.

Pain colonial (en moule) *(suite)*	Couvrez le pain avec un torchon propre et sec, puis laissez la pâte lever jusqu'à ce qu'elle atteigne le haut du moule, pendant 18 à 20 minutes environ. Quand le pain est prêt à cuire, faites rapidement trois entailles diagonales sur le dessus du pain à l'aide d'un couteau à dents. Faites cuire au four à 190 °C (375 °F) pendant 25 à 30 minutes, ou jusqu'à ce que le pain atteigne une température interne de 88 °C (190 °F), que vous pouvez vérifier avec un thermomètre à lecture rapide. Laissez le pain reposer sur une grille à pâtisserie pendant 10 minutes, puis retirez-le avec précaution du moule et laissez-le refroidir complètement avant de découper.

Informations nutritionnelles (par tranche) : 134 kcal (lipides 15 %, protéines 11 %, glucides 74 %) • protéines 4 g lipides totaux 2 g • acides gras saturés 0 g • glucides 25 g • fibres alimentaires 2 g • sucre 3 g • sodium 111 mg cholestérol 18 mg

Une fois le pain colonial refroidi, coupez-le en tranches et régalez-vous...

PETITS PAINS AU BLÉ COMPLET ET AU BABEURRE

préparation : 20 minutes • mixage : 15 secondes • cuisson : 18 à 22 minutes
quantité obtenue : 16 rouleaux

1/3 tasse (80 ml) d'eau tiède, 40 °C à 46 °C (105 °F à 115 °F)

1 1/2 cuillerée à soupe de miel

1 sachet (1 cuillerée à soupe) de levure de boulanger sèche

2 1/2 tasses (300 g) de farine de blé complet fine

1 cuillerée à café de sel

2 cuillerées à soupe (28 g) de beurre doux à température ambiante

2/3 tasse (160 ml) de babeurre à température ambiante

1 gros œuf, légèrement battu

Pour activer la levure, mélangez-la avec l'eau tiède et le miel. Mélangez le tout rapidement. Laissez reposer pendant 5 minutes.

Versez la farine de blé entier et le sel dans le récipient à INGRÉDIENTS SECS Vitamix, et verrouillez le couvercle.

Réglez le commutateur sur la position Variable et la vitesse sur 1.

Mettez l'appareil en marche et augmentez lentement la vitesse jusqu'à la position Variable 10, puis High (Rapide).

Mixez 5 secondes environ, jusqu'à ce qu'une dépression se forme au centre de la préparation.

Réglez le commutateur sur la position Variable et la vitesse sur 3. Mettez l'appareil en marche, puis ôtez le bouchon du couvercle. Ajoutez le beurre, le babeurre, l'œuf et le mélange à base de levure à travers l'orifice du bouchon du couvercle. Arrêtez l'appareil et remettez le bouchon du couvercle en place.

Sélectionnez la vitesse High (Rapide). Démarrez et arrêtez l'appareil par à-coups deux fois de suite. Arrêtez l'appareil et ôtez le couvercle.

Pendant que la pâte repose, huilez légèrement en vaporisant avec une huile végétale ou en enduisant de matière grasse un moule carré de 20 cm (8 pouces) de côté, ou recouvrez une plaque à pâtisserie de papier parcheminé (selon la forme des petits pains).

Avec une spatule en caoutchouc humide, raclez les parois du récipient pour ramener la pâte vers le centre du mélange. Remettez le couvercle en place.

Sélectionnez la vitesse High (Rapide). Démarrez et arrêtez l'appareil par à-coups cinq fois de suite. Ajoutez l'eau supplémentaire, 1 cuillerée à la fois, si la pâte semble particulièrement sèche uniquement. Répétez le processus cinq fois, ou jusqu'à ce que la pâte devienne élastique et compacte.

Placez le couvercle sur le récipient et laissez la pâte lever jusqu'à ce qu'elle ait doublé de volume, pendant 25 à 30 minutes environ.

Aplatissez la pâte avec une spatule en caoutchouc. Replacez le couvercle sur le récipient et laissez la pâte à nouveau lever jusqu'à ce qu'elle ait encore une fois doublé de volume, pendant 20 minutes environ.

Petits pains au blé complet et au babeurre *(suite)*

Renversez la pâte sur une planche à pâtisserie légèrement farinée et roulez-la doucement jusqu'à obtention d'un cylindre de 40 cm (16 pouces). Coupez la pâte en 16 morceaux égaux. Formez des petits pains si vous le souhaitez, puis placez-les dans le moule ou sur la plaque à pâtisserie.

Couvrez les petits pains d'un torchon propre et sec, puis laissez la pâte lever jusqu'à ce qu'elle ait quasiment doublé de volume, pendant 35 à 45 minutes environ.

Faites cuire au four à 190 °C (375 °F) pendant 18 à 22 minutes ou jusqu'à ce que les petits pains soient légèrement dorés. Laissez refroidir sur une grille à pâtisserie.

Informations nutritionnelles (par petit pain) : 95 kcal (lipides 21 %, protéines 15 %, glucides 64 %) • protéines 4 g lipides totaux 2 g • acides gras saturés 1 g • glucides 16 g • fibres alimentaires 2 g • sucre 3 g • sodium 111 mg cholestérol 18 mg

Pour une croûte savoureuse, mélangez deux cuillerées à soupe (30 ml) de beurre fondu et trois cuillerées à soupe (45 ml) de miel. Une fois les petits pains cuits, sortez-les du four et enduisez-les rapidement du glaçage beurre/miel. Laissez refroidir avant de servir.

Petits pains au blé complet et au babeurre

PAIN À LA CANNELLE ET AUX RAISINS SECS

préparation : 30 minutes • mixage : 40 secondes • cuisson : 30 à 40 minutes
quantité obtenue : 1 pain (12 tranches)

1/2 tasse (120 ml) d'eau tiède, 40 °C à 46 °C (105 °F à 115 °F)

1/4 tasse (50 g) de sucre cristallisé

1 sachet (1 cuillerée à soupe) de levure de boulanger sèche

1/2 tasse (112 g) de cottage cheese

1 cuillerée à soupe de beurre doux à température ambiante

2 cuillerées à café de cannelle moulue

3/4 cuillerée à café de sel

1 gros œuf

2 tasses (275 g) de farine à pain, en plusieurs portions

1/2 tasse (104 g) de germe de blé grillé

1/2 tasse (72 g) de raisins secs trempés dans l'eau chaude pendant 30 minutes, puis égouttés, en plusieurs portions

Pour activer la levure, mélangez-la avec l'eau tiède et le sucre. Mélangez le tout rapidement. Laissez reposer pendant 5 minutes.

Mettez le cottage cheese, le beurre, la cannelle, le sel et l'œuf dans le récipient à INGRÉDIENTS HUMIDES Vitamix, et verrouillez le couvercle.

Réglez le commutateur sur la position Variable et la vitesse sur 1.

Mettez l'appareil en marche et augmentez lentement la vitesse jusqu'à la position Variable 10, puis High (Rapide).

Mixer pendant 10 secondes. Arrêtez l'appareil et raclez les parois.

Réglez le commutateur sur la position Variable et la vitesse sur 3. Mettez l'appareil en marche, puis ôtez le bouchon du couvercle. Ajoutez 1 tasse (137 g) de farine et le mélange à base de levure à travers l'orifice du bouchon du couvercle. Mixez 30 secondes. Arrêtez l'appareil et ôtez le couvercle.

Ajoutez le reste de la farine, le germe de blé et 1/4 tasse (72 g) de raisins secs trempés et égouttés, dans le récipient Vitamix, et verrouillez le couvercle.

Sélectionnez la vitesse High (Rapide). Démarrez et arrêtez l'appareil par à-coups deux fois de suite. Arrêtez l'appareil et ôtez le couvercle.

Pendant que la pâte repose, huilez légèrement en vaporisant avec une huile végétale ou en enduisant de matière grasse un moule à pain de 22 cm x 11 cm (8 1/2 pouces x 4 1/2 pouces).

Avec une spatule en caoutchouc humide, raclez les parois du récipient pour ramener la pâte vers le centre du mélange. Ajoutez le reste des raisins secs et verrouillez le couvercle.

Sélectionnez la vitesse High (Rapide). Démarrez et arrêtez l'appareil par à-coups cinq fois de suite. Ajoutez l'eau supplémentaire, 1 cuillerée à la fois, si la pâte semble particulièrement sèche uniquement. Répétez le processus cinq fois, en raclant les parois du récipient jusqu'à ce que la pâte devienne élastique et compacte.

Pour retirer plus facilement la pâte du récipient, démarrez et arrêtez l'appareil par à-coups cinq fois de suite (ce qui va soulever la pâte et la décoller des lames), puis renversez rapidement le récipient au-dessus du moule. Laissez la pâte se déposer dans le moule, en récupérant les restes de pâte avec une spatule humide.

Pain à la cannelle et aux raisins secs *(suite)*

Tassez la pâte dans le moule en vous servant d'une spatule huilée, ou de vos mains légèrement farinées.

Couvrez le pain avec un torchon propre et sec, puis laissez la pâte lever jusqu'à ce qu'elle atteigne le haut du moule, pendant 25 à 35 minutes environ. Quand le pain est prêt à cuire, faites rapidement trois entailles diagonales sur le dessus du pain à l'aide d'un couteau à dents.

Faites cuire au four à 190 °C (375 °F) pendant 30 à 40 minutes, ou jusqu'à ce que le pain atteigne une température interne de 88 °C (190 °F), que vous pouvez vérifier avec un thermomètre à lecture rapide. Laissez le pain reposer sur une grille à pâtisserie pendant 10 minutes, puis retirez-le avec précaution du moule et laissez-le refroidir complètement avant de découper.

Informations nutritionnelles (par tranche) : 162 kcal (lipides 14 %, protéines 15 %, glucides 72 %) • protéines 6 g lipides totaux 3 g • acides gras saturés 1 g • glucides 30 g • fibres alimentaires 2 g • sucre 8 g • sodium 165 mg cholestérol 20 mg

La perfection n'est pas de distribuer les raisins secs régulièrement... C'est l'aspect fait maison qui fait tout le charme de ce pain.

PIZZA AUX CINQ CÉRÉALES

préparation : 20 minutes • mixage : 35 secondes • cuisson : 16 à 20 minutes
quantité obtenue : 1 pizza (8 parts)

1 tasse (240 ml) d'eau tiède, 40 °C à 46 °C (105 °F à 115 °F)

2 cuillerées à café de sucre roux

1 sachet (1 cuillerée à soupe) de levure de boulanger sèche

3/4 tasse (94 g) de farine non blanchie

3/4 tasse (90 g) + 1 cuillerée à soupe de farine de blé complet

1/4 tasse (26 g) de farine de seigle légère

2 cuillerées à soupe (15 g) de farine d'épeautre

2 cuillerées à soupe (15 g) de farine d'orge

2 cuillerées à soupe (21 g) de graines ou de farine de lin

2 cuillerées à soupe (15 g) de farine de maïs entière, plus suffisamment pour saupoudrer le moule à pizza

1/2 cuillerée à café de sel

1 cuillerée à soupe d'huile d'olive

Garniture :

2 cuillerées à soupe (30 ml) d'huile d'olive

/3 tasse (33 g) de armesan râpé

1/3 tasse (320 g) de auce à pizza

utres garnitures selon os goûts

1/4 tasse (141 g) de nozzarella râpée

Pour activer la levure, mélangez-la avec l'eau tiède et le sucre roux. Mélangez le tout rapidement. Laissez reposer pendant 5 minutes.

Versez les farines (farine non blanchie, farine de blé complet, farine de seigle, farine d'épeautre et farine d'orge), le lin, la farine de maïs et le sel dans le récipient à INGRÉDIENTS SECS dans l'ordre indiqué, puis verrouillez le couvercle.

Réglez le commutateur sur la position Variable et la vitesse sur 1.

Mettez l'appareil en marche et augmentez lentement la vitesse jusqu'à la position Variable 10, puis High (Rapide).

Mixez jusqu'à ce le tout soit bien mélangé et qu'une dépression se forme au centre, pendant environ 20 secondes. Arrêtez l'appareil.

Réglez le commutateur sur la position Variable et la vitesse sur 1, puis ôtez le bouchon du couvercle. Mettez l'appareil en marche et augmentez lentement la vitesse jusqu'à la position Variable 6. Ajoutez l'huile d'olive et le mélange à base de levure à travers l'orifice du bouchon du couvercle. Arrêtez l'appareil et remettez le bouchon du couvercle en place.

Sélectionnez la vitesse High (Rapide). Démarrez et arrêtez l'appareil par à-coups deux fois de suite. Arrêtez l'appareil et ôtez le couvercle.

Pendant que la pâte repose, enduisez légèrement le moule à pizza du reste de la farine de maïs.

Avec une spatule en caoutchouc humide, raclez les parois du récipient pour ramener la pâte vers le centre du mélange. Remettez le couvercle en place.

Sélectionnez la vitesse High (Rapide). Démarrez et arrêtez l'appareil par à-coups cinq fois de suite. Ajoutez l'eau supplémentaire, 1 cuillerée à la fois, si la pâte semble particulièrement sèche uniquement. Répétez le processus cinq fois, en raclant les parois du récipient jusqu'à ce que la pâte devienne élastique et compacte.

Pour retirer plus facilement la pâte du récipient, démarrez et arrêtez l'appareil par à-coups cinq fois de suite (ce qui va soulever la pâte et la décoller des lames), puis renversez rapidement le récipient au-dessus d'un plan de travail propre et légèrement saupoudré de farine.

Pizza aux cinq céréales *(suite)*

Couvrez la pâte d'un torchon propre et sec ou d'un saladier renversé, et laissez reposer pendant 15 minutes.

Aplatissez la pâte avec la paume des mains, tout en maintenant la forme arrondie. Avec un rouleau à pâtisserie, étalez régulièrement la pâte du centre vers l'extérieur dans chaque direction, en soulevant et tournant la pâte d'un quart de tour après chaque coup de rouleau. La forme finale doit mesurer 2,5 cm (1 pouce) de plus que votre moule. Placez la pâte dans le moule. Formez un rebord sur tout le tour

Enduisez légèrement la pâte d'huile d'olive avec un pinceau, puis saupoudrez de parmesan râpé. Versez la sauce sur la pâte et étalez-la avec le dos d'une cuillère. Parsemez-la de vos garnitures préférées, puis saupoudrez uniformément de mozzarella râpée.

Faites cuire la pizza sur la grille la plus basse d'un four, à 220 °C (425 °F) pendant 16 à 20 minutes jusqu'à ce que le dessous de la pâte soit légèrement doré et que le fromage fasse des bulles.

Retirez le moule à pizza du four, laissez-la reposer pendant 5 minutes pour laisser le fromage refroidir, puis découpez les parts.

Informations nutritionnelles (par portion, avec garnitures) : 272 kcal (lipides 39 %, protéines 17 %, glucides 44 %) • protéines 12 g • lipides totaux 12 g • acides gras saturés 4 g • glucides 30 g fibres alimentaires 4 g • sucre 5 g • sodium 551 mg • cholestérol 15 mg

En étalant la pâte du centre vers l'extérieur et en la tournant, vous conserverez plus facilement une forme ronde.

PAIN FRANÇAIS

préparation : 10 minutes • mixage : 15 secondes • cuisson : 30 à 40 minutes
quantité obtenue : 1 pain (16 à 18 tranches)

1 tasse (240 ml) d'eau tiède, 40 °C à 46 °C (105 °F à 115 °F), en plusieurs portions

1 sachet (1 cuillerée à soupe) de levure de boulanger sèche

2 1/2 tasses (312 g) de farine non blanchie

1 cuillerée à café de sel

1 cuillerée à soupe d'huile d'olive

2 cuillerées à soupe (15 g) de farine de maïs entière

1 blanc d'œuf battu avec 1 cuillerée à soupe d'eau (pour enduire la pâte avant la cuisson)

Pour activer la levure, mélangez-la avec 1/2 tasse (120 ml) d'eau tiède. Mélangez le tout rapidement. Laissez reposer pendant 5 minutes.

Versez la farine et le sel dans le récipient à INGRÉDIENTS SECS Vitamix, et verrouillez le couvercle.

Réglez le commutateur sur la position Variable et la vitesse sur 1.

Mettez l'appareil en marche et augmentez lentement la vitesse jusqu'à la position Variable 6.

Mixez 5 secondes environ, jusqu'à ce qu'une dépression se forme au centre de la préparation.

Réglez le commutateur sur la position Variable et la vitesse sur 3. Mettez l'appareil en marche, puis ôtez le bouchon du couvercle. Ajoutez le mélange à base de levure et le reste de l'eau (1/2 tasse/120 ml) à travers l'orifice du bouchon du couvercle. Arrêtez l'appareil et remettez le bouchon du couvercle en place.

Sélectionnez la vitesse High (Rapide). Démarrez et arrêtez l'appareil par à-coups deux fois de suite. Arrêtez l'appareil et ôtez le couvercle.

Pendant que la pâte repose, huilez un saladier de taille moyenne avec l'huile d'olive et saupoudrez une plaque à pâtisserie avec la farine de maïs.

Avec une spatule en caoutchouc humide, raclez les parois du récipient pour ramener la pâte vers le centre du mélange. Remettez le couvercle en place.

Sélectionnez la vitesse High (Rapide). Démarrez et arrêtez l'appareil par à-coups cinq fois de suite. Ajoutez l'eau supplémentaire, 1 cuillerée à la fois, si la pâte semble particulièrement sèche uniquement. Répétez le processus cinq fois, en raclant les parois du récipient jusqu'à ce que la pâte devienne élastique et compacte.

Pour retirer plus facilement la pâte du récipient, démarrez et arrêtez l'appareil par à-coups cinq fois de suite (ce qui va soulever la pâte et la décoller des lames), puis renversez rapidement le récipient au-dessus du saladier, en récupérant les restes de pâte avec une spatule humide. Retournez la pâte pour bien l'enduire. Recouvrez de film alimentaire et laissez lever jusqu'à ce que la pâte ait quasiment triplé de volume, pendant 45 minutes à 1 heure.

Pain français *(suite)*

Aplatissez légèrement la pâte avec votre poing et placez-la sur un plan de travail fariné, en ajoutant de la farine afin d'obtenir une pâte malléable, mais encore souple. Étalez-la de façon à obtenir un rectangle de 30 cm x 15 cm (12 pouces x 6 pouces) avec un rouleau à pâtisserie fariné. Étalez suivant le bord le plus long, en pinçant les bords ensemble et en utilisant de l'eau pour les coller.

Déposez la pâte, bords collés vers le bas, sur la plaque à pâtisserie. Couvrez d'un torchon propre et sec, puis laissez la pâte lever jusqu'à ce qu'elle ait quasiment doublé de volume, pendant 45 minutes à 1 heure environ.

Avec un pinceau, enduisez le dessus du pain avec le mélange à base d'œuf et faites-y trois ou quatre entailles diagonales d'environ 6 mm (1/4 pouce) de profondeur avec un couteau à dents bien aiguisé.

Faites cuire au four à 220 °C (425 °F) pendant 30 à 40 minutes, ou jusqu'à ce que le pain soit bien doré et atteigne une température interne de 88 °C (190 °F), que vous pouvez vérifier avec un thermomètre à lecture rapide. Laissez le pain reposer sur une grille à pâtisserie pendant 10 minutes, puis retirez-le avec précaution de la plaque et laissez-le refroidir complètement avant de découper.

Informations nutritionnelles (par tranche) : 86 kcal (lipides 12 %, protéines 12 %, glucides 76 %) • protéines 3 g lipides totaux 1 g • acides gras saturés 0 g • glucides 16 g • fibres alimentaires 1 g • sucre 0 g • sodium 152 mg cholestérol 0 mg

Une spatule en métal peut être utile pour détacher le pain de la plaque à pâtisserie.

PAIN HAWAÏEN

préparation : 15 minutes • mixage : 25 secondes • cuisson : 35 à 40 minutes
quantité obtenue : 1 pain (8 à 10 tranches)

2 cuillerées à soupe (30 ml) d'eau tiède, 40 °C à 46 °C (105 °F à 115 °F)

1/2 tasse (120 ml) de lait tiède, 40 °C à 46 °C (105 °F à 115 °F)

1 sachet (1 cuillerée à soupe) de levure de boulanger sèche

1/2 cuillerée à café plus 1/2 tasse (100 g) de sucre, en plusieurs portions

2 1/2 tasses (312 g) de farine non blanchie

1/4 cuillerée à café de sel

1/4 tasse (56 g) de beurre doux fondu

2 gros œufs battus

1 gros œuf battu avec 1 cuillerée à café d'eau (pour enduire la pâte avant la cuisson)

Sucre à saupoudrer sur le pain

Pour activer la levure, mélangez-la avec l'eau et le lait tièdes et 1/2 cuillerée à café de sucre. Mélangez le tout rapidement. Laissez reposer pendant 5 minutes.

Versez la farine, 1/2 tasse (100 g) de sucre et le sel dans le récipient à INGRÉDIENTS SECS Vitamix, et verrouillez le couvercle.

Réglez le commutateur sur la position Variable et la vitesse sur 1.

Mettez l'appareil en marche et augmentez lentement la vitesse jusqu'à la position Variable 6.

Mixez 5 secondes environ, jusqu'à ce qu'une dépression se forme au centre de la préparation.

Réglez le commutateur sur la position Variable et la vitesse sur 3. Mettez l'appareil en marche, puis ôtez le bouchon du couvercle. Ajoutez le beurre fondu, les œufs et le mélange à base de levure à travers l'orifice du bouchon du couvercle. Arrêtez l'appareil et remettez le bouchon du couvercle en place.

Sélectionnez la vitesse High (Rapide). Démarrez et arrêtez l'appareil par à-coups deux fois de suite. Arrêtez l'appareil et ôtez le couvercle.

Pendant que la pâte repose, huilez légèrement en vaporisant avec une huile végétale ou en enduisant de matière grasse un moule à tarte de 23 cm (9 pouces).

Avec une spatule en caoutchouc humide, raclez les parois du récipient pour ramener la pâte vers le centre du mélange. Remettez le couvercle en place.

Sélectionnez la vitesse High (Rapide). Démarrez et arrêtez l'appareil par à-coups cinq fois de suite. Ajoutez l'eau supplémentaire, 1 cuillerée à la fois, si la pâte semble particulièrement sèche uniquement. Répétez le processus cinq fois, en raclant les parois du récipient jusqu'à ce que la pâte devienne élastique et compacte.

Pour retirer plus facilement la pâte du récipient, démarrez et arrêtez l'appareil par à-coups cinq fois de suite (ce qui va soulever la pâte et la décoller des lames), puis renversez rapidement le récipient au-dessus d'un saladier huilé, en récupérant les restes de pâte avec une spatule humide. Tournez la pâte pour enduire toute la surface.

Pain hawaïen *(suite)*

Recouvrez le saladier avec du film alimentaire préalablement vaporisé d'huile végétale. Laissez lever jusqu'à ce que la pâte ait doublé de volume, pendant 40 à 45 minutes.

Aplatissez la pâte avec votre poing et placez-la sur un plan de travail fariné. Pétrissez-la pendant 1 à 2 minutes. Tassez la pâte dans le moule en vous servant d'une spatule huilée ou de vos mains légèrement farinées.

Couvrez le pain d'un torchon propre et sec, puis laissez la pâte lever jusqu'à ce qu'elle ait doublé de volume, pendant 40 minutes environ. Quand le pain est prêt à cuire, avec un pinceau, enduisez le dessus avec le mélange à base d'œuf, puis saupoudrez de sucre.

Faites cuire au four à 180 °C (350 °F) pendant 35 à 40 minutes, ou jusqu'à ce que le pain soit doré et atteigne une température interne de 88 °C (190 °F), que vous pouvez vérifier avec un thermomètre à lecture rapide. Laissez refroidir sur une grille à pâtisserie.

Informations nutritionnelles (par tranche) : 233 kcal (lipides 29 %, protéines 10 %, glucides 61 %) • protéines 6 g lipides totaux 7 g • acides gras saturés 4 g • glucides 35 g • fibres alimentaires 1 g • sucre 11 g • sodium 126 mg cholestérol 76 mg

PAIN MULTICÉRÉALE

préparation : 20 minutes • mixage : 25 secondes • cuisson : 40 à 50 minutes
quantité obtenue : 1 pain (12 tranches)

1 1/4 tasse (300 ml) d'eau tiède, 40 °C à 46 °C (105 °F à 115 °F)

1 cuillerée à soupe de miel

1 sachet (1 cuillerée à soupe) de levure de boulanger sèche

1 1/2 tasse (156 g) de farine non blanchie

1/2 tasse (60 g) de farine de blé complet

1/4 tasse (26 g) de farine de seigle légère

1 cuillerée à soupe de germe de blé

1 cuillerée à soupe de flocons d'avoine

2 cuillerées à café de farine de maïs complet

2 cuillerées à café de millet

2 cuillerées à café de farine d'orge

2 cuillerées à café de farine de sarrasin

1/4 cuillerée à café de farine de lin

1/2 cuillerée à café de sel

1 cuillerée à soupe d'huile de pépin de raisin ou d'huile d'olive légère

1 cuillerée à soupe de graines de tournesol

1 cuillerée à soupe de mélasse

1/4 cuillerée à café de graines de sésame à saupoudrer

Pour activer la levure, mélangez-la avec l'eau tiède et le miel. Mélangez le tout rapidement. Laissez reposer pendant 5 minutes.

Versez la farine non blanchie, la farine de blé complet, la farine de seigle, le germe de blé, les flocons d'avoine, la farine de maïs, le millet, la farine d'orge, la farine de sarrasin, la farine de lin et le sel dans le récipient à INGRÉDIENTS SECS Vitamix, et verrouillez le couvercle.

Réglez le commutateur sur la position Variable et la vitesse sur 1.

Mettez l'appareil en marche et augmentez lentement la vitesse jusqu'à la position Variable 6.

Mixez 5 secondes environ, jusqu'à ce qu'une dépression se forme au centre de la préparation.

Réglez le commutateur sur la position Variable et la vitesse sur 3. Mettez l'appareil en marche, puis ôtez le bouchon du couvercle. Ajoutez l'huile, les graines de tournesol, la mélasse et le mélange à base de levure à travers l'orifice du bouchon du couvercle. Arrêtez l'appareil et remettez le bouchon du couvercle en place.

Sélectionnez la vitesse High (Rapide). Démarrez et arrêtez l'appareil par à-coups deux fois de suite. Arrêtez l'appareil et ôtez le couvercle.

Pendant que la pâte repose, huilez légèrement en vaporisant avec une huile végétale ou en enduisant de matière grasse un moule à pain de 22 cm x 11 cm (8 1/2 pouces x 4 1/2 pouces).

Avec une spatule en caoutchouc humide, raclez les parois du récipient pour ramener la pâte vers le centre du mélange. Remettez le couvercle en place.

Sélectionnez la vitesse High (Rapide). Démarrez et arrêtez l'appareil par à-coups cinq fois de suite. Ajoutez l'eau supplémentaire, 1 cuillerée à la fois, si la pâte semble particulièrement sèche uniquement. Répétez le processus cinq fois, en raclant les parois du récipient jusqu'à ce que la pâte devienne élastique et compacte.

Pour retirer plus facilement la pâte du récipient, démarrez et arrêtez l'appareil par à-coups cinq fois de suite (ce qui va soulever la pâte et la décoller des lames), puis renversez rapidement le récipient au-dessus du moule. Laissez la pâte se déposer dans le moule, en récupérant les restes de pâte avec une spatule humide.

Pain multicéréale *(suite)*	Tassez la pâte dans le moule en vous servant d'une spatule huilée, ou de vos mains légèrement farinées. Couvrez le pain avec un torchon propre et sec, puis laissez la pâte lever jusqu'à ce qu'elle atteigne le haut du moule, pendant 25 à 30 minutes environ. Quand le pain est prêt à cuire, faites rapidement trois entailles diagonales sur le dessus du pain à l'aide d'un couteau à dents. Saupoudrez des graines de sésame. Faites cuire au four à 180 °C (350 °F) pendant 40 à 50 minutes, ou jusqu'à ce que le pain atteigne une température interne de 88 °C (190 °F), que vous pouvez vérifier avec un thermomètre à lecture rapide. Laissez le pain reposer sur une grille à pâtisserie pendant 10 minutes, puis retirez-le avec précaution du moule et laissez-le refroidir complètement avant de découper.

Informations nutritionnelles (par tranche) : 119 kcal (lipides 13 %, protéines 11 %, glucides 75 %) • protéines 3 g lipides totaux 2 g • acides gras saturés 0 g • glucides 23 g • fibres alimentaires 2 g • sucre 3 g • sodium 101 mg cholestérol 0 mg

Si vous ne trouvez pas certaines des céréales ou farines indiquées ci-dessus, remplacez-les par de la farine de blé complet ou toute autre farine dont vous disposez. (N'oubliez pas que votre appareil peut moudre toutes les céréales ci-dessus pour en faire de la farine.)

PAIN AU SON D'AVOINE

préparation : 10 minutes • mixage : 30 secondes • cuisson : 30 à 35 minutes
quantité obtenue : 1 pain (12 tranches)

1 blanc d'œuf et suffisamment d'eau tiède, 40 °C à 46 °C (105 °F à 115 °F), pour obtenir 1 1/4 tasse (300 ml)

2 cuillerées à soupe (30 ml) de mélasse

1 sachet (1 cuillerée à soupe) de levure de boulanger sèche

1 à 1 1/4 tasse (80 à 100 g) de son d'avoine (ou de flocons d'avoine)

1 1/4 tasse (150 g) de farine de blé complet

1 tasse (125 g) de farine non blanchie

1 cuillerée à café de sel

1 cuillerée à soupe d'huile de pépin de raisin ou d'huile d'olive légère

Pour activer la levure, mélangez-la avec l'eau tiède et la mélasse. Mélangez le tout rapidement. Laissez reposer pendant 5 minutes.

Versez le son d'avoine, les farines et le sel dans le récipient à INGRÉDIENTS SECS Vitamix, et verrouillez le couvercle.

Réglez le commutateur sur la position Variable et la vitesse sur 1.

Mettez l'appareil en marche et augmentez lentement la vitesse jusqu'à la position Variable 6.

Mixez 10 secondes environ, jusqu'à ce qu'une dépression se forme au centre de la préparation, en vous aidant du poussoir si nécessaire.

Réglez le commutateur sur la position Variable et la vitesse sur 3. Mettez l'appareil en marche, puis ôtez le bouchon du couvercle. Ajoutez l'huile et le mélange à base de levure à travers l'orifice du bouchon du couvercle. Arrêtez l'appareil et remettez le bouchon du couvercle en place.

Sélectionnez la vitesse High (Rapide). Démarrez et arrêtez l'appareil par à-coups deux fois de suite. Arrêtez l'appareil et ôtez le couvercle.

Pendant que la pâte repose, huilez légèrement en vaporisant avec une huile végétale ou en enduisant de matière grasse un moule à pain de 22 cm x 11 cm (8 1/2 pouces x 4 1/2 pouces).

Avec une spatule en caoutchouc humide, raclez les parois du récipient pour ramener la pâte vers le centre du mélange. Remettez le couvercle en place.

Sélectionnez la vitesse High (Rapide). Démarrez et arrêtez l'appareil par à-coups cinq fois de suite. Ajoutez l'eau supplémentaire, 1 cuillerée à la fois, si la pâte semble particulièrement sèche uniquement. Répétez le processus cinq fois, en raclant les parois du récipient jusqu'à ce que la pâte devienne élastique et compacte.

Pour retirer plus facilement la pâte du récipient, démarrez et arrêtez l'appareil par à-coups cinq fois de suite (ce qui va soulever la pâte et la décoller des lames), puis renversez rapidement le récipient au-dessus du moule. Laissez la pâte se déposer dans le moule, en récupérant les restes de pâte avec une spatule humide.

Tassez la pâte dans le moule en vous servant d'une spatule huilée, ou de vos mains légèrement farinées.

Pain au son d'avoine *(suite)*

Couvrez le pain avec un torchon propre et sec, puis laissez la pâte lever jusqu'à ce qu'elle atteigne le haut du moule, pendant 15 à 18 minutes environ. Quand le pain est prêt à cuire, faites rapidement trois entailles diagonales sur le dessus du pain à l'aide d'un couteau à dents.

Faites cuire au four à 180 °C (350 °F) pendant 30 à 35 minutes, ou jusqu'à ce que le pain atteigne une température interne de 88 °C (190 °F) , que vous pouvez vérifier avec un thermomètre à lecture rapide. Laissez le pain reposer sur une grille à pâtisserie pendant 10 minutes, puis retirez-le avec précaution du moule et laissez-le refroidir complètement avant de découper.

Informations nutritionnelles (par tranche) : 124 kcal (lipides 13 %, protéines 14 %, glucides 73 %) • protéines 5 g lipides totaux 2 g • acides gras saturés 0 g • glucides 25 g • fibres alimentaires 3 g • sucre 2 g • sodium 8 mg cholestérol 0 mg

FOCACCIA AU SEIGLE

préparation : 15 minutes • mixage : 30 secondes • cuisson : 35 à 40 minutes
quantité obtenue : 1 pain (8 à 10 tranches)

3/4 tasse (180 ml) d'eau tiède, 40 °C à 46 °C (105 °F à 115 °F)

1 cuillerée à soupe de sucre cristallisé

1 sachet (1 cuillerée à soupe) de levure de boulanger sèche

1 1/2 tasse (188 g) de farine non blanchie

1 tasse (104 g) de farine de seigle légère

1/2 tasse (66 g) de gruyère grossièrement coupé

1 cuillerée à café de sel

1 cuillerée à soupe d'aneth

1 cuillerée à soupe de graines de carvi

3/4 tasse (180 ml) de babeurre à température ambiante

Pour garnir :

2 cuillerées à soupe (30 ml) d'huile d'olive extra vierge

1 1/2 cuillerée à café de sel casher

1/2 tasse (66 g) de gruyère grossièrement coupé

1 cuillerée à café d'aneth

Pour activer la levure, mélangez-la avec l'eau tiède et le sucre. Mélangez le tout rapidement. Laissez reposer pendant 5 minutes.

Versez les farines, le fromage, le sel, l'aneth et les graines de carvi dans le récipient à INGRÉDIENTS SECS Vitamix, et verrouillez le couvercle.

Réglez le commutateur sur la position Variable et la vitesse sur 1.

Mettez l'appareil en marche et augmentez lentement la vitesse jusqu'à la position Variable 10, puis High (Rapide).

Mixer pendant 15 secondes. Réduisez la vitesse sur la position Variable 6 et mixez 5 secondes environ, jusqu'à ce qu'une dépression se forme au centre de la préparation. Arrêtez l'appareil.

Réglez le commutateur sur la position Variable et la vitesse sur 1, puis ôtez le bouchon du couvercle. Mettez l'appareil en marche et augmentez progressivement la vitesse jusqu'à la position Variable 6. Ajoutez le babeurre et le mélange à base de levure à travers l'orifice du bouchon du couvercle. Arrêtez l'appareil et remettez le bouchon du couvercle en place.

Sélectionnez la vitesse High (Rapide). Démarrez et arrêtez l'appareil par à-coups deux fois de suite. Arrêtez l'appareil et ôtez le couvercle.

Pendant que la pâte repose, huilez légèrement un moule à tarte de 23 cm (9 pouces).

Avec une spatule en caoutchouc humide, raclez les parois du récipient pour ramener la pâte vers le centre du mélange. Remettez le couvercle en place.

Sélectionnez la vitesse High (Rapide). Démarrez et arrêtez l'appareil par à-coups cinq fois de suite. Ajoutez l'eau supplémentaire, 1 cuillerée à la fois, si la pâte semble particulièrement sèche uniquement. Répétez le processus cinq fois, en raclant les parois du récipient jusqu'à ce que la pâte devienne élastique et compacte.

Pour retirer plus facilement la pâte du récipient, démarrez et arrêtez l'appareil par à-coups cinq fois de suite (ce qui va soulever la pâte et la décoller des lames), puis renversez rapidement le récipient au-dessus du moule. Laissez la pâte se déposer dans le moule, en récupérant les restes de pâte avec une spatule humide.

Focaccia au seigle (*suite*)

Tassez la pâte dans le moule en vous servant d'une spatule huilée, ou de vos mains légèrement farinées.

Couvrez le moule avec un torchon propre et sec, puis laissez la pâte lever jusqu'à ce qu'elle atteigne le haut du moule, pendant 30 minutes environ. Quand le pain est prêt à cuire, du bout des doigts, faites de petites alvéoles dans la pâte, puis enduisez le dessus d'huile d'olive avec un pinceau. Saupoudrez de sel casher, d'aneth et du reste du gruyère.

Faites cuire au four à 180 °C (350 °F) pendant 35 à 40 minutes, ou jusqu'à ce que le pain atteigne une température interne de 88 °C (190 °F), que vous pouvez vérifier avec un thermomètre à lecture rapide. Laissez le pain reposer sur une grille à pâtisserie pendant 10 minutes, puis retirez-le avec précaution du moule et laissez-le refroidir complètement avant de découper.

Informations nutritionnelles (par tranche) : 202 kcal (lipides 32 %, protéines 15 %, glucides 52 %) • protéines 8 g lipides totaux 7 g • acides gras saturés 3 g • glucides 26 g • fibres alimentaires 3 g • sucre 3 g • sodium 448 mg cholestérol 14 mg

Les pâtes à base de seigle sont souvent plus collantes et difficiles à manipuler que celles à base de blé : faites preuve de patience et n'ajoutez pas trop de farine simplement pour éviter que la pâte colle, car le pain serait trop compact.

BRETZELS MOELLEUX

préparation : 10 minutes • mixage : 15 secondes • cuisson : 8 à 10 minutes
quantité obtenue : 12 bretzels

3/4 tasse (180 ml) d'eau tiède, 40 °C à 46 °C (105 °F à 115 °F)

1/4 tasse (55 g) de sucre roux, bien tassé

1 sachet (1 cuillerée à soupe) de levure de boulanger sèche

1/4 tasse (30 g) de farine de blé complet

1/2 tasse (62 g) de farine non blanchie

1 1/2 tasse (205 g) de farine à pain (haute teneur en gluten)

1 pincée de sel

1 gros œuf mélangé à 2 cuillerées à soupe (30 ml) d'eau (pour enduire la pâte avant la cuisson)

Sel casher

Pour activer la levure, mélangez-la avec l'eau tiède et le sucre roux. Mélangez le tout rapidement. Laissez reposer pendant 5 minutes.

Versez les farines et le sel dans le récipient à INGRÉDIENTS SECS Vitamix, et verrouillez le couvercle.

Réglez le commutateur sur la position Variable et la vitesse sur 1.

Mettez l'appareil en marche et augmentez lentement la vitesse jusqu'à la position Variable 6.

Mixez 5 secondes environ, jusqu'à ce qu'une dépression se forme au centre de la préparation.

Réglez le commutateur sur la position Variable et la vitesse sur 3. Mettez l'appareil en marche, puis ôtez le bouchon du couvercle. Ajoutez le mélange à base de levure à travers l'orifice du bouchon du couvercle. Arrêtez l'appareil et remettez le bouchon du couvercle en place.

Sélectionnez la vitesse High (Rapide). Démarrez et arrêtez l'appareil par à-coups deux fois de suite. Arrêtez l'appareil et ôtez le couvercle.

Pendant que la pâte repose, huilez légèrement en vaporisant avec une huile végétale ou en enduisant de matière grasse une plaque à pâtisserie.

Avec une spatule en caoutchouc humide, raclez les parois du récipient pour ramener la pâte vers le centre du mélange. Remettez le couvercle en place.

Sélectionnez la vitesse High (Rapide). Démarrez et arrêtez l'appareil par à-coups cinq fois de suite. Ajoutez l'eau supplémentaire, 1 cuillerée à la fois, si la pâte semble particulièrement sèche uniquement. Répétez le processus cinq fois, en raclant les parois du récipient jusqu'à ce que la pâte devienne élastique et compacte.

Placez le couvercle sur le récipient et laissez la pâte lever jusqu'à ce qu'elle ait doublé de volume, pendant 15 minutes environ.

Transférez la pâte sur une surface légèrement farinée et divisez-la en 12 morceaux. Avec les paumes de vos mains, roulez chaque morceau de façon à former une « corde » de 30 à 46 cm (12 à 18 pouces) de long. Formez une boucle ovale, entrecroisez les extrémités et appuyez doucement pour coller les extrémités au sommet de l'ovale.

Bretzels moelleux *(suite)*	Battez l'œuf avec l'eau. Enduisez rapidement et légèrement chaque bretzel de ce mélange, puis saupoudrez de sel casher. Faites cuire au four à 230 °C (450 °F) pendant 8 à 10 minutes ou jusqu'à ce que les bretzels soient croquants et légèrement dorés. Ces bretzels sont meilleurs chauds.

Informations nutritionnelles (par bretzel) : 117 kcal (lipides 8 %, protéines 13 %, glucides 79 %) • protéines 4 g lipides totaux 1 g • acides gras saturés 0 g • glucides 23 g • fibres alimentaires 1 g • sucre 5 g • sodium 11 mg cholestérol 18 mg

Si vous souhaitez saupoudrer vos bretzels de cannelle et de sucre, ne les saupoudrez pas de gros sel avant de les cuire. Une fois que vous les avez sortis du four, enduisez-les de beurre fondu à l'aide d'un pinceau et saupoudrez d'un mélange de cannelle et de sucre.

PIZZA

préparation : 15 minutes • mixage : 30 secondes • cuisson : 15 à 18 minutes
quantité obtenue : 1 grande pizza (8 parts)

1 tasse (240 ml) d'eau tiède, 40 °C à 46 °C (105 °F à 115 °F)

2 cuillerées à café de sucre cristallisé

1 sachet (1 cuillerée à soupe) de levure de boulanger sèche

2 1/2 tasses (312 g) de farine non blanchie

1/2 cuillerée à café de sel

1 cuillerée à soupe d'huile d'olive

2 cuillerées à soupe (15 g) de farine de maïs complet pour saupoudrer le moule à pizza

Garniture :

2 cuillerées à soupe (30 ml) d'huile d'olive

1/3 tasse (33 g) de parmesan râpé

1 1/3 tasse (320 g) de sauce à pizza

1 1/4 tasse (141 g) de mozzarella râpée

Pour activer la levure, mélangez-la avec l'eau tiède et le sucre. Mélangez le tout rapidement. Laissez reposer pendant 5 minutes.

Versez la farine et le sel dans le récipient à INGRÉDIENTS SECS Vitamix dans l'ordre indiqué, et verrouillez le couvercle.

Réglez le commutateur sur la position Variable et la vitesse sur 1.

Mettez l'appareil en marche et augmentez lentement la vitesse jusqu'à la position Variable 6.

Mixez jusqu'à ce le tout soit bien mélangé et qu'une dépression se forme au centre, pendant environ 5 secondes.

Arrêtez l'appareil et ôtez le bouchon du couvercle. Réglez le commutateur sur la position Variable et la vitesse sur 1. Mettez l'appareil en marche et augmentez lentement la vitesse jusqu'à la position Variable 6. Ajoutez l'huile d'olive et le mélange à base de levure à travers l'orifice du bouchon du couvercle. Arrêtez l'appareil et remettez le bouchon du couvercle en place.

Sélectionnez la vitesse High (Rapide). Démarrez et arrêtez l'appareil par à-coups deux fois de suite. Arrêtez l'appareil et ôtez le couvercle.

Pendant que la pâte repose, saupoudrez légèrement le moule à pizza de la farine de maïs.

Avec une spatule en caoutchouc humide, raclez les parois du récipient pour ramener la pâte vers le centre du mélange. Remettez le couvercle en place.

Sélectionnez la vitesse High (Rapide). Démarrez et arrêtez l'appareil par à-coups cinq fois de suite. Ajoutez l'eau supplémentaire, 1 cuillerée à la fois, si la pâte semble particulièrement sèche uniquement. Répétez le processus cinq fois, en raclant les parois du récipient jusqu'à ce que la pâte devienne élastique et compacte.

Pour retirer plus facilement la pâte du récipient, démarrez et arrêtez l'appareil par à-coups cinq fois de suite (ce qui va soulever la pâte et la décoller des lames), puis renversez rapidement le récipient au-dessus d'un plan de travail propre et légèrement saupoudré de farine.

Couvrez la pâte d'un torchon propre et sec ou d'un saladier renversé, et laissez reposer pendant 15 minutes.

Pizza *(suite)*

Aplatissez la pâte avec la paume des mains, tout en maintenant la forme arrondie. Avec un rouleau à pâtisserie, étalez régulièrement la pâte du centre vers l'extérieur dans chaque direction, en soulevant et tournant la pâte d'un quart de tour après chaque coup de rouleau. La forme finale doit mesurer 2,5 cm (1 pouce) de plus que votre moule. Placez la pâte dans le moule. Formez un rebord sur tout le tour.

Enduisez légèrement la pâte d'huile d'olive avec un pinceau, puis saupoudrez de parmesan râpé. Versez la sauce sur la pâte et étalez-la avec le dos d'une cuillère. Parsemez-la de votre garniture préférée, puis saupoudrez uniformément de mozzarella râpée.

Faites cuire la pizza sur la grille la plus basse d'un four à 220 °C (425 °F) pendant 15 à 18 minutes jusqu'à ce que le dessous de la pâte soit légèrement doré et que le fromage fasse des bulles.

Retirez le moule à pizza du four, laissez-la reposer pendant 5 minutes pour laisser le fromage refroidir, avant de découper les parts.

Informations nutritionnelles (par portion) : 319 kcal (lipides 35 %, protéines 15 %, glucides 51 %) • protéines 12 g lipides totaux 12 g • acides gras saturés 4 g • glucides 40 g • fibres alimentaires 3 g • sucre 6 g • sodium 320 mg cholestérol 13 mg

En étalant la pâte du centre vers l'extérieur et en la tournant, vous conserverez plus facilement une forme ronde.

Pizza

PAIN TRESSÉ AUX GRAINES DE PAVOT

préparation : 15 minutes • mixage : 12 secondes • cuisson : 35 à 40 minutes
quantité obtenue : 1 pain (12 tranches)

4 cuillerées à soupe (60 ml) d'eau tiède, 40 °C à 46 °C (105 °F à 115 °F)

1 sachet (1 cuillerée à soupe) de levure de boulanger sèche

1/3 tasse (80 ml) de lait

1/4 tasse (56 g) de beurre doux

1/3 tasse (80 ml) de miel

1/2 cuillerée à café de sel

1 gros œuf

2 1/4 tasses (281 g) de farine non blanchie, plus quantité nécessaire pour mélanger et étaler la pâte

1 1/3 tasse (320 g) de mélange aux graines de pavot (recette à la page 74)

1 gros œuf et 2 cuillerées à soupe (30 ml) de lait pour enduire le pain

Pour activer la levure, mélangez-la avec l'eau tiède. Mélangez le tout rapidement. Laissez reposer pendant 5 minutes.

Portez le lait à ébullition dans une petite casserole, puis ajoutez le beurre et le miel ; laissez refroidir jusqu'à une température comprise entre 43 °C et 46 °C (110 °F et 115 °F).

Versez la farine et le sel dans le récipient à INGRÉDIENTS SECS Vitamix, et verrouillez le couvercle.

Réglez le commutateur sur la position Variable et la vitesse sur 1.

Mettez l'appareil en marche et augmentez lentement la vitesse jusqu'à la position Variable 6.

Mixez 5 secondes environ, jusqu'à ce qu'une dépression se forme au centre de la préparation.

Réglez le commutateur sur la position Variable et la vitesse sur 3. Mettez l'appareil en marche, puis ôtez le bouchon du couvercle. Versez l'œuf, le mélange à base de levure et le mélange à base de lait à travers l'orifice du bouchon du couvercle. Arrêtez l'appareil et remettez le bouchon du couvercle en place.

Sélectionnez la vitesse High (Rapide). Démarrez et arrêtez l'appareil par à-coups deux fois de suite. Arrêtez l'appareil et ôtez le couvercle.

Pendant que la pâte repose, huilez légèrement un grand saladier en le vaporisant avec une huile végétale ou en l'enduisant de matière grasse.

En vous servant d'une spatule en caoutchouc, raclez les parois du récipient Vitamix. Décollez la pâte des parois du récipient et rassemblez-la au milieu. Remettez le couvercle en place.

Sélectionnez la vitesse High (Rapide). Démarrez et arrêtez l'appareil par à-coups cinq fois de suite. Ajoutez l'eau supplémentaire, 1 cuillerée à la fois, si la pâte semble particulièrement sèche uniquement. Répétez le processus cinq fois, en raclant les parois du récipient jusqu'à ce que la pâte devienne élastique et compacte.

Pour retirer la pâte du récipient, démarrez et arrêtez l'appareil par à-coups cinq fois (ce qui va soulever la pâte et la décoller des lames). Renversez le récipient au-dessus du saladier huilé et laissez la pâte s'y déposer. Retournez la pâte une fois pour enduire toute la surface. Couvrez avec un torchon propre et laissez lever pendant 20 à 30 minutes.

Pain tressé aux graines de pavot *(suite)*

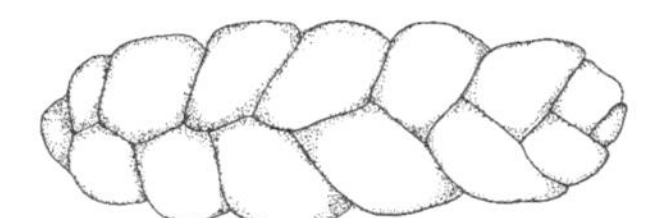

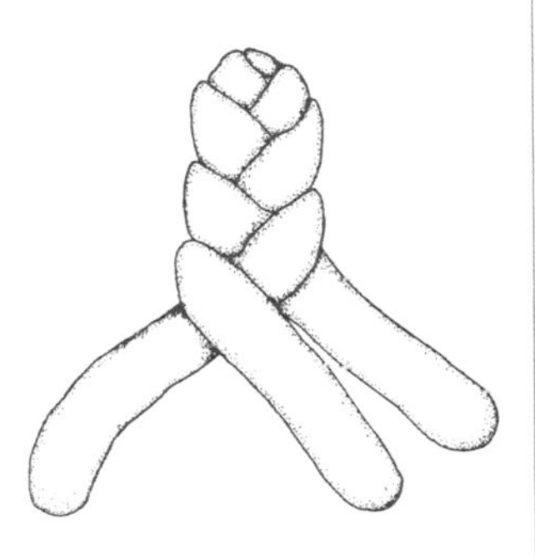

Transférez la pâte sur un plan de travail fariné. En la retournant et la farinant fréquemment, étalez la pâte de façon à former un grand rectangle de 23 cm x 38 cm (9 pouces x 15 pouces).

Coupez la pâte en tiers dans le sens de la longueur de façon à obtenir 3 bandes de 23 cm x 13 cm (9 pouces x 5 pouces, vous pouvez utiliser un découpe-pizza).

Remplissez le centre de chaque section de mélange aux graines de pavot. Humectez les extrémités de chaque bande, ainsi que l'un des côtés longs, avec de l'eau tiède.

Roulez chaque bande sur la longueur pour que les graines de pavot se retrouvent à l'intérieur. Collez les bords humides, puis les extrémités.

Alignez les trois bandes ainsi confectionnées sur une plaque à pâtisserie recouverte de papier parcheminé (côtés collés vers le bas). Tressez les trois bandes, sans trop serrer pour que la pâte ait la place de gonfler. Collez les extrémités avec vos doigts et de l'eau tiède, puis repliez la partie collée sous la tresse pour qu'elle ne se défasse pas pendant la cuisson.

Couvrez d'un torchon propre et sec, puis laissez lever pendant 20 à 25 minutes.

Avec un pinceau, enduisez la surface de la tresse avec le mélange d'œuf et de lait. Faites cuire au four à 180 °C (350 °F) pendant 35 à 40 minutes, ou jusqu'à ce que la tresse soit dorée et atteigne une température interne de 88 °C (190 °F), que vous pouvez vérifier avec un thermomètre à lecture rapide.

Laissez reposer sur une grille à pâtisserie pendant 10 minutes, puis démoulez avec précaution et laissez refroidir complètement avant de découper.

Informations nutritionnelles (par tranche, mélange aux graines de pavot compris) : 282 kcal (lipides 36 %, protéines 10 %, glucides 54 %) • protéines 7 g • lipides totaux 12 g • acides gras saturés 4 g • glucides 39 g fibres alimentaires 2 g • sucre 18 g • sodium 133 mg • cholestérol 48 mg

MÉLANGE AUX GRAINES DE PAVOT

préparation : 10 minutes • mixage : 25 secondes • cuisson : 30 à 45 minutes
quantité obtenue : 1 1/3 tasse (320 g) de mélange, plus graines de pavot moulues supplémentaires pour utilisation ultérieure

2 tasses (282 g) de graines de pavot

1 tasse (240 ml) de lait

1/2 tasse (100 g) de sucre cristallisé

2 cuillerées à café de beurre doux

2 cuillerées à café de zeste de citron

Versez les graines de pavot dans le récipient à INGRÉDIENTS SECS Vitamix, et verrouillez le couvercle.

Réglez le commutateur sur la position Variable et la vitesse sur 1.

Mettez l'appareil en marche et augmentez lentement la vitesse jusqu'à la position Variable 10, puis High (Rapide).

Mixer pendant 10 secondes.

Arrêtez l'appareil et raclez les parois du récipient avec une spatule.

Remettez le couvercle en place et moulez pendant 15 secondes supplémentaires ou jusqu'à obtention de la finesse désirée. Mesurez une tasse (142 g) de graines de pavot moulues. Congelez le surplus des graines de pavot moulues dans un récipient hermétiquement fermé.

Pour le mélange :

Mélangez une tasse (142 g) de graines de pavot moulues, le lait, le sucre, le beurre et le zeste de citron dans une casserole de taille moyenne.

Faites cuire à feux doux, en remuant souvent, pendant 30 à 45 minutes ou jusqu'à obtention de la texture désirée. Retirez du feu et remuez de temps en temps pour refroidir le mélange. Une fois le mélange refroidi, couvrez et mettez au réfrigérateur.

Informations nutritionnelles (pour 2 cuillerées à soupe, soit 30 g) : 132 kcal (lipides 48 %, protéines 10 %, glucides 42 %) • protéines 3 g • lipides totaux 7 g • acides gras saturés 1 g • glucides 15 g • fibres alimentaires 1 g sucre 12 g • sodium 16 mg • cholestérol 3 mg

Mélange aux graines de pavot

PAIN D'ÉPEAUTRE

préparation : 10 minutes • mixage : 1 minute et 30 secondes • cuisson : 35 à 40 minutes
quantité obtenue : 1 pain (12 tranches)

1 tasse (240 ml) d'eau tiède, 40 °C à 46 °C (105 °F à 115 °F)

1 cuillerée à soupe de miel

1 sachet (1 cuillerée à soupe) de levure de boulanger sèche

1 3/4 tasse (315 g) de grains d'épeautre ou 2 1/2 tasses (180 g) de farine d'épeautre

1/2 cuillerée à café de sel

1 cuillerée à soupe d'huile d'olive

Pour activer la levure, mélangez-la avec l'eau tiède et le miel. Mélangez le tout rapidement. Laissez reposer pendant 5 minutes.

Si vous utilisez des grains d'épeautre : Versez l'épeautre et le sel dans le récipient à INGRÉDIENTS SECS Vitamix, et verrouillez le couvercle.

Réglez le commutateur sur la position Variable et la vitesse sur 1.

Mettez l'appareil en marche et augmentez lentement la vitesse jusqu'à la position Variable 10, puis High (Rapide).

Moulez pendant une minute, en utilisant le poussoir (inséré par l'orifice du bouchon) pour pousser le mélange contre les lames. Enlevez le poussoir pendant les 5 dernières secondes pour qu'une dépression se forme au centre de la préparation.

Si vous utilisez de la farine d'épeautre : Versez la farine d'épeautre et le sel dans le récipient à INGRÉDIENTS SECS Vitamix, et verrouillez le couvercle.

Réglez le commutateur sur la position Variable et la vitesse sur 1.

Mettez l'appareil en marche et augmentez lentement la vitesse jusqu'à la position Variable 6.

Mixez 5 secondes environ, jusqu'à ce qu'une dépression se forme au centre de la préparation.

Réglez le commutateur sur la position Variable et la vitesse sur 3. Mettez l'appareil en marche, puis ôtez le bouchon du couvercle. Ajoutez l'huile et le mélange à base de levure à travers l'orifice du bouchon du couvercle. Arrêtez l'appareil et remettez le bouchon du couvercle en place.

Pour mélanger la pâte, sélectionnez la vitesse High (Rapide). Démarrez et arrêtez l'appareil par à-coups deux fois de suite. Arrêtez l'appareil et ôtez le couvercle.

Pendant que la pâte repose, huilez légèrement en vaporisant avec une huile végétale ou en enduisant de matière grasse un moule à pain de 22 cm x 11 cm (8 1/2 pouces x 4 1/2 pouces).

Avec une spatule en caoutchouc humide, raclez les parois du récipient pour ramener la pâte vers le centre du mélange. Remettez le couvercle en place.

Pain d'épeautre (*suite*)

Sélectionnez la vitesse High (Rapide). Démarrez et arrêtez l'appareil par à-coups cinq fois de suite. Ajoutez l'eau supplémentaire, 1 cuillerée à la fois, si la pâte semble particulièrement sèche uniquement. Répétez le processus cinq fois, en raclant les parois du récipient jusqu'à ce que la pâte devienne élastique et compacte.

Pour retirer plus facilement la pâte du récipient, démarrez et arrêtez l'appareil par à-coups cinq fois de suite (ce qui va soulever la pâte et la décoller des lames), puis renversez rapidement le récipient au-dessus du moule. Laissez la pâte se déposer dans le moule, en récupérant les restes de pâte avec une spatule humide.

Tassez la pâte dans le moule en vous servant d'une spatule huilée, ou de vos mains légèrement farinées.

Couvrez le pain avec un torchon propre et sec, puis laissez la pâte lever jusqu'à ce qu'elle atteigne le haut du moule, pendant 15 à 20 minutes environ. Quand le pain est prêt à cuire, faites rapidement trois entailles diagonales sur le dessus du pain à l'aide d'un couteau à dents.

Faites cuire au four à 180 °C (350 °F) pendant 35 à 40 minutes, ou jusqu'à ce que le pain atteigne une température interne de 88 °C (190 °F). Laissez le pain reposer sur une grille à pâtisserie pendant 10 minutes, puis retirez-le avec précaution du moule et laissez-le refroidir complètement avant de découper.

Informations nutritionnelles (par tranche) : 106 kcal (lipides 16 %, protéines 13 %, glucides 71 %) • protéines 4 g lipides totaux 2 g • acides gras saturés 0 g • glucides 21 g • fibres alimentaires 3 g • sucre 3 g • sodium 99 mg cholestérol 0 mg

Le pain tranché quand il est encore chaud, surtout le pain à base de céréales complètes, est souvent humide à l'intérieur. Laissez-le refroidir complètement avant de le couper.

PAIN AU LEVAIN (DE BASE ET RICHE)

préparation : 20 minutes • mixage : 30 secondes • cuisson : 30 à 40 minutes
quantité obtenue : 1 pain (12 tranches)

Recette de base

1 tasse (240 ml) de levain chef à la pomme de terre (recette à la page 75)

1/2 cuillerée à café de sel

1 à 1 1/2 tasse (125 à 188 g) de farine non blanchie

Recette riche

1 tasse (240 ml) de levain chef à la pomme de terre (recette à la page 75)

1/4 tasse (60 ml) de miel

1 cuillerée à soupe de beurre doux, ramolli

1/2 cuillerée à café de sel

1 1/3 à 1 2/3 tasse (166 à 208 g) de farine non blanchie

Choisissez la recette de base ou riche.

Versez tous les ingrédients dans le récipient à INGRÉDIENTS SECS Vitamix dans l'ordre indiqué, et verrouillez le couvercle.

Pour mélanger la pâte, sélectionnez la vitesse High (Rapide). Démarrez et arrêtez l'appareil par à-coups deux fois de suite. Arrêtez l'appareil et ôtez le couvercle.

Pendant que la pâte repose, huilez légèrement en vaporisant avec une huile végétale ou en enduisant de matière grasse un moule à cake de 20 cm x 10 cm (8 pouces x 4 pouces).

Avec une spatule en caoutchouc humide, raclez les parois du récipient pour ramener la pâte vers le centre du mélange. Remettez le couvercle en place.

Sélectionnez la vitesse High (Rapide). Démarrez et arrêtez l'appareil par à-coups cinq fois de suite. Ajoutez l'eau supplémentaire, 1 cuillerée à la fois, si la pâte semble particulièrement sèche uniquement. Répétez le processus cinq fois, en raclant les parois du récipient jusqu'à ce que la pâte devienne élastique et compacte.

Pour retirer plus facilement la pâte du récipient, démarrez et arrêtez l'appareil par à-coups cinq fois de suite (ce qui va soulever la pâte et la décoller des lames), puis renversez rapidement le récipient au-dessus du moule. Laissez la pâte se déposer dans le moule, en récupérant les restes de pâte avec une spatule humide.

Tassez la pâte dans le moule en vous servant d'une spatule huilée, ou de vos mains légèrement farinées.

Couvrez le moule avec un torchon propre et sec, puis laissez la pâte lever jusqu'à ce qu'elle atteigne le haut du moule, pendant 30 minutes environ. Quand le pain est prêt à cuire, du bout des doigts, faites de petites alvéoles dans la pâte, puis enduisez le dessus d'huile d'olive avec un pinceau. Saupoudrez de sel casher, d'aneth et du reste du gruyère.

Pain au levain (de base et riche) *(suite)*	Faites cuire au four à 180 °C (350 °F) pendant 35 à 40 minutes, ou jusqu'à ce que le pain atteigne une température interne de 88 °C (190 °F), que vous pouvez vérifier avec un thermomètre à lecture rapide. Laissez le pain reposer sur une grille à pâtisserie pendant 10 minutes, puis retirez-le avec précaution du moule et laissez-le refroidir complètement avant de découper.

Recette de base : Informations nutritionnelles (par tranche) : 57 kcal (lipides 3 %, protéines 12 %, glucides 85 %) protéines 2 g • lipides totaux 0 g • acides gras saturés 0 g • glucides 12 g • fibres alimentaires 1 g • sucre 0 g sodium 99 mg • cholestérol 0 mg

Recette riche : Informations nutritionnelles (par tranche) : 106 kcal (lipides 10 %, protéines 9 %, glucides 81 %) protéines 2 g • lipides totaux 1 g • acides gras saturés 1 g • glucides 22 g • fibres alimentaires 1 g • sucre 6 g sodium 99 mg • cholestérol 3 mg

PETITS PAINS À LA PATATE DOUCE

préparation : 15 minutes • mixage : 30 secondes • cuisson : 20 à 25 minutes
quantité obtenue : 12 rouleaux

1/2 livre (227 g) de patates douces, pelées et coupées en quartiers

1 sachet (1 cuillerée à soupe) de levure de boulanger sèche

1 cuillerée à soupe de sucre cristallisé

1 tasse (125 g) de farine non blanchie

1 1/3 tasse (160 g) de farine de blé complet, plus si nécessaire

1/2 cuillerée à café de sel

2 cuillerées à soupe (28 g) de beurre doux fondu

2 cuillerées à soupe (30 ml) de miel

1 cuillerée à soupe d'huile végétale

1 gros œuf battu

Faites cuire les patates douces dans une casserole d'eau bouillante jusqu'à ce qu'elles soient tendres, pendant 20 minutes environ. Égouttez-les et réservez 1/3 tasse (80 ml) du liquide de cuisson. Écrasez grossièrement les patates douces et mettez-les de côté. Laissez refroidir le liquide de cuisson jusqu'à ce qu'il atteigne une température de 46 °C (115 °F).

Pour activer la levure, mélangez-la avec 1/3 tasse (80 ml) de liquide de cuisson et le sucre. Mélangez le tout rapidement. Laissez reposer pendant 5 minutes.

Versez les farines et le sel dans le récipient à INGRÉDIENTS SECS Vitamix, et verrouillez le couvercle.

Réglez le commutateur sur la position Variable et la vitesse sur 1.

Mettez l'appareil en marche et augmentez lentement la vitesse jusqu'à la position Variable 10, puis High (Rapide).

Mixez 5 secondes environ, jusqu'à ce qu'une dépression se forme au centre de la préparation. Arrêtez l'appareil.

Réglez le commutateur sur la position Variable et la vitesse sur 3. Mettez l'appareil en marche, puis ôtez le bouchon du couvercle. Ajoutez les patates douces, le beurre, le miel, l'huile, l'œuf et le mélange à base de levure à travers l'orifice du bouchon du couvercle. Arrêtez l'appareil et remettez le bouchon du couvercle en place.

Pour mélanger la pâte, sélectionnez la vitesse High (Rapide). Démarrez et arrêtez l'appareil par à-coups deux fois de suite. Arrêtez l'appareil et ôtez le couvercle.

Avec une spatule en caoutchouc humide, raclez les parois du récipient pour ramener la pâte vers le centre du mélange. Remettez le couvercle en place.

Sélectionnez la vitesse High (Rapide). Démarrez et arrêtez l'appareil par à-coups cinq fois de suite. Ajoutez l'eau supplémentaire, 1 cuillerée à la fois, si la pâte semble particulièrement sèche uniquement. Répétez le processus cinq fois, en raclant les parois du récipient jusqu'à ce que la pâte devienne élastique et compacte.

Huilez légèrement un grand saladier. Placez-y la pâte et retournez-la pour enduire toute la surface. Recouvrez le saladier d'un torchon propre ou de film alimentaire. Laissez la pâte lever à un endroit tiède et sans courant d'air jusqu'à ce qu'elle ait doublé de volume, pendant 20 minutes environ.

Petits pains à la patate douce *(suite)*

Pendant que la pâte repose, huilez légèrement en vaporisant avec une huile végétale ou en enduisant de matière grasse un moule à tarte carré de 23 cm (9 pouces) de côté. Aplatissez la pâte avec votre poing. Retournez la pâte sur une surface légèrement farinée et pétrissez-la doucement jusqu'à ce qu'elle soit bien lisse. Coupez-la en 12 morceaux égaux. Avec chaque morceau, formez une boule et placez-les dans le moule à tarte, relativement près les unes des autres.

Couvrez d'un torchon propre et sec ou de film alimentaire, puis laissez lever pendant 20 minutes. Faites cuire au four à 190 °C (375 °F) pendant 20 à 25 minutes ou jusqu'à ce que les petits pains soient légèrement dorés, en tournant le moule une fois pour que tous les petits pains dorent bien. Laissez refroidir sur une grille à pâtisserie.

Informations nutritionnelles (par petit pain) : 150 kcal (lipides 24 %, protéines 11 %, glucides 66 %) • protéines 4 g lipides totaux 4 g • acides gras saturés 2 g • glucides 25 g • fibres alimentaires 3 g • sucre 5 g • sodium 113 mg cholestérol 23 mg

PAIN COMPLET

préparation : 10 minutes • mixage : 35 secondes • cuisson : 35 minutes
quantité obtenue : 1 pain (12 tranches)

1 sachet (1 cuillerée à soupe) de levure de boulanger sèche

1 1/4 tasse (300 ml) d'eau tiède, 40 °C à 46 °C (105 °F à 115 °F)

1 cuillerée à soupe de miel

1 1/2 tasse (270 g) de grains de blé complet ou 2 1/4 tasses (270 g) de farine de blé complet

1 cuillerée à café de sel

1 cuillerée à soupe d'huile de pépin de raisin ou d'huile d'olive légère

1 cuillerée à café de jus de citron

1 blanc d'œuf battu avec 1 cuillerée à soupe d'eau, facultatif (pour enduire la pâte avant la cuisson)

Pour activer la levure, mélangez-la avec l'eau tiède et le miel. Mélangez le tout rapidement. Laissez reposer pendant 5 minutes.

Si vous utilisez des grains de blé complet : versez les grains de blé et le sel dans le récipient à INGRÉDIENTS SECS Vitamix, et verrouillez le couvercle.

Réglez le commutateur sur la position Variable et la vitesse sur 1.

Mettez l'appareil en marche et augmentez lentement la vitesse jusqu'à la position Variable 10, puis High (Rapide).

Moulez pendant 1 minute (pas plus longtemps). Arrêtez l'appareil pour permettre à la farine de refroidir pendant quelques minutes.

Si vous utilisez de la farine de blé complet : Versez la farine et le sel dans le récipient à INGRÉDIENTS SECS Vitamix, et verrouillez le couvercle.

Réglez le commutateur sur la position Variable et la vitesse sur 1.

Mettez l'appareil en marche et augmentez lentement la vitesse jusqu'à la position Variable 6.

Mixez 5 secondes environ, jusqu'à ce qu'une dépression se forme au centre de la préparation.

Réglez le commutateur sur la position Variable et la vitesse sur 3. Mettez l'appareil en marche, puis ôtez le bouchon du couvercle. Ajoutez l'huile, le jus de citron et le mélange à base de levure à travers l'orifice du bouchon du couvercle. Arrêtez l'appareil et remettez le bouchon du couvercle en place.

Sélectionnez la vitesse High (Rapide). Démarrez et arrêtez l'appareil par à-coups deux fois de suite. Arrêtez l'appareil et ôtez le couvercle.

Pendant que la pâte repose, huilez légèrement en vaporisant avec une huile végétale ou en enduisant de matière grasse un moule à cake de 22 cm x 11 cm (8 1/2 pouces x 4 1/2 pouces).

En vous servant d'une spatule en caoutchouc, raclez les parois du récipient Vitamix. Décollez la pâte des parois du récipient et rassemblez-la au milieu. Remettez le couvercle en place.

Sélectionnez la vitesse High (Rapide). Démarrez et arrêtez l'appareil par à-coups cinq fois de suite. Ajoutez l'eau supplémentaire, 1 cuillerée à la fois, si la pâte semble particulièrement sèche uniquement. Répétez le processus cinq fois, en raclant les parois du récipient jusqu'à ce que la pâte devienne élastique et compacte.

Pain complet *(suite)*

Pour retirer la pâte du récipient, démarrez et arrêtez l'appareil par à-coups cinq fois (ce qui va soulever la pâte et la décoller des lames). Renversez le récipient sur le moule et laissez la pâte s'y déposer. Récupérez les restes de pâte avec une spatule en caoutchouc humide.

Tassez la pâte dans le moule en vous servant d'une spatule en caoutchouc humide ou huilée (ou de vos mains légèrement farinées). Couvrez-la d'un torchon propre et sec, puis laissez-la lever jusqu'à ce qu'elle atteigne le haut du moule, pendant 20 à 25 minutes environ.

Vous pouvez si vous le désirez passer rapidement et légèrement un pinceau trempé dans le mélange de blanc d'œuf sur la pâte et faire trois entailles diagonales d'environ 6 mm (1/4 pouce) de profondeur sur le dessus avec un couteau à dents bien aiguisé.

Faites cuire au four à 180 °C (350 °F) pendant 35 minutes, ou jusqu'à ce que le pain soit bien doré et atteigne une température interne de 88 °C (190 °F) que vous pouvez vérifier avec un thermomètre à lecture rapide.

Laissez le pain reposer sur une grille à pâtisserie pendant 10 minutes, puis retirez-le avec précaution du moule et laissez-le refroidir complètement avant de découper.

Informations nutritionnelles (par tranche) : 102 kcal (lipides 13 %, protéines 13 %, glucides 74 %) • protéines 3 g lipides totaux 2 g • acides gras saturés 0 g • glucides 20 g • fibres alimentaires 3 g • sucre 2 g • sodium 203 mg cholestérol 0 mg

BAGUETTE AUX CÉRÉALES COMPLÈTES

préparation : 15 minutes • mixage : 35 secondes • cuisson : 30 à 40 minutes
quantité obtenue : 1 pain (16 à 18 tranches)

1 tasse (240 ml) d'eau tiède, 40 °C à 46 °C (105 °F à 115 °F), en plusieurs portions

1 sachet (1 cuillerée à soupe) de levure de boulanger sèche

1 1/4 tasse (150 g) de farine de blé complet

3/4 tasse (103 g) de farine à pain

1 1/2 cuillerée à café de sel

2 cuillerées à soupe (21 g) de graines de lin

2 cuillerées à soupe (18 g) de graines de tournesol

1 cuillerée à soupe de graines de citrouille ou de millet

1 cuillerée à soupe de germe de blé

1 cuillerée à soupe d'huile d'olive

2 cuillerées à soupe (15 g) de farine de maïs entière

1 blanc d'œuf mélangé à 1 cuillerée à café d'eau (pour enduire la pâte avant la cuisson)

Pour activer la levure, mélangez-la avec 1/2 tasse (120 ml) d'eau tiède. Mélangez le tout rapidement. Laissez reposer pendant 5 minutes.

Versez la farine de blé complet, la farine à pain, le sel, les graines de lin, les graines de tournesol, de citrouille OU le millet et le germe de blé dans le récipient à INGRÉDIENTS SECS Vitamix, et verrouillez le couvercle.

Réglez le commutateur sur la position Variable et la vitesse sur 1.

Mettez l'appareil en marche et augmentez lentement la vitesse jusqu'à la position Variable 6.

Mixez 5 secondes environ, jusqu'à ce qu'une dépression se forme au centre de la préparation. Arrêtez l'appareil.

Réglez le commutateur sur la position Variable et la vitesse sur 3. Mettez l'appareil en marche, puis ôtez le bouchon du couvercle. Ajoutez le mélange à base de levure et le reste de l'eau (1/2 tasse/120 ml) à travers l'orifice du bouchon du couvercle. Arrêtez l'appareil et remettez le bouchon du couvercle en place.

Pour mélanger la pâte, sélectionnez la vitesse High (Rapide). Démarrez et arrêtez l'appareil par à-coups deux fois de suite. Arrêtez l'appareil et ôtez le couvercle.

Pendant que la pâte repose, huilez un saladier de taille moyenne avec de l'huile d'olive et saupoudrez une plaque à pâtisserie avec la farine de maïs.

Avec une spatule en caoutchouc humide, raclez les parois du récipient pour ramener la pâte vers le centre du mélange. Remettez le couvercle en place.

Sélectionnez la vitesse High (Rapide). Démarrez et arrêtez l'appareil par à-coups cinq fois de suite. Ajoutez l'eau supplémentaire, 1 cuillerée à la fois, si la pâte semble particulièrement sèche uniquement. Répétez le processus cinq fois, en raclant les parois du récipient jusqu'à ce que la pâte devienne élastique et compacte.

Pour retirer plus facilement la pâte du récipient, démarrez et arrêtez l'appareil par à-coups cinq fois de suite (ce qui va soulever la pâte et la décoller des lames), puis renversez rapidement le récipient au-dessus du saladier, en récupérant les restes de pâte avec une spatule humide. Retournez la pâte pour bien l'enduire. Recouvrez de film alimentaire et laissez lever jusqu'à ce que la pâte ait quasiment triplé de volume, pendant 1 heure environ.

Baguette aux céréales complètes *(suite)*

Aplatissez légèrement la pâte avec votre poing et déposez-la sur un plan de travail fariné. Étalez-la de façon à obtenir un rectangle de 30 cm x 15 cm (12 pouces x 6 pouces) avec un rouleau à pâtisserie fariné. Étalez suivant le bord le plus long, en pinçant les bords ensemble et en utilisant de l'eau pour les coller.

Déposez la pâte, bords collés vers le bas, sur la plaque à pâtisserie. Couvrez d'un torchon propre et sec, puis laissez la pâte lever jusqu'à ce qu'elle ait doublé de volume, pendant 45 minutes environ.

Avec un pinceau, enduisez le dessus du pain avec le mélange à base d'œuf et faites-y trois ou quatre entailles diagonales d'environ 0,6 cm (1/4 pouce) de profondeur avec un couteau à dents bien aiguisé.

Faites cuire au four à 220 °C (425 °F) pendant 30 à 40 minutes, ou jusqu'à ce que le pain soit bien doré et atteigne une température interne de 88 °C (190 °F), que vous pouvez vérifier avec un thermomètre à lecture rapide. Laissez le pain reposer sur une grille à pâtisserie pendant 10 minutes, puis retirez-le avec précaution de la plaque et laissez-le refroidir complètement avant de découper.

Informations nutritionnelles (par tranche) : 74 kcal (lipides 23 %, protéines 16 %, glucides 62 %) • protéines 3 g lipides totaux 2 g • acides gras saturés 0 g • glucides 12 g • fibres alimentaires 2 g • sucre 0 g • sodium 202 mg cholestérol 0 mg

Une spatule en métal peut être utile pour détacher le pain de la plaque à pâtisserie.

PAIN AU BLÉ COMPLET, À L'AVOINE ET AUX GRAINES DE LIN

préparation : 10 minutes • mixage : 40 secondes • cuisson : 30 à 35 minutes
quantité obtenue : 1 pain (12 tranches)

1 tasse (240 ml) d'eau tiède, 40 °C à 46 °C (105 °F à 115 °F)

2 cuillerées à soupe (30 ml) de miel

1 sachet (1 cuillerée à soupe) de levure de boulanger sèche

2 cuillerées à soupe (10 g) de flocons d'avoine (pas instantanés)

2 cuillerées à soupe (20 g) de graines de lin

3/4 tasse (135 g) de grains de blé complet ou 1 tasse (120 g) de farine de blé complet

1 1/4 tasse (171 g) de farine à pain

1 cuillerée à café de sel

1 cuillerée à soupe d'huile d'olive

Pour activer la levure, mélangez-la avec l'eau tiède et le miel. Mélangez le tout rapidement. Laissez reposer pendant 5 minutes.

Si vous utilisez des grains de blé complet : Versez les flocons d'avoine, les graines de lin et les grains de blé complet dans le récipient à INGRÉDIENTS SECS Vitamix, et verrouillez le couvercle.

Réglez le commutateur sur la position Variable et la vitesse sur 1.

Mettez l'appareil en marche et augmentez lentement la vitesse jusqu'à la position Variable 10, puis High (Rapide).

Moulez 30 secondes.

Arrêtez l'appareil. Ajoutez la farine et le sel dans le récipient Vitamix et verrouillez le couvercle.

Réglez le commutateur sur la position Variable et la vitesse sur 1.

Mettez l'appareil en marche et augmentez lentement la vitesse jusqu'à la position Variable 10, puis High (Rapide).

Moulez pendant 30 secondes, en utilisant le poussoir (inséré par l'orifice du bouchon) pour pousser le mélange contre les lames. Enlevez le poussoir pendant les 5 dernières secondes pour qu'une dépression se forme au centre de la préparation.

Si vous utilisez de la farine de blé complet : Versez les flocons d'avoine, les graines de lin, la farine de blé complet, la farine et le sel dans le récipient à INGRÉDIENTS SECS Vitamix et verrouillez le couvercle.

Réglez le commutateur sur la position Variable et la vitesse sur 1.

Mettez l'appareil en marche et augmentez lentement la vitesse jusqu'à la position Variable 10, puis High (Rapide).

Moulez pendant 30 secondes, en utilisant le poussoir (inséré par l'orifice du bouchon) pour pousser le mélange contre les lames. Enlevez le poussoir pendant les 5 dernières secondes pour qu'une dépression se forme au centre de la préparation.

Réglez le commutateur sur la position Variable et la vitesse sur 3. Mettez l'appareil en marche, puis ôtez le bouchon du couvercle. Ajoutez l'huile et le mélange à base de levure à travers l'orifice du bouchon du couvercle. Arrêtez l'appareil et remettez le bouchon du couvercle en place.

Pain au blé complet, à l'avoine et aux graines de lin *(suite)*	Sélectionnez la vitesse High (Rapide). Démarrez et arrêtez l'appareil par à-coups deux fois de suite. Arrêtez l'appareil et ôtez le couvercle. Pendant que la pâte repose, huilez légèrement en vaporisant avec une huile végétale ou en enduisant de matière grasse un moule à cake de 20 cm x 10 cm (8 pouces x 4 pouces). Avec une spatule en caoutchouc humide, raclez les parois du récipient pour ramener la pâte vers le centre du mélange. Remettez le couvercle en place. Sélectionnez la vitesse High (Rapide). Démarrez et arrêtez l'appareil par à-coups cinq fois de suite. Ajoutez l'eau supplémentaire, 1 cuillerée à la fois, si la pâte semble particulièrement sèche uniquement. Répétez le processus cinq fois, en raclant les parois du récipient jusqu'à ce que la pâte devienne élastique et compacte. Pour retirer plus facilement la pâte du récipient, démarrez et arrêtez l'appareil par à-coups cinq fois de suite (ce qui va soulever la pâte et la décoller des lames), puis renversez rapidement le récipient au-dessus du moule. Laissez la pâte se déposer dans le moule, en récupérant les restes de pâte avec une spatule humide. Tassez la pâte dans le moule en vous servant d'une spatule huilée, ou de vos mains légèrement farinées. Couvrez le pain avec un torchon propre et sec, puis laissez la pâte lever jusqu'à ce qu'elle atteigne le haut du moule, pendant 20 à 25 minutes environ. Quand le pain est prêt à cuire, faites rapidement trois entailles diagonales sur le dessus du pain à l'aide d'un couteau à dents. Faites cuire au four à 190 °C (375 °F) pendant 30 à 35 minutes, ou jusqu'à ce que le pain atteigne une température interne de 88 °C (190 °F). Laissez le pain reposer sur une grille à pâtisserie pendant 10 minutes, puis retirez-le avec précaution du moule et laissez-le refroidir complètement avant de découper.

Informations nutritionnelles (par tranche) : 130 kcal (lipides 15 %, protéines 12 %, glucides 73 %) • protéines 4 g lipides totaux 2 g • acides gras saturés 0 g • glucides 24 g • fibres alimentaires 3 g • sucre 3 g • sodium 199 mg cholestérol 0 mg

Le pain tranché quand il est encore chaud, surtout le pain à base de céréales complètes, est souvent humide à l'intérieur. Laissez-le refroidir complètement avant de le couper.

Des beurres pour vos pains

Pour sublimer du pain frais, rien ne vaut un beurre parfumé fait maison. Avec l'appareil Vitamix, vous pouvez facilement et rapidement réaliser vos propres beurres parfumés avec des saveurs délicates et des mélanges uniques. Voici cinq idées pour vous aider à vous lancer. Pour chacune d'entre elles, vous devez commencer avec 1/2 tasse (113 g) de beurre doux (que vous avez acheté ou fait vous-même dans votre appareil Vitamix). Ces beurres doivent être servis à température ambiante, car ils s'étalent plus facilement et fondent plus rapidement.

Pour un beurre à la cannelle : Ajoutez au beurre 1 cuillerée à café de cannelle moulue et 3 cuillerées à soupe (24 g) de sucre en poudre. Mélangez à la vitesse Variable 5 pendant 15 à 30 secondes, en utilisant le poussoir pour pousser les ingrédients sur les lames. Le mélange doit être mousseux.

Pour un beurre au miel et aux dattes : Ajoutez au beurre 1/4 tasse (60 ml) de miel et 1/2 à 1 tasse (80 à 160 g) de dattes émincées. Mélangez à la vitesse Variable 5 pendant 15 à 30 secondes, en utilisant le poussoir pour pousser les ingrédients sur les lames. Le mélange doit être mousseux.

Pour un beurre à l'orange : Ajoutez au beurre 1 1/2 cuillerée à café de zeste d'orange râpé et 3 cuillerées à soupe (24 g) de sucre en poudre. Mélangez à la vitesse Variable 5 pendant 15 à 30 secondes, en utilisant le poussoir pour pousser les ingrédients sur les lames. Le mélange doit être mousseux.

Pour un beurre épicé : Ajoutez au beurre 3 cuillerées à soupe (41 g) de sucre roux bien tassé, 1/4 cuillerée à café de cannelle moulue, 1/4 cuillerée à café de piment de la Jamaïque moulu et 1/8 cuillerée à café de noix de muscade moulue. Mélangez à la vitesse Variable 5 pendant 15 à 30 secondes, en utilisant le poussoir pour pousser les ingrédients sur les lames. Le mélange doit être mousseux.

Pour un beurre à la pêche : Pelez, dénoyautez et coupez une pêche ou une nectarine de taille moyenne en morceaux. Dans le récipient Vitamix, réduisez-la en purée avec 1 cuillerée à café de jus de citron en mixant pendant 20 secondes sur la position Variable 10. Ajoutez le beurre, 2 cuillerées à soupe (28 g) de sucre roux léger bien tassé ou de miel, et 1/4 cuillerée à café de noix de muscade moulue. Mélangez à la vitesse Variable 5 pendant 15 à 30 secondes, en utilisant le poussoir pour pousser les ingrédients sur les lames. Le mélange doit être mousseux.

Beurre

marinades sèches

Comment utiliser les marinades sèches

Les marinades sèches ajoutent de la saveur aux aliments grillés. Découvrez nos suggestions et suivez quelques conseils pour obtenir les meilleurs résultats.

- Les marinades sèches ajoutent de la saveur et sont idéalement adaptées aux aliments poêlés, grillés ou cuits au four. Elles sont parfaites pour le tofu, le poisson, les côtes de porc, les blancs de poulet et les légumes.
- Conservez vos marinades sèches dans des bocaux en verre hermétiques, à un endroit frais.
- Trois ou quatre cuillerées à soupe de marinade sèche devraient suffire pour deux livres (1 kilo environ) de nourriture.
- Pour utiliser une marinade sèche, saupoudrez votre viande, votre volaille, votre poisson ou vos légumes puis frottez la surface délicatement avec vos mains. Vous pouvez aussi placer la marinade dans un grand sac en plastique, y ajouter vos ingrédients et secouer le tout. Ensuite, laissez reposer au réfrigérateur pendant plusieurs heures ou toute une nuit avant la cuisson.
- Pour un barbecue plein de saveurs, enduisez généreusement les deux faces de votre viande ou de votre poisson avec une marinade sèche. Recouvrez de film plastique et mettez au réfrigérateur pendant 30 minutes. Enfin, grillez votre viande ou votre poisson.

Remarques importantes :

La mouture d'ingrédients secs pendant plus de 2 minutes risque d'endommager votre appareil. L'utilisation régulière peut causer des rayures du récipient et entraîner l'usure prématurée des lames.

Certaines herbes et épices peuvent libérer des huiles volatiles et décolorer le récipient de façon permanente. D'autres, fortement odorantes, peuvent laisser leur empreinte olfactive sur les parois du récipient, et affecter du même coup la saveur des autres aliments qui y sont préparés. Le broyage de certaines herbes et épices peut entraîner l'usure prématurée de la lame ou fissurer le récipient.

MÉLANGE POUR BARBECUE

préparation : 10 minutes • mixage : 45 secondes • quantité obtenue : 1 tasse (240 g)

1 cuillerée à soupe de sel de mer

1/4 tasse (55 g) de sucre roux foncé

1/4 tasse (28 g) de paprika hongrois doux

2 cuillerées à soupe (24 g) de grains de poivre noir

1 cuillerée à soupe de flocons d'ail séché

1 cuillerée à soupe de flocons d'oignon séché

1 piment Pasilla séché entier, coupé en deux, graines enlevées

1/2 cuillerée à café de graines de céleri

Versez tous les ingrédients dans le récipient à INGRÉDIENTS SECS Vitamix dans l'ordre indiqué, et verrouillez le couvercle.

Réglez le commutateur sur la position Variable et la vitesse sur 1.

Mettez l'appareil en marche et augmentez lentement la vitesse jusqu'à la position Variable 10, puis High (Rapide).

Mixer pendant 45 secondes. Utilisez immédiatement ou conservez dans un récipient hermétique.

REMARQUE : Pour épicer et relever tout ce que vous voulez, des travers de porc au saumon !

Informations nutritionnelles (par cuillerée à café) : 8 kcal (lipides 11 %, protéines 7 %, glucides 82 %) protéines 0 g lipides totaux 0 g • acides gras saturés 0 g • glucides 2 g • fibres alimentaires 0 g • sucre 1 g • sodium 71 mg cholestérol 0 mg

Mélange pour barbecue

MÉLANGE CAJUN

préparation : 10 minutes • mixage : 30 secondes • quantité obtenue : 1 tasse (240 g)

1/4 tasse (67 g) de gros sel de mer

3 cuillerées à soupe (21 g) de paprika doux

2 cuillerées à soupe (17 g) d'ail en poudre

2 cuillerées à soupe (14 g) d'oignon en poudre

2 cuillerées à soupe (5 g) de thym séché

2 cuillerées à soupe (6 g) d'origan séché

1 cuillerée à soupe de poivre noir moulu ou 1 cuillerée à café de grains de poivre noir

1 cuillerée à soupe de poivre blanc moulu ou 1 cuillerée à café de grains de poivre blanc

2 cuillerées à café de feuilles de sauge séchées

2 cuillerées à café de poivre de Cayenne ou 1 piment thaïlandais séché

Versez tous les ingrédients dans le récipient à INGRÉDIENTS SECS Vitamix dans l'ordre indiqué, et verrouillez le couvercle.

Réglez le commutateur sur la position Variable et la vitesse sur 1.

Mettez l'appareil en marche et augmentez lentement la vitesse jusqu'à la position Variable 10, puis High (Rapide).

Mixez pendant 30 secondes, en utilisant le poussoir si nécessaire pour engager le mélange entre les lames. Utilisez immédiatement ou conservez dans un récipient hermétique.

Informations nutritionnelles (pour 2 cuillerées à soupe, soit 30 g) : 31 kcal (lipides 15 %, protéines 14 %, glucides 71 %) • protéines 1 g • lipides totaux 1 g • acides gras saturés 0 g • glucides 7 g • fibres alimentaires 3 g sucre 1 g • sodium 1 683 mg • cholestérol 0 mg

MARINADE SÈCHE AU CAFÉ

préparation : 15 minutes • mixage : 45 secondes • quantité obtenue : 1/2 tasse (120 g)

1 1/2 cuillerée à café de sel de mer

4 cuillerées à café de café moulu ou 1 cuillerée à soupe de grains de café

1 piment Pasilla séché entier, graines enlevées

2 cuillerées à soupe (28 g) de sucre roux foncé

1/2 cuillerée à café de poivre noir moulu ou 1/4 cuillerée à café de grains de poivre noir

1/2 cuillerée à café d'oignon en poudre

1/2 cuillerée à café d'ail en poudre

1/4 cuillerée à café de poivre de Cayenne

1/4 cuillerée à café de grains de coriandre

1/4 cuillerée à café de curcuma

Versez tous les ingrédients dans le récipient à INGRÉDIENTS SECS Vitamix dans l'ordre indiqué, et verrouillez le couvercle.

Réglez le commutateur sur la position Variable et la vitesse sur 1.

Mettez l'appareil en marche et augmentez lentement la vitesse jusqu'à la position Variable 10, puis High (Rapide).

Mixer pendant 45 secondes. Utilisez immédiatement ou conservez dans un récipient hermétique.

Informations nutritionnelles (par cuillerée à café) : 7 kcal (lipides 8 %, protéines 6 %, glucides 86 %)
protéines 0 g • lipides totaux 0 g • acides gras saturés 0 g • glucides 2 g • fibres alimentaires 0 g
sucre 1 g • sodium 71 mg • cholestérol 0 mg

Le café donne un goût de terroir profond à cette marinade. Délicieuse avec du bœuf.

« JERK » JAMAÏCAIN

préparation : 10 minutes • mixage : 45 secondes • quantité obtenue : 1/2 tasse (67 g)

3 cuillerées à soupe (41 g) de sucre roux foncé

1 1/2 cuillerée à soupe de gros sel de mer

1 cuillerée à soupe de grains de coriandre entiers

1 cuillerée à café de grains de poivre noir entiers

1 1/2 cuillerée à café d'ail en poudre

1 1/2 cuillerée à café d'oignon en poudre

1 1/2 cuillerée à café de thym séché

1 cuillerée à café de piment de la Jamaïque entier ou 1 1/2 cuillerée à café de piment de la Jamaïque moulu

1 cuillerée à café de cannelle moulue

1/2 à 1 cuillerée à café de poivre de Cayenne ou 1 piment thaïlandais séché

Versez tous les ingrédients dans le récipient à INGRÉDIENTS SECS Vitamix dans l'ordre indiqué, et verrouillez le couvercle.

Réglez le commutateur sur la position Variable et la vitesse sur 1.

Mettez l'appareil en marche et augmentez lentement la vitesse jusqu'à la position Variable 10, puis High (Rapide).

Mixer pendant 45 secondes. Utilisez immédiatement ou conservez dans un récipient hermétique.

Informations nutritionnelles (par cuillerée à café) : 9 kcal (lipides 6 %, protéines 4 %, glucides 90 %)
protéines 0 g • lipides totaux 0 g • acides gras saturés 0 g • glucides 2 g • fibres alimentaires 0 g
sucre 2 g • sodium 443 mg • cholestérol 0 mg

MÉLANGE « NEW BAY »

préparation : 10 minutes • mixage : 1 minute • quantité obtenue : 1 1/4 tasse (300 g)

1/2 tasse (134 g) de gros sel de mer

1/2 tasse (56 g) de paprika doux

2 cuillerées à soupe (13 g) de graines de céleri

1 cuillerée à soupe de graines de piment de la Jamaïque

1 cuillerée à soupe de grains de poivre noir

1 cuillerée à soupe de moutarde séchée moulue

1 cuillerée à soupe de gingembre moulu

1 cuillerée à soupe de cannelle moulue

1 cuillerée à soupe de poivre de Cayenne moulu

1/2 cuillerée à soupe de grains de cardamome

1/2 cuillerées à soupe de clous de girofle entiers

10 feuilles de laurier

Versez tous les ingrédients dans le récipient à INGRÉDIENTS SECS Vitamix dans l'ordre indiqué, et verrouillez le couvercle.

Réglez le commutateur sur la position Variable et la vitesse sur 1.

Mettez l'appareil en marche et augmentez lentement la vitesse jusqu'à la position Variable 10, puis High (Rapide).

Mixez pendant 1 minute, en utilisant le poussoir si nécessaire pour pousser le mélange sur les lames. Utilisez immédiatement ou conservez dans un récipient hermétique.

Informations nutritionnelles (par cuillerée à café) : 6 kcal (lipides 31 %, protéines 14 %, glucides 55 %)
protéines 0 g • lipides totaux 0 g • acides gras saturés 0 g • glucides 1 g • fibres alimentaires 1 g
sucre 0 g • sodium 449 mg • cholestérol 0 mg

Ce mélange très polyvalent peut servir dans l'eau de cuisson des crevettes et du crabe, pour enduire du poisson ou pour infuser les beurres servis avec le homard et les crevettes.

MÉLANGE POUR VOLAILLE AU PAPRIKA

préparation : 15 minutes • mixage : 1 seconde • quantité obtenue : 3/4 tasse (180 g)

1/3 tasse (9 g) de marjolaine séchée

1/4 tasse (28 g) de paprika hongrois doux

1 piment Pasilla séché, graines enlevées

2 cuillerées à soupe (14 g) d'oignon en poudre

2 cuillerées à soupe (36 g) de zeste de citron séché

1/4 tasse (24 g) de feuilles de sauge séchée

1 cuillerée à soupe de gros sel de mer ou de sel casher

1 cuillerée à soupe de grains de poivre noir

1/2 cuillerée à soupe de graines de céleri

Versez tous les ingrédients dans le récipient à INGRÉDIENTS SECS Vitamix dans l'ordre indiqué, et verrouillez le couvercle.

Réglez le commutateur sur la position Variable et la vitesse sur 1.

Mettez l'appareil en marche et augmentez lentement la vitesse jusqu'à la position Variable 10, puis High (Rapide).

Mélangez pendant 1 minute. Utilisez immédiatement ou conservez dans un récipient hermétique.

Informations nutritionnelles (par cuillerée à café) : 7 kcal (lipides 22 %, protéines 13 %, glucides 65 %)
protéines 0 g • lipides totaux 0 g • acides gras saturés 0 g • glucides 1 g • fibres alimentaires 1 g • sucre 0 g
sodium 94 mg • cholestérol 0 mg

Un mélange facile à utiliser.

MÉLANGE « TARTE À LA CITROUILLE »

préparation : 10 minutes • mixage : 45 secondes • quantité obtenue : 2 cuillerées à soupe (30 g)

1 cuillerée à soupe de cannelle moulue

1 cuillerée à café de gingembre moulu

6 clous de girofle

3 grains de piment de la Jamaïque

1/2 cuillerées à café de macis moulu

1/2 cuillerée à café de noix de muscade fraîchement râpée

Versez tous les ingrédients dans le récipient à INGRÉDIENTS SECS Vitamix dans l'ordre indiqué, et verrouillez le couvercle.

Réglez le commutateur sur la position Variable et la vitesse sur 1.

Mettez l'appareil en marche et augmentez lentement la vitesse jusqu'à la position Variable 10, puis High (Rapide).

Mixer pendant 45 secondes. Utilisez immédiatement ou conservez dans un récipient hermétique.

REMARQUE : Il est possible que ce mélange colore légèrement votre récipient.

Informations nutritionnelles (par cuillerée à café) : 6 kcal (lipides 22 %, protéines 5 %, glucides 73 %)
protéines 0 g • lipides totaux 0 g • acides gras saturés 0 g • glucides 1 g • fibres alimentaires 1 g • sucre 0 g
sodium 1 mg • cholestérol 0 mg

Ce mélange est si apprécié qu'il est utilisé partout, des tartes aux pommes à la purée de pommes de terre en passant, bien sûr, par la tarte à la citrouille. Votre appareil Vitamix vous permet d'exploiter la fraîcheur des aromates. Vous pouvez préparer de petites quantités pour profiter d'une saveur maximum.

MARINADE SÈCHE SUCRÉE SALÉE

préparation : 10 minutes • mixage : 30 secondes • quantité obtenue : 1/4 tasse (60 g)

2 cuillerées à café de sucre roux clair

2 cuillerées à café de moutarde séchée

1 cuillerée à café d'oignon en poudre

1/2 cuillerée à café de sel casher

1/4 cuillerée à soupe de poivre blanc moulu ou 6 grains de poivre blanc

Mettez tous les ingrédients dans le récipient à INGRÉDIENTS SECS Vitamix, et verrouillez le couvercle.

Réglez le commutateur sur la position Variable et la vitesse sur 1.

Mettez l'appareil en marche et augmentez lentement la vitesse jusqu'à la position Variable 10, puis High (Rapide).

Mixez 30 secondes. Utilisez immédiatement ou conservez dans un récipient hermétique.

Informations nutritionnelles (par cuillerée à café) : 7 kcal (lipides 24 %, protéines 10 %, glucides 66 %)
protéines 0 g • lipides totaux 0 g • acides gras saturés 0 g • glucides 1 g • fibres alimentaires 0 g • sucre 1 g
sodium 47 mg • cholestérol 0 mg

CURRY DE LA TRINITÉ

préparation : 10 minutes • mixage : 45 secondes • quantité obtenue : 1/2 tasse (120 g)

3 cuillerées à soupe (15 g) de grains de coriandre entiers

3 cuillerées à soupe (20 g) de curcuma moulu

2 cuillerées à soupe (24 g) de grains de poivre noir

1 cuillerée à soupe de sel casher

1 cuillerée à soupe de graines de cumin

1 cuillerée à café de grains de piment de la Jamaïque

1 cuillerée à café de graines de cardamome

1 cuillerée à café de noix de muscade fraîchement râpée

1 cuillerée à café de cannelle moulue

3/4 cuillerée à café de gingembre moulu

2 piments thaïlandais séchés, graines enlevées

Versez tous les ingrédients dans le récipient à INGRÉDIENTS SECS Vitamix dans l'ordre indiqué, et verrouillez le couvercle.

Réglez le commutateur sur la position Variable et la vitesse sur 1.

Mettez l'appareil en marche et augmentez lentement la vitesse jusqu'à la position Variable 10, puis High (Rapide).

Mixer pendant 45 secondes. Utilisez immédiatement ou conservez dans un récipient hermétique.

REMARQUE : Il est possible que ce mélange colore légèrement votre récipient.

Informations nutritionnelles (par cuillerée à café) : 21 kcal (lipides 29 %, protéines 11 %, glucides 60 %)
protéines 1 g • lipides totaux 1 g • acides gras saturés 0 g • glucides 4 g • fibres alimentaires 2 g • sucre 0 g • sodium 284 mg • cholestérol 0 mg

MÉLANGE D'ÉPICES ADOBO

préparation : 10 minutes • mixage : 1 minute • quantité obtenue : 1 tasse (240 g)

1/4 tasse (34 g) d'ail en poudre

1/4 tasse (28 g) d'oignon en poudre

3 cuillerées à soupe (9 g) d'origan séché

2 cuillerées à soupe (12 g) de graines de cumin

2 cuillerées à soupe (29 g) de sel casher

2 cuillerées à soupe (24 g) de grains de poivre noir

1 cuillerée à soupe de zeste de citron séché

Versez tous les ingrédients dans le récipient à INGRÉDIENTS SECS Vitamix dans l'ordre indiqué, et verrouillez le couvercle.

Réglez le commutateur sur la position Variable et la vitesse sur 1.

Mettez l'appareil en marche et augmentez lentement la vitesse jusqu'à la position Variable 10, puis High (Rapide).

Mélangez pendant 1 minute. Utilisez immédiatement ou conservez dans un récipient hermétique.

Informations nutritionnelles (par cuillerée a café) : 7 kcal (lipides 11 %, protéines 14 %, glucides 74 %)
protéines 0 g • lipides totaux 0 g • acides gras saturés 0 g • glucides 1 g • fibres alimentaires 0 g • sucre 0 g
sodium 141 mg • cholestérol 0 mg

Un mélange d'épices typique d'Amérique latine, parfait avec de la viande ou saupoudré sur des haricots ou des légumes grillés.

Guide de dépannage

Si vous êtes un ou une apprenti(e) boulanger/ère, toutes les variables de la préparation de pain au levain peuvent sembler impressionnantes, et vous craignez peut-être que tout ne se passe pas vraiment comme indiqué dans la recette. Si la fabrication de pain au levain n'est pas une science exacte, elle n'est pas non plus impitoyable. Voici quelques réponses aux questions que vous pouvez vous poser.

Comment savoir si la levure est active ?

Les sachets de levure sèche active portent une date de péremption. Par contre, si vous achetez de la levure au poids, c'est plus compliqué. Vous pouvez tester votre levure en l'activant, une étape simple qui fait partie de nombreuses recettes de pain. Quand vous dissolvez la levure dans l'eau tiède, ajoutez 1 à 3 cuillerées à café du sucre ou du miel que nécessite la recette. (Si la recette ne nécessite ni sucre ni miel, vous pouvez en ajouter 1 cuillerée à café sans modifier le goût du pain.) Laissez le mélange reposer pendant 5 à 15 minutes ou jusqu'à ce que des bulles se forment. Ce sont ces bulles qui vous indiquent que la levure est encore fraîche et active.

Comment gérer les interruptions dans la fabrication du pain ?

Les interruptions courtes, jusqu'à une demi-heure, ne sont pas un problème. Si vous venez de dissoudre la levure, couvrez-la et laissez-la à température ambiante. Un court temps de fermentation ne lui fera pas de mal. Si vous êtes en train de mélanger ou de pétrir la pâte, couvrez-la de film alimentaire pour éviter qu'elle se dessèche.

Si vous n'êtes pas en mesure de former les pains alors que la pâte a doublé de volume, aplatissez-la avec votre poing et laissez-la lever à nouveau, cette fois-ci à température ambiante. Vous pouvez l'aplatir ainsi deux ou trois fois et malgré tout obtenir un pain excellent.

Vous pouvez reporter les dernières étapes (former le pain, laisser la pâte lever une deuxième fois et la cuire) en plaçant la pâte, recouverte de film alimentaire, au réfrigérateur pour la première levée. Vous pouvez l'y laisser pendant plusieurs heures : elle continuera de lever, mais beaucoup plus lentement. Quand vous êtes prêt, laissez la pâte finir de lever, couverte, dans un endroit tiède.

Comment savoir si j'ai utilisé suffisamment de farine ?

Si vous n'êtes pas sûr que votre pâte contienne suffisamment de farine (attention, trop de farine produit un pain très sec), renversez un saladier sur la pâte et laissez-la reposer pendant 15 minutes environ. Si la pâte est très collante et s'est étalée sur les côtés au lieu de commencer à lever, ajoutez de la farine.

Guide de dépannage *(suite)*

Et si la pâte lève pendant trop longtemps ?

Si vous laissez la pâte trop longtemps et qu'elle lève trop (elle devient alors suractive), aplatissez-la avec votre poing, pétrissez-la légèrement pour libérer de l'air et laissez-la lever à nouveau. Une pâte suractive semble avoir plus que doublé de volume. Sa « peau » est fine et transparente, avec des bulles juste sous la surface.

Si vous la laissez reposer assez longtemps, elle peut dégonfler et dans ce cas, il ne vous reste plus qu'à l'aplatir avec votre poing et à la laisser à nouveau lever. Vous pouvez appliquer la même technique si vous avez laissé des pains formés lever trop longtemps. Pétrissez légèrement la pâte pour libérer de l'air, reformez les pains et laissez-les lever à nouveau, mais faites attention, car les pains lèveront plus vite.

Que faire si la face inférieure des pains n'est pas suffisamment dorée quand je les démoule ?

Si vous préférez une croûte plus dorée, vous pouvez remettre vos pains au four, dans leurs moules ou directement sur la grille du four. Quelques minutes de cuisson supplémentaires produiront une croûte plus foncée et plus croustillante.

Remarques

Deutsch

Deutsch

Deutsch

Inhalt

Besondere Hilfe

Vitamix-Rezepte

Frühstücksgerichte

Schnelle Brote

Hefeteige

(Forts. nächste Seite)

Inhalt

Hefeteige

Trockenmarinaden

Informationen zu Klingen und Behältern

Das Vitamix-Gerät wird mit unserem Standard-**Wet**-Blade-Behälter geliefert. Die Rezepte in diesem Buch können zwar im Wet Blade-Behälter zubereitet werden, aber wir empfehlen Ihnen hierfür den Dry Blade-Behälter. Zusätzliche Behälter mit Klingen für feuchte oder trockene Zutaten können separat erworben werden.

⚠ACHTUNG

Rotierende Klingen können schwere Verletzungen hervorrufen.

GREIFEN Sie nicht bei laufendem Gerät in den Behälter.

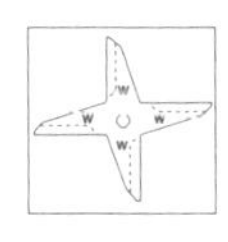

Wet Blade-Behälter: Dafür gedacht, Flüssigkeiten wie Säfte, gefrorene Mischungen, Soßen, Suppen, Pürees und flüssige Teige zu verarbeiten sowie für das Zerkleinern feuchter Zutaten. Die Klingen für feuchte Zutaten können auch Getreide mahlen und Teig kneten, allerdings sind sie dabei nicht ganz so effizient wie die Klingen für trockene Zutaten.

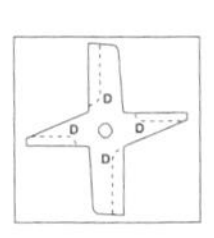

Dry Blade-Behälter: Diese Klingen sind eindeutig mit dem Buchstaben „D" gekennzeichnet und sind dazu gedacht, trockene Materialien wie Getreide, Cerealien und Kaffee zu mahlen sowie zum Kneten von Brotteig. Die Klingen für trockene Zutaten können Flüssigkeiten NICHT effizient verarbeiten.

ACHTUNG: Werden trockene Zutaten länger als zwei Minuten gemahlen, kann dies Ihr Gerät beschädigen. Eine regelmäßige Verwendung kann zu kosmetischen Schäden am Behälter führen und die Klingen können mit der Zeit stumpf werden.

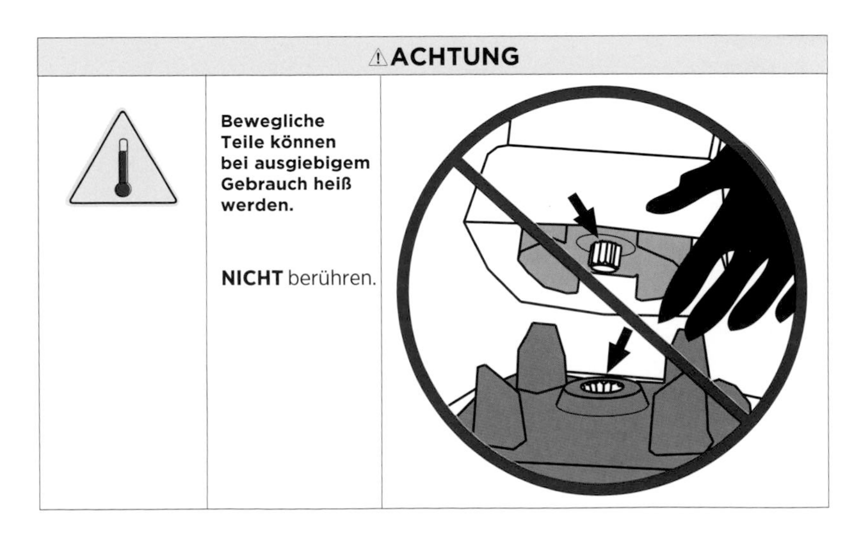

Informationen zu Klingen und Behältern *(Fortsetzung)*

Informationen zum Mahlen von Kräutern und Gewürzen
Beim Mahlen einiger Kräuter können flüchtige Öle freigesetzt werden, die den Behälter dauerhaft verfärben können. Andere haben einen starken Geruch, der im Behälter zurückbleibt und den Geschmack anderer Lebensmittel beeinträchtigen kann. Das Mahlen einiger Kräuter und Gewürze kann außerdem dazu führen, dass die Klingen mit der Zeit stumpf werden oder der Behälter einen Riss bekommt. Wenn Sie regelmäßig Kräuter mahlen ist es gegebenenfalls empfehlenswert, einen weiteren Dry Blade-Behälter zu kaufen und die Klingen ja nach Bedarf zu wechseln.

MAHLEN VON KAFFEEBOHNEN

Verfolgen Sie den Mahlprozess sehr genau. Es gibt 6 verschiedene Feinheitsgrade. Mit diesem Gerät können Sie Ihren eigenen Gourmetkaffee kreieren (siehe folgende Liste).

Geschwindigkeit: variabel • Verarbeitung: 10 Sekunden

2 Tassen (400 g) Kaffeebohnen	2 Tassen (400 g) Kaffeebohnen in den Behälter geben und den Deckel schließen. Variable 1 auswählen. Das Gerät einschalten und die Geschwindigkeit langsam auf Variable 8 erhöhen. Für Filterkaffee 10 Sekunden lang mahlen.

Feinheitsgrade:

1. Perkolator (sehr grob). 7–8 Sekunden lang auf Variable 8 mahlen.
2. Filterkaffee (grob). 10 Sekunden lang auf Variable 8 mahlen.
3. Gewerbliche Kaffeemaschine (weniger grob, wie Maismehl). 12–13 Sekunden auf Variable 8 mahlen.
4. Italienische Kaffeekanne (einigermaßen fein). 15–16 Sekunden auf Variable 8 mahlen.
5. Espresso (feiner, wie Zucker, aber nicht pudrig). 20 Sekunden auf Variable 8 mahlen.
6. Türkischer Kaffee (fein wie Mehl). 25 Sekunden lang auf Variable 8 mahlen.

Je länger die Kaffeebohnen gemahlen werden, desto feiner wird der Kaffee. Gemahlener Kaffee, der innerhalb von zwei Wochen aufgebrüht wird, sollte in einem luftdichten Behälter an einem kühlen, dunklen Ort aufbewahrt werden. Wenn Sie den Kaffee länger als zwei Wochen aufbewahren möchten, dann füllen Sie ihn in einen luftdichten Behälter und stellen Sie ihn in den Gefrierschrank.

Tipps und Tricks für Espressomaschinen: Wenn Ihr Espresso zu langsam (aus der Espressomaschine) läuft und bitter schmeckt, versuchen Sie einen gröberen Mahlgrad. Ist er dünn und wässrig, versuchen Sie einen feineren Mahlgrad.

Das 1-2-3 des Backens

Die Kunst des Backens ist eine therapeutische Entspannung, die jeden Bäcker oder jede Bäckerin mit unwiderstehlichen Aromen, künstlerischem Ausdruck und bewunderndem Lob gefangen nimmt. Es ist eine unglaubliche Befriedigung, etwas von Grund auf selbst zu schaffen und genau zu wissen, was in den Speisen, die auf den Tisch kommen, enthalten ist. Und dank der Vitamix haben Sie die Möglichkeit, Ihr eigenes Mehl zu mahlen und damit Ihre Backwaren noch frischer zu machen.

Ihr Vitamix-Gerät rührt mühelos dünne Teige und knetet feste Teige, mit denen Sie luftige Muffins, weiche Brote, leichte Pizzaböden und vieles mehr herstellen können. Genießen Sie die Rezepte in diesem Kochbuch und nutzen Sie die hilfreichen Tipps unseres Küchenchefs. Er möchte sicherstellen, dass jedes Rezept genau so aus dem Ofen kommt, wie Sie es erwartet haben. Und da man aus dem Vitamix-Behälter direkt in eine Pfanne oder auf ein Blech gießen kann, ist die anschließende Reinigung auch ganz einfach.

Und jetzt lassen Sie uns mit dem Backen mit der Vitamix anfangen - denn Nichts geht über den Geruch frischer Backwaren im Haus.

Die Brotherstellung

Die magischen drei Zutaten

Der Weizen

Die meisten unserer Brote sind eigentlich Weizenbrote. Roggenbrot ist in der Regel ein Weizenbrot mit Roggenanteil. Mehrkornbrot ist Weizenbrot mit kleineren Mengen an Gerste, Hafer, Roggen, Mais, Buchweizen oder anderen Getreidesorten. Kleiebrot ist ein Weizenbrot mit Kleie. Bananenbrot oder Zucchinibrot ist Weizenbrot mit Bananen oder Zucchini. Egal, welche Art von Brot Sie gerne essen, die meisten Brote haben einige Dinge gemeinsam, und eines davon ist der Weizen. Weizen enthält die beste Quelle der Eiweißkomponente von Getreide, das sogenannte Gluten. Wenn Weizenteig geknetet wird, entwickelt sich das Gluten zu einem „Kleber". Die Hefe vergärt die Stärke im Teig und bildet dabei Kohlendioxid. Die daraus entstehenden Bläschen werden von dem Kleber eingeschlossen. Dadurch geht der Teig auf. Ohne Gluten wird das Brot kompakt und flach.

In einem Weizenkorn sorgen die Kleie und der Keim dafür, dass Backwaren schwer werden und nur wenig auf die Hefe oder andere Triebmittel reagieren. Aus diesem Grund ist ein Weizen mit hohem Eiweißgehalt notwendig, um dieser Situation entgegenzuwirken. Wir empfehlen entweder harten Rot- oder neuen harten Weißweizen zu verwenden. (Verwechseln Sie harten Weißweizen nicht mit weichem Weißweizen, der für gewöhnlich für Feingebäck verwendet wird. Hartweizen oder Durumweizen wird hauptsächlich für Nudeln verwendet.) Brot aus hartem Weizen bietet die gesundheitlichen Vorteile von Vollkornweizen und hat einen milden, süßen Geschmack. Harter Weißweizen enthält nicht die starken Geschmacksbestandteile, die Teil des Rotweizens sind. Seine Farbe ist ein goldener Bernsteinton und die daraus hergestellten Backwaren haben einen milderen, leichteren Geschmack. Der Eiweißgehalt von hartem Weißweizen entspricht dem des harten Rotweizens. Sollte harter Weißweizen in Ihrer Gegend nicht erhältlich sein, können Sie sich unter +1 (913) 367-4422 oder +1 (800) 372-4422 an die amerikanische Vereinigung der Weißweizenproduzenten (American White Wheat Producers Association) wenden. Im Internet finden Sie sie unter www.farmerdirectfoods.com. Wir empfehlen außerdem harten Rotweizen aus dem Hochgebirge mit einem Eiweißgehalt von mindestens 14 % und einen Feuchtigkeitsgehalt von höchstens 9 %.

Hefe

Für das Aufgehen von Broten ist ein Triebmittel unerlässlich, und Hefe ist das meistverbreitetste Triebmittel für Brot. Hefe ist ein lebender Organismus und wird „aktiv", wenn warmes Wasser und echter Zucker, beispielsweise Honig, Melasse, Ahornsirup oder raffinierter Zucker zugegeben wird. Künstliche Süßstoffe sind kein echter Zucker und können Hefekulturen nicht befüttern. Mehl, insbesondere Vollkornmehl enthält jedoch genügend natürlichen Zucker, um die Hefe zu befüttern.

Seien Sie vorsichtig, wenn Sie die Hefe-Wasser-Mixtur zu frisch gemahlenem Mehl zugeben. Ist das Mehl zu heiß, wird dadurch die Gesamttemperatur der Mischung erhöht und die Hefe abgetötet. Aus diesem Grund empfehlen wir, zunächst gefrorenes Getreide zu verwenden und dadurch ein Überhitzen des Mehls zu vermeiden.

Flüssigkeit

Wasser, Milch, Kartoffelwasser oder Saft können als Flüssigkeit für den Brotteig dienen. Sie können sogar Eier verwenden, wenn Sie die Eier zuerst in einen Messbecher geben und dann mit einer Flüssigkeit auffüllen, bis die im Rezept angegebene Menge erreicht ist. Wenn Sie Mehl bei Zimmertemperatur verwenden, sollte die Temperatur der Flüssigkeit etwa 40 °C bis 46 °C (105 °F-115 °F) betragen. Wenn Sie mit Ihrer Vitamix-Maschine Brot herstellen, achten Sie besonders auf die Temperatur des Mehls. Wenn Sie frisch gemahlenes Vollkornmehl verwenden, ist das Mehl bereits warm. Entfernen Sie das gemahlene Mehl aus dem Behälter und messen Sie dann die gewünschte Menge ab. Dadurch wird das Mehl abgekühlt.

Andere Inhaltsstoffe

Brot kann mit allerlei Beimischungen angereichert werden.

- Öl als Zutat für Brote sorgt dafür, dass das Brot länger feucht und frisch bleibt.
- Eier verleihen dem Brot einen kräftigeren Geschmack und liefern Eiweiß. Dadurch geht der Laib besser auf und bleibt länger feucht.
- Salz erfüllt zwei Zwecke: 1) es ist ein Hemmstoff für die Hefe, denn das Salz verlangsamt das Aufgehen des Teigs; 2) es verbessert den Geschmack. Ohne Salz schmeckt Brot ein wenig fade.

Gute Nachrichten für Besitzer von Brotbackautomaten

Sie werden auf dem Markt keine bessere Getreidemühle finden als die Vitamix. Verwenden Sie bei Vollkornrezepten für den Brotbackautomaten frisch gemahlenes Mehl. Sie werden von den Ergebnissen begeistert sein.

Die Herausforderungen beim Backen von Vollkornweizenbrot

Die erfolgreiche Herstellung von Vollkornweizenbrot kann eine echte Herausforderung darstellen. Aber verzweifeln Sie nicht, mit ein wenig Übung klappt das schon. Im Folgenden werden wir Ihnen näherbringen, was Sie dabei erwartet und welche Fehler Sie vermeiden sollten.

Wird Vollkornweizen alleine und nicht in Kombination mit anderen Mehlen verwendet, ist das Backergebnis ein schwereres, kompakteres dunkles Brot. Vollkornweizenbrote sind im Vergleich zu Weißmehlbroten desselben Gewichts kleiner. Die Kleie und der Keim machen etwa 15 % des Getreides aus und enthalten kein Gluten. Vergessen Sie nicht, dass Gluten eine Eiweißsubstanz ist, die Backwaren Struktur und Festigkeit gibt. Mit anderen Worten, Vollkornweizenmehl enthält bei gleichem Gewicht weniger Gluten als Weißmehl. Auch wenn frisch gebackenes Vollkornweizenbrot schwerer ist, schmeckt es sehr lecker und ist nahrhaft.

Vollkornweizenbrot wird schneller alt als Weißbrot. Am besten backen Sie nur, was Sie an einem Tag verbrauchen können. Verwenden Sie die Reste vom Vortag für Toast, Füllungen, Brot-und-Milch, Croutons, Semmelbrösel oder Brotpudding.

So wird Ihr Laib gleichmäßiger

Geben Sie den Teig auf ein dünn mit Mehl bestreutes Brett und kneten Sie ihn ein bis zwei Minuten lang. Formen Sie einen Laib und legen Sie ihn in eine gefettete Form. Folgen Sie den Anweisungen für das Gehenlassen und Backen des Brotes.

So verändern Sie Ihre Brotrezepte richtig

Sie können Ihre eigenen Brotrezepte ganz leicht für die Vitamix anpassen. In unserer Testküche halbieren wir die meisten Rezepte für gewöhnlich (Brotrezepte sind traditionell auf zwei Brote ausgelegt). Am besten backen Sie immer nur einen Laib. Reduzieren Sie die Zutaten dafür wie folgt:

Mehl: Verwenden Sie maximal 2 1/2 Tassen (280 g) Mehl. Sie können verschiedene Getreidesorten verwenden, aber achten Sie auf das 1:3-Verhältnis (ein Teil andere Mehlsorten und 3 Teile Weizenmehl).
Wasser: 1 bis 1 1/4 Tassen (240 bis 300 ml)
Hefe: 1 Päckchen pro Laib (1 Esslöffel).

Backen im Gebirge/in großen Höhen

Da der Luftdruck im Gebirge geringer ist, gehen Teige mit Backtriebmittel schneller auf als auf Meereshöhe. Verringern Sie die Gehzeiten für Hefebrote um bis zur Hälfte. Im Gebirge geht auch mehr Feuchtigkeit verloren. Verwenden Sie deshalb zum Kneten mit der Hand nur wenig Mehl. Geben Sie nur gerade so viel Mehl hinzu, dass sich der Teig gut verarbeiten lässt. Fetten Sie Ihre Hände ein, damit der Teig nicht zu sehr an den Fingern klebt.

Das Brot ist schwer und krümelt:

- Versuchen Sie, einen Teil des Vollkornweizenmehls durch herkömmliches Mehl (Type 550) zu ersetzen.
- Versuchen Sie pro Tasse Weizenvollkornmehl einen Teelöffel Gluten (auch Weizenkleber genannt, erhältlich im Reformhaus) hinzuzufügen. Dadurch sollte der Teig besser aufgehen.
- Sollten Sie neben Weizen auch andere Getreidesorten verwenden, achten Sie auf das Verhältnis 1:3 (ein Teil andere Getreidesorten und 3 Teile Weizen).
- Welche Art von Weizen verwenden Sie? Der neue harte Weißweizen ist süßer und ergibt einen leichteren Laib.
- Versuchen Sie den Teig zweimal gehen zu lassen: einmal im Behälter des Geräts und ein weiteres Mal in der Brotform.
- War das Mehl zu grob? Achten Sie beim Mahlen sorgsam auf die Zeit. Die empfohlene Mahldauer beträgt eine Minute.
- Wurde der Teig solange geknetet, bis er dehnbar und elastisch war? Eventuell wurde er nicht lange genug geknetet.

Der Laib hat keine gute Form oder die Kruste ist eingerissen:

- Haben Sie zu viel Wasser hinzugefügt? War der Teig insgesamt zu feucht?
- War der Teig zu trocken? Haben Sie zu viel Mehl verwendet?
- Wie gut wurde der Teig geknetet? War die Hefe nicht gut verteilt?
- Befand die Backform sich in der Mitte des Ofens? War die Temperatur möglicherweise nicht gleichmäßig?
- War der Teig nicht genug gegangen, bevor Sie den Backvorgang eingeleitet haben?

Der Laib ist nicht aufgegangen und die Struktur ist zu kompakt oder zu fest:

- War der Teig kompakt und schwer zu kneten? Vielleicht haben Sie zu wenig Flüssigkeit verwendet.
- War die Hefe zu alt? Überprüfen Sie das Verfallsdatum. Wenn Sie sich nicht sicher sind, lösen Sie 1 Päckchen Hefe mit 1 Teelöffel Zucker in 1/4 Tasse (60 ml) warmem (40 °C–46 °C /105 °F–115 °F) Wasser. Rühren Sie alles um und stellen Sie die Mischung für 5–10 Minuten beiseite. Wenn danach eine deutlich schaumige Schicht entstanden ist, ist die Hefe noch in Ordnung. Hefe sollte im Kühl- oder Gefrierschrank aufbewahrt werden. Bewahren Sie sie keinesfalls bei Zimmertemperatur auf.
- Die Hefe ist aufgrund von zu hohen oder zu niedrigen Temperaturen inaktiv. Hefe ist sehr empfindlich. Die hohen Temperaturen von frisch gemahlenem Mehl können die Hefe abtöten.
- Die Hefe ist nicht aktiv, weil der Teig nicht warm genug ist. Stellen Sie den Teig zum Gehen an einen warmen Ort.
- Ist der Teig vor dem Backen genug aufgegangen? Vielleicht wurde er gebacken, bevor er genug gegangen war.
- Haben Sie zu viel Salz hinzugefügt? Salz kann das Wachstum der Hefe beeinträchtigen.

Die Konsistenz ist zu grob oder offen:

- Haben Sie zu viel Hefe verwendet?
- War der Teig zu feucht?
- Ist der Teig so sehr aufgegangen, dass er über die Form gequillt ist? Vielleicht ist er zu lange gegangen.
- Hatte die Form die richtige Größe?

Hausgemachte Krusten

Welche Kruste mögen Sie am liebsten? Eine weiche, die sich leicht kauen lässt oder eine dicke, harte und zähe? Mithilfe verschiedener Glasuren und einiger Bäckertricks können Sie bei Ihrer Kruste ein weites Spektrum von Texturen, Geschmacksrichtungen und Dunkelgraden erreichen.

Wenn Sie eine zähe, knusprige Kruste wie bei französischem Brot mögen, dann stellen Sie beim Backen eine Schale Wasser auf einen Rost unter dem Brot. Der Dampf, der das Brot beim Backen einhüllt, sorgt dann für eine schöne Kruste. Eine weitere Möglichkeit ist es, das Brot beim Backen alle 10 Minuten mit einem feinen Nebel aus Wasser einzusprühen.

Wenn Sie eine zähe, glänzende Kruste mögen, bepinseln Sie den Teig mit einer einfachen Mischung aus Maisstärke und Wasser. Lösen Sie einen Teelöffel Maisstärke in 2/3 Tasse (160 ml) Wasser auf und bringen Sie die Mischung dann zum Kochen. Lassen Sie sie leicht abkühlen und bestreichen Sie dann vor dem Backen mit einem Pinsel die gesamte freiliegende Oberfläche des Laibs damit. Nehmen Sie das Brot, nachdem es 10 Minuten gebacken hat, aus dem Ofen, wiederholen Sie die Prozedur und schließen Sie dann den Backvorgang ab.

Wenn Sie eine glänzende Kruste mögen, versuchen Sie es mit einer Eiglasur. Weil diese Art von Glasur klebrig ist, kann man sie sehr gut verwenden, um Mohn- oder Sesamsamen zu befestigen. Bestreichen Sie das Brot vor dem Backen mit einem leicht verquirlten Ei, bzw. einem Eigelb oder Eiweiß, verquirlt mit 1 Esslöffel kaltem Wasser. Wenn Sie Eigelb verwenden, erhält das Brot eine goldene Farbe; das Eiweiß macht es glänzend, gibt aber keine zusätzliche Farbe. Bei einem ganzen Ei bekommen Sie von beidem etwas.

Wenn Sie eine weiche Kruste mögen, bestreichen Sie den Laib vor dem Backen oder unmittelbar danach mit geschmolzener Butter. Oder bestreichen Sie den Laib vor dem Backen mit Milch oder Sahne.

Mahlen von Vollkornmehlen

Getreide erhöht sein Volumen beim Mahlen zu Mehl um etwa 25 %. Mais, Sojabohnen und andere Getreidesorten mit einem hohen Feuchtigkeitsgehalt haben die Tendenz, zu klumpen und während des Mahlens nicht mehr zu zirkulieren. Stecken Sie während das Gerät auf die schnellste Geschwindigkeit eingestellt ist, den Stopfen durch die Öffnung im Deckel und schieben Sie das Mehl vorsichtig zurück auf die Klingen. So bleibt es in Bewegung. Damit erreichen Sie, dass alle Getreidesorten gleichmäßig gemahlen werden.

Wichtiger Hinweis:
Am besten bewahren Sie Getreide im Gefrierschrank auf. Mahlen Sie nie mehr als 2 Tassen (400 g) auf einmal.

VOLLKORNMEHL

Geschwindigkeit: Variabel bis Hoch • Verarbeitung: 1 Minute • ergibt: bis zu 3 1/4 Tassen (390 g)

1/4–2 Tassen (50–400 g) Vollkorngetreide

Ein Hinweis unseres Kochs: *Bei Zimmertemperatur bleibt Mehl etwa einen Monat lang frisch. Im Kühlschrank zwei Monate. Wenn Sie es länger aufbewahren möchten, hält es sich gefroren 6 Monate bis 1 Jahr. Erwärmen Sie die für das Backen benötigte Menge auf Zimmertemperatur.*

Bis zu 2 Tassen (400 g) Vollkornweizen in den Vitamix DRY BLADE-Behälter geben und den Deckel schließen.

Variable 1 auswählen.

Das Gerät einschalten und die Geschwindigkeit langsam auf Variable 10 erhöhen.

Bis zum gewünschten Feinheitsgrad mahlen (die empfohlene Mahldauer entnehmen Sie bitte der Tabelle). Je länger das Gerät läuft, desto feiner ist die Konsistenz des Mehls. Maximal 1 Minute mahlen.

Menge Vollkornweizen	Mahldauer	Geschwindigkeit ca.	Menge Mehl	Feinheitsgrad
3/4 Tasse (144 g)	1 Minute	VAR - HIGH	1 Tasse (120 g) + 2 1/2 Teelöffel	sehr fein
1 Tasse (192 g)	1 Minute	VAR - HIGH	1 1/2 Tassen (180 g)	sehr fein
1 1/4 Tassen (240 g)	1 Minute	VAR - HIGH	1 3/4 Tassen (210 g) + 2 Esslöffel (15 g)	sehr fein
1 1/2 Tassen (288 g)	1 Minute	VAR - HIGH	2 1/3 Tassen (280 g) + 1 Esslöffel (8 g)	sehr fein
1 3/4 Tassen (336 g)	1 Minute	VAR - HIGH	2 1/2 Tassen (300 g) + 3 Esslöffel (22 g)	sehr fein
2 Tassen (384 g)	1 Minute	VAR - HIGH	3 1/4 Tassen (390 g)	sehr fein

Hinweis: Die besten Ergebnisse beim Mehlmahlen erzielen Sie mit speziellen Klingen zum Trockenmahlen. Variable 1 auswählen. Das Gerät einschalten und die Geschwindigkeit langsam auf Variable 10 erhöhen.

Mahlen von Vollkornmehlen
(Fortsetzung)

Beim Mehlmahlen bitte beachten:
Bitte halten Sie die empfohlene Mahldauer ein. Ein mehr als zweiminütiges Mahlen trockener Zutaten wie Vollkornweizen kann dazu führen, dass das Mehl klumpt und der Behälter sich überhitzt. Das kann zu einer dauerhaften Beschädigung des Behälters und der Dichtungen des Lagers führen. Beachten Sie unbedingt die empfohlene Mahldauer.

Kochhinweise für geschrotetes Getreide

Geschrotetes Getreide	Menge	Geschw.: Niedrig Variable 7/8	Wasser	Garzeit	Ergibt Müsli
Gerste	1/2 Tasse (90 g)	10 Sekunden	2 Tassen (480 ml)	20 Minuten	1 1/2 Tassen (360 g)
Buchweizen	1/2 Tasse (80 g)	5 Sekunden	2 Tassen (480 ml)	10 Minuten	1 2/3 Tassen (400 g)
Mais	1/2 Tasse (80 g)	10 Sekunden	2 Tassen (480 ml)	20 Minuten	1 1/2 Tassen (360 g)
Hafer	1/2 Tasse (80 g)	10 Sekunden	2 Tassen (480 ml)	20 Minuten	1 1/2 Tassen (360 g)
Reis (weiß)	1/2 Tasse (90 g)	10 Sekunden	2 Tassen (480 ml)	8–10 Minuten	1 3/4 Tassen (420 g)
Reis (braun)	1/2 Tasse (90 g)	10 Sekunden	2 Tassen (480 ml)	20 Minuten	1 3/4 Tassen (420 g)
Roggen	1/2 Tasse (90 g)	10 Sekunden	1 1/2 Tassen (360 ml)	20 Minuten	1 1/2 Tassen (360 g)
Weizen	1/2 Tasse (100 g)	10 Sekunden	1 1/2 Tassen (360 ml)	20 Minuten	1 1/2 Tassen (360 g)
Wilder Reis	1/2 Tasse (90 g)	10 Sekunden	1 1/2 Tassen (360 ml)	20 Minuten	1 1/2 Tassen (360 g)

Hilfreiche Hinweise

1. Beim Mahlen von 2 Tassen (400 g) Getreide in einem Mahlvorgang, wird das Getreide gleichmäßiger gemahlen.
2. 1/4-1/2 Teelöffel Salz kann in das kochende Wasser hinzugegeben werden. Dies dient lediglich dem Geschmack und ist nicht notwendig, wenn Sie versuchen, Ihren Salzkonsum einzuschränken.
3. Wenn Sie die Nährwerte von Vollkorngetreide genießen wollen, aber auch gerne ein fertig vorbereitetes Frühstück haben möchten, können Sie am Vorabend die entsprechende Menge geschrotetes Getreide in einen Topf mit heißem Wasser geben. Schalten Sie den Herd aus, verschließen Sie den Topf gut mit einem Deckel und lassen Sie das Getreide über Nacht einweichen. Am Morgen können Sie sich dann über ein kaltes Frühstück freuen. Wenn Sie das Getreide lieber warm mögen, erwärmen Sie es einfach auf dem Herd oder in der Mikrowelle.

4. Eine weitere einfache Möglichkeit bieten Thermoskannen. 1 Tasse (200 g) Getreide in eine .95 L (1 quart) Thermoskanne (am besten mit einer breiten Öffnung) geben und dann das kochende Wasser bis 2,5 cm (1 Zoll) unter dem Rand auffüllen. Das Getreide und das Wasser mit dem Griff eines Holzlöffels verrühren. Die Thermoskanne schließen. Das Getreide wird darin langsam 8–12 Stunden köcheln.

5. Mehr Abwechslung erhalten Sie, wenn Sie mehrere Getreidesorten kombinieren. Beispielsweise Hafer, Buchweizen, wilden Reis mit braunem Reis usw.

6. Würzen Sie Ihr Frühstück mit Muskat oder Zimt. Ihre Lieblingsfrüchte sorgen für einen anderen Geschmack und noch mehr Nährwerte: Pfirsiche, Erdbeeren, Blaubeeren, Rosinen oder Kokosnuss.

   Ein Hinweis unseres Kochs: *Wenn Sie bei Ihrem Frühstück getrocknete Früchte verwenden, dann denken Sie daran, dass diese wieder Wasser aufnehmen. Deshalb sollten Sie den Wasseranteil Ihres Frühstücksrezeptes leicht erhöhen. So können Sie das durch die getrockneten Früchte aufgenommene Wasser ausgleichen.*

7. Ersetzen Sie für herzhafte Gerichte das Wasser durch Gemüsebrühe.

SCHROTEN VON GETREIDE FÜR MÜSLI UND ANDERE FRÜHSTÜCKSGERICHTE

Geschwindigkeit: Variabel • Verarbeitung: 10 Sekunden

1/4–2 Tassen (50–400 g) Vollkorngetreide (nach Belieben Weizen, Gerste, Hafer, Mais, Reis usw.)

Salz nach Geschmack (etwa 1/4 Teelöffel pro 1/2 Tasse (100 g) Müsli)

Bis zu 2 Tassen (400 g) Vollkorngetreide in den Behälter geben und den Deckel schließen.

Variable 1 auswählen.

Das Gerät einschalten und die Geschwindigkeit langsam auf Variable 7 oder 8 erhöhen.

Mahlen, bis der gewünschte Feinheitsgrad erreicht ist. Je länger das Gerät läuft, desto feiner wird die Konsistenz des Getreides. Schließlich wird es dann zu Mehl.

Kochen von geschrotetem Getreide

In einem schweren Topf (oder einem Wasserbadtopf) Salzwasser zum Kochen bringen. Langsam und unter ständigem Rühren das Getreide hinzugeben, damit es nicht klumpt.

Topf fest verschließen und auf niedrige Temperatur herunterschalten. Kochen, bis das Getreide weich ist (Kochzeiten siehe Tabelle). Dabei häufig umrühren.

Frühstücksgerichte

WEIZENSCHROT-FRÜHSTÜCK MIT ÄPFELN UND ROSINEN

Zubereitung: 15 Minuten • Verarbeitung: 15 Sekunden • Garzeit: 15–20 Minuten
ergibt: 3 Tassen (720 g) zubereitetes Müsli

1 Tasse (180 g) Vollkornweizen

1 1/2 Tassen (360 ml) Wasser

1/4 Teelöffel Salz

1 säuerlicher Apfel (170 g), geschält, entkernt, geviertelt

1/8 Teelöffel Zimt

1/2 Tasse (72 g) Rosinen

2 Esslöffel (18 g) Sonnenblumenkerne

Den Vollkornweizen in den Vitamix DRY BLADE-Behälter geben und den Deckel schließen.

Variable 1 auswählen.

Das Gerät einschalten und die Geschwindigkeit langsam auf Variable 7 oder 8 erhöhen.

Den Weizen etwa 15 Sekunden lang mahlen, bis der gewünschte Feinheitsgrad erreicht ist.

In einem kleinen Topf Salzwasser zum Kochen bringen. Den Weizenschrot unter ständigem Rühren mit einem Schneebesen langsam in das kochende Wasser geben.

Die Temperatur auf „niedrig“ verringern und den Schrot bei geschlossenem Deckel und unter häufigem Rühren etwa 15 bis 20 Minuten lang köcheln.

Während der Weizenschrot gart, die Äpfel im Vitamix WET BLADE-Behälter zerkleinern.

Den Deckel schließen und den Stöpsel des Deckels herausnehmen.

Variable 1 auswählen.

Das Gerät einschalten und die Geschwindigkeit langsam auf Variable 4 erhöhen. Bei laufendem Gerät die Apfelviertel durch die Öffnung im Deckel hineingeben und bei Bedarf den Stopfer verwenden, um die Äpfel zu zerkleinern.

Den Topf vom Herd nehmen und die gehäkselten Äpfel, Zimt, Rosinen und Sonnenblumenkerne zu dem gekochten Weizen geben. Alles gut umrühren.

Die Masse bei geschlossenem Deckel weitere 5 Minuten ziehen lassen und anschließend servieren.

Nährwertinformationen pro Portion (1 Tasse / 240 g): 342 kcal (6 % aus Fett, 9 % aus Eiweiß, 85 % aus Kohlenhydraten) • 9 g Eiweiß • 2 g Fett insgesamt • 0 g gesättigte Fettsäuren
79 g Kohlenhydrate • 10 g Ballaststoffe • 22 g Zucker • 204 mg Natrium • 0 mg Cholesterin

Wenn die Lebensmittel von den Klingen abprallen, ohne dass sie richtig zerkleinert werden, ist die Geschwindigkeit zu niedrig. Wenn die Lebensmittel stark an die Behälterwand geschleudert werden, und die Partikel zu grob oder ungleichmäßig zerkleinert sind, ist die Geschwindigkeit zu hoch.

APRIKOSEN UND BRAUNER REIS FRÜHSTÜCKSGETREIDE

Zubereitung: 10 Minuten • Verarbeitung: 10 Sekunden • Garzeit: 20 Minuten
ergibt: 3 1/2 Tassen (840 g) zubereitetes Müsli

1 Tasse (187 g) brauner Reis, ungekocht

3 1/2 Tassen (840 ml) Wasser

1/2 Teelöffel Salz

8 getrocknete (ungesüßte) Aprikosen

2 Esslöffel (18 g) Sonnenblumenkerne

1/4 Teelöffel Mandelextrakt, optional

Den braunen Reis in den Vitamix DRY BLADE-Behälter geben und den Deckel schließen.

Variable 1 auswählen.

Das Gerät einschalten und die Geschwindigkeit langsam auf Variable 7 oder 8 erhöhen.

Den Reis etwa 10 Sekunden lang mahlen, bis der gewünschte Feinheitsgrad erreicht ist. Wenn Sie feinere Flocken bevorzugen, den Reis länger mahlen.

In einem kleinen Topf Salzwasser zum Kochen bringen. Den Reisschrot unter ständigem Rühren mit einem Schneebesen langsam in das kochende Wasser geben.

Die Temperatur auf „niedrig" verringern und bei geschlossenem Deckel und unter häufigem Rühren etwa 20 Minuten lang köcheln lassen.

Während der Reis gart, die Aprikosen im Vitamix WET BLADE-Behälter zerhäckseln.

Den Deckel schließen und den Stöpsel des Deckels herausnehmen.

Variable 1 auswählen.

Das Gerät einschalten und die Geschwindigkeit langsam auf Variable 5 erhöhen. Bei laufendem Gerät die Aprikosen durch die Öffnung im Deckel hineingeben. Falls nötig, die variable Geschwindigkeit anpassen, um die Aprikosen feiner zu häckseln.

Den Topf vom Herd nehmen und die zerkleinerten Aprikosen, Sonnenblumenkerne und den Mandelextrakt zu dem gekochten Getreide geben. Alles gut umrühren.

Die Masse bei geschlossenem Deckel weitere 5 Minuten ziehen lassen und anschließend servieren.

Nährwertinformationen pro Portion (1 Tasse / 240 g): 224 kcal (10 % aus Fett, 9 % aus Eiweiß, 82 % aus Kohlenhydraten) • 5 g Eiweiß • 2 g Fett insgesamt • 0 g gesättigte Fettsäuren 46 g Kohlenhydrate • 3 g Ballaststoffe • 5 g Zucker • 346 mg Natrium • 0 mg Cholesterin

Wenn die Lebensmittel von den Klingen abprallen, ohne dass sie richtig zerkleinert werden, ist die Geschwindigkeit zu niedrig. Wenn die Lebensmittel stark an die Behälterwand geschleudert werden, und die Partikel zu grob oder ungleichmäßig zerkleinert sind, ist die Geschwindigkeit zu hoch.

BRAUNE REISGRÜTZE

Zubereitung: 10 Minuten • Verarbeitung: 10 Sekunden • Garzeit: 20 Minuten
ergibt: 3 1/2 Tassen (840 g) zubereitetes Müsli

1 Tasse (187 g) brauner Reis, ungekocht

3 1/2 Tassen (840 ml) Wasser

1/2 Teelöffel Salz

Den braunen Reis in den Vitamix DRY BLADE-Behälter geben und den Deckel schließen.

Variable 1 auswählen.

Das Gerät einschalten und die Geschwindigkeit langsam auf Variable 7 oder 8 erhöhen.

Den Reis etwa 10 Sekunden lang mahlen, bis der gewünschte Feinheitsgrad erreicht ist. Wenn Sie feinere Flocken bevorzugen, den Reis länger mahlen.

In einem kleinen Topf Salzwasser zum Kochen bringen. Den Reisschrot unter ständigem Rühren mit einem Schneebesen langsam in das kochende Wasser geben.

Die Temperatur auf „niedrig" verringern und bei geschlossenem Deckel und unter häufigem Rühren etwa 20 Minuten lang köcheln lassen.

Nährwertinformationen pro Portion (1 Tasse / 240 g): 197 kcal (7 % aus Fett, 8 % aus Eiweiß, 85 % aus Kohlenhydraten) • 4 g Eiweiß • 1 g Fett insgesamt • 0 g gesättigte Fettsäuren
41 g Kohlenhydrate • 2 g Ballaststoffe • 0 g Zucker • 344 mg Natrium • 0 mg Cholesterin

WEIZENSCHROT-MÜSLI

Zubereitung: 10 Minuten • Verarbeitung: 15 Sekunden • Garzeit: 15-20 Minuten
ergibt: 3 Tassen (720 g) zubereitetes Müsli

1 Tasse (180 g) Vollkornweizen

3 Tassen (720 ml) Wasser

1/2 Teelöffel Salz

Den Vollkornweizen in den Vitamix DRY BLADE-Behälter geben und den Deckel schließen.

Variable 1 auswählen.

Das Gerät einschalten und die Geschwindigkeit langsam auf Variable 7 oder 8 erhöhen.

Den Weizen etwa 15 Sekunden lang mahlen, bis der gewünschte Feinheitsgrad erreicht ist.

In einem kleinen Topf Salzwasser zum Kochen bringen. Den Weizenschrot unter ständigem Rühren mit einem Schneebesen langsam in das kochende Wasser geben.

Die Temperatur auf „niedrig" verringern und bei geschlossenem Deckel etwa 15–20 Minuten lang köcheln lassen.

Nährwertinformationen pro Portion (1 Tasse / 240 g): 219 kcal (4 % aus Fett, 12 % aus Eiweiß, 83 % aus Kohlenhydraten) • 7 g Eiweiß • 1 g Fett insgesamt • 0 g gesättigte Fettsäuren
49 g Kohlenhydrate • 8 g Ballaststoffe • 0 g Zucker • 399 mg Natrium • 0 mg Cholesterin

CREMIGER REISBREI

Zubereitung: 10 Minuten • Verarbeitung: 10 Sekunden • Garzeit: 8–10 Minuten
ergibt: 1 3/4 Tassen (420 g) zubereiteten Brei

1/2 Tasse (93 g)
Reis, ungekocht

2 Tassen (480 ml)
Wasser

1/4 Teelöffel Salz

Den Reis in den Vitamix DRY BLADE-Behälter geben und den Deckel schließen.

Variable 1 auswählen.

Das Gerät einschalten und die Geschwindigkeit langsam auf Variable 7 oder 8 erhöhen.

Den Reis etwa 10 Sekunden lang mahlen, bis der gewünschte Feinheitsgrad erreicht ist. Wenn Sie feinere Flocken bevorzugen, den Reis länger mahlen.

In einem kleinen Topf Salzwasser zum Kochen bringen. Langsam den geschroteten Reis in das kochende Wasser geben. Mit einem Schneebesen ständig rühren.

Den Reis mit geschlossenem Deckel auf niedriger Stufe 8 bis 10 Minuten lang (bei braunem Reis etwas länger) kochen, bis er gar ist.

Nährwertinformationen pro Portion (1 Tasse / 240 g): 199 kcal (2 % aus Fett, 8 % aus Eiweiß, 90 % aus Kohlenhydraten) • 4 g Eiweiß • 0 g Fett insgesamt • 0 g gesättigte Fettsäuren
44 g Kohlenhydrate • 1 g Ballaststoffe • 0 g Zucker • 355 mg Natrium • 0 mg Cholesterin

MÜSLI

Zubereitung: 15 Minuten • Verarbeitung: 3 Minuten • Backzeit: 15 Minuten • ergibt: 10 Tassen (2,4 kg)

1/2 Tasse (120 ml) Honig

3/4 Tasse (165 g) brauner Zucker

1/2 Tasse (120 ml) heißes Wasser

1 Teelöffel Salz

2 Teelöffel Vanilleextrakt

1 1/2 Teelöffel Zimt

5 Tassen (400 g) Haferflocken

1 Tasse (104 g) Weizenkeime

1/4 Tasse (35 g) Sonnenblumenkerne

1/2 Tasse (42 g) zerhackte Kokosnuss oder Kokosflocken

1/2 Tasse (58 g) gehackte Walnüsse

1 Tasse (145 g) Rosinen

Den Backofen auf 180 °C (350 °F) vorheizen. Zwei 33 cm x 23 cm (13 Zoll x 9 Zoll) große Backformen oder einen großen Bräter dünn mit Backspray oder Backfett einfetten.

Honig, braunen Zucker, Wasser, Salz, Vanille und Zimt in der angegebenen Reihenfolge in den Vitamix WET BLADE-Behälter geben und den Deckel schließen.

Variable 1 auswählen.

Das Gerät einschalten und die Geschwindigkeit langsam auf Variable 10 erhöhen.

3 Minuten lang rühren, oder solange, bis die Mischung dampft.

In einer großen Rührschüssel Hafer, Weizenkeime, Sonnenblumenkerne, Kokosnuss und gehackte Walnüsse vermischen.

Heiße Mischung über die trockenen Zutaten gießen und gut umrühren, bis nur wenige Klümpchen übrig sind. In vorbereiteten Formen verteilen und 15 Minuten backen. Dabei alle 5 Minuten umrühren.

Form(en) aus dem Ofen nehmen und Rosinen einrühren. Auf ein Kuchengitter stellen und vollständig auskühlen lassen. In Gläsern oder einer großen Plastiktüte aufbewahren.

Nährwertinformationen pro Portion (1/2 Tasse / 120 g): 287 kcal (18 % aus Fett, 12 % aus Eiweiß, 69 % aus Kohlenhydraten) • 9 g Eiweiß • 6 g Fett insgesamt • 1 g gesättigte Fettsäuren
52 g Kohlenhydrate • 6 g Ballaststoffe • 20 g Zucker • 124 mg Natrium • 0 mg Cholesterin

Die Mischung kann auch bei niedriger Temperatur gebacken werden, bis sie getrocknet ist.

Dieses einzigartige Rezept kommt ohne zusätzliches Fett aus. Wenn Sie ein feuchtes Müsli bevorzugen, geben Sie 1/4 Tasse (60 ml) helles Olivenöl oder Traubenkernöl in die flüssigen Zutaten.

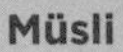

Müsli

Zum Zerkleinern von Nüssen Variable 1 (DRY BLADE-Behälter) wählen. Das Gerät einschalten und die Geschwindigkeit langsam auf Variable 4 erhöhen. Walnüsse durch die Öffnung im Deckel einfüllen und 5 Sekunden lang häckseln.

HAFERBREI

Zubereitung: 10 Minuten • Verarbeitung: 10 Sekunden • Garzeit: 30 Minuten
ergibt: 3 1/2 Tassen (840 g) zubereitetes Müsli

1 Tasse (160 g) Hafergrütze (KEINE Haferflocken)

4 Tassen (960 ml) Wasser

1/2 Teelöffel Salz

Die Vollkorn-Hafergrütze in den Vitamix DRY BLADE-Behälter geben und den Deckel schließen.

Variable 1 auswählen.

Das Gerät einschalten und die Geschwindigkeit langsam auf Variable 7 erhöhen.

Die Hafergrütze etwa 10 Sekunden lang mahlen, bis der gewünschte Feinheitsgrad erreicht ist. Wenn Sie feinere Flocken bevorzugen, die Hafergrütze länger mahlen.

In einem kleinen Topf Salzwasser zum Kochen bringen. Den Haferschrot unter ständigem Rühren mit einem Schneebesen langsam in das kochende Wasser geben.

Die Temperatur auf „niedrig" verringern und den Schrot bei geschlossenem Deckel und unter häufigem Rühren etwa 30 Minuten lang köcheln lassen.

Nährwertinformationen pro Portion (1 Tasse / 240 g): 126 kcal (14 % aus Fett, 18 % aus Eiweiß, 68 % aus Kohlenhydraten) • 8 g Eiweiß • 3 g Fett insgesamt • 1 g gesättigte Fettsäuren
31 g Kohlenhydrate • 5 g Ballaststoffe • 1 g Zucker • 342 mg Natrium • 0 mg Cholesterin

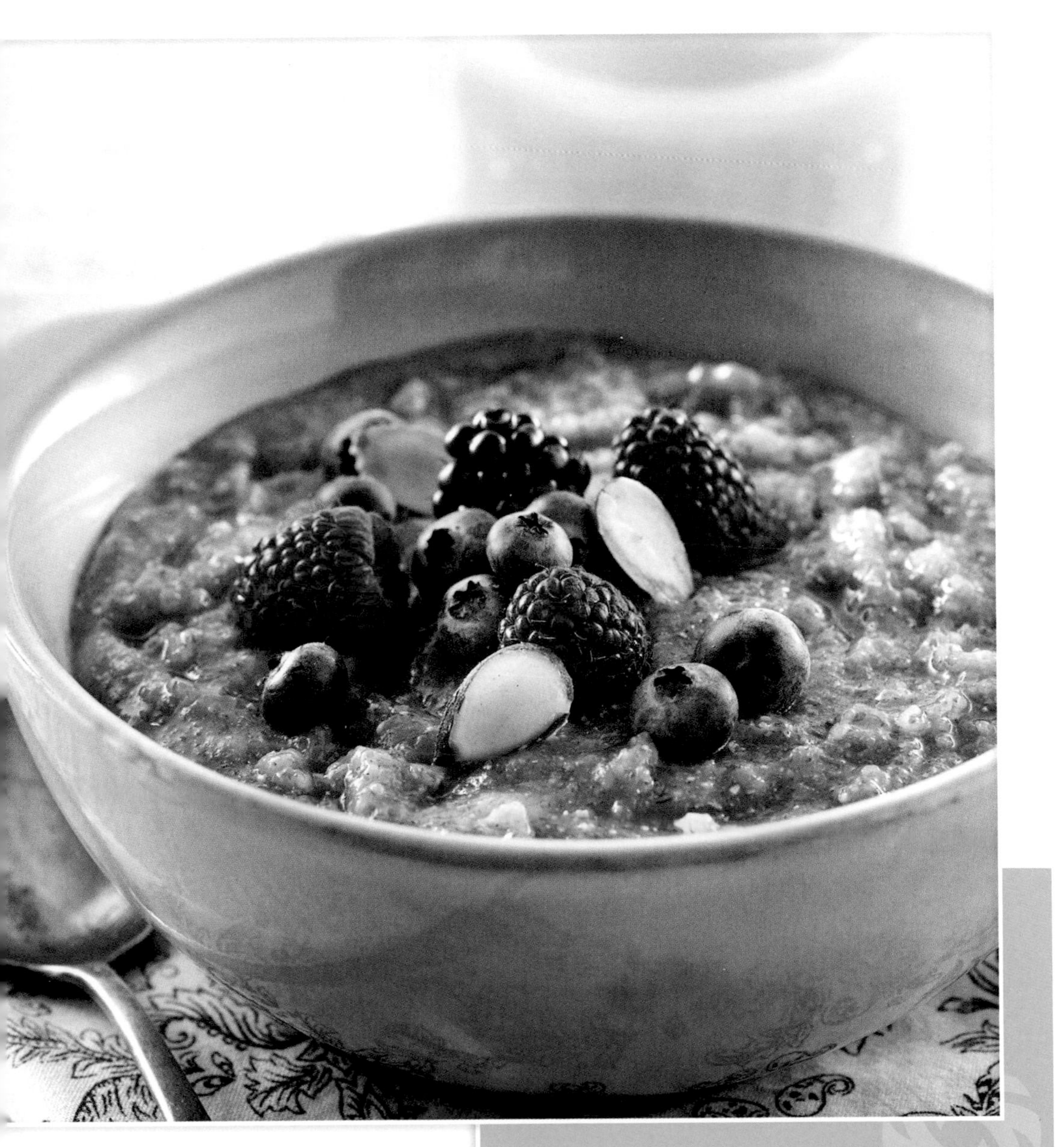

Haferbrei

REIS MIT ROSINEN UND GETREIDE

Zubereitung: 10 Minuten • Verarbeitung: 10 Sekunden • Garzeit: 30 Minuten
ergibt: 3 1/2 Tassen (840 g) zubereitetes Müsli

1/2 Tasse (93 g) ungekochten Reis

2 Tassen (480 ml) Wasser

1/4 Teelöffel Salz

1/2 Tasse (72 g) Rosinen

Eine Messerspitze Zimt

Den Reis in den Vitamix DRY BLADE-Behälter geben und den Deckel schließen.

Variable 1 auswählen.

Das Gerät einschalten und die Geschwindigkeit langsam auf Variable 7 oder 8 erhöhen.

Den Reis etwa 10 Sekunden lang mahlen, bis der gewünschte Feinheitsgrad erreicht ist.

In einem kleinen Topf Salzwasser zum Kochen bringen. Den Reisschrot unter ständigem Rühren mit einem Schneebesen langsam in das kochende Wasser geben.

Den Reis mit geschlossenem Deckel auf niedriger Stufe 8 bis 10 Minuten lang (bei braunem Reis etwas länger) köcheln, bis er gar ist.

Den Topf vom Herd nehmen und die Rosinen und den Zimt hinzugeben.

Die Masse bei geschlossenem Deckel weitere 5 Minuten ziehen lassen. Anschließend Servieren.

Nährwertinformationen pro Portion (1 Tasse / 240 g): 292 kcal (1 % aus Fett, 6 % aus Eiweiß, 92 % aus Kohlenhydraten) • 5 g Eiweiß • 0 g Fett insgesamt • 0 g gesättigte Fettsäuren
70 g Kohlenhydrate • 2 g Ballaststoffe • 24 g Zucker • 306 mg Natrium • 0 mg Cholesterin

HAFERFLOCKEN ZUM SONNENAUFGANG

Zubereitung: 10 Minuten • Verarbeitung: 10 Sekunden • Garzeit: 30 Minuten
ergibt: 3 3/4 Tassen (900 g) zubereitete Haferflocken

1 Tasse (184 g) Vollkorn-Hafergrütze (KEINE Haferflocken)

4 Tassen (960 ml) Wasser

1/2 Teelöffel Salz

6 bis 7 entsteinte Pflaumen

Die Vollkorn-Hafergrütze in den Vitamix DRY BLADE-Behälter geben und den Deckel schließen.

Variable 1 auswählen.

Das Gerät einschalten und die Geschwindigkeit langsam auf Variable 7 erhöhen.

Die Hafergrütze etwa 10 Sekunden lang mahlen, bis der gewünschte Feinheitsgrad erreicht ist. Wenn Sie feinere Flocken bevorzugen, die Hafergrütze länger mahlen.

In einem kleinen Topf Salzwasser zum Kochen bringen. Den Haferschrot unter ständigem Rühren mit einem Schneebesen langsam in das kochende Wasser geben.

Die Temperatur auf „niedrig" verringern und den Schrot bei geschlossenem Deckel und unter häufigem Rühren etwa 30 Minuten lang köcheln lassen.

Während der Haferschrot gart, die Pflaumen im Vitamix WET BLADE-Behälter zerkleinern.

Den Deckel schließen.

Variable 1 auswählen.

Das Gerät einschalten und die Geschwindigkeit langsam auf Variable 5 oder 6 erhöhen. Den Stöpsel im Deckel entfernen. Bei laufendem Gerät die Pflaumen durch die Öffnung im Deckel hineingeben.

Den Topf vom Herd nehmen und die zerkleinerten Pflaumen hinzugeben. Alles gut umrühren.

Die Masse bei geschlossenem Deckel weitere 5 Minuten ziehen lassen und anschließend servieren.

Nährwertinformationen pro Portion (1 Tasse / 240 g): 209 kcal (4 % aus Fett, 12 % aus Eiweiß, 84 % aus Kohlenhydraten) • 7 g Eiweiß • 1 g Fett insgesamt • 0 g gesättigte Fettsäuren
47 g Kohlenhydrate • 6 g Ballaststoffe • 0 g Zucker • 325 mg Natrium • 0 mg Cholesterin

Wenn die Lebensmittel von den Klingen abprallen, ohne dass sie richtig zerkleinert werden, ist die Geschwindigkeit zu niedrig. Wenn die Lebensmittel stark an die Behälterwand geschleudert werden, und die Partikel zu grob oder ungleichmäßig zerkleinert sind, ist die Geschwindigkeit zu hoch.

Schnelle Brote

Erfolgreiches Backen von Schnellbroten

- Wenn in einem Rezept nach weicher Butter verlangt wird, lassen Sie die Butter etwa 20 Minuten bei Zimmertemperatur stehen. Erwärmen Sie die Butter nicht in der Mikrowelle. Das kann dazu führen, dass die Butter schmilzt, anstatt nur weich zu werden und wenn Sie anstatt weicher Butter geschmolzene Butter verwenden, kann dies das Backergebnis negativ beeinträchtigen.
- Wenn Sie den Teig für schnelle Brote zu stark rühren, werden die Brote beim Backen nicht so weich. Danken Sie daran, vorsichtig und wenig zu rühren. Gerade so lange, dass die Zutaten vermischt sind.
- Heizen Sie den Ofen mindestens 10 Minuten vor und stellen Sie das Schnellbrot auf die mittlere Schiene. Wenn Sie ein Schnellbrot in einen zu wenig vorgeheizten Ofen stellen, wird es nicht wie gewünscht aufgehen.
- Schnellbrote können Sie in Frischhaltefolie oder Alufolie eingepackt aufbewahren. Im Kühlschrank hält es sich bis zu drei Tage, eingefroren bis zu drei Monate.

Kinderköche – Mit dem Backen von Schnellbroten oder Muffins kann man Kinder leicht fürs Kochen begeistern. Ermuntern Sie sie zum Mitmachen, indem Sie ihnen zeigen, wie man Formen einfettet oder leckere Zutaten wie Mandeln, Schokoladensplitter und getrocknete Kirschen richtig abmisst.

APFEL-PEKANNUSS-BROT

Zubereitung: 10 Minuten • Verarbeitung: 20 Sekunden • Backzeit: 40–50 Minuten • ergibt: 1 Laib (12 Scheiben)

1 Tasse (125 g) Mehl Type 550

1/2 Tasse (60 g) Vollkornmehl (Type 1600)

1 Teelöffel Backpulver

1/4 Teelöffel Backnatron

1/2 Teelöffel Salz

2 kleine Äpfel, entkernt, geviertelt, etwa 1 1/4 Tassen (156 g)

1 großes Ei

3 Esslöffel (45 ml) helles Olivenöl

2/3 Tasse (147 g) hellbrauner Zucker

1/2 Tasse (54 g) gehackte Pekannüsse

Eine 22 cm x 11 cm (8 1/2 Zoll x 4 1/2 Zoll) große Brotform mit Backspray oder Backfett einfetten. Den Backofen auf 180 °C (350 °F) vorheizen.

In einer großen Rührschüssel Mehl, Weizenvollkornmehl, Backpulver, Backnatron und Salz gut verrühren.

Äpfel, Ei, Öl und braunen Zucker in der angegebenen Reihenfolge in den Vitamix WET BLADE-Behälter geben und den Deckel schließen.

Variable 1 auswählen.

Das Gerät einschalten und die Geschwindigkeit langsam auf Variable 10 erhöhen.

Etwa 20 Sekunden vermischen, bis die Äpfel zerhäckselt sind. Bei Bedarf den Stopfer durch die Öffnung im Deckel stecken, um das Zirkulieren und Häckseln zu unterstützen.

Apfelmischung und Pekannüsse in die Schüssel mit den trockenen Zutaten geben. Von Hand unterheben, NUR solange, bis die trockenen Zutaten angefeuchtet sind; nicht zu viel verkneten.

Den Teig in die vorbereitete Form geben. 40–50 Minuten backen. Wenn an einem in die Mitte des Brots gepieksten Zahnstocher kein Teig mehr hängt, ist es durchgebacken.

30 Minuten lang auf einem Kuchengitter auskühlen lassen und dann vorsichtig aus der Form lösen. Erst anschneiden, wenn es vollständig abgekühlt ist.

Nährwertinformationen pro Portion (1 Scheibe): 175 kcal (36 % aus Fett, 6 % aus Eiweiß, 58 % aus Kohlenhydraten) • 3 g Eiweiß • 7 g Fett insgesamt • 1 g gesättigte Fettsäuren
26 g Kohlenhydrate • 2 g Ballaststoffe • 13 g Zucker • 178 mg Natrium • 18 mg Cholesterin

BROWNIES „BROWNIE POINTS“

Zubereitung: 20 Minuten • Verarbeitung: 20 Sekunden • Backzeit: 25-30 Minuten
ergibt: 2 Dutzend

3/4 Tasse (64 g) Kakaopulver, ungesüßt

1 Teelöffel Backpulver

1 Teelöffel Salz

1 Teelöffel Instant-Espressopulver

1 1/2 Tassen (180 g) Vollkornweizenmehl (Type 1600)

2 Tassen (448 g) Schokoladensplitter, halbbitter

1 Tasse (227 g) ungesalzene Butter, weich und in Stücke geschnitten

2 Tassen (440 g) festgedrückten braunen Zucker, hell oder dunkel

1 Esslöffel Vanilleextrakt

4 große Eier

Eine 23 cm x 33 cm (9 Zoll x 13 Zoll) große Brotform mit Backspray oder Backfett einfetten. Den Backofen auf 180 °C (350 °F) vorheizen.

Bei Zubereitung mit Vollkornweizen: 1 1/2 Tassen (270 g) Vollkornweizen in den Vitamix DRY BLADE-Behälter und den Deckel schließen.

Variable 1 auswählen.

Das Gerät einschalten und die Geschwindigkeit langsam auf Variable 10 erhöhen.

1 Minute lang mahlen. (Nicht zu stark verarbeiten.)

Das Gerät anhalten und das Mehl einige Minuten abkühlen lassen. 1 1/2 Tassen (180 g) Vollkornweizenmehl für das Rezept abmessen. Verbleibendes Mehl zur späteren Verwendung aufbewahren.

Bei Zubereitung mit Vollkornweizenmehl: Kakaopulver, Backpulver, Salz, Espressopulver und Vollkornweizenmehl in eine große Rührschüssel geben. Die Schokoladensplitter zugeben. Zur Seite stellen.

Butter, Zucker, Vanille und Eier in den Vitamix WET BLADE-Behälter geben und Deckel schließen. Variable 1 auswählen.

Das Gerät einschalten und die Geschwindigkeit langsam auf Variable 10 erhöhen.

20 Sekunden lang rühren, oder bis die Masse „cremig“ ist; bei Bedarf den Stopfer verwenden.

Die Buttermischung unter die Mehlmischung heben und mit der Hand gründlich vermischen.

Mithilfe eines Nylonspatels die Masse in die vorbereitete Pfanne schaben. 25–30 Minuten backen. Wenn an einem in die Mitte der Brownies gepieksten Zahnstocher kein Teig mehr hängt, sind sie durchgebacken. Nicht zu lange backen, sonst werden die Brownies trocken.

Aus dem Ofen nehmen und auf einem Kuchengitter abkühlen lassen. In Stücke schneiden und servieren.

Nährwertinformationen pro Portion (1 Brownie): 282 kcal (44% aus Fett, 5 % aus Eiweiß, 51 % aus Kohlenhydraten)
4 g Eiweiß • 14 g Fett insgesamt • 8 g gesättigte Fettsäuren • 37 g Kohlenhydrate • 3 g Ballaststoffe
28 g Zucker • 144 mg Natrium • 56 mg Cholesterin

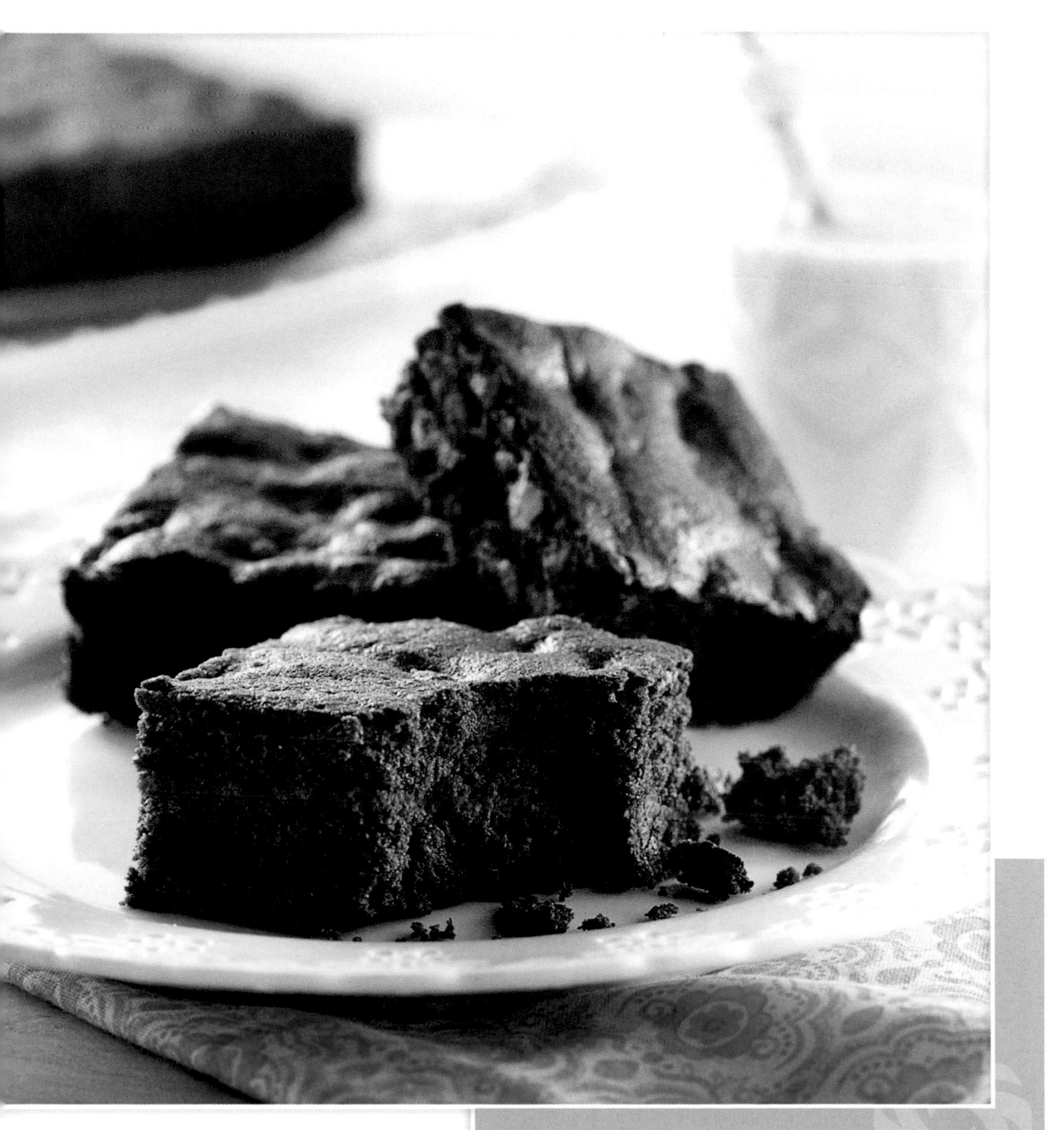

Brownies „Brownie Points“

SCHOKOLADEN-ZUCCHINI-KUCHEN

Zubereitung: 20 Minuten • Verarbeitung: 35-40 Sekunden • Backzeit: 35-40 Minuten
ergibt: 12 Quadrate

1/2 Tasse (114 g) ungesalzene Butter, in Stücke geschnitten, Zimmertemperatur

1 1/2 Tassen (300 g) Kristallzucker

2 große Eier

18 Unzen (511 g) Zucchini, in grobe Stücke geschnitten

1/2 Tasse (120 ml) helles Olivenöl

1 Teelöffel Vanilleextrakt

1/2 Tasse (120 ml) Buttermilch

1 1/2 Tassen (180 g) Vollkornweizenmehl (Type 1600)

1 1/4 Tassen (156 g) Mehl Type 550

1/4 Tasse (21 g) ungesüßtes Kakaopulver

1 1/4 Teelöffel Backnatron

1 Teelöffel Salz

1/4 Tasse (30 g) Puderzucker, gesiebt

Den Backofen auf 160 °C (325 °F) vorheizen. Eine 23 cm (9 Zoll) große Kastenform leicht einfetten.

Butter, Zucker und Eier in der angegebenen Reihenfolge in den Vitamix WET BLADE-Behälter geben und den Deckel schließen.

Variable 1 auswählen.

Das Gerät einschalten und die Geschwindigkeit langsam auf Variable 10 erhöhen. Falls nötig, den Stopfer verwenden, um die Zutaten auf die Klingen zu drücken.

Die Masse 25 Sekunden lang vermischen. Das Gerät ausschalten, Deckel abnehmen und die Masse von den Seiten des Behälters schaben.

Zucchinistücke, Öl, Vanille und Buttermilch in den Vitamix WET BLADE-Behälter geben und Deckel schließen.

Variable 1 auswählen.

Das Gerät einschalten und die Geschwindigkeit langsam auf Variable 10 erhöhen.

10 bis 20 Sekunden lang zerkleinern, oder bis die Zucchinistücke sehr klein sind.

In einer großen Rührschüssel Mehle, Kakaopulver, Backnatron und Salz gut verrühren.

Zucchinimischung in die Schüssel mit den trockenen Zutaten geben. Von Hand unterheben, bis ein gleichmäßiger Teig entstanden ist.

Mit einem Spatel in die vorbereitete Form füllen.

35–40 Minuten backen. Wenn an einem in die Mitte des Kuchens gepieksten Zahnstocher kein Teig mehr hängt, ist der Kuchen durchgebacken.

Schokoladen-Zucchini-Kuchen *(Fortsetzung)*

30 Minuten lang auf einem Kuchengitter auskühlen lassen, anschließend den Rand mithilfe eines Messers vorsichtig ablösen. Auf das Kuchengitter stürzen und vollständig auskühlen lassen. In Quadrate schneiden und vor dem Servieren mit gesiebtem Puderzucker bestäuben.

Zubereitung von Vollkornweizenmehl aus Vollkornweizen: 1 1/2 Tassen (270 g) Vollkornweizen in den Vitamix DRY BLADE-Behälter und den Deckel schließen.

Variable 1 auswählen.

Das Gerät einschalten und die Geschwindigkeit langsam auf Variable 10 erhöhen.

1 Minute lang mahlen. (Nicht zu stark verarbeiten.)

Das Gerät anhalten und das Mehl einige Minuten abkühlen lassen. 1 1/2 Tassen (180 g) Vollkornweizenmehl für das Rezept abmessen. Verbleibendes Mehl zur späteren Verwendung aufbewahren.

Nährwertinformationen pro Portion (1 Quadrat): 386 kcal (42% aus Fett, 6 % aus Eiweiß, 52 % aus Kohlenhydraten)
6 g Eiweiß • 19 g Fett insgesamt • 7 g gesättigte Fettsäuren • 52 g Kohlenhydrate • 3 g Ballaststoffe • 29 g Zucker
359 mg Natrium • 56 mg Cholesterin

CRANBERRY-NUSS-BROT

Zubereitung: 15 Minuten • Verarbeitung: 30 Sekunden • Backzeit: 1 Stunde
ergibt: 1 Laib (12 Scheiben)

1 Tasse (100 g) frische oder gefrorene Cranberrys

1 Orange, geschält, entkernt, geviertelt

2,5 cm–5 cm (1-2-Zoll) Streifen Orangenschale oder Zitronenschale

1/4 Tasse (60 ml) helles Olivenöl

1 Tasse (200 g) Kristallzucker

1 großes Ei

1 Teelöffel Vanilleextrakt

1 1/2 Teelöffel Backpulver

1/2 Teelöffel Backnatron

1 Teelöffel Salz

2 Tassen (240 g) Vollkornweizenmehl (Type 1600)

1/2 Tasse (46 g) gehackte Mandeln

Eine 22 cm x 11 cm (8 1/2 Zoll x 4 1/2 Zoll) große Brotform mit Backspray oder Backfett einfetten. Den Backofen auf 180 °C (350 °F) vorheizen.

Vitamix WET BLADE-Behälter auf Mixerbasis setzen und Variable 1 auswählen.

Das Gerät einschalten und die Geschwindigkeit langsam auf Variable 3 erhöhen. Den Stöpsel aus dem Deckel nehmen und Cranberrys durch die Öffnung im Deckel einfüllen und mixen, bis sie zerkleinert sind. Gerät anhalten; Wände des Behälters abschaben und zerkleinerte Cranberrys herausnehmen.

Orangenviertel, Schale, Olivenöl, Zucker, Eier und Vanille in den Vitamix WET BLADE-Behälter geben und den Deckel schließen.

Variable 1 auswählen.

Das Gerät einschalten und die Geschwindigkeit langsam auf Variable 10 erhöhen.

30 Sekunden lang mixen, bei Bedarf den Stopfer verwenden, um die Zutaten auf die Klingen zu drücken.

In einer großen Rührschüssel Backpulver, Backnatron, Salz und Vollkornweizenmehl gut verrühren.

Orangenmischung in die Schüssel mit den trockenen Zutaten geben. Von Hand unterheben, NUR solange, bis die trockenen Zutaten angefeuchtet sind.

Gehackte Nüsse unter den Teig heben; nicht zu viel verkneten.

Den Teig in die vorbereitete Form geben. 1 Stunde backen. Wenn an einem in die Mitte des Brots gepieksten Zahnstocher kein Teig mehr hängt, ist es durchgebacken.

30 Minuten lang auf einem Kuchengitter auskühlen lassen und dann vorsichtig aus der Form lösen. Erst anschneiden, wenn es vollständig abgekühlt ist.

HINWEIS: Zubereitung von Vollkornweizenmehl aus Vollkornweizen: 1 1/2 Tassen (270 g) Vollkornweizen in den Vitamix DRY BLADE-Behälter und den Deckel schließen.

Cranberry-Nuss-Brot *(Fortsetzung)*	Variable 1 auswählen. Das Gerät einschalten und die Geschwindigkeit langsam auf Variable 10 erhöhen. 1 Minute lang mahlen. (Nicht zu stark verarbeiten.) Das Gerät anhalten und das Mehl einige Minuten abkühlen lassen. 2 Tassen (240 g) Vollkornweizenmehl für das Rezept abmessen. Verbleibendes Mehl zur späteren Verwendung aufbewahren.

Nährwertinformationen pro Portion (1 Scheibe): 224 kcal (32 % aus Fett, 8 % aus Eiweiß, 60 % aus Kohlenhydraten)
4 g Eiweiß • 8 g Fett insgesamt • 1 g gesättigte Fettsäuren • 35 g Kohlenhydrate • 4 g Ballaststoffe • 19 g Zucker
314 mg Natrium • 17 mg Cholesterin

Cranberry-Nuss-Brot

KICHERERBSEN-PFANNKUCHEN

Zubereitung: 10 Minuten • Verarbeitung: 1 Minute • ergibt: 4–5 Pfannkuchen

1 Tasse (172 g) getrocknete Kichererbsen

1 Teelöffel Backpulver

1/2 Teelöffel Backnatron

1/4 Teelöffel Salz

3/4 Tasse (180 ml) kaltes Wasser

2 Esslöffel (30 ml) Olivenöl

1 großes Ei

Bei der Zubereitung mit getrockneten Kichererbsen: Die Kichererbsen in den Vitamix DRY BLADE-Behälter geben und den Deckel schließen.

Variable 1 auswählen.

Das Gerät einschalten und die Geschwindigkeit langsam auf Variable 10 erhöhen.

Etwa 1 Minute lang mahlen, bis der gewünschte Feinheitsgrad erreicht ist. 1 Tasse (120 g) Kichererbsenmehl abmessen; das verbleibende Mehl (etwa 1/3 Tasse (40 g)) zur späteren Verwendung aufbewahren.

Bei der Zubereitung mit Kichererbsenmehl: 1 Tasse (120 g) Mehl, Backpulver, Backnatron und Salz in einer mittelgroßen Rührschüssel vermischen.

Wasser, Öl und Ei in der angegebenen Reihenfolge in den Vitamix DRY BLADE-Behälter geben und den Deckel schließen.

Variable 1 auswählen.

Das Gerät einschalten und die Geschwindigkeit langsam auf Variable 10 erhöhen.

Die Masse 15 Sekunden vermischen.

Wassermischung in die Schüssel mit den trockenen Zutaten geben. Von Hand unterheben, NUR solange, bis die trockenen Zutaten angefeuchtet sind.

Kleine Bratpfanne mit Fett einsprühen oder einpinseln. Pfanne erhitzen.

Etwa 1/3 Tasse (80 ml) des Teigs in die Pfanne gießen und den Teig durch ein leichtes Kippen der Pfanne verteilen. Pfannkuchen braten, bis sich auf der Oberfläche Bläschen bilden. Wenden und braten, bis er eine leichte Bräunung hat. Sofort servieren.

Nährwertinformationen pro Portion (1 Pfannkuchen): 193 kcal (38 % aus Fett, 15 % aus Eiweiß, 47 % aus Kohlenhydraten) • 10 g Eiweiß • 11 g Fett insgesamt • 1 g gesättigte Fettsäuren
29 g Kohlenhydrate • 14 g Ballaststoffe • 1 g Zucker • 476 mg Natrium • 53 mg Cholesterin

WALNUSS-DATTEL-BROT

Zubereitung: 30 Minuten • Verarbeitung: 25-30 Sekunden • Backzeit: 1 1/4-1 1/2 Stunden
ergibt: 1 Laib (12 Scheiben)

1 Tasse (240 ml) kochendes Wasser

2 1/4 Tassen (340 g) entsteinte getrocknete Datteln, grob zerkleinert

4 Esslöffel (56 g) ungesalzene Butter, in Stücke geschnitten

1 1/4 Tassen (125 g) Walnüsse

1 Tasse (120 g) Vollkornmehl (Type 1600)

1 Tasse (125 g) Mehl Type 550

3/4 Tasse (150 g) Kristallzucker

1 Teelöffel Backpulver

1/2 Teelöffel Backnatron

1/2 Teelöffel Meersalz

2 große Eier

1/2 Teelöffel Vanille

Das kochende Wasser über Datteln und Butter in eine große Rührschüssel gießen. Beiseitestellen, bis das Wasser abgekühlt ist; ca. 30 Minuten.

Den Ofen auf 160 °C (325 °F) vorheizen. Blech auf die mittlere Schiene schieben. Die Brotform dünn einfetten; beiseitestellen.

Die Walnüsse in den Vitamix DRY BLADE-Behälter geben. Den Deckel schließen.

Variable 1 auswählen.

Das Gerät einschalten und die Geschwindigkeit langsam auf Variable 3 erhöhen.

10 bis 15 Sekunden lang rühren oder bis die Walnüsse gerade grob zerkleinert sind. Nicht zu stark verarbeiten.

Die zerkleinerten Nüsse in eine kleine Schüssel geben und beiseitestellen.

Das gesamte Mehl, Backpulver, Backnatron und das Salz in den Vitamix DRY BLADE-Behälter geben. Den Deckel schließen.

Variable 1 auswählen.

Das Gerät einschalten und die Geschwindigkeit langsam auf Variable 6 erhöhen.

Die Masse 15 Sekunden vermischen. Mit zerkleinerten Nüssen verrühren.

Eier und Vanille mit einem Schneebesen in die abgekühlte Dattelmasse schlagen, anschließend alles unter die Mehl-/Nuss-Mischung heben.

Gleichmäßig in einer Brotform verteilen und backen. Wenn an einem in die Mitte des Brots gepieksten Zahnstocher kein Teig mehr hängt, ist das Brot durchgebacken.

Das Brot 25 Minuten lang auf einem Kuchengitter auskühlen lassen und es dann vorsichtig auf das Kuchengitter stürzen und vollständig abkühlen lassen.

Nährwertinformationen pro Portion (1 Scheibe): 346 kcal (32 % aus Fett, 9 % aus Eiweiß, 60 % aus Kohlenhydraten)
8 g Eiweiß • 13 g Fett insgesamt • 3 g gesättigte Fettsäuren • 55 g Kohlenhydrate • 2 g Ballaststoffe • 13 g Zucker
208 mg Natrium • 51 mg Cholesterin

Datteln mithilfe der Küchenschere (diese häufig in heißes Wasser tauchen) zerkleinern.

PFIRSICH-GEWÜRZ-SCONES

Zubereitung: 20 Minuten • Verarbeitung: 20 Sekunden • Backzeit: 30-35 Minuten • ergibt: 8 Scones

1 1/2 Tassen (180 g) Vollkornweizenmehl (Type 1600)

1 Tasse (125 g) Mehl Type 550

1/3 Tasse (67 g) Kristallzucker

2 1/4 Teelöffel Backpulver

1/2 Teelöffel Backnatron

1/4 Teelöffel Salz

1/2 Tasse (113 g) ungesalzene Butter, weich und in Stücke geschnitten

1/2 Tasse (120 ml) Milch

1 Teelöffel Vanilleextrakt

1 Tasse (186 g) gefrorene oder frische Pfirsichscheiben, (bei gefroren Pfirsichen: aufgetaut und abgegossen) gewürfelt

Belag:

3 Esslöffel (17 g) Mandelscheiben

1 Esslöffel Kristallzucker

1 Teelöffel gemahlener Zimt

Zusätzlich Milch oder Zucker nach Bedarf zum Einpinseln des Teigs

Mehle, Zucker, Backpulver, Backnatron und Salz in einer großen Rührschüssel vermischen.

Butter, Milch und Vanilleextrakt in den Vitamix WET BLADE-Behälter geben und Deckel schließen.

Variable 1 auswählen.

Das Gerät einschalten und die Geschwindigkeit langsam auf Variable 6 erhöhen.

Etwa 20 Sekunden lang mixen, bis die Butter gut untergerührt ist.

Butter-Milch-Mischung und Pfirsichstückchen vorsichtig unter den Mehlmix heben (nur so lange rühren, bis alles grob vermischt ist). Den Teig zu einer Kugel formen und dann auf einem mit Backpapier ausgelegten Blech vorsichtig zu einem 20 cm (8 Zoll) großen Kreis klopfen. Mithilfe eines Messers oder Pizzarollers den Kreis in 8 Dreiecke unterteilen (einschneiden, aber nicht durchschneiden).

Mandeln, Zucker und Zimt in den Vitamix DRY BLADE-Behälter geben und den Deckel schließen.

Variable 1 auswählen.

Das Gerät einschalten und die Geschwindigkeit langsam auf Variable 4 erhöhen.

Etwa 10 Sekunden mixen, bis die Mischung fein gehackt und vermischt ist.

Den Teig mit Milch oder Sahne bestreichen und die Mandelmischung darüberstreuen.

Im vorgeheizten Backofen bei 200 °C (400 °F) 30 bis 35 Minuten backen, bis die Scones knusprig und im Innern nicht mehr feucht sind. 10 Minuten abkühlen lassen, dann die Dreiecke mit einem scharfen Messer oder Pizzaroller durchschneiden. Warm oder bei Zimmertemperatur servieren.

Pfirsich-Gewürz-Scones
(Fortsetzung)

HINWEIS: Zubereitung von Vollkornweizenmehl aus Vollkornweizen: 1 1/2 Tassen (270 g) Vollkornweizen in den Vitamix DRY BLADE-Behälter und den Deckel schließen.

Variable 1 auswählen.

Das Gerät einschalten und die Geschwindigkeit langsam auf Variable 10 erhöhen.

1 Minute lang mahlen. (Nicht zu stark verarbeiten.) Das Gerät anhalten und das Mehl einige Minuten abkühlen lassen. 1 1/2 Tassen (180 g) Vollkornweizenmehl für das Rezept abmessen. Verbleibendes Mehl zur späteren Verwendung aufbewahren.

Nährwertinformationen pro Portion (1 Scone): 311 kcal (39 % aus Fett, 8 % aus Eiweiß, 53 % aus Kohlenhydraten)
6 g Eiweiß • 14 g Fett insgesamt • 8 g gesättigte Fettsäuren • 42 g Kohlenhydrate • 4 g Ballaststoffe • 12 g Zucker
302 mg Natrium • 31 mg Cholesterin

VOLLKORNWEIZEN-MUFFINS MIT FRÜCHTEN UND KAROTTEN

Zubereitung: 15 Minuten • Verarbeitung: 10-15 Sekunden • Backzeit: 20–25 Minuten
ergibt: 6 Muffins

1 Tasse (165 g) Ananasstücke

1/2 Tasse (64 g) grob gehackte Karotten

1 Esslöffel helles Olivenöl

1/4 Tasse (55 g) hellbrauner Zucker

1 großes Ei

1 Tasse (120 g) Vollkornmehl (Type 1600)

1 Teelöffel gemahlenen Leinsamen

1 Teelöffel Zimt

1 Teelöffel Backpulver

1/2 Teelöffel Backnatron

1/2 Teelöffel Salz

1/2 Tasse (72 g) Rosinen

Den Backofen auf 190 °C (375 °F) vorheizen. Muffinblech dünn mit Backspray einsprühen oder Muffin-Papierförmchen verwenden.

Ananas, Karotten, Öl, braunen Zucker und Ei in der angegebenen Reihenfolge in den Vitamix WET BLADE-Behälter geben und den Deckel schließen.

Variable 1 auswählen.

Das Gerät einschalten und die Geschwindigkeit langsam auf Variable 4 erhöhen.

10 bis 15 Sekunden lang mixen (Karotten und Ananas sollten noch in groben Stücken sein).

In einer großen Rührschüssel Mehl, gemahlenen Leinsamen, Zimt, Backpulver, Backnatron und Salz gut verrühren.

Ananasmischung in die Schüssel mit den trockenen Zutaten geben. Von Hand unterheben, NUR solange, bis die trockenen Zutaten angefeuchtet sind. Schnell aber vorsichtig die Rosinen unterheben.

Mit einem Löffel das vorbereitete Muffinblech füllen. Jedes Förmchen dabei komplett füllen.

20–25 Minuten backen. Wenn an einem in die Mitte der Muffins gepieksten Zahnstocher kein Teig mehr hängt, sind sie durchgebacken.

Auf einem Kuchengitter 5 Minuten abkühlen lassen, dann vorsichtig jeden Muffin aus dem Muffinblech lösen. Warm oder bei Zimmertemperatur servieren.

Nährwertinformationen pro Portion (1 Muffin): 203 kcal (17 % aus Fett, 9 % aus Eiweiß, 74 % aus Kohlenhydraten)
5 g Eiweiß • 4 g Fett insgesamt • 1 g gesättigte Fettsäuren • 40 g Kohlenhydrate • 4 g Ballaststoffe • 18 g Zucker
412 mg Natrium • 35 mg Cholesterin

Keinesfalls weniger Öl verwenden. Die angegebene Menge ist nötig, um saftige Muffins zu bekommen. Wenn Sie Honig verwenden oder weniger braunen Zucker, werden Sie das Natron durchschmecken.

Vollkornweizen-Muffins mit Früchten und Karotten

ZUCCHINIBROT

Zubereitung: 15 Minuten • Verarbeitung: 15-20 Sekunden • Backzeit: 1 Stunde
ergibt: 1 Laib (12 Scheiben)

1 großes Ei

2/3 Tasse (133 g) Kristallzucker

1/4 Tasse (60 ml) helles Olivenöl oder Traubenkernöl

1 Teelöffel Vanilleextrakt

7 Unzen (200 g) Zucchini, in grobe Stücke geschnitten, etwa 1 1/2 Tassen

2 Tassen (250 g) Mehl Type 550

1 Teelöffel Backnatron

1/4 Teelöffel Backpulver

1/4 Teelöffel Salz

1/4 Teelöffel gemahlener Muskat

1/2 Teelöffel gemahlener Zimt

1/2 Teelöffel gemahlener Piment

Optionale Zutaten:

1/2 Tasse (58 g) grob gehackte Walnüsse

1/2 Tasse (72 g) Rosinen

Eine 22 cm x 11 cm (8 1/2 Zoll x 4 1/2 Zoll) große Brotform mit Backspray oder Backfett einfetten. Den Backofen auf 180 °C (350 °F) vorheizen.

Ei, Zucker, Öl und Vanilleextrakt in der angegebenen Reihenfolge in den Vitamix WET BLADE-Behälter geben und den Deckel schließen.

Variable 1 auswählen.

Das Gerät einschalten und die Geschwindigkeit langsam auf Variable 5 erhöhen.

15 bis 20 Sekunden lang mixen, oder bis die Masse vermischt und die Zucchinistücke zerkleinert sind.

In einer großen Rührschüssel Mehl, Backnatron, Backpulver, Salz, Muskat, Zimt und Piment gut verrühren.

Zucchinimischung in die Schüssel mit den trockenen Zutaten geben. Von Hand unterheben, NUR solange, bis die trockenen Zutaten angefeuchtet sind; dann schnell die Walnüsse und/oder Rosinen unterheben. Nicht zu lange rühren.

Den Teig in die vorbereitete Form geben. 1 Stunde backen. Wenn an einem in die Mitte des Brots gepieksten Zahnstocher kein Teig mehr hängt, ist es durchgebacken.

30 Minuten lang auf einem Kuchengitter auskühlen lassen und dann vorsichtig aus der Form lösen. Erst anschneiden, wenn es vollständig abgekühlt ist.

Nährwertinformationen pro Portion (1 Scheibe, ohne optionale Zutaten): 171 kcal (28 % aus Fett, 7 % aus Eiweiß, 65 % aus Kohlenhydraten) • 3 g Eiweiß • 5 g Fett insgesamt • 1 g gesättigte Fettsäuren • 28 g Kohlenhydrate 1 g Ballaststoffe • 12 g Zucker • 174 mg Natrium • 18 mg Cholesterin

KÜRBISMUFFINS

Zubereitung: 15 Minuten • Verarbeitung: 10 Sekunden • Backzeit: 20–25 Minuten • ergibt: 12 Muffins

2 große Eier

1/4 Tasse (60 ml) helles Olivenöl

1 Tasse (245 g) Kürbis, frisch gekocht oder aus der Dose

1/4 Tasse (60 ml) Milch

3/4 Tasse (150 g) Kristallzucker

1/2 Teelöffel Salz

2 Teelöffel Backnatron

1 Teelöffel Piment

1 Teelöffel Zimt

1 3/4 Tasse (219 g) Mehl Type 550

1/2 Tasse (120 g) Schokoladensplitter, klein oder normal

Den Backofen auf 180 °C (350 °F) vorheizen. Muffinblech dünn mit Backspray einsprühen oder Muffin-Papierförmchen verwenden.

Eier, Öl, Kürbis, Milch und Zucker in der angegebenen Reihenfolge in den Vitamix WET BLADE-Behälter geben und den Deckel schließen.

Variable 1 auswählen.

Das Gerät einschalten und die Geschwindigkeit langsam auf Variable 5 erhöhen.

Die Masse 10 Sekunden lang verrühren.

In einer mittelgroßen Rührschüssel Salz, Backnatron, Piment, Zimt, Mehl und Schokoladensplitter in der angegebenen Reihenfolge vermischen.

Kürbismischung in die Schüssel mit den trockenen Zutaten geben. Von Hand unterheben, NUR solange, bis die trockenen Zutaten angefeuchtet sind.

Mit einem Löffel das vorbereitete Muffinblech füllen. Jedes Förmchen dabei zu 3/4 füllen.

20–25 Minuten backen. Wenn an einem in die Mitte der Muffins gepieksten Zahnstocher kein Teig mehr hängt, sind sie durchgebacken.

Auf einem Kuchengitter 5 Minuten abkühlen lassen, dann vorsichtig jeden Muffin aus dem Muffinblech lösen. Warm oder bei Zimmertemperatur servieren.

Nährwertinformationen pro Portion (1 Muffin): 228 kcal (32 % aus Fett, 7 % aus Eiweiß, 61 % aus Kohlenhydraten)
4 g Eiweiß • 8 g Fett insgesamt • 2 g gesättigte Fettsäuren • 35 g Kohlenhydraten • 2 g Ballaststoffe • 18 g Zucker
326 mg Natrium • 41 mg Cholesterin

Hefeteige

Anleitung für Hefebrote

Hier einige hilfreiche Tipps für die Zubereitung von Hefeteig.

Abmessen des Mehls

Es ist nicht nötig, das Mehl zu sieben, aber um ein genaues Messergebnis zu gewährleisten, sollten Sie das Mehl mit einem Löffel in einen trockenen Messbecher mit Tassenmaßen füllen und den Messbecher dann mit einem Spatel oder Messer abstreichen. Alternativ können Sie das Mehl auch abwiegen.

Temperatur der Flüssigkeiten

Das Ansetzen eines Vorteigs garantiert, dass die Hefekultur noch aktiv ist und beim Rezept gut funktionieren wird. Hefe reagiert äußerst empfindlich auf Temperaturen: zu viel Hitze tötet die Hefe ab, zu wenig schränkt ihr Wachstum ein. Daher ist es wichtig, dass die Flüssigkeit die richtige Temperatur hat, wenn die Hefe hinzugefügt wird.

Meistens wird ein Temperaturbereich zwischen 40 °C bis 46 °C (105 °F-115 °F) empfohlen, wenn die Hefe direkt mit der Flüssigkeit vermischt wird.

Gehen lassen

Lassen Sie den Teig leicht zugedeckt an einem warmen Ort ohne Zugluft gehen. Am besten ist es, den Teig bei Zimmertemperatur gehen zu lassen. Höhere Temperaturen können dem fertigen Produkt einen Geschmack nach roher Hefe geben; niedrigere Temperaturen können dazu führen, dass der Teig versauert, bevor er aufgeht.

SAUERTEIG-BLAUBEER-BROT

Zubereitung: 15 Minuten • Verarbeitung: 15 Sekunden • Backzeit: 35–40 Minuten
ergibt: 1 runder Laib (8–10 Scheiben)

1 großes Ei

1/2 Tasse (120 ml) Pflanzenöl

1/2 Tasse (120 ml) Milch

3/4 Tasse (180 ml) Kartoffel-Starter (Rezept auf Seite 75), bei Zimmertemperatur

1/2 Tasse (100 g) Kristallzucker

1 1/2 Tassen (188 g) Mehl Type 550

1/2 Tasse (60 g) Vollkornmehl (Type 1600)

1/2 Teelöffel Salz

3/4 Teelöffel Backnatron

1 Tasse (148 g) frische oder gefrorene (auftauen und trocken tupfen) Blaubeeren

Zucker zum Bestäuben, optional

Den Backofen auf 190 °C (375 °F) vorheizen. Eine Bratpfanne oder Kuchenform dünn einfetten.

Ei, Öl, Milch, Kartoffel-Starter und Zucker in der angegebenen Reihenfolge in den Vitamix WET BLADE-Behälter geben und den Deckel schließen.

Variable 1 auswählen.

Das Gerät einschalten und die Geschwindigkeit langsam auf Variable 10 erhöhen.

Die Masse 15 Sekunden vermischen.

In einer mittelgroßen Rührschüssel Mehle, Salz und Backnatron verrühren.

Startermischung in die Schüssel mit den trockenen Zutaten geben. Von Hand unterheben, NUR solange, bis die trockenen Zutaten angefeuchtet sind. Schnell aber vorsichtig die Blaubeeren unterheben.

In die vorbereitete Form löffeln. Bei Bedarf mit dem zusätzlichen Zucker besprenkeln.

35–40 Minuten backen. Wenn an einem in die Mitte des Kuchens gepieksten Zahnstocher kein Teig mehr hängt, ist der Kuchen durchgebacken. Warm oder kalt servieren, in Dreiecke schneiden.

Nährwertinformationen pro Portion (1 Scheibe): 249 kcal (7 % aus Fett, 12 % aus Eiweiß, 81 % aus Kohlenhydraten)
8 g Eiweiß • 2 g Fett insgesamt • 0 g gesättigte Fettsäuren • 51 g Kohlenhydrate • 5 g Ballaststoffe • 3 g Zucker
23 mg Natrium • 0 mg Cholesterin

ZIMTSCHNECKEN

Zubereitung: 20 Minuten • Verarbeitung: 30 Sekunden • Backzeit: 30-35 Minuten
ergibt: 9 Brötchen

1 Packung (1 Esslöffel) aktive Trockenhefe

4 Esslöffel (60 ml) warmes Wasser, 40 °C bis 46 °C (105 °F-115 °F)

2 Esslöffel (30 ml) Honig

2 1/4 Tassen (281 g) Mehl Type 550 sowie zusätzliches Mehl für später und zum Ausrollen des Teigs

1/2 Teelöffel Salz

1/3 Tasse (80 ml) Milch

1/4 Tasse (56 g) ungesalzene Butter, weich und in Stücke geschnitten

1 großes Ei

Füllung:

4 Esslöffel (50 g) Kristallzucker

1 Esslöffel gemahlener Zimt

1/4 Tasse (56 g) ungesalzene Butter, geschmolzen

1 großes Ei plus 2 Esslöffel (30 ml) Milch (um die Brötchen vor dem Backen einzupinseln)

Puderzuckerguss (Rezept auf Seite 46)

Hefe ansetzen, indem Hefe, Wasser und Honig vermischt werden. Alles zügig umrühren. Die Mischung für 5 Minuten beiseitestellen.

Das Mehl und das Salz in den Vitamix DRY BLADE-Behälter geben und den Deckel schließen.

Variable 1 auswählen.

Das Gerät einschalten und die Geschwindigkeit langsam auf Variable 6 erhöhen.

Die Mischung etwa 5 Sekunden lang verrühren, bis sich in der Mitte ein Loch bildet.

Variable 3 auswählen. Gerät einschalten und den Stöpsel aus dem Deckel nehmen. Hefemischung, Milch, Butter und Eier durch die Öffnung im Deckel hinzugeben. Das Gerät ausschalten und den Stöpsel wieder einsetzen.

Die schnellste Geschwindigkeitsstufe auswählen. Das Gerät zwei Mal hintereinander schnell ein- und wieder ausschalten. Das Gerät ausschalten und den Stöpsel abnehmen.

Während der Teig ruht, eine 20 cm (8 Zoll) große quadratische Kuchenform mit Backspray oder Backfett dünn einfetten.

Mithilfe eines nassen Nylonspatels die Wand des Behälters freischaben und den Teig von der Behälterwand in die Mitte der Mixtur schieben. Den Deckel wieder aufsetzen.

Die schnellste Geschwindigkeitsstufe auswählen. Das Gerät fünfmal hintereinander schnell ein- und ausschalten. Sollte der Teig besonders trocken sein, esslöffelweise zusätzliches Wasser hinzugeben. Die Prozedur fünf Mal wiederholen und die Behälterwand freischaben, bis der Teig eine weiche, elastische Masse gebildet hat.

Um den Teig aus dem Behälter lösen zu können, Gerät fünfmal ein- und ausschalten (dadurch wird der Teig an- und von den Klingen abgehoben). Den Behälter anschließend kopfüber über die vorbereitete Schüssel halten und den Teig hineinfallen lassen. Den Teig einmal wenden, um die gesamte Oberfläche zu bedecken; mit einem sauberen Geschirrtuch zudecken und 25 bis 30 Minuten gehen lassen.

Zucker und Zimt vermischen; mit der geschmolzenen und abgekühlten Butter beiseitestellen.

Zimtschnecken
(Fortsetzung)

Den Teig auf eine bemehlte Arbeitsfläche geben. Zu einem großen Rechteck (ca. 20 cm x 40 cm / 8 Zoll x 16 Zoll) ausrollen. Den Teig dabei häufig wenden und mit Mehl bestäuben. Mit der geschmolzenen Butter bestreichen und dabei an allen Seiten einen ca. 1,3 cm (1/2 Zoll) großen Rand lassen. Die Zucker-Zimtmischung auf die Butter streuen.

Eng zusammenrollen, wie eine Biskuitrolle. In 9 Stücke schneiden. Nach oben klappen und in die Form legen.

Mit einem sauberen, trockenen Geschirrtuch abdecken und etwa 45 bis 60 Minuten gehen lassen.

Die Oberseite der Schnecken mit der Ei-Milch-Mischung einpinseln. Im vorgeheizten Backofen bei 160 °C (325 °F) 30 bis 35 Minuten backen, bis sie goldbraun sind.

Die Schnecken 10 Minuten lang auf einem Kuchengitter auskühlen lassen und sie dann vorsichtig aus der Form nehmen. Auf einem Kuchengitter auskühlen lassen und erst anschneiden, wenn sie vollständig abgekühlt sind. Mit Puderzuckerglasur überziehen und servieren.

Nährwertinformationen pro Portion (1 Schnecke): 422 kcal (37% aus Fett, 5% aus Eiweiß, 58% aus Kohlenhydraten)
6 g Eiweiß • 18 g Fett insgesamt • 11 g gesättigte Fettsäuren • 62 g Kohlenhydrate • 2 g Ballaststoffe
35 g Zucker • 162 mg Natrium • 88 mg Cholesterin

Zimtschnecken

PUDERZUCKERGUSS

Der perfekte Guss für Zimtschnecken.
Zubereitung: 20 Minuten • Verarbeitung: 25 Sekunden • ergibt: 1 Tasse (240 g)

2 Tassen (240 g) Puderzucker

1/4 Tasse (56 g) ungesalzene Butter, weich

1 Teelöffel Vanille

1 bis 2 Esslöffel heißes Wasser, evtl. mehr nach Bedarf

Puderzucker, Butter, Vanille und heißes Wasser in den Vitamix WET BLADE-Behälter geben und den Deckel schließen.

Variable 1 auswählen.

Das Gerät einschalten und die Geschwindigkeit langsam auf Variable 10 erhöhen.

Die Masse 10 Sekunden lang verrühren. Das Gerät ausschalten, den Deckel abnehmen und die Masse von den Seiten des Behälters schaben. Bei Bedarf teelöffelweise zusätzliches Wasser hinzugeben, bis ein streichfähiger (aber nicht zu dünnflüssiger) Guss entsteht.

Die Variable 1 auswählen und den Deckel schließen.

Das Gerät einschalten und die Geschwindigkeit langsam auf Variable 10 erhöhen.

Die Masse etwa 15 Sekunden lang glatt und cremig rühren. Sofort verwenden.

Nährwertinformationen pro Portion (2 Esslöffel / 30 g): 169 kcal (30 % aus Fett, 0 % aus Eiweiß, 70 % aus Kohlenhydraten) • 0 g Eiweiß • 6 g Fett insgesamt • 4 g gesättigte Fettsäuren
30 g Kohlenhydrate • 0 g Ballaststoffe • 29 g Zucker • 1 mg Natrium • 15 mg Cholesterin

KARTOFFELSTARTER

Zubereitung: 10 Minuten

1 Packung (1 Esslöffel) aktive Trockenhefe

2 Teelöffel Zucker

2 Tassen (480 ml) warmes Kartoffelwasser, 43 °C (110 °F)

2 Tassen (480 ml) warmes Wasser, 43 °C (110 °F) oder zusätzliches Kartoffelwasser, erwärmt

1 Tasse (125 g) Mehl Type 550

1 Tasse (120 g) Vollkornmehl (Type 1600)

Hefe und Zucker in 2 Tassen (480 ml) Kartoffelwasser in einer großen Rührschüssel auflösen.

Mit einem sauberen, trockenen Geschirrtuch abdecken und 24 Stunden an einem warmen Ort stehen lassen.

2 Tassen (480 ml) warmes Wasser hinzugeben und in die Mehle rühren.

Abdecken und über Nacht oder bis die Mischung Blasen wirft und sauer riecht stehen lassen. Im Kühlschrank in einem großen Gefäß mit Deckel aufbewahren.

Aus dem Kühlschrank nehmen und „füttern". 1 Tasse (240 ml) für einen Laib Brot verwenden, wenn das Rezept nach einem Starter verlangt.

Nährwertinformationen pro Portion (1 Tasse / 240 ml): 232 kcal (4 % aus Fett, 14 % aus Eiweiß, 82 % aus Kohlenhydraten) 8 g Eiweiß • 1 g Fett insgesamt • 0 g gesättigte Fettsäuren 49 g Kohlenhydrate • 5 g Ballaststoffe • 2 g Zucker • 6 mg Natrium • 0 mg Cholesterin

Füttern des Starters: Am Morgen auf Zimmertemperatur bringen und 1 Tasse (240 ml) warmes Wasser 43 °C (110 °F) und 1 Tasse (125 g) Mehl Typ 550 einrühren. Über Nacht stehen lassen. Benötigte Menge verwenden und den Rest in den Kühlschrank stellen. Alle 2 bis 3 Wochen erneuern.

KOLONIALBROT (OVALE FORM)

Zubereitung: 15 Minuten • Verarbeitung: 30 Sekunden • Backzeit: 25 Minuten
ergibt: 1 ovalen Laib (8–10 Scheiben)

1 1/4 Tassen (300 ml) warmes Wasser, 40 °C bis 46 °C (105 °F-115 °F)

3 Esslöffel (41 g) brauner Zucker

1 Packung (1 Esslöffel) aktive Trockenhefe

1 1/2 Tassen (188 g) Mehl Type 550

1/2 Tasse (60 g) Vollkornmehl (Type 1600)

1/4 Tasse (26 g) helles Roggenmehl (Type 1150)

1/4 Tasse (30 g) Vollkorn-Maismehl

1/2 Teelöffel Salz

1 Esslöffel helles Olivenöl

1/4 Tasse (30 g) Vollkorn-Maismehl fürs Blech

1 Ei, vermischt mit 1 Teelöffel Wasser (zum Bestreichen des Teigs vor dem Backen)

Die Hefe ansetzen, indem warmes Wasser, brauner Zucker und Hefe vermischt werden. Alles zügig umrühren. Die Mischung für 5 Minuten beiseitestellen.

Mehl Type 550, Vollkornmehl, Roggenmehl, Maismehl und Salz in den Vitamix DRY BLADE-Behälter geben und den Deckel.

Variable 1 auswählen.

Das Gerät einschalten und die Geschwindigkeit langsam auf Variable 6 erhöhen.

Die Mischung etwa 5 Sekunden lang rühren, bis sich in der Mitte ein Loch bildet.

Variable 3 auswählen. Das Gerät einschalten und den Stöpsel aus dem Deckel nehmen. Das Öl und die Hefemischung durch die Öffnung im Deckel hinzugeben. Das Gerät ausschalten und den Stöpsel wieder einsetzen.

Die schnellste Geschwindigkeitsstufe auswählen. Das Gerät zwei Mal hintereinander schnell ein- und wieder ausschalten. Das Gerät ausschalten und den Stöpsel abnehmen.

Während der Teig ruht, 1/4 Tasse (30 g) Maismehl aufs Backblech streuen; beiseitelegen.

Mithilfe eines nassen Nylonspatels die Wand des Behälters freischaben und den Teig von der Behälterwand in die Mitte der Mixtur schieben. Den Deckel wieder aufsetzen.

Die schnellste Geschwindigkeitsstufe auswählen. Das Gerät fünfmal hintereinander schnell ein- und ausschalten. Sollte der Teig besonders trocken sein, esslöffelweise zusätzliches Wasser hinzugeben. Die Prozedur fünf Mal wiederholen und die Behälterwand freischaben, bis der Teig eine weiche, elastische Masse gebildet hat.

Den Deckel auf den Behälter setzen und den Teig 15 Minuten lang gehen lassen.

Den Teig mit einem Nylonspatel zusammenstoßen und ihn dann auf ein leicht mit Mehl besprenkeltes Stück Backpapier legen. (Der Teig ist klebrig.) Den Teig mit bemehlten Händen schnell vom Backpapier ziehen und auf das Backblech legen. Den Teig mit Mehl bestäuben und in ein großes Oval formen.

Den Laib mit einem sauberen und trockenen Geschirrtuch bedecken und ihn etwa 15 bis 20 Minuten gehen lassen, bis er ungefähr doppelt so groß geworden ist.

Kolonialbrot (ovale Form) *(Fortsetzung)*	Den Teig vor dem Backen mit der Ei-Wasser-Mischung bestreichen und ihn mit 3 schnellen, schrägen Schnitten mit einem gezahnten Messer einschneiden. Das Brot im vorgeheizten Ofen bei 190 °C (375 °F) 25 Minuten lang backen oder bis das Brot eine Innentemperatur von 88 °C (190 °F) aufweist (mit Backthermometer messen). Das Brot 10 Minuten lang auf einem Kuchengitter auskühlen lassen und es dann vorsichtig vom Backblech nehmen. Das Brot erst anschneiden, wenn es vollständig abgekühlt ist.

Nährwertinformationen pro Portion (1 Scheibe): 160 kcal (15 % aus Fett, 11 % aus Eiweiß, 74 % aus Kohlenhydraten) • 5 g Eiweiß • 3 g Fett insgesamt • 0 g gesättigte Fettsäuren 30 g Kohlenhydrate • 2 g Ballaststoffe • 4 g Zucker • 133 mg Natrium • 21 mg Cholesterin

Ideal als ein flacher, hausgemachter Laib, der geschnitten oder zum Dippen in Olivenöl verwendet werden kann.

KOLONIALBROT (LAIBFORM)

Zubereitung: 10 Minuten • Verarbeitung: 30 Sekunden • Backzeit: 25-30 Minuten
ergibt: 1 Laib (12 Scheiben)

1 1/4 Tassen (300 ml) warmes Wasser, 40 °C bis 46 °C (105 °F-115 °F)

3 Esslöffel (41 g) brauner Zucker

1 Packung (1 Esslöffel) aktive Trockenhefe

1 1/2 Tassen (188 g) Mehl Type 550

1/2 Tasse (60 g) Vollkornmehl (Type 1600)

1/4 Tasse (26 g) helles Roggenmehl (Type 1150)

1/4 Tasse (30 g) Vollkorn-Maismehl

1/2 Teelöffel Salz

1 Esslöffel helles Olivenöl

1 großes Ei, vermischt mit 1 Teelöffel Wasser (zum Bestreichen des Teigs vor dem Backen)

Die Hefe ansetzen, indem warmes Wasser, brauner Zucker und Hefe vermischt werden. Alles zügig umrühren. Die Mischung für 5 Minuten beiseitestellen.

Mehl Type 550, Vollkornmehl, Roggenmehl, Maismehl und Salz in den Vitamix DRY BLADE-Behälter geben und den Deckel.

Variable 1 auswählen.

Das Gerät einschalten und die Geschwindigkeit langsam auf Variable 6 erhöhen.

Die Mischung etwa 5 Sekunden lang rühren, bis sich in der Mitte ein Loch bildet.

Variable 3 auswählen. Das Gerät einschalten und den Stöpsel aus dem Deckel nehmen. Das Öl und die Hefemischung durch die Öffnung im Deckel hinzugeben. Das Gerät ausschalten und den Stöpsel wieder einsetzen.

Die schnellste Geschwindigkeitsstufe auswählen. Das Gerät zwei Mal hintereinander schnell ein- und wieder ausschalten. Das Gerät ausschalten und den Stöpsel abnehmen.

Während der Teig ruht, eine 22 cm x 11 cm (8 1/2 Zoll x 4 1/2 Zoll) große Brotform mit Backspray oder Backfett einfetten.

Mithilfe eines nassen Nylonspatels die Wand des Behälters freischaben und den Teig von der Behälterwand in die Mitte der Mixtur schieben. Den Deckel wieder aufsetzen.

Die schnellste Geschwindigkeitsstufe auswählen. Das Gerät fünfmal hintereinander schnell ein- und ausschalten. Sollte der Teig besonders trocken sein, esslöffelweise zusätzliches Wasser hinzugeben. Die Prozedur fünf Mal wiederholen und die Behälterwand freischaben, bis der Teig eine weiche, elastische Masse gebildet hat.

Um den Teig leichter aus dem Behälter lösen zu können, Gerät fünfmal ein- und ausschalten (dadurch wird der Teig an- und von den Klingen abgehoben) und den Behälter anschließend schnell kopfüber über die vorbereitete Form halten. Teig in die Form fallen lassen und mithilfe eines feuchten Spatels Teigreste ausschaben.

Mit leicht bemehlten Fingern oder einem eingeölten Spatel den Laib unter leichtem Druck gleichmäßig in der Form verteilen.

Kolonialbrot (Laibform) *(Fortsetzung)*	Den Laib mit einem sauberen und trockenen Geschirrtuch bedecken und ihn etwa 18 bis 20 Minuten gehen lassen, bis er den oberen Rand der Form erreicht hat. Den Teig vor dem Backen mit 3 schnellen, schrägen Schnitten mit einem gezahnten Messer einschneiden. Das Brot im vorgeheizten Ofen bei 190 °C (375 °F) 25 bis 30 Minuten oder bis das Brot eine Innentemperatur von 88 °C (190 °F) aufweist (mit Backthermometer messen) backen. 10 Minuten lang auf einem Kuchengitter auskühlen lassen und dann vorsichtig aus der Form lösen. Brot erst anschneiden, wenn es vollständig abgekühlt ist.

Nährwertinformationen pro Portion (1 Scheibe): 134 kcal (15% aus Fett, 11% aus Eiweiß, 74% aus Kohlenhydraten)
4 g Eiweiß • 2 g Fett insgesamt • 0 g gesättigte Fettsäuren • 25 g Kohlenhydrate • 2 g Ballaststoffe
3 g Zucker • 111 mg Natrium • 18 mg Cholesterin

Kolonialbrot nach dem Abkühlen in Scheiben schneiden ... wunderbare Konsistenz und geht sehr gut auf.

BUTTERMILCH-VOLLKORNWEIZENBRÖTCHEN

Zubereitung: 20 Minuten • Verarbeitung: 15 Sekunden • Backzeit: 18-22 Minuten
ergibt: 16 Brötchen

1/3 Tasse (80 ml) warmes Wasser, 40 °C bis 46 °C (105 °F-115 °F)

1 1/2 Esslöffel Honig

1 Packung (1 Esslöffel) aktive Trockenhefe

2 1/2 Tassen (300 g) fein gemahlenes Vollkornweizenmehl

1 Teelöffel Salz

2 Esslöffel (28 g) ungesalzene Butter, Zimmertemperatur

2/3 Tasse (160 ml) Buttermilch, Zimmertemperatur

1 großes Ei, leicht verquirlt

Hefe ansetzen, indem warmes Wasser, Honig und Hefe vermischt werden. Alles zügig umrühren. Die Mischung für 5 Minuten beiseitestellen.

Das Vollkornweizenmehl und das Salz in den Vitamix DRY BLADE-Behälter geben und den Deckel schließen.

Variable 1 auswählen.

Das Gerät einschalten und die Geschwindigkeit langsam auf Variable 10 erhöhen.

Die Mischung etwa 5 Sekunden lang rühren, bis sich in der Mitte ein Loch bildet.

Variable 3 auswählen. Gerät einschalten und den Stöpsel aus dem Deckel nehmen. Butter, Buttermilch, Ei und Hefemischung durch die Öffnung im Deckel hinzugeben. Das Gerät ausschalten und den Stöpsel wieder einsetzen.

Die schnellste Geschwindigkeitsstufe auswählen. Das Gerät zwei Mal hintereinander schnell ein- und wieder ausschalten. Das Gerät ausschalten und den Stöpsel abnehmen.

Während der Teig geht, eine 20 cm (8 Zoll) große quadratische Backform mit Backspray oder Backfett dünn einfetten oder ein Backblech mit Backpapier auslegen (abhängig von der Form Ihrer Brötchen).

Mithilfe eines nassen Nylonspatels die Wand des Behälters freischaben und den Teig von der Behälterwand in die Mitte der Mixtur schieben. Den Deckel wieder aufsetzen.

Die schnellste Geschwindigkeitsstufe auswählen. Das Gerät fünfmal hintereinander schnell ein- und ausschalten. Sollte der Teig besonders trocken sein, esslöffelweise zusätzliches Wasser hinzugeben. Die Prozedur fünf Mal wiederholen bzw. bis der Teig eine weiche, elastische Masse gebildet hat.

Den Behälter mit dem Deckel verschließen und Teig etwa 25 bis 30 Minuten gehen lassen, bis er ungefähr doppelt so groß geworden ist.

Den Teig mit einem Nylonspatel zusammenkneten. Den Behälter erneut verschließen und den Teig weitere 20 Minuten gehen lassen, bis er seine Größe erneut verdoppelt hat.

Teig auf eine leicht bemehlte Knetfläche geben und vorsichtig eine 40 cm (16 Zoll) große Rolle formen; anschließend in 16 gleichgroße Stücke schneiden. Nach Belieben Brötchen formen; in Backform oder auf Backblech legen.

Buttermilch-Vollkornweizenbrötchen *(Fortsetzung)*

Die Brötchen mit einem sauberen und trockenen Geschirrtuch bedecken und sie etwa 35 bis 45 Minuten gehen lassen, bis sie ungefähr doppelt so groß geworden sind.

Im vorgeheizten Backofen bei 190 °C (375 °F) 18 bis 22 Minuten backen, bis die Brötchen eine leichte Bräunung haben. Auf Kuchengitter abkühlen lassen.

NährwertInformationen pro Portion (1 Brötchen): 95 kcal (21% aus Fett, 15% aus Eiweiß, 64% aus Kohlenhydraten) 4 g Eiweiß • 2 g Fett insgesamt • 1 g gesättigte Fettsäuren • 16 g Kohlenhydrate • 2 g Ballaststoffe • 3 g Zucker 111 mg Natrium • 18 mg Cholesterin

Um eine leckere Kruste zu bekommen, 2 Esslöffel (30 ml) geschmolzene Butter mit 3 Esslöffeln (45 ml) Honig vermischen. Die Brötchen aus dem Ofen holen, sobald sie fertig sind und die heißen Brötchen rasch mit der Butter-Honig-Mischung glasieren. Abkühlen lassen und anschließend servieren.

Buttermilch-Vollkornweizenbrötchen

ZIMT-ROSINEN-BROT

Zubereitung: 30 Minuten • Verarbeitung: 40 Sekunden • Backzeit: 30-40 Minuten
ergibt: 1 Laib (12 Scheiben)

1/2 Tasse (120 ml) warmes Wasser, 40-46 °C (105 °F-115 °F)

1/4 Tasse (50 g) Kristallzucker

1 Packung (1 Esslöffel) aktive Trockenhefe

1/2 Tasse (112 g) cremigen Hüttenkäse

1 Esslöffel (14 g) ungesalzene Butter, Zimmertemperatur

2 Teelöffel gemahlener Zimt

3/4 Teelöffel Salz

1 großes Ei

2 Tassen (275 g) Mehl Type 812, wird aufgeteilt

1/2 Tasse (104 g) geröstete Weizenkeime

1/2 Tasse (72 g) Rosinen, 30 Minuten lang in heißem Wasser eingeweicht und anschließend gut abgetropft, werden aufgeteilt

Hefe ansetzen, indem warmes Wasser, Zucker und Hefe vermischt werden. Alles zügig umrühren. Die Mischung für 5 Minuten beiseitestellen.

Hüttenkäse, Butter, Zimt, Salz und Ei in den Vitamix WET BLADE-Behälter geben und Deckel schließen.

Variable 1 auswählen.

Das Gerät einschalten und die Geschwindigkeit langsam auf Variable 10 erhöhen.

Die Masse 10 Sekunden lang verrühren. Anhalten und Behälterwand abschaben.

Variable 3 auswählen. Gerät einschalten und den Stöpsel aus dem Deckel nehmen. 1 Tasse (137 g) Mehl und die Hefemischung durch die Öffnung im Deckel hinzugeben. Die Masse 30 Sekunden lang verkneten. Das Gerät ausschalten und den Stöpsel abnehmen.

Das verbleibende Mehl, Weizenkeime und 1/4 Tasse (72 g) eingeweichte/abgetropfte Rosinen in den Vitamix-Behälter geben und Deckel schließen.

Die schnellste Geschwindigkeitsstufe auswählen. Das Gerät zwei Mal hintereinander schnell ein- und wieder ausschalten. Das Gerät ausschalten und den Stöpsel abnehmen.

Während der Teig ruht, eine 22 cm x 11 cm (8 1/2 Zoll x 4 1/2 Zoll) große Brotform mit Backspray oder Backfett einfetten.

Mithilfe eines nassen Nylonspatels die Wand des Behälters freischaben und den Teig von der Behälterwand in die Mitte der Mixtur schieben. Verbleibende Rosinen hinzugeben und Deckel schließen.

Die schnellste Geschwindigkeitsstufe auswählen. Das Gerät fünfmal hintereinander schnell ein- und ausschalten. Sollte der Teig besonders trocken sein, esslöffelweise zusätzliches Wasser hinzugeben. Die Prozedur fünf Mal wiederholen und die Behälterwand freischaben, bis der Teig eine weiche, elastische Masse gebildet hat.

Um den Teig leichter aus dem Behälter lösen zu können, Gerät fünfmal ein- und ausschalten (dadurch wird der Teig an- und von den Klingen abgehoben) und den Behälter anschließend schnell kopfüber über die vorbereitete Form halten. Teig in die Form fallen lassen und mithilfe eines feuchten Spatels Teigreste ausschaben.

Zimt-Rosinen-Brot
(Fortsetzung)

Mit leicht bemehlten Fingern oder einem eingeölten Spatel den Laib unter leichtem Druck gleichmäßig in der Form verteilen.

Den Laib mit einem sauberen und trockenen Geschirrtuch bedecken und ihn etwa 25 bis 35 Minuten gehen lassen, bis er den oberen Rand der Form erreicht hat. Den Teig vor dem Backen mit 3 schnellen, schrägen Schnitten mit einem gezahnten Messer einschneiden.

Das Brot im vorgeheizten Ofen bei 190 °C (375 °F) 30 bis 40 Minuten oder bis das Brot eine Innentemperatur von 88 °C (190 °F) aufweist (mit Backthermometer messen) backen. 10 Minuten lang auf einem Kuchengitter auskühlen lassen und dann vorsichtig aus der Form lösen. Brot erst anschneiden, wenn es vollständig abgekühlt ist.

Nährwertinformationen pro Portion (1 Scheibe): 162 kcal (14 % aus Fett, 15 % aus Eiweiß, 72 % aus Kohlenhydraten)
6 g Eiweiß • 3 g Fett insgesamt • 1 g gesättigte Fettsäuren • 30 g Kohlenhydrate • 2 g Ballaststoffe • 8 g Zucker
165 mg Natrium • 20 mg Cholesterin

Die Rosinen lassen sich im Teig nicht völlig gleichmäßig verteilen. Das gibt dem Brot noch einen zusätzlichen hausgemachten Charme.

FÜNFKORNPIZZA

Zubereitung: 20 Minuten • Verarbeitung: 35 Sekunden • Backzeit: 16–20 Minuten
ergibt: 1 Pizza (8 Stücke)

1 Tasse (240 ml) warmes Wasser, 40 °C bis 46 °C (105 °F-115 °F)

2 Teelöffel brauner Zucker

1 Packung (1 Esslöffel) aktive Trockenhefe

3/4 Tasse (94 g) Mehl Type 550

3/4 Tasse (90 g) + 1 Teelöffel Vollkornmehl (Type 1600)

1/4 Tasse (26 g) helles Roggenmehl (Type 1150)

2 Esslöffel (15 g) Dinkelmehl

2 Esslöffel (15 g) Gerstenmehl

2 Esslöffel (21 g) Leinsamenkörner oder gemahlenen Leinsamen

2 Esslöffel (15 g) Vollkorn-Maismehl plus zusätzliches Maismehl, um das Pizzablech zu bestäuben

1/2 Teelöffel Salz

1 Esslöffel Olivenöl

Belag:

2 Esslöffel (30 ml) Olivenöl

1/3 Tasse (33 g) frisch geriebenen Parmesan

1 1/3 Tassen (320 g) Pizzasoße

Weitere Beläge nach Wunsch

1 1/4 Tassen (141 g) geriebenen Mozzarella

Die Hefe ansetzen, indem warmes Wasser, brauner Zucker und Hefe vermischt werden. Alles zügig umrühren. Die Mischung für 5 Minuten beiseitestellen.

Das gesamte Mehl (Brot-, Vollkornweizen-, Roggen-, Dinkel- und Gerstenmehl), Leinsamen, Maismehl und Salz in der angegebenen Reihenfolge in den Vitamix DRY BLADE-Behälter geben und Deckel schließen.

Variable 1 auswählen.

Das Gerät einschalten und die Geschwindigkeit langsam auf Variable 10 erhöhen.

Die Masse etwa 20 Sekunden lang verkneten, bis sich ein Teig gebildet hat und sich in der Mitte der Zutaten ein Loch formt. Das Gerät anhalten.

Variable 1 auswählen und Deckel schließen. Das Gerät einschalten und die Geschwindigkeit langsam auf Variable 6 erhöhen. Die Hefemischung und das Olivenöl durch die Öffnung im Deckel hinzugeben. Das Gerät ausschalten und den Stöpsel wieder einsetzen.

Die schnellste Geschwindigkeitsstufe auswählen. Das Gerät zwei Mal hintereinander schnell ein- und wieder ausschalten. Das Gerät ausschalten und den Stöpsel abnehmen.

Während der Teig geht, das Pizzablech mit dem zusätzlichen Maismehl leicht bedecken.

Mithilfe eines nassen Nylonspatels die Wand des Behälters freischaben und den Teig von der Behälterwand in die Mitte der Mixtur schieben. Den Deckel wieder aufsetzen.

Die schnellste Geschwindigkeitsstufe auswählen. Das Gerät fünfmal hintereinander schnell ein- und ausschalten. Sollte der Teig besonders trocken sein, esslöffelweise zusätzliches Wasser hinzugeben. Die Prozedur fünf Mal wiederholen und die Behälterwand freischaben, bis der Teig eine weiche, elastische Masse gebildet hat.

Um den Teig leichter aus dem Behälter lösen zu können, Gerät fünfmal ein- und ausschalten (dadurch wird der Teig an- und von den Klingen abgehoben) und den Behälter anschließend schnell kopfüber über eine saubere und mit Mehl bestäubte Arbeitsfläche halten.

Den Teig mit einem sauberen, trockenen Geschirrtuch oder einer umgedrehten Schüssel bedecken und 15 Minuten gehen lassen.

Fünfkornpizza
(Fortsetzung)

Den Teig mit den Handballen zusammenstoßen und eine runde Form beibehalten. Mit einem Nudelholz mit gleichmäßigen Bewegungen von der Mitte aus leicht in alle Richtungen auswellen. Nach jeder Ausrollbewegung den Teig anheben und um eine 1/4-Umdrehung drehen. Der ausgerollte Teig sollte etwa 2,5 cm (1 Zoll) größer sein als Ihr Pizzablech. Den Teig auf das Blech legen. Einen Rand hochdrücken, damit der Belag nicht auslaufen kann.

Den Teig leicht mit Olivenöl bepinseln und anschließend mit dem Parmesan bestreuen. Mit einem Löffel die Pizzasoße darauf geben und mit der Rückseite des Löffels verteilen. Mit den gewünschten Zutaten belegen und anschließend gleichmäßig mit Mozzarella bestreuen.

Im vorgeheizten Backofen auf der untersten Schiene bei 220 °C (425 °F) 16 bis 20 Minuten backen, bis der Boden eine leichte Bräunung hat und der Käse Blasen wirft.

Die Pizza aus dem Ofen nehmen und 5 Minuten warten, damit der Käse fest werden kann. Anschließen in Stücke schneiden.

Nährwertinformationen pro Portion (1 Scheibe, mit Belag): 272 kcal (39% aus Fett, 17% aus Eiweiß, 44% aus Kohlenhydraten) 12 g Eiweiß • 12 g Fett insgesamt • 4 g gesättigte Fettsäuren
30 g Kohlenhydrate • 4 g Ballaststoffe • 5 g Zucker • 551 mg Natrium • 15 mg Cholesterin

Wenn Sie den Teig von der Mitte her nach außen ausrollen, behält er seine runde Grundform.

FRANZÖSISCHES BROT

Zubereitung: 10 Minuten • Verarbeitung: 15 Sekunden • Backzeit: 30–40 Minuten
ergibt: 1 Laib (16-18 Scheiben)

1 Tasse (240 ml) warmes Wasser, wird aufgeteilt, 40 °C bis 46 °C (105 °F-115 °F)

1 Packung (1 Esslöffel) aktive Trockenhefe

2 1/2 Tassen (312 g) Mehl Type 550

1 Teelöffel Salz

1 Esslöffel Olivenöl

2 Esslöffel (15 g) Vollkorn-Maismehl

1 Ei, vermischt mit 1 Esslöffel Wasser (zum Bestreichen des Teigs vor dem Backen)

Hefe ansetzen, indem 1/2 Tasse (120 ml) warmes Wasser und Hefe vermischt werden. Alles zügig umrühren. Die Mischung für 5 Minuten beiseitestellen.

Das Mehl und das Salz in den Vitamix DRY BLADE-Behälter geben und den Deckel schließen.

Variable 1 auswählen.

Das Gerät einschalten und die Geschwindigkeit langsam auf Variable 6 erhöhen.

Die Mischung etwa 5 Sekunden lang rühren, bis sich in der Mitte ein Loch bildet.

Variable 3 auswählen. Gerät einschalten und den Stöpsel aus dem Deckel nehmen. Hefemischung und die verbleibende 1/2 Tasse (120 ml) warmes Wasser durch die Öffnung im Deckel in den Behälter geben. Das Gerät ausschalten und den Stöpsel wieder einsetzen.

Die schnellste Geschwindigkeitsstufe auswählen. Das Gerät zwei Mal hintereinander schnell ein- und wieder ausschalten. Das Gerät ausschalten und den Stöpsel abnehmen.

Während der Teig ruht, eine mittelgroße Rührschüssel mit Olivenöl einfetten und das Maismehl auf ein Backblech streuen.

Mithilfe eines nassen Nylonspatels die Wand des Behälters freischaben und den Teig von der Behälterwand in die Mitte der Mixtur schieben. Den Deckel wieder aufsetzen.

Die schnellste Geschwindigkeitsstufe auswählen. Das Gerät fünfmal hintereinander schnell ein- und ausschalten. Sollte der Teig besonders trocken sein, esslöffelweise zusätzliches Wasser hinzugeben. Die Prozedur fünf Mal wiederholen und die Behälterwand freischaben, bis der Teig eine weiche, elastische Masse gebildet hat.

Um den Teig leichter aus dem Behälter lösen zu können, Gerät fünfmal ein- und ausschalten (dadurch wird der Teig an- und von den Klingen abgehoben) und den Behälter anschließend schnell kopfüber über die vorbereitete Schüssel halten. Mit einem feuchten Spatel den verbleibenden Teig aus der Schüssel kratzen. Den Teig mehrmals umdrehen und gleichmäßig mit dem Öl überziehen. Mit Frischhaltefolie bedecken und etwa 45 Minuten bis 1 Stunde gehen lassen, bis der Teig sich im Umfang fast verdreifacht hat.

Französisches Brot
(Fortsetzung)

Den Teig zusammenstoßen und auf eine bemehlte Arbeitsfläche legen. Bei Bedarf weiteres Mehl hinzugeben, damit der Teig gut zu handhaben, aber dennoch weich ist. Mit einem bemehlten Nudelholz in ein 30 cm x 15 cm (12 Zoll x 6 Zoll) großes Rechteck ausrollen. Von der langen Seite her aufrollen und dabei die Ansatzstellen zusammendrücken und mit Wasser verkleben.

Den Teig mit den Ansatzstellen nach unten auf das vorbereitete Backblech legen. Mit einem sauberen und trockenen Geschirrtuch bedecken und den Teig etwa 45 Minuten bis 1 Stunde gehen lassen, bis er ungefähr doppelt so groß geworden ist.

Den Laib mit der Ei-Mischung einpinseln und die Oberseite mit einem scharfen, gezahnten Messer drei- oder viermal diagonal einschneiden (etwa 1/2 cm / 1/4 Zoll tief).

Das Brot im vorgeheizten Ofen bei 220 °C (425 °F) 30 bis 40 Minuten oder bis das Brot gut gebräunt ist und eine Innentemperatur von 88 °C (190 °F) aufweist (mit Backthermometer messen) backen. Das Backblech 10 Minuten lang auf einem Kuchengitter auskühlen lassen und dann das Brot vorsichtig vom Backblech nehmen. Das Brot erst anschneiden, wenn es vollständig abgekühlt ist.

Nährwertinformationen pro Portion (1 Scheibe): 86 kcal (12 % aus Fett, 12 % aus Eiweiß, 76 % aus Kohlenhydraten)
3 g Eiweiß • 1 g Fett insgesamt • 0 g gesättigte Fettsäuren • 16 g Kohlenhydrate • 1 g Ballaststoffe • 0 g Zucker
152 mg Natrium • 0 mg Cholesterin

Mithilfe eines Metallspatels kann das Brot auf dem Backblech platziert werden.

HAWAIIANISCHES BROT

Zubereitung: 15 Minuten • Verarbeitung: 25 Sekunden • Backzeit: 35–40 Minuten
ergibt: 1 Laib (8-10 Scheiben)

2 Esslöffel (30 ml) warmes Wasser, 40 °C bis 46 °C (105 °F-115 °F)

1/2 Tasse (120 ml) warme Milch 40 °C bis 46 °C (105 °F-115 °F)

1 Packung (1 Esslöffel) aktive Trockenhefe

1/2 Teelöffel plus 1/2 Tasse (100 g) Zucker, wird aufgeteilt

2 1/2 Tassen (312 g) Mehl Type 550

1/4 Teelöffel Salz

1/4 Tasse (56 g) ungesalzene Butter, geschmolzen

2 große Eier, verquirlt

1 großes Ei, verquirlt mit 1 Teelöffel Wasser (zum Bestreichen des Teigs vor dem Backen)

Zusätzlich Zucker zum Bestäuben des Laibs

Hefe ansetzen, indem warmes Wasser, warme Milch, Hefe und 1/2 Teelöffel des Zuckers vermischt werden. Alles zügig umrühren. Die Mischung für 5 Minuten beiseitestellen.

Mehl, 1/2 Tasse (100 g) Zucker und Salz in den Vitamix DRY BLADE-Behälter geben und den Deckel schließen.

Variable 1 auswählen.

Das Gerät einschalten und die Geschwindigkeit langsam auf Variable 6 erhöhen.

Die Mischung etwa 5 Sekunden lang rühren, bis sich in der Mitte ein Loch bildet.

Variable 3 auswählen. Gerät einschalten und den Stöpsel aus dem Deckel nehmen. Geschmolzene Butter, Eier und Hefemischung durch die Öffnung im Deckel hinzugeben. Das Gerät ausschalten und den Stöpsel wieder einsetzen.

Die schnellste Geschwindigkeitsstufe auswählen. Das Gerät zwei Mal hintereinander schnell ein- und wieder ausschalten. Das Gerät ausschalten und den Stöpsel abnehmen.

Während der Teig ruht, eine 23 cm (9 Zoll) große Kuchenform mit Backspray oder Backfett dünn einfetten.

Mithilfe eines nassen Nylonspatels die Wand des Behälters freischaben und den Teig von der Behälterwand in die Mitte der Mixtur schieben. Den Deckel wieder aufsetzen.

Die schnellste Geschwindigkeitsstufe auswählen. Das Gerät fünfmal hintereinander schnell ein- und ausschalten. Sollte der Teig besonders trocken sein, esslöffelweise zusätzliches Wasser hinzugeben. Die Prozedur fünf Mal wiederholen und die Behälterwand freischaben, bis der Teig eine weiche, elastische Masse gebildet hat.

Um den Teig leichter aus dem Behälter lösen zu können, Gerät fünfmal ein- und ausschalten (dadurch wird der Teig an- und von den Klingen abgehoben) und den Behälter anschließend schnell kopfüber über die eingefettete Schüssel halten (mit einem feuchten Spatel den verbleibenden Teig aus der Schüssel kratzen) und den Teig mehrmals wenden, um ihn gleichmäßig mit Zucker zu bedecken.

Schüssel mit Frischhaltefolie (vorher mit Backfett einsprühen) bedecken. Den Teig 40 bis 45 Minuten gehen lassen, bis er seine Größe verdoppelt hat.

Hawaiianisches Brot *(Fortsetzung)*	Teig zusammenstoßen und auf eine bemehlte Arbeitsfläche geben. Erneut 1 bis 2 Minuten lang durchkneten. In die vorbereitete Form geben und mit leicht bemehlten Fingern oder einem eingeölten Spatel den Laib unter leichtem Druck gleichmäßig in der Form verteilen. Den Teig mit einem sauberen und trockenen Geschirrtuch bedecken und etwa 40 Minuten gehen lassen, bis er ungefähr doppelt so groß geworden ist. Vor dem Backen die Oberfläche mit der verquirlten Ei-Mischung einpinseln und mit Zucker besprenkeln. Im vorgeheizten Ofen bei 180 °C (350 °F) 35 bis 40 Minuten oder bis das Brot eine goldene Farbe hat und eine Innentemperatur von 88 °C (190 °F) aufweist (mit Backthermometer messen) backen. Auf einem Kuchengitter abkühlen lassen.

Nährwertinformationen pro Portion (1 Scheibe): 233 kcal (29% aus Fett, 10% aus Eiweiß, 61% aus Kohlenhydraten)
6 g Eiweiß • 7 g Fett insgesamt • 4 g gesättigte Fettsäuren • 35 g Kohlenhydrate • 1 g Ballaststoffe • 11 g Zucker
126 mg Natrium • 76 mg Cholesterin

HERZHAFTES MEHRKORNBROT

Zubereitung: 20 Minuten • Verarbeitung: 25 Sekunden • Backzeit: 40–50 Minuten
ergibt: 1 Laib (12 Scheiben)

1 1/4 Tassen (300 ml) warmes Wasser, 40 °C bis 46 °C (105 °F-115 °F)

1 Esslöffel Honig

1 Packung (1 Esslöffel) aktive Trockenhefe

1 1/2 Tassen (156 g) Mehl Type 550

1/2 Tasse (60 g) Vollkornmehl (Type 1600)

1/4 Tasse (26 g) helles Roggenmehl (Type 1150)

1 Esslöffel Weizenkeime

1 Esslöffel Haferflocken

2 Teelöffel Vollkorn-Weizenmehl

2 Teelöffel Hirse

2 Teelöffel Gerstenmehl

2 Teelöffel Buchweizenmehl

1/4 Teelöffel gemahlenen Leinsamen

1/2 Teelöffel Salz

1 Esslöffel helles Olivenöl oder Traubenkernöl

1 Esslöffel Sonnenblumenkerne

1 Esslöffel Melasse

1/4 Teelöffel Sesamkörner, zum Bestreuen

Hefe ansetzen, indem warmes Wasser, Honig und Hefe vermischt werden. Alles zügig umrühren. Die Mischung für 5 Minuten beiseitestellen.

Brotmehl, Vollkornweizenmehl, Roggenmehl, Weizenkeime, Haferflocken, Maismehl, Hirse, Gerstemehl, Buchweizenmehl, gemahlenen Leinsamen und Salz in den Vitamix DRY BLADE-Behälter geben und Deckel schließen.

Variable 1 auswählen.

Das Gerät einschalten und die Geschwindigkeit langsam auf Variable 6 erhöhen.

Die Mischung etwa 5 Sekunden lang rühren, bis sich in der Mitte ein Loch bildet.

Variable 3 auswählen. Gerät einschalten und den Stöpsel aus dem Deckel nehmen. Öl, Sonnenblumenkerne, Melasse und Hefemischung durch die Öffnung im Deckel hinzufügen. Das Gerät ausschalten und den Stöpsel wieder einsetzen.

Die schnellste Geschwindigkeitsstufe auswählen. Das Gerät zwei Mal hintereinander schnell ein- und wieder ausschalten. Das Gerät ausschalten und den Stöpsel abnehmen.

Während der Teig ruht, eine 22 cm x 11 cm (8 1/2 Zoll x 4 1/2 Zoll) große Brotform mit Backspray oder Backfett einfetten.

Mithilfe eines nassen Nylonspatels die Wand des Behälters freischaben und den Teig von der Behälterwand in die Mitte der Mixtur schieben. Den Deckel wieder aufsetzen.

Die schnellste Geschwindigkeitsstufe auswählen. Das Gerät fünfmal hintereinander schnell ein- und ausschalten. Sollte der Teig besonders trocken sein, esslöffelweise zusätzliches Wasser hinzugeben. Die Prozedur fünf Mal wiederholen und die Behälterwand freischaben, bis der Teig eine weiche, elastische Masse gebildet hat.

Um den Teig leichter aus dem Behälter lösen zu können, Gerät fünfmal ein- und ausschalten (dadurch wird der Teig an- und von den Klingen abgehoben) und den Behälter anschließend schnell kopfüber über die vorbereitete Form halten. Teig in die Form fallen lassen und mithilfe eines feuchten Spatels Teigreste ausschaben.

Mit leicht bemehlten Fingern oder einem eingeölten Spatel den Laib unter leichtem Druck gleichmäßig in der Form verteilen.

Herzhaftes Mehrkornbrot *(Fortsetzung)*	Den Laib mit einem sauberen und trockenen Geschirrtuch bedecken und ihn etwa 25 bis 30 Minuten gehen lassen, bis er den oberen Rand der Form erreicht hat. Den Teig vor dem Backen mit 3 schnellen, schrägen Schnitten mit einem gezahnten Messer einschneiden. Mit 1/4 Teelöffel Sesamkörner bestreuen Das Brot im vorgeheizten Ofen bei 180 °C (350 °F) 40 bis 50 Minuten oder bis das Brot eine Innentemperatur von 88 °C (190 °F) aufweist (mit Backthermometer messen) backen. 10 Minuten lang auf einem Kuchengitter auskühlen lassen und dann vorsichtig aus der Form lösen. Brot erst anschneiden, wenn es vollständig abgekühlt ist.

Nährwertinformationen pro Portion (1 Scheibe): 119 kcal (13% aus Fett, 11% aus Eiweiß, 75% aus Kohlenhydraten)
3 g Eiweiß • 2 g Fett insgesamt • 0 g gesättigte Fettsäuren • 23 g Kohlenhydrate • 2 g Ballaststoffe • 3 g Zucker
101 mg Natrium • 0 mg Cholesterin

Sollten Sie einige der oben aufgeführten Spezialgetreide oder -mehle nicht zur Hand haben, können Sie diese stattdessen durch Vollkornweizenmehl oder ein beliebiges anderes Spezialmehl ersetzen. (Denken Sie daran, dass Ihr Gerät jedes der oben genannten Getreide zu Mehl mahlen kann.)

HAFERKLEIE-BROT

Zubereitung: 10 Minuten • Verarbeitung: 30 Sekunden • Backzeit: 30-35 Minuten
ergibt: 1 Laib (12 Scheiben)

1 Eiweiß und genug warmes Wasser, 40 °C bis 46 °C (105 °F-115 °F), für 1 1/4 Tassen (300 ml)

2 Esslöffel (30 ml) Melasse

1 Packung (1 Esslöffel) aktive Trockenhefe

1-1 1/4 Tassen (80-100g) Haferkleie (Haferflocken)

1 1/4 Tassen (150 g) Vollkornweizenmehl (Type 1600)

1 Tasse (125 g) Mehl Type 550

1 Teelöffel Salz

1 Esslöffel helles Olivenöl oder Traubenkernöl

Hefe ansetzen, indem warmes Wasser, Melasse und Hefe vermischt werden. Alles zügig umrühren. Die Mischung für 5 Minuten beiseitestellen.

Haferkleie, Mehle und Salz in den Vitamix DRY BLADE-Behälter geben und den Deckel schließen.

Variable 1 auswählen.

Das Gerät einschalten und die Geschwindigkeit langsam auf Variable 6 erhöhen.

Solange verkneten, bis sich in der Mitte der Mehlmischung ein Loch bildet (etwa 10 Sekunden lang). Bei Bedarf den Stopfer verwenden.

Variable 3 auswählen. Gerät einschalten und den Stöpsel aus dem Deckel nehmen. Die Hefemischung und das Öl durch die Öffnung im Deckel hinzugeben. Das Gerät ausschalten und den Stöpsel wieder einsetzen.

Die schnellste Geschwindigkeitsstufe auswählen. Das Gerät zwei Mal hintereinander schnell ein- und wieder ausschalten. Das Gerät ausschalten und den Stöpsel abnehmen.

Während der Teig ruht, eine 22 cm x 11 cm (8 1/2 Zoll x 4 1/2 Zoll) große Brotform mit Backspray oder Backfett einfetten.

Mithilfe eines nassen Nylonspatels die Wand des Behälters freischaben und den Teig von der Behälterwand in die Mitte der Mixtur schieben. Den Deckel wieder aufsetzen.

Die schnellste Geschwindigkeitsstufe auswählen. Das Gerät fünfmal hintereinander schnell ein- und ausschalten. Sollte der Teig besonders trocken sein, esslöffelweise zusätzliches Wasser hinzugeben. Die Prozedur fünf Mal wiederholen und die Behälterwand freischaben, bis der Teig eine weiche, elastische Masse gebildet hat.

Um den Teig leichter aus dem Behälter lösen zu können, Gerät fünfmal ein- und ausschalten (dadurch wird der Teig an- und von den Klingen abgehoben) und den Behälter anschließend schnell kopfüber über die vorbereitete Form halten. Teig in die Form fallen lassen und mithilfe eines feuchten Spatels Teigreste ausschaben.

Mit leicht bemehlten Fingern oder einem eingeölten Spatel den Laib unter leichtem Druck gleichmäßig in der Form verteilen.

Haferkleie-Brot *(Fortsetzung)*	Den Laib mit einem sauberen und trockenen Geschirrtuch bedecken und ihn etwa 15 bis 18 Minuten gehen lassen, bis er den oberen Rand der Form erreicht hat. Den Teig vor dem Backen mit 3 schnellen, schrägen Schnitten mit einem gezahnten Messer einschneiden. Das Brot im vorgeheizten Ofen bei 180 °C (350 °F) 30 bis 35 Minuten oder bis das Brot eine Innentemperatur von 88 °C (190 °F) aufweist (mit Backthermometer messen) backen. 10 Minuten lang auf einem Kuchengitter auskühlen lassen und dann vorsichtig aus der Form lösen. Brot erst anschneiden, wenn es vollständig abgekühlt ist.

Nährwertinformationen pro Portion (1 Scheibe): 124 kcal (13 % aus Fett, 14 % aus Eiweiß, 73 % aus Kohlenhydraten)
5 g Eiweiß • 2 g Fett insgesamt • 0 g gesättigte Fettsäuren • 25 g Kohlenhydrate • 3 g Ballaststoffe • 2 g Zucker
8 mg Natrium • 0 mg Cholesterin

ROGGEN-FOCACCIA

Zubereitung: 15 Minuten • Verarbeitung: 30 Sekunden • Backzeit: 35–40 Minuten
ergibt: 1 Laib (8-10 Scheiben)

3/4 Tasse (180 ml) warmes Wasser, 40 °C bis 46 °C (105 °F-115 °F)

1 Esslöffel Kristallzucker

1 Packung (1 Esslöffel) aktive Trockenhefe

1 1/2 Tassen (188 g) Mehl Type 550

1 Tasse (104 g) helles Roggenmehl (Type 1150)

1/2 Tasse (66 g) grob gehackten Schweizer Käse

1 Teelöffel Salz

1 Esslöffel Dillkraut

1 Esslöffel Kümmelkörner

3/4 Tasse (180 ml) Buttermilch, Zimmertemperatur

Zusätzlich für den Belag:

2 Esslöffel (30 ml) natives (kalt gepresstes) Olivenöl

1 1/2 Teelöffel koscheres Salz

1/2 Tasse (66 g) grob gehackten Schweizer Käse

1 Teelöffel Dillkraut

Hefe ansetzen, indem warmes Wasser, Zucker und Hefe vermischt werden. Alles zügig umrühren. Die Mischung für 5 Minuten beiseitestellen.

Mehle, Käse, Salz, Dill und Kümmel in den Vitamix DRY BLADE-Behälter geben und den Deckel schließen.

Variable 1 auswählen.

Das Gerät einschalten und die Geschwindigkeit langsam auf Variable 10 erhöhen.

Die Masse 15 Sekunden vermischen. Die Geschwindigkeit auf Variable 6 reduzieren und die Mischung etwa 5 Sekunden lang verrühren, bis sich in der Mitte ein Loch bildet. Das Gerät anhalten.

Variable 1 auswählen und Deckel schließen. Das Gerät einschalten und die Geschwindigkeit langsam auf Variable 6 erhöhen. Buttermilch und Hefemischung durch die Öffnung im Deckel hinzugeben. Das Gerät ausschalten und den Stöpsel wieder einsetzen.

Die schnellste Geschwindigkeitsstufe auswählen. Das Gerät zwei Mal hintereinander schnell ein- und wieder ausschalten. Das Gerät ausschalten und den Stöpsel abnehmen.

Während der Teig ruht, eine 23 cm (9 Zoll) große Kuchenform mit Backspray oder Backfett einfetten.

Mithilfe eines nassen Nylonspatels die Wand des Behälters freischaben und den Teig von der Behälterwand in die Mitte der Mixtur schieben. Den Deckel wieder aufsetzen.

Die schnellste Geschwindigkeitsstufe auswählen. Das Gerät fünfmal hintereinander schnell ein- und ausschalten. Sollte der Teig besonders trocken sein, esslöffelweise zusätzliches Wasser hinzugeben. Die Prozedur fünf Mal wiederholen und die Behälterwand freischaben, bis der Teig eine weiche, elastische Masse gebildet hat.

Um den Teig leichter aus dem Behälter lösen zu können, Gerät fünfmal ein- und ausschalten (dadurch wird der Teig an- und von den Klingen abgehoben) und den Behälter anschließend schnell kopfüber über die vorbereitete Form halten. Teig in die Form fallen lassen und mithilfe eines feuchten Spatels Teigreste ausschaben.

Mit leicht bemehlten Fingern oder einem eingeölten Spatel den Laib unter leichtem Druck gleichmäßig in der Form verteilen.

Roggen-Focaccia *(Fortsetzung)*	Die Form mit einem sauberen und trockenen Geschirrtuch bedecken und ihn etwa 30 Minuten gehen lassen, bis er den oberen Rand der Form erreicht hat. Vor dem Backen den Teig mit sauberen Fingerspitzen eindrücken und anschließend mit Olivenöl einpinseln. Mit koscherem Salz, Dillkraut und verbleibendem Schweizer Käse besprenkeln. Das Brot im vorgeheizten Ofen bei 180 °C (350 °F) 35 bis 40 Minuten oder bis das Brot eine Innentemperatur von 88 °C (190 °F) aufweist (mit Backthermometer messen) backen. Das Brot 10 Minuten lang auf einem Kuchengitter auskühlen lassen und es dann vorsichtig aus der Form lösen. Brot erst anschneiden, wenn es vollständig abgekühlt ist.

Nährwertinformationen pro Portion (1 Scheibe): 202 kcal (32 % aus Fett, 15 % aus Eiweiß, 52 % aus Kohlenhydraten)
8 g Eiweiß • 7 g Fett insgesamt • 3 g gesättigte Fettsäuren • 26 g Kohlenhydrate • 3 g Ballaststoffe • 3 g Zucker
448 mg Natrium • 14 mg Cholesterin

Roggenteige sind stets klebriger und schwieriger zu bearbeiten als Weizenteige. Haben Sie also Geduld und fügen Sie nicht zu viel Mehl hinzu, wenn der Teig noch etwas klebrig ist. Sonst wird das Brot zu fest.

WEICHE BREZELN

Zubereitung: 10 Minuten • Verarbeitung: 15 Sekunden • Backzeit: 8–10 Minuten • ergibt: 12 Brezeln

3/4 Tasse (180 ml) warmes Wasser, 40 °C bis 46 °C (105 °F-115 °F)

1/4 Tasse (55 g) brauner Zucker

1 Packung (1 Esslöffel) aktive Trockenhefe

1/4 Tasse (30 g) Vollkornmehl (Type 1600)

1/2 Tasse (62 g) Mehl Type 550

1 1/2 Tassen (205 g) Brotmehl Type 812 (hoher Glutengehalt)

eine Prise Salz

1 großes Ei, vermischt mit 2 Esslöffeln (30 ml) Wasser (zum Bestreichen des Teigs vor dem Backen)

Koscheres Salz

Die Hefe ansetzen, indem warmes Wasser, brauner Zucker und Hefe vermischt werden. Alles zügig umrühren. Die Mischung für 5 Minuten beiseitestellen.

Das gesamte Mehl und das Salz in den Vitamix DRY BLADE-Behälter geben und den Deckel schließen.

Variable 1 auswählen.

Das Gerät einschalten und die Geschwindigkeit langsam auf Variable 6 erhöhen.

Die Mischung etwa 5 Sekunden lang rühren, bis sich in der Mitte ein Loch bildet.

Variable 3 auswählen. Gerät einschalten und den Stöpsel aus dem Deckel nehmen. Die Hefemischung durch die Öffnung im Deckel hinzugeben. Das Gerät ausschalten und den Stöpsel wieder einsetzen.

Die schnellste Geschwindigkeitsstufe auswählen. Das Gerät zwei Mal hintereinander schnell ein- und wieder ausschalten. Das Gerät ausschalten und den Stöpsel abnehmen.

Während der Teig ruht, ein Backblech dünn mit Backspray oder Backfett einfetten.

Mithilfe eines nassen Nylonspatels die Wand des Behälters freischaben und den Teig von der Behälterwand in die Mitte der Mixtur schieben. Den Deckel wieder aufsetzen.

Die schnellste Geschwindigkeitsstufe auswählen. Das Gerät fünfmal hintereinander schnell ein- und ausschalten. Sollte der Teig besonders trocken sein, esslöffelweise zusätzliches Wasser hinzugeben. Die Prozedur fünf Mal wiederholen und die Behälterwand freischaben, bis der Teig eine weiche, elastische Masse gebildet hat.

Den Teig bei geschlossenem Deckel etwa 15 Minuten gehen lassen, bis er seinen Umfang ungefähr verdoppelt hat.

Den Teig auf eine leicht mit Mehl bestäubte Arbeitsfläche geben und in 12 Stücke aufteilen. Mit den Händen aus jedem Stück eine etwa 30–46 cm (12–18 Zoll) lange Rolle formen. Diese zu einem Oval formen, die Enden verzwirbeln und sie dann vorsichtig ans obere Ende des Ovals pressen.

Weiche Brezeln
(Fortsetzung)

Ei und Wasser miteinander verquirlen. Die Ei-Mischung rasch und vorsichtig auf die Brezeln streichen und diese anschließend mit dem koscheren Salz bestreuen.

Im vorgeheizten Backofen bei 230 °C (450 °F) 8 bis 10 Minuten backen, bis die Brezeln knusprig sind und eine leichte Bräunung haben. Am besten warm servieren.

Nährwertinformationen pro Portion (1 Brezel): 117 kcal (8 % aus Fett, 13 % aus Eiweiß, 79 % aus Kohlenhydraten)
4 g Eiweiß • 1 g Fett insgesamt • 0 g gesättigte Fettsäuren • 23 g Kohlenhydrate • 1 g Ballaststoffe • 5 g Zucker
11 mg Natrium • 18 mg Cholesterin

Besprenkeln Sie die Brezeln vor dem Backen nicht mit grobem Salz, wenn Sie sie später mit Zimt und Zucker garnieren möchten. Bestreichen Sie sie, sobald sie aus dem Ofen kommen, mit geschmolzener Butter und streuen Sie eine Mischung aus Zimt und Zucker darüber.

PIZZA

Zubereitung: 15 Minuten • Verarbeitung: 30 Sekunden • Backzeit: 15–18 Minuten
ergibt: 1 große Pizza (8 Stücke)

1 Tasse (240 ml) warmes Wasser, 40 °C bis 46 °C (105 °F-115 °F)

2 Teelöffel Kristallzucker

1 Packung (1 Esslöffel) aktive Trockenhefe

2 1/2 Tassen (312 g) Mehl Type 550

1/2 Teelöffel Salz

1 Esslöffel helles Olivenöl

2 Esslöffel (15 g) Vollkorn-Maismehl, um das Pizzablech zu bestäuben

Belag:

2 Esslöffel (30 ml) Olivenöl

1/3 Tasse (33 g) frisch geriebenen Parmesan

1 1/3 Tassen (320 g) Pizzasoße

1 1/4 Tassen (141 g) geriebenen Mozzarella

Hefe ansetzen, indem warmes Wasser, Zucker und Hefe vermischt werden. Alles zügig umrühren. Die Mischung für 5 Minuten beiseitestellen.

Mehl und Salz in der angegebenen Reihenfolge in den Vitamix DRY BLADE-Behälter geben und den Deckel schließen.

Variable 1 auswählen.

Das Gerät einschalten und die Geschwindigkeit langsam auf Variable 6 erhöhen.

Die Masse etwa 5 Sekunden lang verkneten, bis sich ein Teig gebildet hat und sich in der Mitte der Zutaten ein Loch formt.

Das Gerät ausschalten und den Stöpsel abnehmen. Variable 1 auswählen. Das Gerät einschalten und die Geschwindigkeit langsam auf Variable 6 erhöhen. Die Hefemischung und das Olivenöl durch die Öffnung im Deckel hinzugeben. Das Gerät ausschalten und den Stöpsel wieder einsetzen.

Die schnellste Geschwindigkeitsstufe auswählen. Das Gerät zwei Mal hintereinander schnell ein- und wieder ausschalten. Das Gerät ausschalten und den Stöpsel abnehmen.

Während der Teig geht, das Pizzablech mit dem Maismehl leicht bedecken.

Mithilfe eines nassen Nylonspatels die Wand des Behälters freischaben und den Teig von der Behälterwand in die Mitte der Mixtur schieben. Den Deckel wieder aufsetzen.

Die schnellste Geschwindigkeitsstufe auswählen. Das Gerät fünfmal hintereinander schnell ein- und ausschalten. Sollte der Teig besonders trocken sein, esslöffelweise zusätzliches Wasser hinzugeben. Die Prozedur fünf Mal wiederholen und die Behälterwand freischaben, bis der Teig eine weiche, elastische Masse gebildet hat.

Um den Teig leichter aus dem Behälter lösen zu können, Gerät fünfmal ein- und ausschalten (dadurch wird der Teig an- und von den Klingen abgehoben) und den Behälter anschließend schnell kopfüber über eine saubere und mit Mehl bestäubte Arbeitsfläche halten.

Den Teig mit einem sauberen, trockenen Geschirrtuch oder einer umgedrehten Schüssel bedecken und 15 Minuten gehen lassen.

Pizza *(Fortsetzung)*

Den Teig mit den Handballen zusammenstoßen und eine runde Form beibehalten. Mit einem Nudelholz mit gleichmäßigen Bewegungen von der Mitte aus leicht in alle Richtungen auswellen. Nach jeder Ausrollbewegung den Teig anheben und um eine 1/4-Umdrehung drehen. Der ausgerollte Teig sollte etwa 2,5 cm (1 Zoll) größer sein als Ihr Pizzablech. Den Teig auf das Blech legen. Einen Rand hochdrücken, damit der Belag nicht auslaufen kann.

Den Teig leicht mit Olivenöl bepinseln und anschließend mit dem Parmesan bestreuen. Mit einem Löffel die Pizzasoße darauf geben und mit der Rückseite des Löffels verteilen. Mit den gewünschten Zutaten belegen und anschließend gleichmäßig mit Mozzarella bestreuen.

Im vorgeheizten Backofen auf der untersten Schiene bei 220 °C (425 °F) 15 bis 18 Minuten backen, bis der Boden eine leichte Bräunung hat und der Käse Blasen wirft.

Die Pizza aus dem Ofen nehmen und 5 Minuten warten, damit der Käse fest werden kann. Anschließen in Stücke schneiden.

Nährwertinformationen pro Portion (1 Scheibe): 319 kcal (35 % aus Fett, 15 % aus Eiweiß, 51 % aus Kohlenhydraten)
12 g Eiweiß • 12 g Fett insgesamt • 4 g gesättigte Fettsäuren • 40 g Kohlenhydrate • 3 g Ballaststoffe • 6 g Zucker
320 mg Natrium • 13 mg Cholesterin

Wenn Sie den Teig von der Mitte her nach außen ausrollen, behält er seine runde Grundform.

Pizza

MOHNZOPF

Zubereitung: 15 Minuten • Verarbeitung: 12 Sekunden • Backzeit: 35-40 Minuten
ergibt: 1 Laib (12 Scheiben)

4 Esslöffel (60 ml) warmes Wasser, 40 °C bis 46 °C (105 °F-115 °F)

1 Packung (1 Esslöffel) aktive Trockenhefe

1/3 Tasse (80 ml) Milch

1/4 Tasse (56 g) ungesalzene Butter

1/3 Tasse (80 ml) Honig

1/2 Teelöffel Salz

1 großes Ei

2 1/4 Tassen (281 g) Mehl Type 550 sowie zusätzliches Mehl für später und zum Ausrollen des Teigs

1 1/3 Tassen (320 g) Mohnfüllung (Rezept siehe Seite 74)

1 großes Ei plus 2 Esslöffel (30 ml) Milch zum Bestreichen des Zopfes

Hefe ansetzen, indem warmes Wasser und Hefe vermischt werden. Alles zügig umrühren. Die Mischung für 5 Minuten beiseitestellen.

Milch in einem kleinen Topf erhitzen und anschließend Butter und Honig hinzugeben; auf 43 °C-46 °C (105 °F-115 °F) abkühlen lassen.

Das Mehl und das Salz in den Vitamix DRY BLADE-Behälter geben und den Deckel schließen.

Variable 1 auswählen.

Das Gerät einschalten und die Geschwindigkeit langsam auf Variable 6 erhöhen.

Die Mischung etwa 5 Sekunden lang verrühren, bis sich in der Mitte ein Loch bildet.

Variable 3 auswählen. Gerät einschalten und den Stöpsel aus dem Deckel nehmen. Ei, Hefemischung und Milchgemisch durch die Öffnung im Deckel hinzugeben. Das Gerät ausschalten und den Stöpsel wieder einsetzen.

Die schnellste Geschwindigkeitsstufe auswählen. Das Gerät zwei Mal hintereinander schnell ein- und wieder ausschalten. Das Gerät ausschalten und den Stöpsel abnehmen.

Während der Teig geht, eine große Schüssel dünn mit Backspray oder Backfett einfetten.

Mit einem feuchten Nylonspachtel die Wände des Vitamix-Behälters abkratzen. Den Teig von den Behälterwänden in die Mitte der Mischung ziehen. Den Deckel wieder aufsetzen.

Die schnellste Geschwindigkeitsstufe auswählen. Das Gerät fünfmal hintereinander schnell ein- und ausschalten. Sollte der Teig besonders trocken sein, esslöffelweise zusätzliches Wasser hinzugeben. Die Prozedur fünf Mal wiederholen und die Behälterwand freischaben, bis der Teig eine weiche, elastische Masse gebildet hat.

Um den Teig aus dem Behälter lösen zu können, Gerät fünfmal ein- und ausschalten (dadurch wird der Teig an- und von den Klingen abgehoben). Den Behälter anschließend kopfüber über die vorbereitete Schüssel halten und den Teig hineinfallen lassen. Den Teig einmal wenden, um die gesamte Oberfläche zu bedecken; mit einem sauberen Geschirrtuch zudecken und 20 bis 30 Minuten gehen lassen.

Den Teig auf eine bemehlte Arbeitsfläche geben. Zu einem großen Rechteck (ca. 23 cm x 38 cm / 9 Zoll x 15 Zoll) ausrollen. Den Teig dabei häufig wenden und mit Mehl bestäuben.

Mohnzopf *(Fortsetzung)*

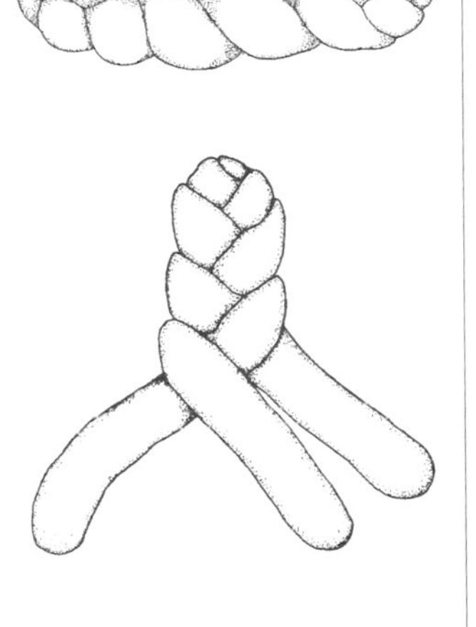

Den Teig längs dritteln, sodass 3 Streifen à 23 cm x 13 cm (9 Zoll x 5 Zoll) entstehen (das geht sehr leicht mit einem Pizzaroller).

Die Mitte jedes Stücks mit der Mohnfüllung bestreichen. Beide Enden der Streifen mit warmem Wasser anfeuchten, ebenso eine lange Seite.

Jedes Drittel der Länge nach rollen, sodass die Mohnsamen wie bei einer Zitronenrolle innen aufgerollt werden. Die feuchten Enden versiegeln und anschließend die beiden Enden des Strangs versiegeln.

Die drei Stränge nebeneinander auf ein mit Backpapier ausgelegtes Backblech legen (mit den Nahtstellen nach unten). Die drei Stränge lose verflechten, damit der Teig Platz hat sich auszudehnen. Die Enden mit den Fingern und etwas zusätzlichem Wasser versiegeln und die versiegelte Stelle unter den Zopf stecken, sodass die Stränge während des Backens nicht auseinandergehen.

Mit einem sauberen, trockenen Geschirrtuch abdecken und etwa 20 bis 25 Minuten gehen lassen.

Die Oberseite des Zopfes mit der Ei-Milch-Mischung einpinseln. Den Zopf im vorgeheizten Ofen bei 180 °C (350 °F) 35 bis 40 Minuten oder bis das Brot eine goldbraune Farbe hat und eine Innentemperatur von 88 °C (190 °F) aufweist (mit Backthermometer messen) backen.

Den Zopf 10 Minuten lang auf einem Kuchengitter auskühlen lassen und ihn dann vorsichtig vom Backblech nehmen. Erst anschneiden, wenn er vollständig abgekühlt ist.

Nährwertinformationen pro Portion (1 Scheibe, mit Füllung): 282 kcal (36 % aus Fett, 10 % aus Eiweiß, 54 % aus Kohlenhydraten) • 7 g Eiweiß • 12 g Fett insgesamt • 4 g gesättigte Fettsäuren • 39 g Kohlenhydrate 2 g Ballaststoffe • 18 g Zucker • 133 mg Natrium • 48 mg Cholesterin

DINKELBROT

Zubereitung: 10 Minuten • Verarbeitung: 1 Minute 30 Sekunden • Backzeit: 35–40 Minuten
ergibt: 1 Laib (12 Scheiben)

1 Tasse (240 ml) warmes Wasser, 40 °C bis 46 °C (105 °F-115 °F)

1 Esslöffel Honig

1 Packung (1 Esslöffel) aktive Trockenhefe

1 3/4 Tassen (315 g) Vollkorndinkel oder 2 1/2 Tasse (180 g) Dinkelmehl

1/2 Teelöffel Salz

1 Esslöffel helles Olivenöl

Hefe ansetzen, indem warmes Wasser, Honig und Hefe vermischt werden. Alles zügig umrühren. Die Mischung für 5 Minuten beiseitestellen.

Für Zubereitung mit Vollkorndinkel: Dinkel und Salz in den Vitamix DRY BLADE-Behälter geben und den Deckel schließen.

Variable 1 auswählen.

Das Gerät einschalten und die Geschwindigkeit langsam auf Variable 10 erhöhen.

1 Minute lang mahlen, dabei den Stopfer durch die Öffnung im Deckel in den Behälter einführen und die Mehlmischung auf die Klingen drücken. Den Stopfer während der letzten 5 Sekunden herausnehmen, damit sich in der Mitte ein Loch bilden kann.

Für Zubereitung mit Dinkelmehl: Dinkelmehl und Salz in den Vitamix DRY BLADE-Behälter geben und den Deckel schließen.

Variable 1 auswählen.

Das Gerät einschalten und die Geschwindigkeit langsam auf Variable 6 erhöhen.

Die Mischung etwa 5 Sekunden lang rühren, bis sich in der Mitte ein Loch bildet.

Variable 3 auswählen. Gerät einschalten und den Stöpsel aus dem Deckel nehmen. Öl und Hefemischung durch die Öffnung im Deckel hinzugeben. Das Gerät ausschalten und den Stöpsel wieder einsetzen.

Den Teig auf Geschwindigkeitsstufe HIGH verkneten. Das Gerät zwei Mal hintereinander schnell ein- und wieder ausschalten. Das Gerät ausschalten und den Stöpsel abnehmen.

Während der Teig ruht, eine 22 cm x 11 cm (8 1/2 Zoll x 4 1/2 Zoll) große Brotform mit Backspray oder Backfett einfetten.

Mithilfe eines nassen Nylonspatels die Wand des Behälters freischaben und den Teig von der Behälterwand in die Mitte der Mixtur schieben. Den Deckel wieder aufsetzen.

Die schnellste Geschwindigkeitsstufe auswählen. Das Gerät fünfmal hintereinander schnell ein- und ausschalten. Sollte der Teig besonders trocken sein, esslöffelweise zusätzliches Wasser hinzugeben. Die Prozedur fünf Mal wiederholen und die Behälterwand freischaben, bis der Teig eine weiche, elastische Masse gebildet hat.

Dinkelbrot *(Fortsetzung)*

Um den Teig leichter aus dem Behälter lösen zu können, Gerät fünfmal ein- und ausschalten (dadurch wird der Teig an- und von den Klingen abgehoben) und den Behälter anschließend schnell kopfüber über die vorbereitete Form halten. Teig in die Form fallen lassen und mithilfe eines feuchten Spatels Teigreste ausschaben.

Mit leicht bemehlten Fingern oder einem eingeölten Spatel den Laib unter leichtem Druck gleichmäßig in der Form verteilen.

Den Laib mit einem sauberen und trockenen Geschirrtuch bedecken und ihn etwa 15 bis 20 Minuten gehen lassen, bis er den oberen Rand der Form erreicht hat. Den Teig vor dem Backen mit 3 schnellen, schrägen Schnitten mit einem gezahnten Messer einschneiden.

Das Brot im vorgeheizten Ofen bei 180 °C (350 °F) 35 bis 40 Minuten oder bis das Brot eine Innentemperatur von 88 °C (190 °F) aufweist, backen. 10 Minuten lang auf einem Kuchengitter auskühlen lassen und dann vorsichtig aus der Form lösen. Brot erst anschneiden, wenn es vollständig abgekühlt ist.

Nährwertinformationen pro Portion (1 Scheibe): 106 kcal (16 % aus Fett, 13 % aus Eiweiß, 71 % aus Kohlenhydraten) • 4 g Eiweiß • 2 g Fett insgesamt • 0 g gesättigte Fettsäuren 21 g Kohlenhydrate • 3 g Ballaststoffe • 3 g Zucker • 99 mg Natrium • 0 mg Cholesterin

Brot, das angeschnitten wird, solange es noch warm ist, ist oftmals im Innern noch feucht; das gilt besonders für Vollkornbrot. Lassen Sie es daher vor dem Anschneiden abkühlen.

SAUERTEIGBROT (EINFACH UND REICHHALTIG)

Zubereitung: 20 Minuten • Verarbeitung: 30 Sekunden • Backzeit: 30-40 Minuten
ergibt: 1 Laib (12 Scheiben)

Einfaches Rezept

1 Tasse (240 ml) Kartoffel-Starter (Rezept auf Seite 75)

1/2 Teelöffel Salz

1-1 1/2 Tassen (125-188 g) Mehl Type 550

Reichhaltiges Rezept

1 Tasse (240 ml) Kartoffel-Starter (Rezept auf Seite 75)

1/4 Tasse (60 ml) Honig

1 Esslöffel ungesalzene Butter, weich

1/2 Teelöffel Salz

1 1/3 -1 2/3 Tassen (166-208 g) Mehl Type 550

Bereiten Sie entweder das einfache oder das reichhaltige Rezept zu.

Alle Zutaten in der angegebenen Reihenfolge in den Vitamix DRY BLADE-Behälter geben und den Deckel schließen.

Den Teig auf Geschwindigkeitsstufe HIGH verkneten. Das Gerät zwei Mal hintereinander schnell ein- und wieder ausschalten. Das Gerät ausschalten und den Stöpsel abnehmen.

Während der Teig ruht, eine 20 cm x 10 cm (8 Zoll x 4 Zoll) große Brotform mit Backspray oder Backfett dünn einfetten.

Mithilfe eines nassen Nylonspatels die Wand des Behälters freischaben und den Teig von der Behälterwand in die Mitte der Mixtur schieben. Den Deckel wieder aufsetzen.

Die schnellste Geschwindigkeitsstufe auswählen. Das Gerät fünfmal hintereinander schnell ein- und ausschalten. Sollte der Teig besonders trocken sein, esslöffelweise zusätzliches Wasser hinzugeben. Die Prozedur fünf Mal wiederholen und die Behälterwand freischaben, bis der Teig eine weiche, elastische Masse gebildet hat.

Um den Teig leichter aus dem Behälter lösen zu können, Gerät fünfmal ein- und ausschalten (dadurch wird der Teig an- und von den Klingen abgehoben) und den Behälter anschließend schnell kopfüber über die vorbereitete Form halten. Teig in die Form fallen lassen und mithilfe eines feuchten Spatels Teigreste ausschaben.

Mit leicht bemehlten Fingern oder einem eingeölten Spatel den Laib unter leichtem Druck gleichmäßig in der Form verteilen.

Die Form mit einem sauberen und trockenen Geschirrtuch bedecken und ihn etwa 30 Minuten gehen lassen, bis er den oberen Rand der Form erreicht hat. Vor dem Backen den Teig mit sauberen Fingerspitzen eindrücken und anschließend mit Olivenöl einpinseln. Mit koscherem Salz, Dillkraut und verbleibendem Schweizer Käse besprenkeln.

Das Brot im vorgeheizten Ofen bei 180 °C (350 °F) 35 bis 40 Minuten oder bis das Brot eine Innentemperatur von 88 °C (190 °F) aufweist (mit Backthermometer messen) backen. Das Brot 10 Minuten lang auf einem Kuchengitter auskühlen lassen und es dann vorsichtig aus der Form lösen. Brot erst anschneiden, wenn es vollständig abgekühlt ist.

Sauerteigbrot *(Fortsetzung)*	Das Brot im vorgeheizten Ofen bei 180 °C (350 °F) 35 bis 40 Minuten oder bis das Brot eine Innentemperatur von 88 °C (190 °F) aufweist (mit Backthermometer messen) backen. Das Brot 10 Minuten lang auf einem Kuchengitter auskühlen lassen und es dann vorsichtig aus der Form lösen. Brot erst anschneiden, wenn es vollständig abgekühlt ist.

Einfaches Rezept: Nährwertinformationen pro Portion (1 Scheibe): 57 kcal (3 % aus Fett, 12 % aus Eiweiß, 85 % aus Kohlenhydraten) • 2 g Eiweiß 0 g Fett insgesamt • 0 g gesättigte Fettsäuren • 12 g Kohlenhydrate 1 g Ballaststoffe • 0 g Zucker • 99 mg Natrium • 0 mg Cholesterin

Reichhaltiges Rezept: Nährwertinformationen pro Portion (1 Scheibe): 106 kcal (10 % aus Fett, 9 % aus Eiweiß, 81 % aus Kohlenhydraten) • 2 g Eiweiß 1 g Fett insgesamt • 1 g gesättigte Fettsäuren • 22 g Kohlenhydrate 1 g Ballaststoffe • 6 g Zucker • 99 mg Natrium • 3 mg Cholesterin

SÜSSKARTOFFELBRÖTCHEN

Zubereitung: 15 Minuten • Verarbeitung: 30 Sekunden • Backzeit: 20–25 Minuten
ergibt: 12 Brötchen

1/2 Pfund (227 g) Süßkartoffeln, geschält, geviertelt

1 Packung (1 Esslöffel) aktive Trockenhefe

1 Esslöffel Kristallzucker

1 Tasse (125 g) Mehl Type 550

1 1/3 Tassen (160 g) Vollkornweizenmehl (Type 1600), plus zusätzliches Mehl nach Bedarf

1/2 Teelöffel Salz

2 Esslöffel (28 g) ungesalzene Butter, geschmolzen

2 Esslöffel (30 ml) Honig

1 Esslöffel Pflanzenöl

1 großes Ei, verquirlt

Die Kartoffeln in einem Topf mit köchelndem Wasser etwa 20 Minuten lang abkochen, bis sie gar sind. Das Wasser abgießen, 1/3 Tasse (80 ml) der Kochflüssigkeit auffangen. Kartoffeln leicht zerdrücken, anschließend beiseitestellen. Kochflüssigkeit auf 46 °C (115 °F) abkühlen lassen.

Hefe ansetzen, indem 1/3 Tasse (80 ml) der Kochflüssigkeit, Hefe und Zucker vermischt werden. Alles zügig umrühren. Die Mischung für 5 Minuten beiseitestellen.

Das gesamte Mehl und das Salz in den Vitamix DRY BLADE-Behälter geben und den Deckel schließen.

Variable 1 auswählen.

Das Gerät einschalten und die Geschwindigkeit langsam auf Variable 10 erhöhen.

Die Mischung etwa 5 Sekunden lang rühren, bis sich in der Mitte ein Loch bildet. Das Gerät anhalten.

Variable 3 auswählen. Gerät einschalten und den Stöpsel aus dem Deckel nehmen. Kartoffeln, Butter, Honig, Öl, Ei und Hefemischung durch die Öffnung im Deckel hinzugeben. Das Gerät ausschalten und den Stöpsel wieder einsetzen.

Den Teig auf Geschwindigkeitsstufe HIGH verkneten. Das Gerät zwei Mal hintereinander schnell ein- und wieder ausschalten. Das Gerät ausschalten und den Stöpsel abnehmen.

Mithilfe eines nassen Nylonspatels die Wand des Behälters freischaben und den Teig von der Behälterwand in die Mitte der Mixtur schieben. Den Deckel wieder aufsetzen.

Die schnellste Geschwindigkeitsstufe auswählen. Das Gerät fünfmal hintereinander schnell ein- und ausschalten. Sollte der Teig besonders trocken sein, esslöffelweise zusätzliches Wasser hinzugeben. Die Prozedur fünf Mal wiederholen und die Behälterwand freischaben, bis der Teig eine weiche, elastische Masse gebildet hat.

Eine große Schüssel leicht einfetten. Den Teig hineingeben und mehrmals wenden, um die gesamte Oberfläche zu bedecken. Schüssel mit einem sauberen Geschirrtuch oder Frischhaltefolie abdecken. Den Teig an einem warmen, windstillen Ort etwa 20 Minuten gehen lassen, bis er seine Größe verdoppelt hat.

Süßkartoffelbrötchen *(Fortsetzung)*	Während der Teig geht, eine 23 cm (9 Zoll) große quadratische Kuchenform mit Backspray oder Backfett dünn einfetten. Den Teig zusammenstoßen. Den Teig auf eine leicht bemehlte Oberfläche geben und leicht durchkneten, bis er glatt ist. Teig in 12 gleichmäßige Stücke schneiden. Jedes Stück zu einem Ball formen und nacheinander und dicht beieinander in die vorbereitete Form legen. Die Form mit einem sauberen, trockenen Geschirrtuch oder Frischhaltefolie abdecken und etwa 20 Minuten gehen lassen. Im vorgeheizten Backofen bei 190 °C (375 °F) 20 bis 25 Minuten backen, bis die Brötchen eine leichte Bräunung haben. Die Form dabei einmal drehen, um eine gleichmäßige Bräunung zu erzielen. Auf einem Kuchengitter abkühlen lassen.

Nährwertinformationen pro Portion (1 Brötchen): 150 kcal (24 % aus Fett, 11 % aus Eiweiß, 66 % aus Kohlenhydraten) • 4 g Eiweiß • 4 g Fett insgesamt • 2 g gesättigte Fettsäuren 25 g Kohlenhydrate • 3 g Ballaststoffe • 5 g Zucker • 113 mg Natrium • 23 mg Cholesterin

WEIZENVOLLKORNBROT

Zubereitung: 10 Minuten • Verarbeitung: 35 Sekunden • Backzeit: 35 Minuten
ergibt: 1 Laib (12 Scheiben)

1 Packung (1 Esslöffel) aktive Trockenhefe

1 1/4 Tassen (300 ml) warmes Wasser, 40 °C bis 46 °C (105 °F-115 °F)

1 Esslöffel Honig

1 1/2 Tassen (270 g) Vollkornweizen oder 2 1/4 Tasse (270 g) Vollkornweizenmehl

1 Teelöffel Salz

1 Esslöffel helles Olivenöl oder Traubenkernöl

1 Teelöffel Zitronensaft

1 Eiweiß, vermischt mit 1 Esslöffel Wasser, optional (zum Bestreichen des Teigs vor dem Backen)

Hefe ansetzen, indem warmes Wasser, Honig und Hefe vermischt werden. Alles zügig umrühren. Die Mischung für 5 Minuten beiseitestellen.

Bei Zubereitung mit Vollkornweizen: Weizen und Salz in den Vitamix DRY BLADE-Behälter geben und den Deckel schließen.

Variable 1 auswählen.

Das Gerät einschalten und die Geschwindigkeit langsam auf Variable 10 erhöhen.

1 Minute lang mahlen. (Nicht zu stark verarbeiten.) Das Gerät anhalten und das Mehl einige Minuten abkühlen lassen.

Bei Zubereitung mit Vollkornweizenmehl: Das Mehl und das Salz in den Vitamix DRY BLADE-Behälter geben und den Deckel schließen.

Variable 1 auswählen.

Das Gerät einschalten und die Geschwindigkeit langsam auf Variable 6 erhöhen.

Die Mischung etwa 5 Sekunden lang verrühren, bis sich in der Mitte ein Loch bildet.

Variable 3 auswählen. Gerät einschalten und den Stöpsel aus dem Deckel nehmen. Öl, Zitronensaft und Hefemischung durch die Öffnung im Deckel hinzugeben. Das Gerät ausschalten und den Stöpsel wieder einsetzen.

Die schnellste Geschwindigkeitsstufe auswählen. Das Gerät zwei Mal hintereinander schnell ein- und wieder ausschalten. Das Gerät ausschalten und den Stöpsel abnehmen.

Während der Teig ruht, eine 22 cm x 11 cm (8 1/2 Zoll x 4 1/2 Zoll) große Brotform mit Backspray oder Backfett dünn einfetten.

Mit einem Nylonspatel die Wände des Vitamix-Behälters abkratzen. Den Teig von den Behälterwänden in die Mitte der Mischung ziehen. Den Deckel wieder aufsetzen.

Die schnellste Geschwindigkeitsstufe auswählen. Das Gerät fünfmal hintereinander schnell ein- und ausschalten. Sollte der Teig besonders trocken sein, esslöffelweise zusätzliches Wasser hinzugeben. Die Prozedur fünf Mal wiederholen und die Behälterwand freischaben, bis der Teig eine weiche, elastische Masse gebildet hat.

Weizenvollkornbrot
(Fortsetzung)

Um den Teig aus dem Behälter lösen zu können, Gerät fünfmal ein- und ausschalten (dadurch wird der Teig an- und von den Klingen abgehoben). Den Behälter anschließend kopfüber über die vorbereitete Form halten und den Teig hineinfallen lassen. Mithilfe eines feuchten Nylonspatels verbleibende Teigreste ausschaben.

Den Laib mithilfe eines feuchten oder eingeölten Spatels (oder leicht mit Mehl bestäubter Finger) formen. Den Laib mit einem sauberen und trockenen Geschirrtuch bedecken und ihn etwa 20 bis 25 Minuten gehen lassen, bis er den oberen Rand der Form erreicht hat.

Bei Bedarf den Laib rasch und vorsichtig mit der Eiweißmischung einpinseln und die Oberseite mit einem scharfen, gezahnten Messer drei- oder viermal diagonal einschneiden (etwa 1/2 cm / 1/4 Zoll tief).

Das Brot im vorgeheizten Ofen bei 180 °C (350 °F) 35 Minuten oder bis das Brot gut gebräunt ist und eine Innentemperatur von 88 °C (190 °F) aufweist (mit Backthermometer messen) backen.

10 Minuten lang auf einem Kuchengitter auskühlen lassen und es dann vorsichtig aus der Form lösen. Brot erst anschneiden, wenn es vollständig abgekühlt ist.

Nährwertinformationen pro Portion (1 Scheibe): 102 kcal (13 % aus Fett, 13 % aus Eiweiß, 74 % aus Kohlenhydraten) • 3 g Eiweiß • 2 g Fett insgesamt • 0 g gesättigte Fettsäuren
20 g Kohlenhydrate • 3 g Ballaststoffe • 2 g Zucker • 203 mg Natrium • 0 mg Cholesterin

VOLLKORNBAGUETTE

Zubereitung: 15 Minuten • Verarbeitung: 35 Sekunden • Backzeit: 30–40 Minuten
ergibt: 1 Laib (16-18 Scheiben)

1 Tasse (240 ml) warmes Wasser, wird aufgeteilt, 40 °C bis 46 °C (105 °F-115 °F)

1 Packung (1 Esslöffel) aktive Trockenhefe

1 1/4 Tassen (150 g) Vollkornweizenmehl (Type 1600)

3/4 Tasse (103 g) Brotmehl Type 812

1 1/2 Teelöffel Salz

2 Esslöffel (21 g) Leinsamensaat

2 Esslöffel (18 g) Sonnenblumenkerne

1 Esslöffel Kürbiskerne oder 1 Esslöffel Hirse

1 Esslöffel Weizenkeime

1 Esslöffel Olivenöl

2 Esslöffel (15 g) Vollkorn-Maismehl

1 Eiweiß, vermischt mit 1 Teelöffel Wasser (zum Bestreichen des Teigs vor dem Backen)

Hefe ansetzen, indem 1/2 Tasse (120 ml) warmes Wasser und Hefe vermischt werden. Alles zügig umrühren. Die Mischung für 5 Minuten beiseitestellen.

Vollkornweizenmehl, Brotmehl, Salz, Leinsamensaat, Sonnenblumenkerne, Kürbiskerne ODER Hirse sowie Weizenkeime in den Vitamix DRY BLADE-Behälter geben und Deckel schließen.

Variable 1 auswählen.

Das Gerät einschalten und die Geschwindigkeit langsam auf Variable 6 erhöhen.

Die Mischung etwa 5 Sekunden lang rühren, bis sich in der Mitte ein Loch bildet. Das Gerät anhalten.

Variable 3 auswählen. Gerät einschalten und den Stöpsel aus dem Deckel nehmen. Hefemischung und die verbleibende 1/2 Tasse (120 ml) warmes Wasser durch die Öffnung im Deckel in den Behälter geben. Das Gerät ausschalten und den Stöpsel wieder einsetzen.

Den Teig auf Geschwindigkeitsstufe HIGH verkneten. Das Gerät zwei Mal hintereinander schnell ein- und wieder ausschalten. Das Gerät ausschalten und den Stöpsel abnehmen.

Während der Teig ruht eine mittelgroße Rührschüssel mit Olivenöl einfetten und das Maismehl auf ein Backblech streuen.

Mithilfe eines nassen Nylonspatels die Wand des Behälters freischaben und den Teig von der Behälterwand in die Mitte der Mixtur schieben. Den Deckel wieder aufsetzen.

Die schnellste Geschwindigkeitsstufe auswählen. Das Gerät fünfmal hintereinander schnell ein- und ausschalten. Sollte der Teig besonders trocken sein, esslöffelweise zusätzliches Wasser hinzugeben. Die Prozedur fünf Mal wiederholen und die Behälterwand freischaben, bis der Teig eine weiche, elastische Masse gebildet hat.

Um den Teig leichter aus dem Behälter lösen zu können, Gerät fünfmal ein- und ausschalten (dadurch wird der Teig an- und von den Klingen abgehoben) und den Behälter anschließend schnell kopfüber über die vorbereitete Schüssel halten. Mit einem feuchten Spatel den verbleibenden Teig aus der Schüssel kratzen. Den Teig mehrmals umdrehen und gleichmäßig mit dem Öl überziehen. Mit Frischhaltefolie bedecken und etwa 1 Stunde gehen lassen, bis der Teig sich im Umfang fast verdreifacht hat.

Vollkornbaguette
(Fortsetzung)

Teig leicht zusammenstoßen und auf eine bemehlte Arbeitsfläche legen. Mit einem bemehlten Nudelholz in ein 30 cm x 15 cm (12 Zoll x 6 Zoll) großes Rechteck ausrollen. Von der langen Seite her aufrollen und dabei die Ansatzstellen zusammendrücken und mit Wasser verkleben.

Den Teig mit den Ansatzstellen nach unten auf das vorbereitete Backblech legen. Mit einem sauberen und trockenen Geschirrtuch bedecken und den Teig etwa 45 Minuten gehen lassen, bis er seinen Umfang ungefähr verdoppelt hat.

Mit der Ei-Mischung einpinseln und die Oberseite mit einem scharfen, gezahnten Messer drei- oder viermal diagonal einschneiden (etwa 0,6 cm / 1/4 Zoll tief).

Das Brot im vorgeheizten Ofen bei 220 °C (425 °F) 30 bis 40 Minuten oder bis das Brot gut gebräunt ist und eine Innentemperatur von 88 °C (190 °F) aufweist (mit Backthermometer messen) backen. Das Backblech 10 Minuten lang auf einem Kuchengitter auskühlen lassen und dann das Brot vorsichtig vom Backblech nehmen. Das Brot erst anschneiden, wenn es vollständig abgekühlt ist.

Nährwertinformationen pro Portion (1 Scheibe): 74 kcal (23 % aus Fett, 16 % aus Eiweiß, 62 % aus Kohlenhydraten)
3 g Eiweiß • 2 g Fett insgesamt • 0 g gesättigte Fettsäuren • 12 g Kohlenhydrate • 2 g Ballaststoffe • 0 g Zucker
202 mg Natrium • 0 mg Cholesterin

Mithilfe eines Metallspatels kann das Brot auf dem Backblech platziert werden.

VOLLKORNWEIZEN-, HAFER- UND LEINSAMENBROT

Zubereitung: 10 Minuten • Verarbeitung: 40 Sekunden • Backzeit: 30-35 Minuten
ergibt: 1 Laib (12 Scheiben)

1 Tasse (240 ml) warmes Wasser, 40 °C bis 46 °C (105 °F-115 °F)

2 Esslöffel (30 ml) Honig

1 Packung (1 Esslöffel) aktive Trockenhefe

2 Esslöffel (10 g) Haferflocken (keine Instant-Flocken)

2 Esslöffel (20 g) Leinsamensaat

3/4 Tasse (135 g) Vollkornweizen oder 1 Tasse (120 g) Vollkornweizenmehl

1 1/4 Tassen (171 g) Brotmehl Type 812

1 Teelöffel Salz

1 Esslöffel helles Olivenöl

Hefe ansetzen, indem warmes Wasser, Honig und Hefe vermischt werden. Alles zügig umrühren. Die Mischung für 5 Minuten beiseitestellen.

Bei Zubereitung mit Vollkornweizen: Haferflocken, Leinsamen und Vollkornweizen in den Vitamix DRY BLADE-Behälter geben und Deckel schließen.

Variable 1 auswählen.

Das Gerät einschalten und die Geschwindigkeit langsam auf Variable 10 erhöhen.

30 Sekunden lang mahlen.

Das Gerät anhalten. Brotmehl und Salz hinzugeben und den Deckel schließen.

Variable 1 auswählen.

Das Gerät einschalten und die Geschwindigkeit langsam auf Variable 10 erhöhen.

30 Sekunden lang mahlen, dabei den Stopfer durch die Öffnung im Deckel in den Behälter stecken und die Mehlmischung auf die Klingen drücken. Den Stopfer während der letzten 5 Sekunden herausnehmen, damit sich in der Mitte ein Loch bilden kann.

Bei Zubereitung mit Vollkornweizenmehl: Haferflocken, Leinsamensaat, Vollkornweizenmehl, Brotmehl und Salz in den Vitamix DRY BLADE-Behälter geben und Deckel schließen.

Variable 1 auswählen.

Das Gerät einschalten und die Geschwindigkeit langsam auf Variable 10 erhöhen.

30 Sekunden lang mahlen, dabei den Stopfer durch die Öffnung im Deckel in den Behälter stecken und die Mehlmischung auf die Klingen drücken. Den Stopfer während der letzten 5 Sekunden herausnehmen, damit sich in der Mitte ein Loch bilden kann.

Variable 3 auswählen. Gerät einschalten und den Stöpsel aus dem Deckel nehmen. Öl und Hefemischung durch die Öffnung im Deckel hinzugeben. Das Gerät ausschalten und den Stöpsel wieder einsetzen.

Vollkornweizen-, Hafer- und Leinsamenbrot *(Fortsetzung)*

Die schnellste Geschwindigkeitsstufe auswählen. Das Gerät zwei Mal hintereinander schnell ein- und wieder ausschalten. Das Gerät ausschalten und den Stöpsel abnehmen.

Während der Teig ruht, eine 20 cm x 10 cm (8 Zoll x 4 Zoll) große Brotform mit Backspray oder Backfett dünn einfetten.

Mithilfe eines nassen Nylonspatels die Wand des Behälters freischaben und den Teig von der Behälterwand in die Mitte der Mixtur schieben. Den Deckel wieder aufsetzen.

Die schnellste Geschwindigkeitsstufe auswählen. Das Gerät fünfmal hintereinander schnell ein- und ausschalten. Sollte der Teig besonders trocken sein, esslöffelweise zusätzliches Wasser hinzugeben. Die Prozedur fünf Mal wiederholen und die Behälterwand freischaben, bis der Teig eine weiche, elastische Masse gebildet hat.

Um den Teig leichter aus dem Behälter lösen zu können, Gerät fünfmal ein- und ausschalten (dadurch wird der Teig an- und von den Klingen abgehoben) und den Behälter anschließend schnell kopfüber über die vorbereitete Form halten. Teig in die Form fallen lassen und mithilfe eines feuchten Spatels Teigreste ausschaben.

Mit leicht bemehlten Fingern oder einem eingeölten Spatel den Laib unter leichtem Druck gleichmäßig in der Form verteilen.

Den Laib mit einem sauberen und trockenen Geschirrtuch bedecken und ihn etwa 20 bis 25 Minuten gehen lassen, bis er den oberen Rand der Form erreicht hat. Den Teig vor dem Backen mit 3 schnellen, schrägen Schnitten mit einem gezahnten Messer einschneiden.

Das Brot im vorgeheizten Ofen bei 190 °C (375 °F) 30 bis 35 Minuten oder bis das Brot eine Innentemperatur von 88 °C (190 °F) aufweist, backen. 10 Minuten lang auf einem Kuchengitter auskühlen lassen und dann vorsichtig aus der Form lösen. Brot erst anschneiden, wenn es vollständig abgekühlt ist.

Nährwertinformationen pro Portion (1 Scheibe): 130 kcal (15 % aus Fett, 12 % aus Eiweiß, 73 % aus Kohlenhydraten)
4 g Eiweiß • 2 g Fett insgesamt • 0 g gesättigte Fettsäuren • 24 g Kohlenhydrate • 3 g Ballaststoffe
3 g Zucker • 199 mg Natrium • 0 mg Cholesterin

Brot, das angeschnitten wird, solange es noch warm ist, ist oftmals im Innern noch feucht; das gilt besonders für Vollkornbrot. Lassen Sie es daher vor dem Anschneiden abkühlen.

Trockenmarinaden

Verwenden von Trockenmarinaden

Durch Trockenmarinaden erhalten Ihre gegrillten Speisen noch mehr Geschmack. Versuchen Sie unsere Mischungen und halten Sie sich an einige einfache Tipps.

- Trockenmarinaden sorgen für eine Extraportion Geschmack und eignen sich am besten zum Braten, Grillen oder Backen. Sie sind wunderbar für Tofu, Fisch, Schweinekoteletts, Hähnchenbrust und Gemüse.
- Bewahren Sie Ihre Marinaden in einem luftdichten Glasgefäß an einem kühlen Ort auf und verwenden Sie sie nach Bedarf.
- Drei oder vier Esslöffel einer Trockenmarinade reichen für etwa 1 kg Fleisch oder Gemüse.
- Bestreuen Sie Fleisch, Geflügel, Fisch oder Gemüse mit der Trockenmarinade und reiben Sie sie leicht mit den Händen ein. Alternativ können Sie die Marinade in eine große Plastikschüssel geben, die Zutaten hinzufügen und alles gut durchschütteln. Lassen Sie die marinierten Speisen mehrere Stunden oder über Nacht im Kühlschrank ziehen.
- Wenn Sie beim Grillen einen besonderen Geschmack erzielen möchten, bedecken Sie Fleisch, Fisch oder andere Eiweißprodukte großzügig auf beiden Seiten mit der Marinade. Bedecken Sie das Ganze mit Frischhaltefolie und lassen Sie es 30 Minuten im Kühlschrank stehen. Anschließend Grillen.

Wichtige Hinweise:

Werden trockene Zutaten länger als zwei Minuten gemahlen, kann dies Ihr Gerät beschädigen. Eine regelmäßige Verwendung kann zu kosmetischen Schäden am Behälter führen und die Klingen können mit der Zeit stumpf werden.

Beim Mahlen einiger Kräuter können flüchtige Öle freigesetzt werden, die den Behälter dauerhaft verfärben. Andere haben einen starken Geruch, der im Behälter zurückbleibt und den Geschmack anderer Lebensmittel beeinträchtigen kann. Das Mahlen einiger Kräuter und Gewürze kann außerdem dazu führen, dass die Klingen mit der Zeit stumpf werden oder der Behälter einen Riss bekommt.

ALLZWECK-BARBECUE-TROCKENMARINADE

Zubereitung: 10 Minuten • Verarbeitung: 45 Sekunden • ergibt: 1 Tasse (240 g)

1 Esslöffel Meersalz

1/4 Tasse (55 g) dunkelbrauner Zucker

1/4 Tasse (28 g) ungarischer Paprika, edelsüß

2 Esslöffel (24 g) schwarze Pfefferkörner

1 Esslöffel getrocknete Knoblauchflocken

1 Esslöffel getrocknete Zwiebelflocken

1 ganze Pasilla-Chilischote, getrocknet, entkernt und halbiert

1/2 Teelöffel Selleriesamen

Alle Zutaten in der angegebenen Reihenfolge in den Vitamix DRY BLADE-Behälter geben und den Deckel schließen.

Variable 1 auswählen.

Das Gerät einschalten und die Geschwindigkeit langsam auf Variable 10 erhöhen.

Die Zutaten 45 Sekunden lang vermischen. Sofort verwenden oder in einem luftdichten Behälter bei den Gewürzen aufbewahren und später verwenden.

HINWEIS: Würzt Rippchen, Lachs und andere Gerichte und verleiht ihnen eine angenehme Schärfe.

Nährwertinformationen pro Portion (1 Teelöffel): 8 kcal (11 % aus Fett, 7 % aus Eiweiß, 82 % aus Kohlenhydraten)
0 g Eiweiß • 0 g Fett insgesamt • 0 g gesättigte Fettsäuren • 2 g Kohlenhydrate • 0 g Ballaststoffe • 1 g Zucker
71 mg Natrium • 0 mg Cholesterin

Allzweck-Barbecue-Trockenmarinade

CAJUN-TROCKENMARINADE

Zubereitung: 10 Minuten • Verarbeitung: 30 Sekunden • ergibt: 1 Tasse (240 g)

1/4 Tasse (67 g)
grobes Meersalz

3 Esslöffel (21 g)
ungarischer Paprika,
edelsüß

2 Esslöffel (17 g)
Knoblauchpulver

2 Esslöffel (14 g)
Zwiebelpulver

2 Esslöffel (5 g)
getrockneter Thymian

2 Esslöffel (6 g)
getrockneter Oregano

1 Esslöffel schwarzer
Pfeffer, gemahlen oder
1 Teelöffel schwarze
Pfefferkörner

1 Esslöffel weißer Pfeffer,
gemahlen oder 1 Teelöffel
weiße Pfefferkörner

2 Teelöffel
getrocknete Salbeiblätter

2 Teelöffel
Cayennepfeffer oder
1 getrocknete Thai-
Chilischote

Alle Zutaten in der angegebenen Reihenfolge in den Vitamix DRY BLADE-Behälter geben und den Deckel schließen.

Variable 1 auswählen.

Das Gerät einschalten und die Geschwindigkeit langsam auf Variable 10 erhöhen.

30 Sekunden lang mixen, bei Bedarf den Stopfer verwenden, um die Zutaten auf die Klingen zu drücken. Sofort verwenden oder in einem luftdichten Behälter bei den Gewürzen aufbewahren und später verwenden.

Nährwertinformationen pro Portion (2 Esslöffel / 30 g): 31 kcal (15 % aus Fett, 14 % aus Eiweiß, 71 % aus Kohlenhydraten) 1 g Eiweiß • 1 g Fett insgesamt • 0 g gesättigte Fettsäuren • 7 g Kohlenhydrate 3 g Ballaststoffe • 1 g Zucker • 1683 mg Natrium • 0 mg Cholesterin

KAFFEE-TROCK-ENMARINADE

Zubereitung: 15 Minuten • Verarbeitung: 45 Sekunden • ergibt: 1/2 Tasse (120 g)

1 1/2 Teelöffel Meersalz

4 Teelöffel gemahlenen Kaffee oder 1 Esslöffel ganze Kaffeebohnen

1 ganze Pasilla-Chilischote, getrocknet und entkernt

2 Esslöffel (28 g) dunkelbrauner Zucker

1/2 Teelöffel schwarzer Pfeffer, gemahlen oder 1/4 Teelöffel schwarze Pfefferkörner, ganz

1/2 Teelöffel Zwiebelpulver

1/2 Teelöffel Knoblauchpulver

1/4 Teelöffel Cayennepfeffer

1/4 Teelöffel Korianderkörner, ganz

1/4 Teelöffel Kurkuma

Alle Zutaten in der angegebenen Reihenfolge in den Vitamix DRY BLADE-Behälter geben und den Deckel schließen.

Variable 1 auswählen.

Das Gerät einschalten und die Geschwindigkeit langsam auf Variable 10 erhöhen.

Die Zutaten 45 Sekunden lang vermischen. Sofort verwenden oder in einem luftdichten Behälter bei den Gewürzen aufbewahren und später verwenden.

Nährwertinformationen pro Portion (1 Teelöffel): 7 kcal (8 % aus Fett, 6 % aus Eiweiß, 86 % aus Kohlenhydraten)
0 g Eiweiß • 0 g Fett insgesamt • 0 g gesättigte Fettsäuren • 2 g Kohlenhydrate • 0 g Ballaststoffe • 1 g Zucker
71 mg Natrium • 0 mg Cholesterin

Der Kaffee sorgt bei dieser Marinade für einen vollen, erdigen Geschmack. Besonders lecker zu Rind.

DÖRRFLEISCH-GEWÜRZMISCHUNG

Zubereitung: 10 Minuten • Verarbeitung: 45 Sekunden • ergibt: 1/2 Tasse (67 g)

3 Esslöffel (41 g) dunkelbrauner Zucker

1 1/2 Esslöffel grobes Meersalz

1 Esslöffel Korianderkörner, ganz

1 Teelöffel schwarze Pfefferkörner, ganz

1 1/2 Teelöffel Knoblauchpulver

1 1/2 Teelöffel Zwiebelpulver

1 1/2 Teelöffel getrockneter Thymian

1/2 Teelöffel Pimentkörner oder 1 1/2 Teelöffel gemahlenen Piment

1 Teelöffel gemahlener Zimt

1/2 bis 1 Teelöffel Cayennepfeffer oder 1 getrocknete Thai-Chilischote

Alle Zutaten in der angegebenen Reihenfolge in den Vitamix DRY BLADE-Behälter geben und den Deckel schließen.

Variable 1 auswählen.

Das Gerät einschalten und die Geschwindigkeit langsam auf Variable 10 erhöhen.

Die Zutaten 45 Sekunden lang vermischen. Sofort verwenden oder in einem luftdichten Behälter bei den Gewürzen aufbewahren und später verwenden.

Nährwertinformationen pro Portion (1 Teelöffel): 9 kcal (6% aus Fett, 4% aus Eiweiß, 90% aus Kohlenhydraten)
0 g Eiweiß • 0 g Fett insgesamt • 0 g gesättigte Fettsäuren • 2 g Kohlenhydrate • 0 g Ballaststoffe • 2 g Zucker
443 mg Natrium • 0 mg Cholesterin

LORBEER-GEWÜRZMISCHUNG „NEW BAY“

Zubereitung: 10 Minuten • Verarbeitung: 1 Minute • ergibt: 1 1/4 Tassen (300 g)

- 1/2 Tasse (134 g) grobes Meersalz
- 1/2 Tasse (56 g) ungarischer Paprika, edelsüß
- 2 Esslöffel (13 g) Selleriesamen
- 1 Esslöffel Pimentkörner
- 1 Esslöffel schwarze Pfefferkörner
- 1 Esslöffel getrocknete und gemahlene Senfkörner
- 1 Esslöffel gemahlener Ingwer
- 1 Esslöffel gemahlener Zimt
- 1 Esslöffel gemahlener Cayennepfeffer
- 1/2 Esslöffel Kardamomsamen
- 1/2 Esslöffel ganze Gewürznelken
- 10 Lorbeerblätter

Alle Zutaten in der angegebenen Reihenfolge in den Vitamix DRY BLADE-Behälter geben und den Deckel schließen.

Variable 1 auswählen.

Das Gerät einschalten und die Geschwindigkeit langsam auf Variable 10 erhöhen.

1 Minute lang mixen, bei Bedarf den Stopfer verwenden, um die Zutaten auf die Klingen zu drücken. Sofort verwenden oder in einem luftdichten Behälter bei den Gewürzen aufbewahren und später verwenden.

Nährwertinformationen pro Portion (1 Teelöffel): 6 kcal (31 % aus Fett, 14 % aus Eiweiß, 55 % aus Kohlenhydraten)
0 g Eiweiß • 0 g Fett insgesamt • 0 g gesättigte Fettsäuren • 1 g Kohlenhydrate • 1 g Ballaststoffe • 0 g Zucker
449 mg Natrium • 0 mg Cholesterin

Diese Gewürzmischung ist so vielseitig, dass Sie sie als Kochgewürz für Garnelen und Krabben verwenden können, als Marinade für Fisch oder sogar um Dip-Butter für Hummer und Garnelen zu würzen.

PAPRIKA-GEFLÜGEL-TROCKENMARINADE

Zubereitung: 15 Minuten • Verarbeitung: 1 Sekunde • ergibt: 3/4 Tasse (180 g)

1/3 Tasse (9 g)
getrockneter Majoran

1/4 Tasse (28 g)
ungarischer Paprika,
edelsüß

1 getrocknete
Pasilla-Chilischote,
entkernt

2 Esslöffel (14 g)
Zwiebelpulver

2 Esslöffel (36 g)
getrocknete abgeriebene
Zitrone

1/4 Tasse (24 g)
getrocknete Salbeiblätter

1 Esslöffel
grobes Meersalz
oder koscheres Salz

1 Esslöffel
schwarze Pfefferkörner

1/2 Esslöffel
Selleriesamen

Alle Zutaten in der angegebenen Reihenfolge in den Vitamix DRY BLADE-Behälter geben und den Deckel schließen.

Variable 1 auswählen.

Das Gerät einschalten und die Geschwindigkeit langsam auf Variable 10 erhöhen.

1 Minute lang rühren. Sofort verwenden oder in einem luftdichten Behälter bei den Gewürzen aufbewahren und später verwenden.

Nährwertinformationen pro Portion (1 Teelöffel): 7 kcal (22 % aus Fett, 13 % aus Eiweiß, 65 % aus Kohlenhydraten)
0 g Eiweiß • 0 g Fett insgesamt • 0 g gesättigte Fettsäuren • 1 g Kohlenhydrate • 1 g Ballaststoffe • 0 g Zucker
94 mg Natrium • 0 mg Cholesterin

Eine Gewürzmischung für den „Alltag“.

KÜRBISKUCHEN-GEWÜRZMISCHUNG

Zubereitung: 10 Minuten • Verarbeitung: 45 Sekunden • ergibt: 2 Esslöffel (30 g)

1 Esslöffel gemahlener Zimt

1 Teelöffel gemahlener Ingwer

6 Zehen

3 ganze Pimentkörner

1/2 Teelöffel gemahlene Muskatblüte

1/2 Teelöffel frisch gemahlener Muskat

Alle Zutaten in der angegebenen Reihenfolge in den Vitamix DRY BLADE-Behälter geben und den Deckel schließen.

Variable 1 auswählen.

Das Gerät einschalten und die Geschwindigkeit langsam auf Variable 10 erhöhen.

Die Zutaten 45 Sekunden lang vermischen. Sofort verwenden oder in einem luftdichten Behälter bei den Gewürzen aufbewahren und später verwenden.

HINWEIS: Diese Masse kann Ihren Behälter leicht verfärben.

Nährwertinformationen pro Portion (1 Teelöffel): 6 kcal (22 % aus Fett, 5 % aus Eiweiß, 73 % aus Kohlenhydraten)
0 g Eiweiß • 0 g Fett insgesamt • 0 g gesättigte Fettsäuren • 1 g Kohlenhydrate • 1 g Ballaststoffe • 0 g Zucker
1 mg Natrium • 0 mg Cholesterin

Diese Gewürzmischung ist so beliebt, dass sie nicht nur beim klassischen Kürbiskuchen Verwendung findet, sondern auch bei zahlreichen anderen Gerichten, wie Apfeltorte oder Kartoffelpüree. Mit Ihrer Vitamix können Sie ganz einfach die Vorteile von frischen, aromatischen Zutaten nutzen. Bereiten Sie also nur kleine Mengen vor, um den Geschmack besonders zur Geltung zu bringen.

SÜSS-WÜRZIGE & TROCKENMARINADE

Zubereitung: 10 Minuten • Verarbeitung: 30 Sekunden • ergibt: 1/4 Tasse (60 g)

2 Teelöffel hellbrauner Zucker

2 Teelöffel getrocknetes Senfmehl

1 Teelöffel Zwiebelpulver

1/2 Teelöffel koscheres Salz

6 weiße Pfefferkörner oder 1/4 Teelöffel weißer Pfeffer, gemahlen

Alle Zutaten in den Vitamix DRY BLADE-Behälter und den Deckel schließen.

Variable 1 auswählen.

Das Gerät einschalten und die Geschwindigkeit langsam auf Variable 10 erhöhen.

Die Masse 30 Sekunden lang verkneten. Sofort verwenden oder in einem luftdichten Behälter bei den Gewürzen aufbewahren und später verwenden.

Nährwertinformationen pro Portion (1 Teelöffel): 7 kcal (24 % aus Fett, 10 % aus Eiweiß, 66 % aus Kohlenhydraten)
0 g Eiweiß • 0 g Fett insgesamt • 0 g gesättigte Fettsäuren • 1 g Kohlenhydrate • 0 g Ballaststoffe • 1 g Zucker
47 mg Natrium • 0 mg Cholesterin

CURRY-GEWÜRZMISCHUNG TRINIDAD

Zubereitung: 10 Minuten • Verarbeitung: 45 Sekunden • ergibt: 1/2 Tasse (120 g)

3 Esslöffel (15 g) ganze Korianderkörner

3 Esslöffel (20 g) gemahlener Kurkuma

2 Esslöffel (24 g) schwarze Pfefferkörner

1 Esslöffel koscheres Salz

1 Esslöffel Kreuzkümmelsamen

1 Teelöffel Pimentkörner

1 Teelöffel Kardamomsamen

1 Teelöffel frisch gemahlener Muskat

1 Teelöffel gemahlener Zimt

3/4 Teelöffel gemahlener Ingwer

2 getrocknete Thai-Chilischoten, entkernt

Alle Zutaten in der angegebenen Reihenfolge in den Vitamix DRY BLADE-Behälter geben und den Deckel schließen.

Variable 1 auswählen.

Das Gerät einschalten und die Geschwindigkeit langsam auf Variable 10 erhöhen.

Die Zutaten 45 Sekunden lang vermischen. Sofort verwenden oder in einem luftdichten Behälter bei den Gewürzen aufbewahren und später verwenden.

HINWEIS: Diese Masse kann Ihren Behälter leicht verfärben.

Nährwertinformationen pro Portion (1 Teelöffel): 21 kcal (29 % aus Fett, 11 % aus Eiweiß, 60 % aus Kohlenhydraten)
1 g Eiweiß • 1 g Fett insgesamt • 0 g gesättigte Fettsäuren • 4 g Kohlenhydrate • 2 g Ballaststoffe • 0 g Zucker
284 mg Natrium • 0 mg Cholesterin

ADOBO TROCKENMARINADE

Zubereitung: 10 Minuten • Verarbeitung: 1 Minute • ergibt: 1 Tasse (240 g)

1/4 Tasse (34 g) Knoblauchpulver

1/4 Tasse (28 g) Zwiebelpulver

3 Esslöffel (9 g) getrockneten Oregano

2 Esslöffel (12 g) Kreuzkümmelsamen

2 Esslöffel (29 g) koscheres Salz

2 Esslöffel (24 g) schwarze Pfefferkörner

1 Esslöffel getrocknete abgeriebene Zitrone

Alle Zutaten in der angegebenen Reihenfolge in den Vitamix DRY BLADE-Behälter geben und den Deckel schließen.

Variable 1 auswählen.

Das Gerät einschalten und die Geschwindigkeit langsam auf Variable 10 erhöhen.

1 Minute lang rühren. Sofort verwenden oder in einem luftdichten Behälter bei den Gewürzen aufbewahren und später verwenden.

Nährwertinformationen pro Portion (1 Teelöffel): 7 kcal (11 % aus Fett, 14 % aus Eiweiß, 74 % aus Kohlenhydraten)
0 g Eiweiß • 0 g Fett insgesamt • 0 g gesättigte Fettsäuren • 1 g Kohlenhydrate • 0 g Ballaststoffe • 0 g Zucker
141 mg Natrium • 0 mg Cholesterin

Eine lateinamerikanische Gewürzmischung die sehr gut zu Fleisch, Bohnen oder geröstetem Gemüse passt.

Tipps zur Fehlersuche und -behebung

Wenn Sie ein Backanfänger sind, scheinen all die Feinheiten der Hefezubereitung eine Herausforderung darzustellen. Und Sie fragen sich vielleicht, was Sie tun sollen, wenn die Dinge nicht wie geplant laufen. Es ist richtig, dass das Backen mit Hefe keine exakte Wissenschaft ist. Aber es ist auch richtig, dass kleine Fehler oft keine gravierenden Auswirkungen haben. Hier einige Antworten auf mögliche Fragen.

Woher weiß ich, ob die Hefe aktiv ist?

Päckchen mit aktiver Trockenhefe sind mit einem Mindesthaltbarkeitsdatum versehen. Daran können Sie sehen, wie lange die Hefe aktiv ist. Aber wenn Sie Hefe in größeren Mengen kaufen ist es nicht immer so einfach festzustellen. Sie können die Hefe mithilfe eines Vorteigs testen. Dieser einfache Schritt wird bei vielen Rezepten angewendet. Lösen Sie die Hefe in warmem Wasser auf und geben Sie 1 bis 3 Teelöffel Zucker oder Honig hinzu (je nachdem, was das Rezept vorsieht). (Wenn im Rezept kein Zucker oder Honig vorgesehen ist, können Sie 1 Teelöffel hinzugeben, ohne den Geschmack des Brotes zu beeinträchtigen.) Lassen Sie die Mischung 5 bis 15 Minuten stehen, oder bis sich Bläschen bilden. Diese sind ein Anzeichen dafür, dass die Hefe noch frisch und aktiv ist.

Was mache ich, wenn ich beim Brotbacken unterbrochen werde?

Wenn die Unterbrechung nicht länger als eine halbe Stunde dauert, brauchen Sie sich keine Sorgen zu machen. Wenn Sie gerade die Hefe aufgelöst haben, dann decken Sie sie ab und lassen Sie sie bei Zimmertemperatur stehen. Sie nimmt keinen Schaden, wenn sie für eine Weile fermentiert. Wenn Sie den Teig gerade kneten oder rühren, können Sie ihn mit Frischhaltefolie zudecken, damit er nicht austrocknet.

Wenn der Teig sich bereits verdoppelt hat, aber Sie noch keine Zeit haben, die Laibe zu formen, können Sie ihn kurz zusammenstoßen und erneut gehen lassen. Dieses Mal bei Zimmertemperatur. Hefeteig kann zwei- bis dreimal zusammengestoßen werden und dennoch ein ausgezeichnetes Backergebnis erzielen.

Sie können die letzten Schritte hinauszögern – das Formen der Brote, das zweite Mal gehen lassen und das Backen – indem Sie den Teig während des ersten Gehens mit Frischhaltefolie bedecken und in den Kühlschrank stellen. Dort kann er mehrere Stunden verbleiben. Der Teig geht trotzdem weiter, nur viel langsamer. Wenn Sie bereit sind, können Sie den Teig zugedeckt an einem warmen Ort zu Ende gehen lassen.

Woher weiß ich, ob ich genug Mehl eingeknetet habe?

Wenn Sie sich nicht sicher sind, ob genug Mehl im Teig ist (denken Sie daran, zu viel Mehl macht das Brot sehr trocken), drehen Sie eine Schüssel um und stülpen Sie sie über Ihren Teig. Lassen Sie ihn dann 15 Minuten lang ruhen. Wenn Sie nach den 15 Minuten feststellen, dass der Teig sehr klebrig ist und sich zur Seite hin ausgebreitet hat, anstatt weiter aufzugehen, benötigen Sie mehr Mehl.

Tipps zur Fehlersuche und -behebung (Fortsetzung)

Was passiert, wenn der Teig zu lange geht?

Wenn Sie den Teig aus Versehen zu lange gehen lassen und er zu hoch aufgeht (wenn er sozusagen „übergeht"), können Sie ihn einfach zusammenstoßen, ihn ein wenig kneten, damit die Luft entweichen kann, und ihn dann erneut gehen lassen. Teig, der zu lange gegangen ist, sieht aus als wäre er wie ein Ballon aufgegangen und ist mehr als doppelt so groß wie zu Anfang. Die „Haut" des Teigs ist dünn und transparent und es befinden sich Bläschen direkt unter der Oberfläche.

Wenn man ihn noch länger gehen lässt, geht er von selbst wieder zurück. Auch dann müssen Sie ihn zusammenstoßen und erneut gehen lassen. Genauso können Sie vorgehen, wenn Sie Ihre fertig geformten Laibe zu lange haben gehen lassen. Kneten Sie den Teig leicht durch, um die Luft entweichen zu lassen. Formen Sie anschließend erneut einen Laib und lassen Sie ihn gehen. Passen Sie dabei allerdings gut auf, denn der Teig geht jetzt schneller.

Was ist, wenn die Unterseite der Brote nicht braun genug ist, wenn ich sie aus der Form nehme?

Wenn Sie lieber eine braune Kruste mögen, können Sie die Brote in den Ofen zurückstellen. Entweder in der entsprechenden Brotform oder direkt auf den Rost. Einige zusätzliche Minuten im Ofen werden die Kruste dunkler und knuspriger machen.

Notizen:

Español

Español

índice

ayuda especial

recetas vitamix

cereales

panes rápidos

masas con levadura

(continúa en la página siguiente)

índice

masas con levadura

adobos secos

Acerca de las cuchillas y el recipiente

La máquina Vitamix incluye nuestro recipiente estándar con cuchillas para ingredientes **húmedos**. Aunque las recetas de este libro se pueden realizar en el recipiente con cuchillas para ingredientes húmedos, Vitamix recomienda utilizar el recipiente con cuchillas para ingredientes secos para obtener mejores resultados. Se pueden adquirir por separado recipientes con cuchillas para ingredientes secos o húmedos adicionales.

⚠ADVERTENCIA		
	**Las cuchillas en funcionamiento pueden causar lesiones graves.** **NO** introduzca la mano en el recipiente mientras la máquina está en funcionamiento.	

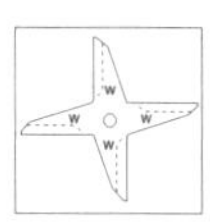

Recipiente con cuchillas para ingredientes húmedos: diseñado para procesar líquidos, incluidos zumos, mezclas congeladas, salsas, sopas, purés, masas líquidas y para trocear ingredientes húmedos. Las cuchillas para ingredientes húmedos también pueden moler granos y amasar, pero no son tan eficientes como las cuchillas para ingredientes secos para estas aplicaciones.

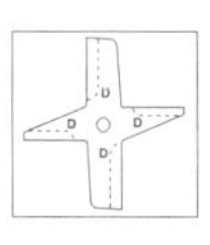

Recipiente con cuchillas para ingredientes secos: estas cuchillas están claramente marcadas con la letra "D" (de "Dry", seco en inglés) y están diseñadas específicamente para moler ingredientes secos, tales como los granos, los cereales y el café, y también se utilizan para amasar. Las cuchillas para ingredientes secos NO pueden procesar líquidos de forma eficiente.

PRECAUCIÓN: moler ingredientes secos durante más de 2 minutos puede dañar la máquina. El uso habitual puede provocar deterioros estéticos en el recipiente y desafilar las cuchillas con el tiempo.

⚠PRECAUCIÓN		
	Las piezas móviles pueden recalentarse con un uso prolongado. **NO** tocar.	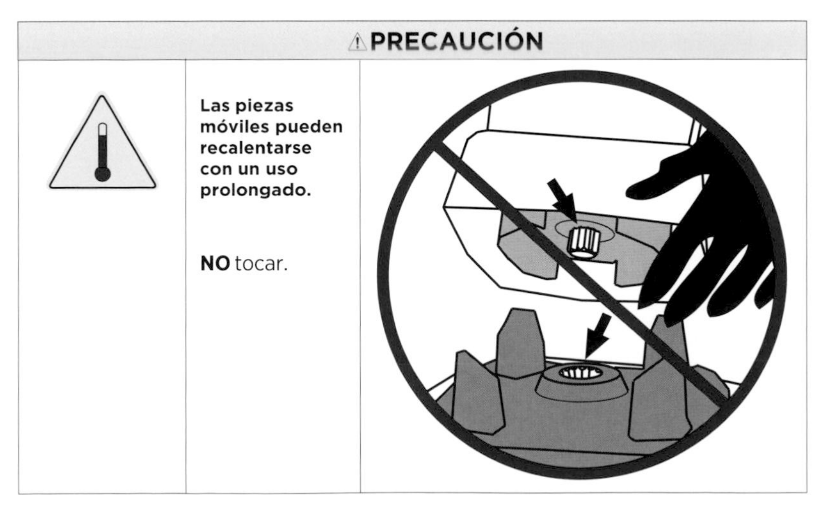

Acerca de las cuchillas y el recipiente *(continuación)*

Acerca de la molienda de hierbas aromáticas y especias
Algunas hierbas aromáticas pueden desprender aceites volátiles al molerlas, lo que puede causar la decoloración del recipiente de forma permanente. Otras hierbas tienen aromas muy intensos que pueden permanecer en el recipiente y afectar al sabor de otros alimentos. La molienda de algunas hierbas aromáticas y especias también puede causar que las cuchillas se desafilen con el tiempo o que se agriete el recipiente. Si muele hierbas aromáticas habitualmente, es posible que le convenga adquirir un recipiente con cuchillas para ingredientes secos adicional y sustituir las cuchillas cuando sea necesario.

MOLER CAFÉ EN GRANO

Observe el proceso de molienda atentamente, hay 6 niveles de finura. Con esta máquina puede crear su propio estilo de café gourmet (véase la lista a continuación).

velocidad: variable • procesamiento: 10 segundos

2 tazas (400 g) de café en grano	Verter 2 tazas (400 g) de café en grano en el recipiente y ajustar la tapa. Seleccionar la Variable 1. Poner en marcha la máquina y aumentar gradualmente la velocidad hasta la Variable 8. Moler durante 10 segundos para obtener un café de tipo filtro.

Niveles de finura:

1. Cafetera eléctrica (muy grueso). Moler en la Variable 8 durante 7-8 segundos.
2. Filtro (grueso). Moler en la Variable 8 durante 10 segundos
3. En forma de cono (menos grueso que la harina de maíz). Moler en la Variable 8 durante 12-13 segundos.
4. Cocina tradicional (moderadamente fino). Moler en la Variable 8 durante 15-16 segundos.
5. Espresso (más fino, como el azúcar, pero no en polvo). Moler en la Variable 8 durante 20 segundos.
6. Molienda turca (fino, como la harina). Moler en la Variable 8 durante 25 segundos.

Cuanto más tiempo se muelan los granos de café, más fino es el resultado. El café molido que se vaya a consumir en las dos semanas posteriores se debe guardar en un recipiente hermético y mantener en un lugar fresco sin luz directa. Si se desea conservar durante más de dos semanas, guardar en un recipiente hermético en el congelador.

Resolución de problemas para el café espresso: si el café espresso sale lentamente (de la cafetera express) y es muy amargo, pruebe una molienda más gruesa. Si queda flojo y aguado, pruebe una molienda más fina.

Horneado fácil

El arte del horneado es una experiencia terapéutica que cautiva con sus aromas embriagadores, la expresión artística y los halagos de admiración. Se experimenta una gran satisfacción cuando se crea algo desde el principio, y cuando se sabe exactamente lo que contiene la comida del plato. Y, con la capacidad de elaborar sus propias harinas integrales, Vitamix le permite llevar su afición a un nivel de frescura totalmente nuevo.

Su máquina Vitamix mezcla fácilmente masas líquidas y prepara masas sólidas para elaborar magdalenas esponjosas, panes tiernos, pizzas finas y mucho más. Disfrute con las recetas de este libro y con los consejos útiles de nuestro cocinero para asegurarse de que cada receta salga del horno tal y como había esperado. Y, puesto que puede verter las mezclas desde el recipiente Vitamix directamente en el molde o la plancha, la limpieza también es fácil.

Empecemos a elaborar nuestros productos con Vitamix, porque no hay nada como el aroma de los alimentos recién horneados en casa para reunir a la familia.

Acerca de la elaboración de pan

La magia de tres ingredientes

Trigo

La mayoría de los panes que consumimos son de trigo. El pan de centeno es en realidad pan de trigo con centeno. El pan multicereales es pan de trigo que contiene cantidades más pequeñas de cebada, avena, centeno, maíz, trigo sarraceno u otros cereales. El pan integral es pan de trigo con salvado. El pan de plátano o de calabacín es pan de trigo con plátano o calabacín. Independientemente del tipo de pan que nos guste, la mayoría de los panes tienen cosas en común, y el trigo es una de ellas. El trigo es la mejor fuente de proteína de cereal, denominada gluten. Cuando se trabaja la masa de trigo, el gluten forma una red esponjosa. Esta red atrapa las burbujas de dióxido de carbono que se producen cuando la levadura digiere el almidón de la masa, lo que provoca que la masa suba. Sin gluten, el resultado es un pan compacto y plano.

En un grano de trigo, el salvado y el germen tienden a provocar que el producto horneado sea compacto y que no reaccione a la levadura o a otros agentes de fermentación. Por tanto, se necesita un trigo con alto contenido en proteína para contrarrestar esta situación. Recomendamos utilizar trigo duro rojo o el nuevo trigo duro blanco. (No confundir el trigo duro blanco con el trigo blando blanco, que se utiliza habitualmente en repostería. El trigo duro se utiliza principalmente para hacer pasta). El pan elaborado con trigo duro blanco combina las propiedades beneficiosas del trigo integral con un sabor suave y dulce. El trigo duro blanco no contiene los compuestos con sabores fuertes que forman parte del trigo duro rojo. Es de color ámbar dorado y consigue que el producto horneado tenga un sabor suave y un color más claro. El contenido de proteína del trigo duro blanco es similar al del trigo duro rojo. Si no hay disponibilidad de trigo duro blanco en su zona, puede ponerse en contacto con la Asociación Estadounidense de Productores de Trigo Blanco en los números +1 (913) 367-4422 o +1 (800) 372-4422, o visitar su sitio web en www.farmerdirectfoods.com. Se recomienda el trigo duro rojo de altura y de invierno con un contenido de proteína de al menos un 14% y una humedad del 9% o menos.

Levadura

La fermentación es fundamental en la elaboración del pan, y la levadura es el agente de fermentación más utilizado. La levadura es un organismo vivo que se activa con agua templada y azúcar natural, como el que encontramos en la miel, la melaza o el jarabe de arce, o azúcares refinados. Los edulcorantes artificiales no son azúcares naturales y no ofrecen alimento para el cultivo de levadura. Sin embargo, la harina, especialmente la harina integral, contiene una cantidad suficiente de azúcar natural para alimentar el cultivo.

Es necesario tener precaución al añadir la mezcla de levadura/agua a la harina recién molida. Si la harina está demasiado caliente, aumentará la temperatura general de la mezcla y matará la levadura. Por este motivo, sugerimos empezar con granos congelados para evitar el sobrecalentamiento de la harina.

Líquido

Se necesitará líquido para la masa de pan, y puede ser agua, leche, agua de patata o zumo. Se pueden utilizar incluso huevos. Para ello, primero hay que echar los huevos en la taza de medir y, a continuación, añadir el líquido que falte para alcanzar la cantidad especificada en la receta. Si se utiliza harina a temperatura ambiente, la temperatura del líquido debe ser de 40-46 ºC (105°F-115°F). Al hacer pan con la máquina Vitamix, es necesario prestar atención a la temperatura de la harina. Si se utiliza harina integral recién molida, ya estará caliente. Para facilitar que se enfríe, es conveniente retirar la harina del recipiente y medir la cantidad deseada.

Otros ingredientes

El pan admite todo tipo de variaciones.

- El aceite, cuando lo encontramos en la lista de ingredientes de una receta, ayuda a mantener la humedad y a conservar el pan fresco durante más tiempo.
- Los huevos potencian el sabor del pan y le aportan las proteínas que contribuyen a que la masa crezca más; además, también ayudan a evitar que se seque.
- La sal tiene dos funciones: 1) es un inhibidor de la levadura, ya que la sal ralentiza el proceso de fermentación; 2) potencia el sabor. Sin sal, el pan tiene un sabor un poco insípido.

Buenas noticias para los que tienen una panificadora

No encontrará en el mercado ningún electrodoméstico mejor que Vitamix para moler el grano. Utilice harina recién molida en sus recetas de pan integral para panificadoras. Estamos convencidos de que le gustarán los resultados.

Los retos de hacer pan de trigo integral

Sí, conseguir hacer un buen pan integral puede ser complicado. Pero se puede hacer. Las siguientes pautas le enseñarán a saber qué esperar y cómo evitar fallos comunes.

Cuando se utiliza sola, la harina integral produce un pan oscuro, más pesado y compacto. Los panes integrales son generalmente de menor tamaño en comparación con los panes blancos del mismo peso. El salvado y el germen constituyen el 15% del grano y no contienen gluten. Recuerde, el gluten es una proteína que aporta estructura y fuerza a los productos horneados. En otras palabras, la harina de trigo integral contiene menos gluten que la misma cantidad de harina blanca. Aunque el pan integral recién horneado es más pesado, también es delicioso y saciante.

El pan integral se seca antes que el pan blanco. Es mejor hacer solo la cantidad a consumir en un día. Se puede usar el pan del día anterior para hacer tostadas, rellenos, torrijas, picatostes, pan rallado o pudin de pan.

Cómo obtener un pan más liso

Trasladar la masa a una superficie ligeramente enharinada y amasar uno o dos minutos. Dar forma al pan y colocarlo en un molde engrasado. Dejar que la masa suba y hornear según las instrucciones.

Cómo adaptar las recetas de pan

Adaptar sus propias recetas de pan es fácil con Vitamix. En la cocina de prueba, dividimos la mayoría de las recetas en dos partes (puesto que las recetas de pan normalmente rinden dos hogazas). Para obtener mejores resultados, se recomienda hacer una hogaza cada vez y reducir los ingredientes de la siguiente forma:

Harina: utilizar hasta 2 1/2 tazas (280 g) de harina. Esta harina puede ser de una mezcla de cereales, pero hay que tener en cuenta la proporción 1:3 (una parte de otros cereales y tres partes de trigo o harina de trigo).
Agua: entre 1 y 1 1/4 tazas (240-300 ml).
Levadura: 1 sobre por cada hogaza (1 cucharada).

Hornear en regiones altas

Puesto que la presión atmosférica disminuye en lugares altos, las masas fermentadas suben más rápidamente que al nivel del mar. Hay que disminuir el tiempo de fermentación de los panes con levaduras a la mitad. La altitud también puede provocar una mayor pérdida de humedad. Utilizar harina con moderación a la hora de amasar a mano. Añadir solo la harina necesaria para trabajar la masa. Engrasarse las manos facilita la manipulación de la masa.

Si el pan queda pesado y quebradizo:

- Pruebe a sustituir la harina sin blanquear por un poco de harina integral.
- Pruebe a añadir una cucharadita de harina de gluten (de venta en tiendas de alimentación natural) a cada taza de harina de trigo integral para que la masa suba más fácilmente.
- En caso de añadir otros cereales al trigo, debemos asegurarnos de mantener la proporción 1:3 (una parte de otros cereales por cada tres partes de trigo).
- ¿Qué tipo de trigo utiliza? El nuevo trigo blanco duro es más dulce y produce un pan más ligero.
- Pruebe a dejar que la masa suba dos veces: la primera en el recipiente de la máquina y la segunda en el molde de pan.
- ¿La harina era demasiado gruesa? Controle atentamente el tiempo de molienda de los granos. El tiempo de molienda recomendado es de un minuto.
- ¿Hemos amasado el pan hasta que la masa ha quedado elástica? Es posible que no se amasara lo suficiente.

Si la hogaza tiene una forma deficiente o la corteza quebrada:

- ¿Hemos añadido demasiado líquido? ¿La masa estaba demasiado húmeda en general?
- ¿La masa estaba demasiado seca? ¿Hemos añadido demasiada harina?
- ¿Hemos amasado la masa bien? ¿La distribución de la levadura no era uniforme?
- ¿Hemos colocado el molde en la mitad del horno? ¿Es posible que el calor no se distribuya de manera uniforme?
- ¿No hemos dejado que la masa subiera lo suficiente antes de meterla en el horno?

Si el pan queda bajo y la textura es demasiado compacta o granulada:

- ¿La masa era demasiado densa y difícil de amasar? Es posible que no tuviera suficiente líquido.
- ¿La levadura es vieja? Compruebe la fecha de caducidad. En caso de duda, disuelva un sobre de levadura y una cucharadita de azúcar en 1/4 de taza (60 ml) de agua templada 40-46 ºC (105°F-115°F). Remueva y reserve durante 5-10 minutos. Si produce una característica capa de espuma significa que está en buenas condiciones. La levadura se debe conservar en la nevera o el congelador. Nunca se debe conservar a temperatura ambiente.
- La levadura no se activa debido al calor o al frío. La levadura es muy frágil. La alta temperatura de la harina recién molida matará la levadura.
- La levadura no se activa porque la masa no tiene la temperatura suficiente. Deje reposar la masa en un lugar templado para que suba.
- ¿Hemos dejado que la masa suba lo suficiente antes de hornearla? Puede ser que la horneáramos antes de que terminara de subir.
- ¿Hemos añadido demasiada sal? La sal puede inhibir el crecimiento de la levadura.

Si la textura es demasiado gruesa o abierta:

- ¿Hemos añadido demasiada levadura?
- ¿La masa estaba demasiado húmeda?
- ¿La masa subió por encima del borde del molde? Puede ser que haya subido demasiado tiempo.
- ¿El molde era del tamaño adecuado?

Cortezas a medida

¿Cómo le gusta la corteza: tierna o gruesa, correosa y dura? Con los diferentes glaseados y algunos consejos de panadería, es posible conseguir una amplia gama de texturas, sabores y colores de corteza.

Para conseguir una corteza crujiente, como la del pan francés, coloque un recipiente con agua en la rejilla del horno inferior a la del pan mientras se hornea. El vapor que rodea al pan en el horno caliente consigue este resultado. Otra técnica consiste en vaporizar agua sobre el pan en intervalos de 10 minutos durante el horneado.

Para conseguir una corteza crujiente y brillante, pinte la masa con una mezcla simple de almidón de maíz y agua. Disuelva 1 cucharadita de almidón de maíz en 2/3 de taza (160 ml) de agua y lleve la mezcla a ebullición. Deje enfriar la mezcla y, con un pincel suave, pinte todas las superficies expuestas justo antes de hornear. Después de hornear durante 10 minutos, saque el pan, píntelo de nuevo y termine de hornear.

Para conseguir una corteza lustrosa, pruebe con un glaseado de huevo. Puesto que es pegajoso, es muy útil para fijar las semillas de amapola o de sésamo. Justo antes de hornear, pinte el pan con un huevo entero ligeramente batido, o use una yema o una clara batida con 1 cucharada de agua fría. Si usa la yema, obtendrá un color más dorado; la clara añade brillo pero no aporta color. Un huevo entero produce los dos resultados.

Para conseguir una corteza tierna, pinte el pan con mantequilla derretida justo antes de hornearlo o nada más sacarlo del horno. O también puede pintar el pan con leche o nata antes de hornearlo.

Acerca de la molienda de harinas integrales

Los cereales en grano crecen aproximadamente un 25% en volumen cuando se muelen hasta conseguir harina. El maíz, la soja y otros granos con alto contenido de humedad suelen apelmazarse y atascarse durante la molienda. Para mantener la harina en movimiento, introduzca el empujador a través de la abertura del tapón y, mientras la máquina está en funcionamiento en la posición de velocidad High (Alta), dirija suavemente la harina hacia las cuchillas. Esta acción garantiza que el grano se muela de manera uniforme.

Nota importante:
Para obtener mejores resultados, conservar el grano en el congelador. No se debe moler más de 2 tazas (400 g) cada vez.

HARINA INTEGRAL

velocidad: variable en posición alta • procesamiento: 1 minuto
rendimiento: hasta 3 1/4 tazas (390 g)

1/4-2 tazas (50-400 g) de trigo entero

Nota del cocinero:
a temperatura ambiente, la harina se conserva fresca durante un mes. En la nevera, durante dos meses. Para conservarla durante más tiempo, se puede congelar de 6 meses a un año. Separe la cantidad que va a necesitar y deje que alcance la temperatura ambiente.

Coloque 2 tazas (400 g) de trigo entero en el recipiente Vitamix y ajuste la tapa.

Seleccionar la Variable 1.

Poner en marcha la máquina y aumentar gradualmente la velocidad hasta la Variable 10, después hasta la posición de velocidad High (Alta).

Muela hasta conseguir la consistencia deseada (consulte la tabla de los tiempos de molienda recomendados). Cuanto más tiempo lo tenga en la máquina, más fina será la consistencia de la harina, con un máximo de 1 minuto.

Medida de trigo integral entero	Tiempo de molienda	Velocidad	Rendimiento de harina aproximado	Grado de finura
3/4 de taza (144 g)	1 minuto	VAR - HIGH (ALTA)	1 taza (120 g) + 2 1/2 cucharaditas	muy fina
1 taza (192 g)	1 minuto	VAR - HIGH (ALTA)	1 1/2 tazas (180 g)	muy fina
1 1/4 tazas (240 g)	1 minuto	VAR - HIGH (ALTA)	1 3/4 tazas (210 g) + 2 cucharadas (15 g)	muy fina
1 1/2 tazas (288 g)	1 minuto	VAR - HIGH (ALTA)	2 1/3 tazas (280 g) + 1 cucharadas (8 g)	muy fina
1 3/4 tazas (336 g)	1 minuto	VAR - HIGH (ALTA)	2 1/2 tazas (300 g) + 3 cucharadas (22 g)	muy fina
2 tazas (384 g)	1 minuto	VAR - HIGH (ALTA)	3 1/4 tazas (390 g)	muy fina

Nota: para obtener mejores resultados, utilice las cuchillas especiales para ingredientes secos cuando elabore harinas. Seleccionar la Variable 1. Poner en marcha la máquina y aumentar gradualmente la velocidad hasta la Variable 10, después hasta la posición de velocidad High (Alta).

Acerca de la molienda de harinas integrales *(continuación)*

Precaución al moler harina:
Siga los siguientes tiempos de molienda recomendados. Moler los ingredientes secos, como el trigo entero, durante más de dos minutos puede provocar que la harina se apelmace y el recipiente se sobrecaliente. Pueden producirse daños permanentes en el recipiente y las juntas. Observe atentamente los tiempos de molienda recomendados.

Guía de cocción de granos partidos

Grano partido	Cantidad	Velocidad: baja Variable 7 u 8	Agua	Tiempo de cocción	Rendimiento de cereal
Cebada	1/2 taza (90 g)	10 segundos	2 tazas (480 ml)	20 minutos	1 1/2 tazas (360 g)
Trigo sarraceno	1/2 taza (80 g)	5 segundos	2 tazas (480 ml)	10 minutos	1 2/3 tazas (400 g)
Maíz	1/2 taza (80 g)	10 segundos	2 tazas (480 ml)	20 minutos	1 1/2 tazas (360 g)
Avena	1/2 taza (80 g)	10 segundos	2 tazas (480 ml)	20 minutos	1 1/2 tazas (360 g)
Arroz (blanco)	1/2 taza (90 g)	10 segundos	2 tazas (480 ml)	8-10 minutos	1 3/4 tazas (420 g)
Arroz (integral)	1/2 taza (90 g)	10 segundos	2 tazas (480 ml)	20 minutos	1 3/4 tazas (420 g)
Centeno	1/2 taza (90 g)	10 segundos	1 1/2 tazas (360 ml)	20 minutos	1 1/2 tazas (360 g)
Trigo	1/2 taza (100 g)	10 segundos	1 1/2 tazas (360 ml)	20 minutos	1 1/2 tazas (360 g)
Arroz salvaje	1/2 taza (90 g)	10 segundos	1 1/2 tazas (360 ml)	20 minutos	1 1/2 tazas (360 g)

Consejos útiles

1. Moler 2 tazas (400 g) de grano cada vez produce una molienda más uniforme.
2. Se puede añadir 1/4-1/2 cucharadita de sal al agua hirviendo. El único propósito es mejorar el sabor y no es necesaria si desea reducir su consumo de sal.
3. Una forma de aprovechar las propiedades nutritivas del grano entero y la comodidad de los cereales preparados es añadir la cantidad adecuada de grano partido en un cazo con agua hirviendo la noche anterior antes de irse a dormir. Apague el fuego, tape bien el cazo y deje que el cereal en remojo toda la noche. Por la mañana ya estará listo para consumirse como cereal frío. Si lo prefiere caliente, solo tiene que calentarlo en el cazo o en el microondas.

4. Otro método práctico es el uso de un termo. Vierta 1 taza (200 g) de grano en un termo (más cómodo si es de boca grande) con capacidad 0,95 l y añada agua hirviendo hasta 2,5 cm (1 pulg.) del borde. Utilice una cuchara de madera para remover el grano y el agua. Cierre el termo y el cereal se cocinará lentamente en 8-12 horas.
5. Para mayor variedad, mezcle diferentes granos. Por ejemplo, avena y trigo sarraceno, arroz salvaje y arroz integral, etc.
6. Condimente el cereal con nuez moscada o canela. Añada sus frutas favoritas para conseguir sabores nuevos y mayores propiedades nutricionales: melocotón, fresas, arándanos, pasas o coco.

   Nota del cocinero: *si añade frutas deshidratadas a sus cereales, recuerde que estas absorben agua y se rehidratan. Es conveniente aumentar la proporción de agua especificada en la receta para compensar el agua que absorbe la fruta deshidratada.*
7. Para utilizarlo en guisos, sustituya el agua de cocción por caldo.

PARTIR GRANOS PARA HACER CEREALES

velocidad: variable • procesamiento: 10 segundos

1/4-2 tazas (50-400 g) cereal de grano entero (trigo, cebada, avena, maíz, arroz, etc.)

Sal al gusto (aproximadamente 1/4 de cucharadita por cada 1/2 taza (100 g) de cereal)

Verter hasta 2 tazas (400 g) de grano entero en el recipiente y ajustar la tapa.

Seleccionar la Variable 1.

Poner la máquina en marcha y aumentar gradualmente la velocidad hasta la Variable 7 u 8.

Moler hasta conseguir la consistencia deseada. Cuanto más tiempo se tenga en la máquina, más fina será la consistencia del cereal, hasta el punto de convertirse en harina.

Cómo cocinar los granos partidos

En un cazo pesado (o a baño maría), llevar el agua con sal a ebullición. Añadir el cereal lentamente, removiendo constantemente para evitar la formación de grumos.

Tapar bien el cazo y bajar el fuego. Cocer hasta que esté tierno (consultar los tiempos de cocción en la tabla anterior), removiendo con frecuencia.

CEREALES CON TRIGO PARTIDO, MANZANA Y PASAS

preparación: 15 minutos • procesamiento: 15 segundos • tiempo de cocción: 15-20 minutos
rendimiento: 3 tazas (720 g) de cereales cocidos

1 taza (180 g) de trigo entero

1 1/2 tazas (360 ml) de agua

1/4 de cucharadita de sal

1 manzana (170 g) ácida, pelada, sin pepitas y en cuartos

1/8 de cucharadita de canela

1/2 taza (72 g) de pasas

2 cucharadas (18 g) de pipas de girasol

Colocar el trigo integral en el recipiente Vitamix con CUCHILLAS PARA INGREDIENTES SECOS y ajustar la tapa.

Seleccionar la Variable 1.

Poner la máquina en marcha y aumentar gradualmente la velocidad hasta la Variable 7 u 8.

Moler hasta conseguir el grosor deseado, alrededor de 15 segundos.

En un cazo, llevar a ebullición el agua con la sal. Añadir lentamente el trigo partido al agua hirviendo, removiendo constantemente con un batidor de varillas.

Bajar el fuego, tapar y cocer de 15 a 20 minutos removiendo con frecuencia.

Mientras se cocina el trigo partido, trocear las manzanas en el recipiente Vitamix con CUCHILLAS PARA INGREDIENTES HÚMEDOS.

Ajustar la tapa y retirar el tapón.

Seleccionar la Variable 1.

Poner en marcha la máquina y aumentar gradualmente la velocidad hasta la Variable 4. Mientras la máquina está en funcionamiento, añadir las manzanas en cuartos a través de la abertura del tapón, utilizando el empujador según sea necesario para trocearlas.

Retirar el cazo del fuego y añadir las manzanas troceadas, la canela, las pasas y las pipas de girasol al trigo cocido. Remover para mezclar los ingredientes.

Tapar y dejar reposar la mezcla durante 5 minutos más antes de servir.

Información nutricional por ración de 1 taza (240 g): 342 calorías (6% de grasas, 9% de proteína, 85% de hidratos de carbono) • proteínas 9 g • grasas totales 2 g • grasas saturadas 0 g
hidratos de carbono 79 g • fibra 10 g • azúcar 22 g • sodio 204 mg • colesterol 0 mg

Si los ingredientes rebotan contra la parte superior de las cuchillas y no se trocean correctamente significa que la velocidad es demasiado baja. Si rebotan violentamente contra las paredes del recipiente y el resultado son partículas demasiado gruesas o troceadas irregularmente significa que la velocidad es demasiado alta.

CEREALES DE ARROZ INTEGRAL Y ALBARICOQUE

preparación: 10 minutos • procesamiento: 10 segundos • tiempo de cocción: 20 minutos
rendimiento: 3 1/2 tazas (840 g) de cereales cocidos

1 taza (185 g) de arroz integral crudo

3 1/2 tazas (840 ml) de agua

1/2 cucharadita de sal

8 albaricoques deshidratados (sin azúcar añadida)

2 cucharadas (18 g) de pipas de girasol

1/4 de cucharadita de extracto de almendra, opcional

Colocar el arroz integral en el recipiente Vitamix con CUCHILLAS PARA INGREDIENTES SECOS y ajustar la tapa.

Seleccionar la Variable 1.

Poner la máquina en marcha y aumentar gradualmente la velocidad hasta la Variable 7 u 8.

Moler hasta conseguir el grosor deseado, aproximadamente 10 segundos. Si se desea un cereal más fino, moler durante más tiempo.

En un cazo, llevar a ebullición el agua con la sal. Añadir lentamente el arroz partido al agua hirviendo, removiendo constantemente con un batidor de varillas.

Bajar el fuego, tapar y cocer durante 20 minutos hasta que se cocine, removiendo con frecuencia.

Mientras se cocina el arroz, trocear los albaricoques en el recipiente Vitamix con CUCHILLAS PARA INGREDIENTES HÚMEDOS.

Ajustar la tapa y retirar el tapón.

Seleccionar la Variable 1.

Poner en marcha la máquina y aumentar gradualmente la velocidad hasta la Variable 5. Con la máquina en funcionamiento, añadir los albaricoques a través de la abertura del tapón. Si es necesario, ajustar la variable de velocidad para trocearlos más finos.

Retirar el cazo del fuego y añadir los albaricoques troceados, las pipas de girasol y el extracto de almendras al cereal cocido. Remover para mezclar los ingredientes.

Tapar y dejar reposar la mezcla durante 5 minutos más antes de servir.

Información nutricional por ración de 1 taza (240 g): 224 calorías (10% de grasa, 9% de proteína, 82% de hidratos de carbono) • proteínas 5 g • grasas totales 2 g • grasas saturadas 0 g hidratos de carbono 46 g • fibra 3 g • azúcar 5 g • sodio 346 mg • colesterol 0 mg

Si los ingredientes rebotan contra la parte superior de las cuchillas y no se trocean correctamente significa que la velocidad es demasiado baja. Si rebotan violentamente contra las paredes del recipiente y el resultado son partículas demasiado gruesas o troceadas irregularmente significa que la velocidad es demasiado alta.

SÉMOLA DE ARROZ INTEGRAL

preparación: 10 minutos • procesamiento: 10 segundos • tiempo de cocción: 20 minutos
rendimiento: 3 1/2 tazas (840 g) de cereales cocidos

1 taza (185 g) de arroz integral crudo

3 1/2 tazas (840 ml) de agua

1/2 cucharadita de sal

Colocar el arroz integral en el recipiente Vitamix con CUCHILLAS PARA INGREDIENTES SECOS y ajustar la tapa.

Seleccionar la Variable 1.

Poner la máquina en marcha y aumentar gradualmente la velocidad hasta la Variable 7 u 8.

Moler hasta conseguir el grosor deseado, aproximadamente 10 segundos. Si se desea un cereal más fino, moler durante más tiempo.

En un cazo, llevar a ebullición el agua con la sal. Añadir lentamente el arroz partido al agua hirviendo, removiendo constantemente con un batidor de varillas.

Bajar el fuego, tapar y cocer durante 20 minutos hasta que se cocine, removiendo con frecuencia.

Información nutricional por ración de 1 taza (240 g): 197 calorías (7% de grasas, 8% de proteínas, 85% de hidratos de carbono) • proteínas 4 g • grasas totales 1 g • grasas saturadas 0 g
hidratos de carbono 41 g • fibra 2 g • azúcar 0 g • sodio 344 mg • colesterol 0 mg

CEREALES DE TRIGO PARTIDO

preparación: 10 minutos • procesamiento: 15 segundos • tiempo de cocción: 15-20 minutos
rendimiento: 3 tazas (720 g) de cereales cocidos

1 taza (180 g) de trigo entero

3 tazas (720 ml) de agua

1/2 cucharadita de sal

Colocar el trigo integral en el recipiente Vitamix con CUCHILLAS PARA INGREDIENTES SECOS y ajustar la tapa.

Seleccionar la Variable 1.

Poner la máquina en marcha y aumentar gradualmente la velocidad hasta la Variable 7 u 8.

Moler hasta conseguir el grosor deseado, alrededor de 15 segundos.

En un cazo, llevar a ebullición el agua con la sal. Añadir lentamente el trigo partido al agua hirviendo, removiendo constantemente con un batidor de varillas.

Bajar el fuego, tapar y cocer durante 15-20 minutos hasta que se cocine.

Información nutricional por ración de 1 taza (240 g): 219 calorías (4% de grasa, 12% de proteínas, 83% de hidratos de carbono) • proteínas 7 g • grasas totales 1 g • grasas saturadas 0 g
hidratos de carbono 49 g • fibra 8 g • azúcar 0 g • sodio 399 mg • colesterol 0 mg

CEREALES DE ARROZ CREMOSO

preparación: 10 minutos • procesamiento: 10 segundos • tiempo de cocción: 8-10 minutos
rendimiento: 1 3/4 tazas (420 g) de cereales cocidos

1/2 taza (93 g) de arroz crudo

2 tazas (480 ml) de agua

1/4 de cucharadita de sal

Colocar el arroz en el recipiente Vitamix con CUCHILLAS PARA INGREDIENTES SECOS y ajustar la tapa.

Seleccionar la Variable 1.

Poner la máquina en marcha y aumentar gradualmente la velocidad hasta la Variable 7 u 8.

Moler hasta conseguir el grosor deseado, aproximadamente 10 segundos. Si se desea un cereal más fino, moler durante más tiempo.

En un cazo, llevar a ebullición el agua con la sal. Verter el arroz partido lentamente en agua hirviendo. Remover constantemente con un batidor de varillas.

Bajar el fuego, tapar y cocer de 8 a 10 minutos (un poco más si se utiliza arroz integral) hasta que se cocine, removiendo frecuentemente.

Información nutricional por ración de 1 taza (240 g): 199 calorías (2% de grasa, 8% de proteínas, 90% de hidratos de carbono) • proteínas 4 g • grasas totales 0 g • grasas saturadas 0 g
hidratos de carbono 44 g • fibra 1 g • azúcar 0 g • sodio 355 mg • colesterol 0 mg

MUESLI

preparación: 15 minutos • procesamiento: 3 minutos • tiempo de cocción: 15 minutos
rendimiento: 10 tazas (2,4 kg)

1/2 taza (120 ml) de miel

3/4 de taza (165 g) de azúcar moreno, colmada

1/2 taza (120 ml) de agua caliente

1 cucharadita de sal

2 cucharaditas de extracto de vainilla

1 1/2 cucharaditas de canela

5 tazas (400 g) de copos de avena

1 taza (104 g) de germen de trigo

1/4 de taza (35 g) de pipas de girasol

1/2 taza (42 g) de coco rallado o en copos

1/2 taza (58 g) de nueces troceadas

1 taza (145 g) de pasas

Precalentar el horno a 180 °C (350°F). Engrasar ligeramente dos fuentes de horno de 33 x 23 cm (13 pulg. x 9 pulg.) o una bandeja de asar grande con aceite vegetal.

Verter la miel, el azúcar moreno, el agua, la sal, la vainilla y la canela en el recipiente Vitamix con CUCHILLAS PARA INGREDIENTES HÚMEDOS en el orden especificado y ajustar la tapa.

Seleccionar la Variable 1.

Poner en marcha la máquina y aumentar gradualmente la velocidad hasta la Variable 10, después hasta la posición de velocidad High (Alta).

Procesar durante 3 minutos o hasta que la mezcla desprenda vapor.

En un recipiente grande, mezclar la avena, el germen de trigo, las pipas de girasol, el coco y las nueces troceadas.

Verter la mezcla caliente sobre los ingredientes secos y remover, dejando únicamente unos pocos grumos. Verter en las fuentes preparadas y hornear durante 15 minutos, removiendo cada 5 minutos.

Sacar los moldes del horno y añadir las pasas. Colocar los moldes en una rejilla y dejar enfriar por completo. Conservar en tarros de cristal o en una bolsa de plástico grande.

Información nutricional por ración de 1/2 taza (120 g): 287 calorías (18% de grasa, 12% de proteína, 69% de hidratos de carbono) • proteínas 9 g • grasas totales 6 g • grasas saturadas 1 g hidratos de carbono 52 g • fibra 6 g • azúcar 20 g • sodio 124 mg • colesterol 0 mg

La mezcla también se puede hornear a una temperatura más baja hasta que se seque.

Esta receta única no necesita grasas añadidas. Para obtener un muesli menos seco, añadir 1/4 de taza (60 ml) de aceite de oliva ligero o de pepitas de uva a los ingredientes líquidos.

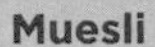

Muesli

Para trocear las nueces (en el recipiente con CUCHILLAS PARA INGREDIENTES SECOS), seleccionar la Variable 1. Poner en marcha la máquina y aumentar gradualmente la velocidad hasta la Variable 4. Verter las nueces a través de la abertura de la tapa y procesar durante 5 segundos.

GACHAS DE AVENA

preparación: 10 minutos • procesamiento: 10 segundos • tiempo de cocción: 30 minutos
rendimiento: 3 1/2 tazas (840 g) de cereales cocidos

1 taza (160 g) de avena descascarillada (NO harina de avena)

4 tazas (960 ml) de agua

1/2 cucharadita de sal

Colocar la avena integral descascarillada en el recipiente Vitamix con CUCHILLAS PARA INGREDIENTES SECOS y ajustar la tapa.

Seleccionar la Variable 1.

Poner en marcha la máquina y aumentar gradualmente la velocidad hasta la Variable 7.

Moler hasta conseguir el grosor deseado, aproximadamente 10 segundos. Si se desea un cereal más fino, moler durante más tiempo.

En un cazo, llevar a ebullición el agua con la sal. Añadir lentamente la avena partida al agua hirviendo, removiendo constantemente con un batidor de varillas.

Bajar el fuego, tapar y cocer durante 30 minutos o hasta que se cocine, removiendo con frecuencia.

Información nutricional por ración de 1 taza (240 g): 126 calorías (14% de grasas, 18% de proteínas, 68% de hidratos de carbono) • proteína 8 g • grasas saturadas 3 g • grasas totales 1 g
hidratos de carbono 31 g • fibra 5 g • azúcar 1 g • sodio 342 mg • colesterol 0 mg

Gachas de avena

CEREALES DE ARROZ CON PASAS

preparación: 10 minutos • procesamiento: 10 segundos • tiempo de cocción: 30 minutos
rendimiento: 3 1/2 tazas (840 g) de cereales cocidos

1/2 taza (93 g) de arroz crudo

2 tazas (480 ml) de agua

1/4 de cucharadita de sal

1/2 taza (72 g) de pasas

Una pizca de canela

Colocar el arroz en el recipiente Vitamix con CUCHILLAS PARA INGREDIENTES SECOS y ajustar la tapa.

Seleccionar la Variable 1.

Poner la máquina en marcha y aumentar gradualmente la velocidad hasta la Variable 7 u 8.

Moler hasta conseguir el grosor deseado, aproximadamente 10 segundos.

En un cazo, llevar a ebullición el agua con la sal. Añadir lentamente el arroz partido al agua hirviendo, removiendo constantemente con un batidor de varillas.

Bajar el fuego, tapar y cocer de 8 a 10 minutos (un poco más si se utiliza arroz integral) hasta que se cocine.

Retirar el cazo del fuego y añadir las pasas y la canela.

Tapar y dejar reposar durante 5 minutos más antes de servir.

Información nutricional por ración de 1 taza (240 g): 292 calorías (1% de grasas, 6% de proteína, 92% de hidratos de carbono) • proteínas 5 g • grasas totales 0 g • grasas saturadas 0 g
hidratos de carbono 70 g • fibra 2 g • azúcar 24 g • sodio 306 mg • colesterol 0 mg

CEREALES DE DESAYUNO CON AVENA

preparación: 10 minutos • procesamiento: 10 segundos • tiempo de cocción: 30 minutos
rendimiento: 3 3/4 tazas (900 g) de cereales cocidos

1 taza (184 g) de avena integral descascarillada (NO harina de avena)

4 tazas (960 ml) de agua

1/2 cucharadita de sal

6 a 7 ciruelas pasas deshuesadas

Colocar la avena integral descascarillada en el recipiente Vitamix con CUCHILLAS PARA INGREDIENTES SECOS y ajustar la tapa.

Seleccionar la Variable 1.

Poner en marcha la máquina y aumentar gradualmente la velocidad hasta la Variable 7.

Moler hasta conseguir el grosor deseado, aproximadamente 10 segundos. Si se desea un cereal más fino, moler durante más tiempo.

En un cazo, llevar a ebullición el agua con la sal. Añadir lentamente la avena partida al agua hirviendo, removiendo constantemente con un batidor de varillas.

Bajar el fuego, tapar y cocer durante 30 minutos o hasta que se cocine, removiendo con frecuencia.

Mientras se cocina la avena, cortar las ciruelas en el recipiente Vitamix con CUCHILLAS PARA INGREDIENTES HÚMEDOS.

Ajustar la tapa.

Seleccionar la Variable 1.

Poner en marcha la máquina y aumentar gradualmente la velocidad hasta la Variable 5 o 6. Retirar el tapón de la tapa. Con la máquina en funcionamiento, añadir las ciruelas a través de la abertura del tapón.

Retirar el cazo del fuego y añadir las ciruelas troceadas. Remover para mezclar los ingredientes.

Tapar y dejar reposar la mezcla durante 5 minutos más antes de servir.

Información nutricional por ración de 1 taza (240 g): 209 calorías (4% de grasas, 12% de proteínas, 84% de hidratos de carbono) • proteínas 7 g • grasas totales 1 g • grasas saturadas 0 g hidratos de carbono 47 g • fibra 6 g • azúcar 0 g • sodio 325 mg • colesterol 0 mg

Si los ingredientes rebotan contra la parte superior de las cuchillas y no se trocean correctamente significa que la velocidad es demasiado baja. Si rebotan violentamente contra las paredes del recipiente y el resultado son partículas demasiado gruesas o troceadas irregularmente significa que la velocidad es demasiado alta.

panes rápidos

Claves para elaborar pan rápido con éxito

- Si conviene utilizar mantequilla ablandada en una receta, deje la mantequilla a temperatura ambiente durante aproximadamente 20 minutos. No caliente la mantequilla en el microondas, ya que la alta temperatura puede derretirla en lugar de ablandarla y esta consistencia afectará de forma desfavorable al resultado del producto horneado.
- Si se bate la masa en exceso para los panes rápidos, estos quedarán menos tiernos al hornearlos. Hay que removerlos con cuidado y moderación, solo hasta que los ingredientes se mezclen.
- Se debe precalentar el horno durante al menos 10 minutos antes de introducir el pan rápido en la rejilla central. Si se introduce el pan rápido en el horno cuando no tiene la temperatura adecuada, el pan no subirá como debería.
- Guarde los panes rápidos envueltos en film transparente o en papel de aluminio. Se conservan en la nevera hasta tres días o en el congelador hasta tres meses.

Cocina para niños: elaborar panes rápidos o magdalenas es una forma fantástica de fomentar el interés de los niños en la cocina. Anímelos a participar mostrándoles cómo engrasar un molde o cómo medir adecuadamente los ingredientes más sabrosos, como las almendras, las virutas de chocolate o las frutas deshidratadas.

PAN DE MANZANA Y NUECES PECANAS

preparación: 10 minutos • procesamiento: 20 segundos • tiempo de cocción: 40-50 minutos
rendimiento: 1 hogaza (12 rebanadas)

1 taza (125 g) de harina común sin blanquear

1/2 taza (60 g) de harina de trigo integral

1 cucharadita de levadura en polvo

1/4 de cucharadita de bicarbonato

1/2 cucharadita de sal

2 manzanas pequeñas, sin pepitas, cortadas en cuartos, aproximadamente 1 1/4 tazas (156 g)

1 huevo grande

3 cucharadas (45 ml) de aceite de oliva suave

2/3 de taza (147 g) de azúcar moreno, colmada

1/2 taza (54 g) de nueces pecanas troceadas

Engrasar un molde para pan de 22 x 11 cm (8 1/2 pulg. x 4 1/2 pulg.) con aceite vegetal u otro tipo de grasa. Precalentar el horno a 180 °C (350°F).

En un recipiente grande, mezclar la harina común, la harina de trigo integral, la levadura en polvo, el bicarbonato y la sal; mezclar bien.

Verter las manzanas, el huevo y el azúcar moreno en el recipiente Vitamix con CUCHILLAS PARA INGREDIENTES HÚMEDOS en el orden especificado y ajustar la tapa.

Seleccionar la Variable 1.

Poner en marcha la máquina y aumentar gradualmente la velocidad hasta la Variable 10, después hasta la posición de velocidad High (Alta).

Procesar hasta trocear las manzanas, aproximadamente 20 segundos. Si es necesario, introducir el empujador a través de la abertura de la tapa para que la mezcla circule y se troceen los ingredientes.

Verter la mezcla de manzanas y las nueces pecanas en el recipiente con los ingredientes secos. Mezclar a mano SOLO hasta que los ingredientes secos se humedezcan; no mezclar en exceso.

Verter la mezcla en la fuente preparada. Hornear entre 40 y 50 minutos o hasta que al introducir un palillo en el centro, este salga limpio.

Dejar enfriar en una rejilla durante 30 minutos y, a continuación, retirar del molde con cuidado. Dejar que se enfríe por completo antes de cortarlo en rebanadas.

Información nutricional por rebanada: 175 calorías (36% de grasas, 6% de proteínas, 58% de hidratos de carbono)
proteína 3 g • grasas totales 7 g • grasas saturadas 1 g • hidratos de carbono 26 g • fibra 2 g • azúcar 13 g
sodio 178 mg • colesterol 18 mg

BROWNIES "BROWNIE POINTS"

preparación: 20 minutos • procesamiento: 20 segundos • tiempo de cocción: 25-30 minutos
rendimiento: 2 docenas

3/4 de taza (64 g) de cacao en polvo sin azúcar

1 cucharadita de levadura en polvo

1 cucharadita de sal

1 cucharadita de café instantáneo

1 1/2 tazas (180 g) de harina de trigo integral

2 tazas (448 g) de virutas de chocolate semidulce

1 taza (227 g) de mantequilla sin sal, ablandada y cortada en trozos

2 tazas (440 g) de azúcar blanco o moreno colmadas

1 cucharada de extracto de vainilla

4 huevos grandes

Engrasar un molde para pan de 23 x 33 cm (9 pulg. x 13 pulg.) con aceite vegetal u otro tipo de grasa. Precalentar el horno a 180 °C (350°F).

Si se empieza con el trigo integral: colocar 1 1/2 tazas (270 g) de trigo entero en el recipiente Vitamix con CUCHILLAS PARA INGREDIENTES SECOS y ajustar la tapa.

Seleccionar la Variable 1.

Poner en marcha la máquina y aumentar gradualmente la velocidad hasta la Variable 10, después hasta la posición de velocidad High (Alta).

Moler el trigo durante 1 minuto. (No moler en exceso).

Detener la máquina y dejar que la harina se enfríe durante unos minutos. Medir 1 1/2 tazas (180 g) de harina de trigo integral para la receta. Reservar y guardar la harina restante para otro uso.

Si se empieza con la harina de trigo integral: verter el cacao en polvo, la levadura en polvo, la sal, el café instantáneo y la harina de trigo integral en un recipiente grande. Añadir las virutas de chocolate. Reservar.

Verter la mantequilla, el azúcar, la vainilla y los huevos en el recipiente Vitamix con cuchillas para ingredientes HÚMEDOS y ajustar la tapa. Seleccionar la Variable 1.

Poner en marcha la máquina y aumentar gradualmente la velocidad hasta la Variable 10, después hasta la posición de velocidad High (Alta).

Procesar durante 20 segundos hasta que adquiera una consistencia cremosa, utilizando el empujador si es necesario.

Añadir la mezcla de mantequilla a la mezcla de harina y remover a mano para mezclarlas completamente.

Utilizar una espátula de nailon para trasladar la mezcla a la fuente preparada. Hornear entre 25 y 30 minutos o hasta que al introducir un palillo en el centro, este salga con algunas migas húmedas adheridas. No hornear en exceso o los brownies quedarán secos.

Sacar del horno y dejar enfriar en una rejilla. Cortar en porciones y servir.

Información nutricional por brownie: 282 calorías (44% de grasas, 5% de proteínas, 51% de hidratos de carbono)
proteínas 4 g • grasas totales 14 g • grasas saturadas 8 g • hidratos de carbono 37 g • fibra 3 g • azúcar 28 g
sodio 144 mg • colesterol 56 mg

Brownies “Brownie Points”

TARTA DE CALABACÍN CON CHOCOLATE

preparación: 20 minutos • procesamiento: 35-40 segundos • tiempo de cocción: 35-40 minutos
rendimiento: 12 porciones

1/2 taza (114 g) de mantequilla sin sal, en cubos, a temperatura ambiente

1 1/2 tazas (300 g) de azúcar granulado

2 huevos grandes

511 g de calabacín, troceado

1/2 taza (120 ml) de aceite de oliva suave

1 cucharadita de extracto de vainilla

1/2 taza (120 ml) de suero de leche

1 1/2 tazas (180 g) de harina de trigo integral

1 1/4 tazas (156 g) de harina común sin blanquear

1/4 de taza (21 g) de cacao en polvo sin azúcar

1 1/4 cucharaditas de bicarbonato

1 cucharadita de sal

1/4 de taza (30 g) de azúcar glas, tamizado

Precalentar el horno a 160 °C (325°F). Engrasar un molde cuadrado para tarta de 23 cm (9 pulg.).

Verter la mantequilla, el azúcar y los huevos en el recipiente Vitamix con CUCHILLAS PARA INGREDIENTES HÚMEDOS en el orden especificado y ajustar la tapa.

Seleccionar la Variable 1.

Poner en marcha la máquina y aumentar gradualmente la velocidad hasta la Variable 10, después cambiar a la posición de velocidad High (Alta) y utilizar el empujador si es necesario para empujar los ingredientes hacia las cuchillas.

Procesar durante 25 segundos. Detener la máquina, retirar la tapa y raspar las paredes del recipiente.

Añadir el calabacín troceado, el aceite, la vainilla y el suero de leche al recipiente Vitamix con CUCHILLAS PARA INGREDIENTES HÚMEDOS y ajustar la tapa.

Seleccionar la Variable 1.

Poner en marcha la máquina y aumentar gradualmente la velocidad hasta la Variable 10, después hasta la posición de velocidad High (Alta).

Procesar de 10 a 20 segundos o hasta que el calabacín se pique en trozos pequeños.

En un recipiente grande, mezclar las harinas, el cacao en polvo, el bicarbonato y la sal.

Verter la mezcla de calabacín en el recipiente con los ingredientes secos. Mezclar a mano hasta que la masa sea uniforme.

Con una espátula, trasladar la mezcla a la fuente preparada.

Hornear entre 35 y 40 minutos o hasta que al introducir un palillo en el centro, este salga limpio.

Tarta de calabacín con chocolate *(continuación)*

Dejar enfriar en una rejilla durante 30 minutos y, a continuación, pasar un cuchillo con cuidado a lo largo del borde de la tarta para que se desprenda. Invertir en una rejilla y dejar enfriar por completo. Cortar en porciones cuadradas y tamizar el azúcar glas por encima cuando se vaya a servir.

Para hacer harina de trigo integral con trigo entero: colocar 1 1/2 tazas (270 g) de trigo entero en el recipiente Vitamix con CUCHILLAS PARA INGREDIENTES SECOS y ajustar la tapa.

Seleccionar la Variable 1.

Poner en marcha la máquina y aumentar gradualmente la velocidad hasta la Variable 10, después hasta la posición de velocidad High (Alta).

Moler el trigo durante 1 minuto. (No moler en exceso).

Detener la máquina y dejar que la harina se enfríe durante unos minutos. Medir 1 1/2 tazas (180 g) de harina de trigo integral para la receta. Reservar y guardar la harina restante para otro uso.

Información nutricional por porción: 386 calorías (42% de grasas, 6% de proteínas, 52% de hidratos de carbono) proteínas 6 g • grasas totales 19 g • grasas saturadas 7 g • hidratos de carbono 52 g • fibra 3 g • azúcar 29 g sodio 359 mg • colesterol 56 mg

PAN DE ALMENDRAS Y ARÁNDANOS

preparación: 15 minutos • procesamiento: 30 segundos • tiempo de cocción: 1 hora
rendimiento: 1 hogaza (12 rebanadas)

1 taza (100 g) de arándanos frescos o congelados

1 naranja, pelada, sin semillas, cortada en cuartos

2,5-5 cm (1-2 pulg.) de piel de naranja o de limón

1/4 de taza (60 ml) de aceite de oliva suave

1 taza (200 g) de azúcar granulado

1 huevo grande

1 cucharadita de extracto de vainilla

1 1/2 cucharaditas de levadura

1/2 cucharadita de bicarbonato

1 cucharadita de sal

2 tazas (240 g) de harina de trigo integral

1/2 taza (46 g) de almendras troceadas

Engrasar un molde para pan de 22 x 11 cm (8 1/2 pulg. x 4 1/2 pulg.) con aceite vegetal u otro tipo de grasa. Precalentar el horno a 180 °C (350°F).

Colocar el recipiente Vitamix con CUCHILLAS PARA INGREDIENTES HÚMEDOS en la base de la licuadora y seleccionar la Variable 1.

Poner en marcha la máquina y aumentar gradualmente la velocidad hasta la Variable 3. Retirar el tapón y verter los arándanos a través de la abertura hasta picarlos en trozos pequeños. Detener la máquina; raspar las paredes y sacar los arándanos picados.

Verter la naranja en cuartos, la piel, el aceite de oliva, el azúcar, el huevo y la vainilla en el recipiente Vitamix con CUCHILLAS PARA INGREDIENTES SECOS y ajustar la tapa.

Seleccionar la Variable 1.

Poner en marcha la máquina y aumentar gradualmente la velocidad hasta la Variable 10, después hasta la posición de velocidad High (Alta).

Procesar durante 30 segundos; utilizar el empujador si es necesario para empujar los ingredientes hacia las cuchillas.

En un recipiente grande, mezclar la levadura en polvo, el bicarbonato, la sal y la harina de trigo integral; mezclar bien.

Verter la mezcla de naranja en el recipiente con los ingredientes secos. Mezclar a mano SOLO hasta que los ingredientes secos se humedezcan.

Añadir las almendras picadas a la mezcla; no mezclar en exceso.

Verter la mezcla en la fuente preparada. Hornear durante 1 hora o hasta que al introducir un palillo, este salga limpio.

Dejar enfriar en una rejilla durante 30 minutos y, a continuación, retirar del molde con cuidado. Dejar que se enfríe por completo antes de cortarlo en rebanadas.

NOTA: para hacer harina de trigo integral con trigo entero: colocar 1 1/2 tazas (270 g) de trigo entero en el recipiente Vitamix con CUCHILLAS PARA INGREDIENTES SECOS y ajustar la tapa.

Pan de almendras y arándanos *(continuación)*	Seleccionar la Variable 1. Poner en marcha la máquina y aumentar gradualmente la velocidad hasta la Variable 10, después hasta la posición de velocidad High (Alta). Moler el trigo durante 1 minuto. (No moler en exceso). Detener la máquina y dejar que la harina se enfríe durante unos minutos. Medir 2 tazas (240 g) de harina de trigo integral para la receta. Reservar y guardar la harina restante para otro uso.

Información nutricional por rebanada: 224 calorías (32% de grasas, 8% de proteínas, 60% de hidratos de carbono)
proteínas 4 g • grasas totales 8 g • grasas saturadas 1 g • hidratos de carbono 35 g • fibra 4 g • azúcar 19 g
sodio 314 mg • colesterol 17 mg

Pan de almendras y arándanos

TORTITAS DE GARBANZO

preparación: 10 minutos • procesamiento: 1 minuto • rendimiento: 4-5 tortitas

1 taza (172 g) de garbanzos crudos

1 cucharadita de levadura en polvo

1/2 cucharadita de bicarbonato

1/4 de cucharadita de sal

3/4 de taza (180 ml) de agua fría

2 cucharadas (30 ml) de aceite de oliva

1 huevo grande

Si se empieza con los garbanzos crudos: colocar los garbanzos en el recipiente Vitamix con CUCHILLAS PARA INGREDIENTES SECOS y ajustar la tapa.

Seleccionar la Variable 1.

Poner en marcha la máquina y aumentar gradualmente la velocidad hasta la Variable 10, después hasta la posición de velocidad High (Alta).

Moler hasta conseguir el grosor deseado, aproximadamente 1 minuto. Medir 1 taza (120 g) de harina de garbanzo de la mezcla molida; reservar el resto (aproximadamente 1/3 de taza [40 g]) para otro uso.

Si se empieza con la harina de garbanzo: verter 1 taza (120 g) de harina, la levadura en polvo, el bicarbonato y la sal en un recipiente mediano.

Verter el agua, el aceite y el huevo en el recipiente Vitamix con CUCHILLAS PARA INGREDIENTES SECOS en el orden especificado y ajustar la tapa.

Seleccionar la Variable 1.

Poner en marcha la máquina y aumentar gradualmente la velocidad hasta la Variable 10, después hasta la posición de velocidad High (Alta).

Procesar durante 15 segundos.

Añadir la mezcla de agua en el recipiente con los ingredientes secos. Mezclar a mano SOLO hasta que los ingredientes secos se humedezcan.

Engrasar una plancha o sartén pequeña. Calentar la plancha o sartén hasta que esté caliente.

Verter 1/3 de taza (80 ml) de masa en la sartén dar forma de tortita. Freír la tortita hasta que se formen burbujas en la superficie. Dar la vuelta a la tortita y cocinar hasta que se dore ligeramente. Servir inmediatamente.

Información nutricional por tortita: 193 calorías (38% de grasas, 15% de proteínas, 47% de hidratos de carbono)
proteínas 10 g • grasas totales 11 g • grasas saturadas 1 g • hidratos de carbono 29 g • fibra 14 g • azúcar 1 g
sodio 476 mg • colesterol 53 mg

PAN DE NUECES Y DÁTILES

preparación: 30 minutos • procesamiento: 25-30 segundos • tiempo de cocción: 1 1/4-1 1/2 horas
rendimiento: 1 hogaza (12 rebanadas)

1 taza (240 ml) de agua hirviendo

2 1/4 tazas (340 g) de dátiles deshidratados sin hueso, en trozos

4 cucharadas (56 g) de mantequilla sin sal, en trozos

1 1/4 tazas (125 g) de nueces

1 taza (120 g) de harina de trigo integral

1 taza (125 g) de harina común sin blanquear

3/4 1 1/4 tazas (150 g) de azúcar granulado

1 cucharadita de levadura en polvo

1/2 cucharadita de bicarbonato

1/2 cucharadita de sal marina

2 huevos grandes

1/2 cucharadita de vainilla

Verter agua hirviendo sobre los dátiles y la mantequilla en un recipiente grande. Dejar reposar hasta que se enfríe, aproximadamente 30 minutos.

Precalentar el horno a 160 ºC (325°F) con la rejilla en la posición central. Engrasar ligeramente un molde para pan y reservar.

Verter las nueces en el recipiente Vitamix con CUCHILLAS PARA INGREDIENTES SECOS. Ajustar la tapa.

Seleccionar la Variable 1.

Poner en marcha la máquina y aumentar gradualmente la velocidad hasta la Variable 3.

Procesar durante 10 o 15 segundos o hasta que las nueces tengan una consistencia gruesa. No picar en exceso.

Trasladar las nueces troceadas a un recipiente pequeño y reservar.

Verter las harinas, el azúcar, la levadura en polvo, el bicarbonato y la sal en el recipiente Vitamix con CUCHILLAS PARA INGREDIENTES SECOS. Ajustar la tapa.

Seleccionar la Variable 1.

Poner en marcha la máquina y aumentar gradualmente la velocidad hasta la Variable 6.

Procesar durante 15 segundos. Añadir las nueces troceadas.

Batir los huevos con la vainilla y añadir a la mezcla de dátiles enfriada. A continuación, añadir a la mezcla de harina/ nueces y remover solo hasta mezclar los ingredientes.

Verter uniformemente en el molde para pan y hornear hasta que al introducir un palillo en el centro, este salga limpio, aproximadamente 1 1/4 a 1 1/2 horas.

Dejar enfriar el pan en el molde sobre una rejilla durante 25 minutos y después sacarlo y dejarlo enfriar completamente en la rejilla.

Información nutricional por rebanada: 346 calorías (32% de grasas, 9% de proteínas, 60% de hidratos de carbono)
proteínas 8 g • grasas totales 13 g • grasas saturadas 3 g • hidratos de carbono 55 g • fibra 2 g • azúcar 13 g
sodio 208 mg • colesterol 51 mg

Con unas tijeras de cocina, trocear los dátiles remojados en agua caliente.

PANECILLOS DE MELOCOTÓN CON ESPECIAS

preparación: 20 minutos • procesamiento: 20 segundos • tiempo de cocción: 30-35 minutos
rendimiento: 8 panecillos

1 1/2 tazas (180 g) de harina de trigo integral

1 taza (125 g) de harina común sin blanquear

1/3 de taza (67 g) de azúcar granulado

2 1/4 cucharaditas de levadura en polvo

1/2 cucharadita de bicarbonato

1/4 de cucharadita de sal

1/2 taza (113 g) de mantequilla sin sal, ablandada y cortada en trozos

1/2 taza (120 ml) de leche

1 cucharadita de extracto de vainilla

1 taza (186 g) de rodajas de melocotón fresco o congelado (descongelado y escurrido), en dados

Cobertura:

3 cucharadas (17 g) de almendras laminadas

1 cucharada de azúcar granulado

1 cucharadita de canela molida

Leche o nata en la cantidad necesaria para pintar la masa

Mezclar las harinas, el azúcar, la levadura en polvo, el bicarbonato y la sal en un recipiente grande.

Verter la mantequilla, la leche y el extracto de vainilla en el recipiente Vitamix con CUCHILLAS PARA INGREDIENTES HÚMEDOS y ajustar la tapa.

Seleccionar la Variable 1.

Poner en marcha la máquina y aumentar gradualmente la velocidad hasta la Variable 6.

Procesar hasta que la mantequilla se mezcle bien, aproximadamente 20 segundos.

Verter con cuidado la mezcla de mantequilla/leche y las rodajas de melocotón sobre la mezcla de harinas y mezclar ligeramente. Formar una bola con la masa, colocarla sobre una lámina de papel para hornear en una bandeja de horno y aplastarla con cuidado hasta formar un círculo de 20 cm (8 pulg.). Con un cuchillo o cortador de pizza, marcar el círculo en 8 porciones triangulares sin llegar a separarlas.

Verter las almendras, el azúcar y la canela en el recipiente Vitamix con CUCHILLAS PARA INGREDIENTES SECOS y ajustar la tapa.

Seleccionar la Variable 1.

Poner en marcha la máquina y aumentar gradualmente la velocidad hasta la Variable 4.

Procesar hasta que la mezcle tenga una consistencia fina y bien mezclada, aproximadamente 10 segundos.

Pintar la parte superior de la masa con leche o nata y espolvorear la mezcla de almendras por encima.

Introducir en el horno precalentado a 200 ºC (400°F) y hornear entre 30 y 35 minutos o hasta que los bollos adquieran un color ligeramente dorado y no estén húmedos en el centro. Dejar enfriar durante 10 minutos, después cortar las porciones con un cuchillo afilado o un cortador de pizza. Servir templado o a temperatura ambiente.

Panecillos de melocotón con especias *(continuación)*

NOTA: para hacer harina de trigo integral con trigo entero: colocar 1 1/2 tazas (270 g) de trigo entero en el recipiente Vitamix con CUCHILLAS PARA INGREDIENTES SECOS y ajustar la tapa.

Seleccionar la Variable 1.

Poner en marcha la máquina y aumentar gradualmente la velocidad hasta la Variable 10, después hasta la posición de velocidad High (Alta).

Moler el trigo durante 1 minuto. (No moler en exceso). Detener la máquina y dejar que la harina se enfríe durante unos minutos. Medir 1 1/2 tazas (180 g) de harina de trigo integral para la receta. Reservar y guardar la harina restante para otro uso.

Información nutricional por panecillo: 311 calorías (39% de grasas, 8% de proteínas, 53% de hidratos de carbono)
proteínas 6 g • grasas totales 14 g • grasas saturadas 8 g • hidratos de carbono 42 g • fibra 4 g • azúcar 12 g
sodio 302 mg • colesterol 31 mg

MAGDALENAS DE TRIGO INTEGRAL CON FRUTA Y ZANAHORIA

preparación: 15 minutos • procesamiento: 10-15 segundos • tiempo de cocción: 20-25 minutos
rendimiento: 6 magdalenas

1 taza (165 g) de piña en trozos

1/2 taza (64 g) de zanahoria en trozos

1 cucharada de aceite de oliva suave

1/4 de taza (55 g) de azúcar moreno, colmada

1 huevo grande

1 taza (120 g) de harina de trigo integral

1 cucharadita de semillas de lino

1 cucharadita de canela

1 cucharadita de levadura en polvo

1/2 cucharadita de bicarbonato

1/2 cucharadita de sal

1/2 taza (72 g) de pasas

Precalentar el horno a 190 °C (375°F). Engrasar los moldes de magdalena con aceite vegetal o utilizar moldes de papel para magdalenas.

Verter la piña, la zanahoria, el aceite, el azúcar moreno y el huevo en el recipiente Vitamix con CUCHILLAS PARA INGREDIENTES HÚMEDOS en el orden especificado y ajustar la tapa.

Seleccionar la Variable 1.

Poner en marcha la máquina y aumentar gradualmente la velocidad hasta la Variable 4.

Procesar de 10 a 15 segundos (la zanahoria y la piña deben quedar en trozos pequeños).

En un recipiente grande, mezclar las harinas, las semillas de lino, la canela, la levadura en polvo, el bicarbonato y la sal.

Verter la mezcla de piña en el recipiente con los ingredientes secos. Mezclar a mano SOLO hasta que los ingredientes secos se humedezcan. Añadir las pasas y mezclar rápidamente pero con cuidado.

Verter la mezcla con una cuchara en cada molde de magdalena.

Hornear entre 20 y 25 minutos o hasta que al introducir un palillo en el centro, este salga limpio.

Dejar enfriar en una rejilla durante 5 minutos y después retirar cada magdalena de su molde. Servir templado o a temperatura ambiente.

Información nutricional por magdalena: 203 calorías (17% de grasas, 9% de proteínas, 74% de hidratos de carbono)
proteínas 5 g • grasas totales 4 g • grasas saturadas 1 g • hidratos de carbono 40 g • fibra 4 g • azúcar 18 g
sodio 412 mg • colesterol 35 mg

No reducir la medida de aceite. Es la cantidad mínima necesaria para producir magdalenas jugosas. Si se utiliza miel o se reduce la cantidad de azúcar moreno, se apreciará un sabor a bicarbonato.

Magdalenas de trigo integral con fruta y zanahoria

PAN DE CALABACÍN

preparación: 15 minutos • procesamiento: 15-20 segundos • tiempo de cocción: 1 hora
rendimiento: 1 hogaza (12 rebanadas)

1 huevo grande

2/3 de taza (133 g) de azúcar granulado

1/4 de taza (60 ml) de aceite de oliva ligero o de pepitas de uva

1 cucharadita de extracto de vainilla

200 g de calabacín, troceado, aproximadamente 1 1/2 tazas

2 tazas (250 g) de harina común sin blanquear

1 cucharadita de bicarbonato

1/4 de cucharadita de levadura en polvo

1/4 de cucharadita de sal

1/4 de cucharadita de nuez moscada molida

1/2 cucharadita de canela molida

1/2 cucharadita de pimienta inglesa

Ingredientes opcionales:

1/2 taza (58 g) de nueces troceadas

1/2 taza (72 g) de pasas

Engrasar un molde para pan de 22 x 11 cm con (8 1/2 pulg. x 4 1/2 pulg.) aceite vegetal u otro tipo de grasa. Precalentar el horno a 180 °C (350°F).

Verter el huevo, el azúcar, el aceite y el extracto de vainilla en el recipiente Vitamix con CUCHILLAS PARA INGREDIENTES HÚMEDOS en el orden especificado y ajustar la tapa.

Seleccionar la Variable 1.

Poner en marcha la máquina y aumentar gradualmente la velocidad hasta la Variable 5.

Procesar de 15 a 20 segundos o hasta que la mezcla quede uniforme y el calabacín en trozos pequeños.

En un recipiente grande, mezclar la harina, el bicarbonato, la levadura en polvo, la sal, la nuez moscada, la canela y la pimienta inglesa.

Verter la mezcla de calabacín en el recipiente con los ingredientes secos. Mezclar a mano SOLO hasta que los ingredientes secos se humedezcan; después, añadir rápidamente las nueces o las pasas y mezclar ligeramente. No mezclar en exceso.

Verter la mezcla en la fuente preparada. Hornear durante 1 hora o hasta que al introducir un palillo, este salga limpio.

Dejar enfriar en una rejilla durante 30 minutos y, a continuación, retirar del molde con cuidado. Dejar que se enfríe por completo antes de cortarlo en rebanadas.

Información nutricional por rebanada (sin los ingredientes opcionales): 171 calorías (28% de grasas, 7% de proteínas, 65% de hidratos de carbono) • proteínas 3 g • grasas totales 5 g • grasas saturadas 1 g • hidratos de carbono 28 g fibra 1 g • azúcar 12 g • sodio 174 mg • colesterol 18 mg

MAGDALENAS DE CALABAZA

preparación: 15 minutos • procesamiento: 10 segundos • tiempo de cocción: 20-25 minutos
rendimiento: 12 magdalenas

2 huevos grandes

1/4 de taza (60 ml) de aceite de oliva suave

1 taza (245 g) de calabaza recién cocida o en lata

1/4 de taza (60 ml) de leche

3/4 de taza (150 g) de azúcar granulado

1/2 cucharadita de sal

2 cucharaditas de bicarbonato

1 cucharadita de pimienta inglesa

1 cucharadita de canela

1 3/4 tazas (219 g) de harina común sin blanquear

1/2 taza (120 g) de virutas de chocolate pequeñas o medianas

Precalentar el horno a 180 °C (350°F). Engrasar los moldes de magdalena con aceite vegetal o utilizar moldes de papel para magdalenas.

Verter los huevos, el aceite, la calabaza, la leche y el azúcar en el recipiente Vitamix con CUCHILLAS PARA INGREDIENTES HÚMEDOS en el orden especificado y ajustar la tapa.

Seleccionar la Variable 1.

Poner en marcha la máquina y aumentar gradualmente la velocidad hasta la Variable 5.

Procesar durante 10 segundos.

En un recipiente mediano, mezclar la sal, el bicarbonato, la pimienta inglesa, la canela, la harina y las virutas de chocolate en el orden especificado.

Verter la mezcla de calabaza en el recipiente con los ingredientes secos. Mezclar a mano SOLO hasta que los ingredientes secos se humedezcan.

Verter la mezcla con una cuchara en cada molde de magdalena a 3/4 de su capacidad.

Hornear entre 20 y 25 minutos o hasta que al introducir un palillo en el centro, este salga limpio.

Dejar enfriar en una rejilla durante 5 minutos y después retirar cada magdalena de su molde. Servir templado o a temperatura ambiente.

Información nutricional por magdalena: 228 calorías (32% de grasas, 7% de proteínas, 61% de hidratos de carbono)
proteínas 4 g • grasas totales 8 g • grasas saturadas 2 g • hidratos de carbono 35 g • fibra 2 g • azúcar 18 g
sodio 326 mg • colesterol 41 mg

masas con levadura

Tutorial sobre pan de levadura

A continuación se incluyen algunos consejos útiles para preparar masa de levadura.

Medida de la harina

No es necesario tamizar la harina antes de medirla, pero para medir con mayor exactitud, vierta la harina en una taza de medir seca y retire el exceso al ras con el lado recto de una espátula o un cuchillo.

Temperatura de los líquidos

Al activar la levadura nos aseguramos de que está viva y de que funcionará con nuestra receta. La levadura es extremadamente sensible a la temperatura: si hay demasiado calor, la levadura se muere; por otro lado, si hay muy poco, el crecimiento se retarda. Por tanto, es importante que la temperatura del líquido sea la adecuada al verterlo sobre la levadura.

El rango de temperatura recomendado con mayor frecuencia cuando se mezcla la levadura directamente con el líquido es de 40-46 ºC (105°F-115°F).

Dejar que suba

Es necesario dejar que la masa suba, tapada ligeramente en un lugar templado sin corrientes de aire. Para conseguir mejores resultados, es conveniente dejar que la masa suba a temperatura ambiente. Una temperatura más alta puede producir un sabor a levadura cruda en el producto final; una temperatura más baja puede hacer que la masa quede ácida antes de subir.

PAN DE MASA MADRE CON ARÁNDANOS

preparación: 15 minutos • procesamiento: 15 segundos • tiempo de cocción: 35-40 minutos
rendimiento: 1 hogaza redonda (8-10 rebanadas)

1 huevo grande

1/2 taza (120 ml) de aceite vegetal

1/2 taza (120 ml) de leche

3/4 de taza (180 ml) de fermento base de patata (receta en la página 75) a temperatura ambiente

1/2 taza (100 g) de azúcar granulado

1 1/2 tazas (188 g) de harina común sin blanquear

1/2 taza (60 ml) de harina de trigo integral

1/2 cucharadita de sal

3/4 de cucharadita de bicarbonato

1 taza (148 g) de arándanos frescos o congelados (descongelados y secados con un paño)

Azúcar para la cobertura, opcional

Precalentar el horno a 190 °C (375°F). Engrasar una sartén o molde para tarta.

Verter el huevo, el aceite, la leche, el fermento de patata y el azúcar en el recipiente Vitamix con CUCHILLAS PARA INGREDIENTES HÚMEDOS en el orden especificado y ajustar la tapa.

Seleccionar la Variable 1.

Poner en marcha la máquina y aumentar gradualmente la velocidad hasta la Variable 10, después hasta la posición de velocidad High (Alta).

Procesar durante 15 segundos.

En un recipiente mediano, mezclar las harinas, la sal y el bicarbonato.

Verter la mezcla de fermento base en el recipiente con los ingredientes secos. Mezclar a mano SOLO hasta que los ingredientes secos se humedezcan. Añadir los arándanos y remover rápidamente pero con cuidado.

Verter en el molde preparado. Espolvorear la parte superior con azúcar si se desea.

Hornear entre 35 y 40 minutos o hasta que al introducir un palillo en el centro, este salga limpio. Servir caliente o frío, cortado en cuñas.

Información nutricional por rebanada: 249 calorías (7% de grasas, 12% de proteínas, 81% de hidratos de carbono)
proteínas 8 g • grasas totales 2 g • grasas saturadas 0 g • hidratos de carbono 51 g • fibra 5 g • azúcar 3 g
sodio 23 mg • colesterol 0 mg

ROLLOS DE CANELA

preparación: 20 minutos • procesamiento: 30 segundos • tiempo de cocción: 30-35 minutos
rendimiento: 9 rollos

1 sobre (1 cucharada) de levadura seca activa

4 cucharadas (60 ml) de agua templada a 40-46 ºC (105°F-115°F)

2 cucharadas (30 ml) de miel

2 1/4 tazas (281 g) de harina común sin blanquear, más una cantidad adicional para el amasado final y el estirado.

1/2 cucharadita de sal

1/3 de taza (80 ml) de leche

1/4 de taza (56 g) de mantequilla sin sal, ablandada y cortada en trozos

1 huevo grande

Relleno:

4 cucharadas (50 g) de azúcar granulado

1 cucharada de canela molida

1/4 de taza (56 g) de mantequilla sin sal, derretida

1 huevo grande más 2 cucharadas (30 ml) de leche (para pintar los rollos antes de hornearlos)

Cobertura de azúcar glas (receta en la página 46)

Para activar la levadura, mezclar la levadura, el agua y la miel. Remover rápidamente para mezclar los ingredientes. Reposar la masa 5 minutos.

Verter la harina y la sal en el recipiente Vitamix con CUCHILLAS PARA INGREDIENTES SECOS y ajustar la tapa.

Seleccionar la Variable 1.

Poner en marcha la máquina y aumentar gradualmente la velocidad hasta la Variable 6.

Procesar hasta que se forme un hueco en el centro de la mezcla, aproximadamente 5 segundos.

Seleccionar la Variable 3. Poner en marcha la máquina y retirar el tapón de la tapa. Añadir la mezcla de levadura, la leche, la mantequilla y el huevo a través de la abertura de la tapa. Detener la máquina y volver a poner el tapón en la abertura.

Seleccionar la posición de velocidad High (Alta). Encender y detener la máquina rápidamente dos veces. Detener la máquina y retirar la tapa.

Mientras reposa la masa, engrasar ligeramente un molde cuadrado para tartas de 20 cm (8 pulg.) con aceite de cocina en espray u otro tipo de grasa.

Utilizar una espátula de nailon húmeda para raspar las paredes del recipiente, separando la masa de las paredes y llevándola hacia el centro de la mezcla. Volver a colocar la tapa.

Seleccionar la posición de velocidad High (Alta). Encender y detener la máquina rápidamente cinco veces. Añadir más agua, 1 cucharada cada vez, únicamente si parece que la masa está muy seca. Repetir el proceso cinco veces, raspando las paredes del recipiente hasta que la masa forme una mezcla blanda y elástica.

Para sacar la masa del recipiente, encender y apagar la máquina cinco veces (esta acción levanta la masa y la separa de las cuchillas). Invertir el recipiente sobre la fuente engrasada y dejar que la masa caiga en la fuente. Invertir la masa una vez para cubrir toda la superficie; cubrir con un paño de cocina limpio y dejar que suba entre 25 y 30 minutos.

Mezclar el azúcar con la canela; reservar con la mantequilla derretida y enfriada.

Rollos de canela
(continuación)

Trasladar la masa a una superficie de trabajo enharinada. Estirar la masa, girándola y enharinándola con frecuencia, hasta formar un rectángulo de aproximadamente 20 x 40 cm (8 pulg. x 16 pulg.). Untar con la mantequilla derretida, dejando aproximadamente 1,3 cm (1/2 pulg.) de borde en todos los lados. Espolvorear la mezcla de azúcar/canela sobre la mantequilla.

Enrollar la masa firmemente en forma de brazo de gitano. Cortar en 9 porciones. Darle la vuelta y colocar en un molde.

Cubrir con un paño de cocina limpio y seco y dejar que suba aproximadamente entre 45 y 60 minutos.

Pintar la parte superior de los rollos con la mezcla de huevo y leche. Introducir en el horno precalentado a 160 ºC (325°F) y hornear entre 30 y 35 minutos o hasta que se dore ligeramente.

Dejar enfriar en una rejilla durante 10 minutos y, a continuación, retirar de la bandeja con cuidado. Dejar que se enfríe por completo en una rejilla antes de cortarlo en rebanadas. Glasear con la cobertura de azúcar glas y servir.

Información nutricional por rollo con cobertura: 422 calorías (37% de grasa, 5% de proteínas, 58% de hidratos de carbono) proteínas 6 g • grasas totales 18 g • grasas saturadas 11 g hidratos de carbono 62 g • fibra 2 g • azúcar 35 g • sodio 162 mg • colesterol 88 mg

Rollos de canela

COBERTURA DE AZÚCAR GLAS

La cobertura perfecta para los rollos de canela.
preparación: 20 minutos • procesamiento: 25 segundos • rendimiento: 1 taza (240 g)

2 tazas (240 g) de azúcar glas

1/4 de taza (56 g) de mantequilla sin sal ablandada

1 cucharadita de vainilla

1 o 2 cucharadas de agua caliente, y más si es necesario

Verter el azúcar glas, la mantequilla, la vainilla y el agua caliente en el recipiente Vitamix con CUCHILLAS PARA INGREDIENTES HÚMEDOS y ajustar la tapa.

Seleccionar la Variable 1.

Poner en marcha la máquina y aumentar gradualmente la velocidad hasta la Variable 10, después hasta la posición de velocidad High (Alta).

Procesar durante 10 segundos. Detener la máquina, retirar la tapa y raspar las paredes del recipiente. Añadir más agua (por cucharaditas) si es necesario en este momento para hacer un glaseado que se pueda extender (pero sin que quede demasiado fino).

Seleccionar la Variable 1 y ajustar la tapa.

Poner en marcha la máquina y aumentar gradualmente la velocidad hasta la Variable 10, después hasta la posición de velocidad High (Alta).

Batir hasta que quede suave y cremoso, aproximadamente 15 segundos más. Utilizar inmediatamente.

Información nutricional por ración de 2 cucharadas (30 g): 169 calorías (30% de grasas, 0% de proteínas, 70% de hidratos de carbono) • proteínas 0 g • grasas totales 6 g • grasas saturadas 4 g • hidratos de carbono 30 g fibra 0 g • azúcar 29 g • sodio 1 mg • colesterol 15 mg

FERMENTO BASE DE PATATA

preparación: 10 minutos

1 sobre (1 cucharada) de levadura seca activa

2 cucharaditas de azúcar

2 tazas (480 ml) de agua de patata emplada, a 43 ºC (110°F)

2 tazas (480 ml) de agua templada a 43 ºC (110°F) o agua de patata templada

1 taza (125 g) de harina común sin blanquear

1 taza (120 g) de harina de trigo integral

Disolver la levadura y el azúcar en 2 tazas (480 ml) de agua de patata en un recipiente grande.

Cubrir con un paño de cocina limpio y seco y dejar reposar en un lugar templado durante 24 horas.

Añadir 2 tazas (480 ml) de agua templada y mezclar con las harinas.

Cubrir y dejar reposar toda la noche o hasta que la mezcla produzca burbujas y desprenda un olor ácido. Refrigerar en un recipiente grande y tapado.

Sacar de la nevera y "activar". Usar 1 taza (240 ml) por cada hogaza de pan en cualquier receta que necesite un fermento base.

Información nutricional por ración de 1 taza (240 ml): 232 calorías (4% de grasa, 14% de proteína, 82% de hidratos de carbono) proteínas 8 g • grasas totales 1 g • grasas saturadas 0 g hidratos de carbono 49 g • fibra 5 g • azúcar 2 g • sodio 6 mg • colesterol 0 mg

Activar el fermento: por la mañana, dejar que alcance la temperatura ambiente y añadir 1 taza (240 ml) de agua templada a 43 ºC (110°F) y 1 taza (125 g) de harina común. Dejar reposar toda la noche. Utilizar la cantidad necesaria para el pan y refrigerar el resto. Renovar cada 2 o 3 semanas.

PAN COLONIAL (FORMA LIBRE)

preparación: 15 minutos • procesamiento: 30 segundos • tiempo de cocción: 25 minutos
rendimiento: 1 hogaza ovalada (8-10 rebanadas)

1 1/4 tazas (300 ml) de agua templada a 40-46 ºC (105°F-115°F)

3 cucharadas (41 g) de azúcar moreno

1 sobre (1 cucharada) de levadura seca activa

1 1/2 tazas (188 g) de harina común sin blanquear

1/2 taza (60 g) de harina de trigo integral

1/4 de taza (26 g) de harina de centeno ligera

1/4 de taza (30 g) de harina de maíz integral

1/2 cucharadita de sal

1 cucharada de aceite de oliva suave

1/4 de taza (30 g) de harina de maíz integral para la bandeja de horno

1 huevo mezclado con 1 cucharadita de agua (para pintar la masa antes del horneado)

Para activar la levadura, mezclar el agua templada, el azúcar moreno y la levadura. Remover rápidamente para mezclar los ingredientes. Reposar la masa 5 minutos.

Verter la harina común, la harina de trigo integral, la harina de centeno, la harina de maíz y la sal en el recipiente Vitamix con CUCHILLAS PARA INGREDIENTES SECOS y ajustar la tapa.

Seleccionar la Variable 1.

Poner en marcha la máquina y aumentar gradualmente la velocidad hasta la Variable 6.

Procesar hasta que se forme un hueco en el centro de la mezcla de harinas, aproximadamente 5 segundos.

Seleccionar la Variable 3. Poner en marcha la máquina y retirar el tapón de la tapa. Añadir el aceite a la mezcla de levadura a través de la abertura del tapón. Detener la máquina y volver a poner el tapón en la abertura.

Seleccionar la posición de velocidad High (Alta). Encender y detener la máquina rápidamente dos veces. Detener la máquina y retirar la tapa.

Mientras la masa reposa, espolvorear 1/4 de taza (30 g) de harina de maíz sobre una bandeja de horno; reservar.

Utilizar una espátula de nailon húmeda para raspar las paredes del recipiente, separando la masa de las paredes y llevándola hacia el centro de la mezcla. Volver a colocar la tapa.

Seleccionar la posición de velocidad High (Alta). Encender y detener la máquina rápidamente cinco veces. Añadir más agua, 1 cucharada cada vez, únicamente si parece que la masa está muy seca. Repetir el proceso cinco veces, raspando las paredes del recipiente hasta que la masa forme una mezcla blanda y elástica.

Colocar la tapa del recipiente y dejar que la masa suba durante 15 minutos.

Desinflar la masa con una espátula de nailon y, a continuación, volcarla sobre una lámina de papel encerado espolvoreado ligeramente con harina. (La masa será pegajosa). Retirar rápidamente la masa del papel encerado con las manos enharinadas y colocarla sobre una bandeja de horno. Espolvorear harina por encima y dar a la masa una forma ovalada.

Cubrir el pan con un paño de cocina limpio y seco y dejar que la masa suba hasta casi duplicar su tamaño, aproximadamente entre 15 y 20 minutos.

Pan colonial (forma libre) *(continuación)*	Una vez listo para hornear, pintar la masa con la mezcla de huevo y realizar 3 incisiones en diagonal en la parte superior con un cuchillo de sierra. Introducir en el horno precalentado a 190 ºC (375°F) y hornear durante 25 minutos o hasta que el pan alcance una temperatura interna de 88 ºC (190°F), medida con un termómetro de lectura instantánea. Dejar enfriar en una rejilla durante 10 minutos y, a continuación, retirar la bandeja del horno. Dejar que se enfríe por completo antes de cortarlo en rebanadas.

Información nutricional por rebanada: 160 calorías (15% de grasas, 11% de proteínas, 74% de hidratos de carbono)
proteínas 5 g • grasas totales 3 g • grasas saturadas 0 g • hidratos de carbono 30 g • fibra 2 g • azúcar 4 g
sodio 133 mg • colesterol 21 mg

Perfecto para hacer una hogaza plana de estilo artesano que se puede cortar en rebanadas y comer con aceite de oliva.

PAN COLONIAL (FORMA DE HOGAZA)

preparación: 10 minutos • procesamiento: 30 segundos • tiempo de cocción: 25-30 minutos
rendimiento: 1 hogaza (12 rebanadas)

1 1/4 tazas (300 ml) de agua templada a 40-46 ºC (105°F-115°F)

3 cucharadas (41 g) de azúcar moreno

1 sobre (1 cucharada) de levadura seca activa

1 1/2 tazas (188 g) de harina común sin blanquear

1/2 taza (60 g) de harina de trigo integral

1/4 de taza (26 g) de harina de centeno ligera

1/4 de taza (30 g) de harina de maíz

1/2 cucharadita de sal

1 cucharada de aceite de oliva suave

1 huevo grande mezclado con 1 cucharadita de agua (para pintar la masa antes del horneado)

Para activar la levadura, mezclar el agua templada, el azúcar moreno y la levadura. Remover rápidamente para mezclar los ingredientes. Reposar la masa 5 minutos.

Verter la harina común, la harina de trigo integral, la harina de centeno, la harina de maíz y la sal en el recipiente Vitamix con CUCHILLAS PARA INGREDIENTES SECOS y ajustar la tapa.

Seleccionar la Variable 1.

Poner en marcha la máquina y aumentar gradualmente la velocidad hasta la Variable 6.

Procesar hasta que se forme un hueco en el centro de la mezcla de harinas, aproximadamente 5 segundos.

Seleccionar la Variable 3. Poner en marcha la máquina y retirar el tapón de la tapa. Añadir el aceite a la mezcla de levadura a través de la abertura del tapón. Detener la máquina y volver a poner el tapón en la abertura.

Seleccionar la posición de velocidad High (Alta). Encender y detener la máquina rápidamente dos veces. Detener la máquina y retirar la tapa.

Mientras la masa reposa, engrasar un molde para pan de 22 x 11 cm (8 1/2 pulg. x 4 1/2 pulg.) con aceite vegetal u otro tipo de grasa.

Utilizar una espátula de nailon húmeda para raspar las paredes del recipiente, separando la masa de las paredes y llevándola hacia el centro de la mezcla. Volver a colocar la tapa.

Seleccionar la posición de velocidad High (Alta). Encender y detener la máquina rápidamente cinco veces. Añadir más agua, 1 cucharada cada vez, únicamente si parece que la masa está muy seca. Repetir el proceso cinco veces, raspando las paredes del recipiente hasta que la masa forme una mezcla blanda y elástica.

Para ayudar a sacar la masa del recipiente, encender y apagar la máquina cinco veces (esta acción levanta la masa y la separa de las cuchillas) e invertir el recipiente rápidamente sobre el molde preparado. Dejar caer la masa en el molde y utilizar una espátula para retirar la masa restante.

Usar los dedos ligeramente enharinados o una espátula engrasada para dar forma al pan dentro del molde, presionando con cuidado para dejar la masa uniforme.

Pan colonial (forma de hogaza) *(continuación)*	Cubrir el pan con un paño de cocina limpio y seco y dejar que la masa suba hasta que alcance el borde del molde, aproximadamente entre 18 y 20 minutos. Una vez listo para hornear, realizar 3 incisiones en diagonal en la parte superior con un cuchillo de sierra. Introducir en el horno precalentado a 190 ºC (375°F) y hornear entre 25 y 30 minutos o hasta que el pan alcance una temperatura interna de 88 ºC (190°F), medida con un termómetro de lectura instantánea. Dejar enfriar en una rejilla durante 10 minutos y, a continuación, retirar del molde con cuidado. Dejar que se enfríe por completo antes de cortarlo en rebanadas.

Información nutricional por rebanada: 134 calorías (15% de grasas, 11% de proteínas, 74% de hidratos de carbono)
proteínas 4 g • grasas totales 2 g • grasas saturadas 0 g • hidratos de carbono 25 g • fibra 2 g • azúcar 3 g
sodio 111 mg • colesterol 18 mg

Cortar en rebanadas una vez frío.

BOLLOS DE TRIGO INTEGRAL CON SUERO DE LECHE

preparación: 20 minutos • procesamiento: 15 segundos • tiempo de cocción: 18-22 minutos
rendimiento: 16 bollos

1/3 de taza (80 ml) de agua templada a 40-46 ºC (105°F-115°F)

1 1/2 cucharadas de miel

1 sobre (1 cucharada) de levadura seca activa

2 1/2 tazas (300 g) de harina de trigo integral de molienda fina

1 cucharadita de sal

2 cucharadas (28 g) de mantequilla sin sal a temperatura ambiente

2/3 de taza (160 ml) de suero de leche a temperatura ambiente

1 huevo grande, ligeramente batido

Para activar la levadura, mezclar el agua templada, la miel y la levadura. Remover rápidamente para mezclar los ingredientes. Reposar la masa 5 minutos.

Verter la harina de trigo integral y la sal en el recipiente Vitamix con CUCHILLAS PARA INGREDIENTES SECOS y ajustar la tapa.

Seleccionar la Variable 1.

Poner en marcha la máquina y aumentar gradualmente la velocidad hasta la Variable 10, después hasta la posición de velocidad High (Alta).

Procesar hasta que se forme un hueco en el centro de la mezcla de harinas, aproximadamente 5 segundos.

Seleccionar la Variable 3. Poner en marcha la máquina y retirar el tapón de la tapa. Añadir la mantequilla, el suero de leche, el huevo y la mezcla de levadura a través de la abertura del tapón. Detener la máquina y volver a poner el tapón en la abertura.

Seleccionar la posición de velocidad High (Alta). Encender y detener la máquina rápidamente dos veces. Detener la máquina y retirar la tapa.

Mientras la masa reposa, engrasar ligeramente una fuente cuadrada de 20 cm (8 pulg.) con aceite vegetal u otro tipo de grasa, o colocar una lámina de papel para hornear en una bandeja de horno (en función de la forma de los bollos).

Utilizar una espátula de nailon húmeda para raspar las paredes del recipiente, separando la masa de las paredes y llevándola hacia el centro de la mezcla. Volver a colocar la tapa.

Seleccionar la posición de velocidad High (Alta). Encender y detener la máquina rápidamente cinco veces. Añadir más agua, 1 cucharada cada vez, únicamente si parece que la masa está muy seca. Repetir el proceso cinco veces hasta que la masa forme una mezcla blanda y elástica.

Poner la tapa del recipiente y dejar que la masa suba hasta duplicar su tamaño, aproximadamente entre 25 y 30 minutos.

Desinflar la masa con una espátula de nailon. Dejar que vuelva a subir con la tapa puesta hasta que la masa haya duplicado su tamaño otra vez, aproximadamente 20 minutos.

Volcar en una superficie ligeramente enharinada y formar un bollo de unos 40 cm (16 pulg.); cortar la masa en 16 partes iguales. Dar la forma deseada a los bollos; colocar en una fuente o bandeja de horno.

Bollos de trigo integral con suero de leche *(continuación)*

Cubrir los bollos con un paño de cocina limpio y seco y dejar que la masa suba hasta casi duplicar su tamaño, aproximadamente entre 35 y 45 minutos.

Introducir en el horno precalentado a 190 ºC (375°F) y hornear entre 18 y 22 minutos o hasta que se dore ligeramente. Dejar enfriar en una rejilla.

Información nutricional por bollo: 95 calorías (21% de grasas, 15% de proteínas, 64% de hidratos de carbono)
proteína 4 g • grasas totales 2 g • grasas saturadas 1 g • hidratos de carbono 16 g • fibra 2 g • azúcar 3 g
sodio 111 mg • colesterol 18 mg

Para obtener una corteza deliciosa, mezclar 2 cucharadas (30 ml) de mantequilla derretida con 3 cucharadas (45 ml) de miel. Cuando los bollos estén horneados, sacarlos del horno y pintarlos rápidamente con el glaseado de mantequilla/miel. Dejar enfriar antes de servir.

Bollos de trigo integral con suero de leche

PAN DE PASAS Y CANELA

preparación: 30 minutos • procesamiento: 40 segundos • tiempo de cocción: 30-40 minutos
rendimiento: 1 hogaza (12 rebanadas)

1/2 taza (120 ml) de agua templada a 40-46 ºC (105°F-115°F)

1/4 de taza (50 g) de azúcar granulado

1 sobre (1 cucharada) de levadura seca activa

1/2 taza (112 g) de queso crema

1 cucharada de mantequilla sin sal a temperatura ambiente

2 cucharaditas de canela molida

3/4 de cucharadita de sal

1 huevo grande

2 tazas (275 g) de harina de pan, uso dividido

1/2 taza (104 g) de germen de trigo tostado

1/2 taza (72 g) de pasas, remojadas en agua caliente durante 30 minutos, escurridas, uso dividido

Para activar la levadura, mezclar el agua templada, el azúcar y la levadura. Remover rápidamente para mezclar los ingredientes. Reposar la masa 5 minutos.

Verter el queso crema, la mantequilla, la canela, la sal y el huevo en el recipiente Vitamix con CUCHILLAS PARA INGREDIENTES HÚMEDOS y ajustar la tapa.

Seleccionar la Variable 1.

Poner en marcha la máquina y aumentar gradualmente la velocidad hasta la Variable 10, después hasta la posición de velocidad High (Alta).

Procesar durante 10 segundos. Detener y raspar las paredes.

Seleccionar la Variable 3. Poner en marcha la máquina y retirar el tapón de la tapa. Añadir 1 taza (137 g) de harina y la mezcla de levadura a través de la abertura de la tapa. Procesar durante 30 segundos. Detener la máquina y retirar la tapa.

Añadir la harina restante, el germen de trigo y 1/4 de taza (72 g) de pasas remojadas previamente y escurridas al recipiente Vitamix y ajustar la tapa.

Seleccionar la posición de velocidad High (Alta). Encender y detener la máquina rápidamente dos veces. Detener la máquina y retirar la tapa.

Mientras la masa reposa, engrasar un molde para pan de 22 x 11 cm (8 1/2 pulg. x 4 1/2 pulg.) con aceite vegetal u otro tipo de grasa.

Utilizar una espátula de nailon húmeda para raspar las paredes del recipiente, separando la masa de las paredes y llevándola hacia el centro de la mezcla. Añadir el resto de las pasas y ajustar la tapa.

Seleccionar la posición de velocidad High (Alta). Encender y detener la máquina rápidamente cinco veces. Añadir más agua, 1 cucharada cada vez, únicamente si parece que la masa está muy seca. Repetir el proceso cinco veces, raspando las paredes del recipiente hasta que la masa forme una mezcla blanda y elástica.

Para ayudar a sacar la masa del recipiente, encender y apagar la máquina cinco veces (esta acción levanta la masa y la separa de las cuchillas) e invertir el recipiente rápidamente sobre el molde preparado. Dejar caer la masa en el molde y utilizar una espátula para retirar la masa restante.

Pan de pasas y canela
(continuación)

Usar los dedos ligeramente enharinados o una espátula engrasada para dar forma al pan dentro del molde, presionando con cuidado para dejar la masa uniforme.

Cubrir el pan con un paño de cocina limpio y seco y dejar que la masa suba hasta que alcance el borde del molde, aproximadamente entre 25 y 35 minutos. Una vez listo para hornear, realizar 3 incisiones en diagonal en la parte superior con un cuchillo de sierra.

Introducir en el horno precalentado a 190 ºC (375°F) y hornear entre 30 y 40 minutos o hasta que el pan alcance una temperatura interna de 88 ºC (190°F), medida con un termómetro de lectura instantánea. Dejar enfriar en una rejilla durante 10 minutos y, a continuación, retirar del molde con cuidado. Dejar que se enfríe por completo antes de cortarlo en rebanadas.

Información nutricional por rebanada: 162 calorías (14% de grasas, 15% de proteínas, 72% de hidratos de carbono)
proteínas 6 g • grasas totales 3 g • grasas saturadas 1 g • hidratos de carbono 30 g • fibra 2 g • azúcar 8 g
sodio 165 mg • colesterol 20 mg

La distribución de las pasas en la masa no tiene que ser perfecta... eso es precisamente lo que confiere a este pan su aspecto casero.

PIZZA CINCO CEREALES

preparación: 20 minutos • procesamiento: 35 segundos • tiempo de cocción: 16-20 minutos
rendimiento: 1 pizza (8 porciones)

1 taza (240 ml) de agua templada a 40-46 ºC (105°F-115°F)

2 cucharaditas de azúcar moreno

1 sobre (1 cucharada) de levadura seca activa

3/4 de taza (94 g) de harina común sin blanquear

3/4 de taza (90 g) + 1 cucharada de harina de trigo integral

1/4 de taza (26 g) de harina de centeno ligera

2 cucharadas (15 g) de harina de espelta

2 cucharadas (15 g) de harina de cebada

2 cucharadas (21 g) de semillas o harina de lino

2 cucharadas (15 g) de harina de maíz integral más una pequeña cantidad para enharinar la fuente

1/2 cucharadita de sal

1 cucharada de aceite de oliva

Cobertura:

2 cucharadas (30 ml) de aceite de oliva

1/3 de taza (33 g) de queso parmesano rallado

1 1/3 tazas (320 g) de salsa para pizza

Otros ingredientes si se desea

1 1/4 tazas (141 g) de queso mozzarella rallado

Para activar la levadura, mezclar el agua templada, el azúcar moreno y la levadura. Remover rápidamente para mezclar los ingredientes. Reposar la masa 5 minutos.

Verter las harinas (común, trigo integral, centeno, espelta y cebada), las semillas de lino, la harina de maíz y la sal en el recipiente Vitamix con CUCHILLAS PARA INGREDIENTES SECOS en el orden especificado y ajustar la tapa.

Seleccionar la Variable 1.

Poner en marcha la máquina y aumentar gradualmente la velocidad hasta la Variable 10, después hasta la posición de velocidad High (Alta).

Procesar hasta que se mezclen los ingredientes y la mezcla forme un hueco en el centro, aproximadamente 20 segundos. Detener la máquina.

Seleccionar la Variable 1 y retirar la tapa. Poner en marcha la máquina y aumentar gradualmente la velocidad hasta la Variable 6. Añadir la mezcla de levadura y el aceite de oliva a través de la abertura de la tapa. Detener la máquina y volver a poner el tapón en la abertura.

Seleccionar la posición de velocidad High (Alta). Encender y detener la máquina rápidamente dos veces. Detener la máquina y retirar la tapa.

Mientras la masa reposa, enharinar ligeramente la fuente con un poco de harina de maíz.

Utilizar una espátula de nailon húmeda para raspar las paredes del recipiente, separando la masa de las paredes y llevándola hacia el centro de la mezcla. Volver a colocar la tapa.

Seleccionar la posición de velocidad High (Alta). Encender y detener la máquina rápidamente cinco veces. Añadir más agua, 1 cucharada cada vez, únicamente si parece que la masa está muy seca. Repetir el proceso cinco veces, raspando las paredes del recipiente hasta que la masa forme una mezcla blanda y elástica.

Para ayudar a sacar la masa del recipiente, encender y apagar la máquina cinco veces (esta acción levanta la masa y la separa de las cuchillas) e invertir el recipiente rápidamente sobre una superficie de trabajo limpia y ligeramente enharinada.

Cubrir la masa con un paño de cocina limpio y seco o con el recipiente invertido y dejar reposar durante 15 minutos.

Pizza cinco cereales
(continuación)

Desinflar la masa con la palma de la mano, manteniendo la forma redonda. Con un rodillo, estirar desde el centro hacia fuera con movimientos uniformes en cada dirección, levantando y girando la masa 1/4 después de cada estiramiento. La forma final deberá ser de 2,5 cm (1 pulg.) más grande que la fuente. Colocar en la fuente. Enrollar los bordes para sostener el relleno.

Pintar la masa ligeramente con aceite de oliva y espolvorear queso parmesano. Añadir la salsa y extenderla con el reverso de una cuchara. Añadir los ingredientes preferidos y, a continuación, cubrir uniformemente con queso mozzarella.

Introducir en la rejilla inferior del horno precalentado a 220 ºC (425°F) durante 16 a 20 minutos hasta que la corteza inferior se dore ligeramente y el queso forme burbujas.

Retirar la pizza del horno, dejar reposar 5 minutos para que el queso se asiente y, a continuación, cortar en porciones.

Información nutricional por porción (con ingredientes): 272 calorías (39% de grasa, 17% de proteínas, 44% de hidratos de carbono) proteínas 12 g • grasas totales 12 g • grasas saturadas 4 g hidratos de carbono 30 g • fibra 4 g • azúcar 5 g • sodio 551 mg • colesterol 15 mg

Estirar la masa desde el centro hacia fuera y girarla ayuda a mantener la forma redonda.

PAN FRANCÉS

preparación: 10 minutos • procesamiento: 15 segundos • tiempo de cocción: 30-40 minutos
rendimiento: 1 hogaza (16-18 rebanadas)

1 taza (240 ml) de agua templada a 40-46 ºC (105°F-115°F), uso dividido

1 sobre (1 cucharada) de levadura seca activa

2 1/2 tazas (312 g) de harina común sin blanquear

1 cucharadita de sal

1 cucharada de aceite de oliva

2 cucharadas (15 g) de harina de maíz entero

1 clara de huevo batida con 1 cucharada de agua (para pintar la masa antes de hornear)

Para activar la levadura, mezclar 1/2 taza (120 ml) de agua templada con la levadura. Remover rápidamente para mezclar los ingredientes. Reposar la masa 5 minutos.

Verter la harina y la sal en el recipiente Vitamix con CUCHILLAS PARA INGREDIENTES SECOS y ajustar la tapa.

Seleccionar la Variable 1.

Poner en marcha la máquina y aumentar gradualmente la velocidad hasta la Variable 6.

Procesar hasta que se forme un hueco en el centro de la mezcla de harinas, aproximadamente 5 segundos.

Seleccionar la Variable 3. Poner en marcha la máquina y retirar el tapón de la tapa. Añadir la mezcla de levadura y la 1/2 taza (120 ml) de agua templada restante a través de la abertura de la tapa. Detener la máquina y volver a poner el tapón en la abertura.

Seleccionar la posición de velocidad High (Alta). Encender y detener la máquina rápidamente dos veces. Detener la máquina y retirar la tapa.

Mientras la masa reposa, engrasar una fuente de tamaño mediano con aceite de oliva y espolvorear harina de maíz en una bandeja de horno.

Utilizar una espátula de nailon húmeda para raspar las paredes del recipiente, separando la masa de las paredes y llevándola hacia el centro de la mezcla. Volver a colocar la tapa.

Seleccionar la posición de velocidad High (Alta). Encender y detener la máquina rápidamente cinco veces. Añadir más agua, 1 cucharada cada vez, únicamente si parece que la masa está muy seca. Repetir el proceso cinco veces, raspando las paredes del recipiente hasta que la masa forme una mezcla blanda y elástica.

Para ayudar a sacar la masa del recipiente, encender y apagar la máquina cinco veces (esta acción levanta la masa y la separa de las cuchillas) e invertir el recipiente rápidamente sobre la fuente preparada, utilizando una espátula húmeda para retirar la masa restante. Invertir la masa para se cubra bien con la mezcla de la fuente. Tapar con film transparente y dejar que suba hasta prácticamente triplicar su tamaño, entre 45 minutos y 1 hora.

Pan francés
(continuación)

Aplastar ligeramente la masa y trasladarla a una superficie de trabajo enharinada, añadiendo la harina necesaria para poder amasarla y que siga siendo una masa blanda. Estirar en forma rectangular de 30 x 15 cm (12 pulg. x 6 pulg.) con un rodillo enharinado. Estirar desde el extremo largo hacia abajo, presionando los bordes y añadiendo agua para sellarlos.

Colocar la masa con los bordes hacia abajo sobre la bandeja de horno preparada. Cubrir con un paño de cocina limpio y seco y dejar que la masa suba hasta duplicar su tamaño, aproximadamente entre 45 minutos y 1 hora.

Pintar la parte superior de la masa con la mezcla de huevo y realizar tres o cuatro incisiones en diagonal de aproximadamente 0,6 cm (1/4 pulg.) con un cuchillo de sierra afilado.

Introducir en el horno precalentado a 220 ºC (425°F) y hornear entre 30 y 40 minutos o hasta que el pan alcance una temperatura interna de 88 ºC (190°F), medida con un termómetro de lectura instantánea. Dejar enfriar en una rejilla durante 10 minutos y, a continuación, sacarlo de la bandeja de horno. Dejar que se enfríe por completo antes de cortarlo en rebanadas.

Información nutricional por rebanada: 86 calorías (12% de grasas, 12% de proteínas, 76% de hidratos de carbono) proteínas 3 g • grasas totales 1 g • grasas saturadas 0 g • hidratos de carbono 16 g • fibra 1 g • azúcar 0 g sodio 152 mg • colesterol 0 mg

Una espátula metálica es útil para sacar el pan de la bandeja del horno.

PAN HAWAIANO

preparación: 15 minutos • procesamiento: 25 segundos • tiempo de cocción: 35-40 minutos
rendimiento: 1 hogaza (8-10 rebanadas)

2 cucharadas (30 ml) de agua templada a 40-46 ºC (105°F-115°F)

1/2 taza (120 ml) de leche templada a 40-46 ºC (105°F-115°F)

1 sobre (1 cucharada) de levadura seca activa

1/2 cucharadita más 1/2 taza (100 g) de azúcar, uso dividido

2 1/2 tazas (312 g) de harina común, sin blanquear

1/4 de cucharadita de sal

1/4 de taza (56 g) de mantequilla sin sal, derretida

2 huevos grandes, batidos

1 huevo grande batido con 1 cucharadita de agua (para pintar la masa antes del horneado)

Azúcar para espolvorear sobre el pan

Para activar la levadura, mezclar el agua templada, la leche templada, la levadura y 1/2 cucharadita de azúcar. Remover rápidamente para mezclar los ingredientes. Reposar la masa 5 minutos.

Verter la harina, 1/2 taza (100 g) de azúcar y la sal en el recipiente Vitamix con CUCHILLAS PARA INGREDIENTES SECOS y ajustar la tapa.

Seleccionar la Variable 1.

Poner en marcha la máquina y aumentar gradualmente la velocidad hasta la Variable 6.

Procesar hasta que se forme un hueco en el centro de la mezcla de harinas, aproximadamente 5 segundos.

Seleccionar la Variable 3. Poner en marcha la máquina y retirar el tapón de la tapa. Añadir la mantequilla derretida, los huevos y la mezcla de levadura a través de la abertura de la tapa. Detener la máquina y volver a poner el tapón en la abertura.

Seleccionar la posición de velocidad High (Alta). Encender y detener la máquina rápidamente dos veces. Detener la máquina y retirar la tapa.

Mientras la masa reposa, engrasar un molde para tarta de 23 cm (9 pulg.) con aceite vegetal u otro tipo de grasa.

Utilizar una espátula de nailon húmeda para raspar las paredes del recipiente, separando la masa de las paredes y llevándola hacia el centro de la mezcla. Volver a colocar la tapa.

Seleccionar la posición de velocidad High (Alta). Encender y detener la máquina rápidamente cinco veces. Añadir más agua, 1 cucharada cada vez, únicamente si parece que la masa está muy seca. Repetir el proceso cinco veces, raspando las paredes del recipiente hasta que la masa forme una mezcla blanda y elástica.

Para ayudar a sacar la masa del recipiente, encender y apagar la máquina cinco veces (esta acción levanta la masa y la separa de las cuchillas), invertir el recipiente rápidamente sobre una fuente engrasada (utilizando una espátula húmeda para retirar la masa restante) e invertir la masa para cubrir toda la superficie.

Tapar la fuente con film transparente engrasado con aceite vegetal en espray. Dejar que la masa suba hasta duplicar su tamaño, aproximadamente entre 40 y 45 minutos.

Pan hawaiano *(continuación)*	Aplastar la masa y trasladarla a una superficie de trabajo enharinada. Amasar de nuevo entre 1 y 2 minutos. Verter la masa en el molde, usar los dedos ligeramente enharinados o una espátula engrasada para dar forma al pan dentro del molde, presionando con cuidado para dejar la masa uniforme. Cubrir la masa con un paño de cocina limpio y seco y dejar que la masa suba hasta duplicar su tamaño, aproximadamente 40 minutos. Cuando esté listo para hornear, pintar la parte superior con la mezcla de huevo batido y espolvorear con azúcar. Introducir en el horno precalentado a 180 ºC (350°F) y hornear durante 35 a 40 minutos o hasta que el pan alcance una temperatura interna de 88 ºC (190°F), medida con un termómetro de lectura instantánea. Dejar enfriar en una rejilla.

Información nutricional por rebanada: 233 calorías (29% de grasas, 10% de proteínas, 61% de hidratos de carbono)
proteínas 6 g • grasas totales 7 g • grasas saturadas 4 g • hidratos de carbono 35 g • fibra 1 g • azúcar 11 g
sodio 126 mg • colesterol 76 mg

PAN MULTICEREALES CRUJIENTE

preparación: 20 minutos • procesamiento: 25 segundos • tiempo de cocción: 40-50 minutos
rendimiento: 1 hogaza (12 rebanadas)

1 1/4 tazas (300 ml) de agua templada a 40-46 ºC (105°F-115°F)

1 cucharada de miel

1 sobre (1 cucharada) de levadura seca activa

1 1/2 tazas (156 g) de harina común sin blanquear

1/2 taza (60 g) de harina de trigo integral

1/4 de taza (26 g) de harina de centeno ligera

1 cucharada de germen de trigo

1 cucharada de copos de avena

2 cucharaditas de harina de maíz integral

2 cucharaditas de mijo

2 cucharaditas de harina de cebada

2 cucharaditas de harina de trigo sarraceno

1/4 de cucharadita de semillas de lino

1/2 cucharadita de sal

1 cucharada de aceite de oliva suave o de pepitas de uva

1 cucharada de pipas de girasol

1 cucharada de melaza

1/4 de cucharadita de semillas de sésamo para espolvorear por encima

Para activar la levadura, mezclar el agua templada, la miel y la levadura. Remover rápidamente para mezclar los ingredientes. Reposar la masa 5 minutos.

Verter la harina común, la harina de trigo integral, la harina de centeno, el germen de trigo, los copos de avena, la harina de trigo, el mijo, la harina de cebada, la harina de trigo sarraceno, las semillas de lino y la sal en el recipiente Vitamix con CUCHILLAS PARA INGREDIENTES SECOS y ajustar la tapa.

Seleccionar la Variable 1.

Poner en marcha la máquina y aumentar gradualmente la velocidad hasta la Variable 6.

Procesar hasta que se forme un hueco en el centro de la mezcla de harinas, aproximadamente 5 segundos.

Seleccionar la Variable 3. Poner en marcha la máquina y retirar el tapón de la tapa. Añadir el aceite, las pipas de girasol, la melaza y la mezcla de levadura a través de la abertura de la tapa. Detener la máquina y volver a poner el tapón en la abertura.

Seleccionar la posición de velocidad High (Alta). Encender y detener la máquina rápidamente dos veces. Detener la máquina y retirar la tapa.

Mientras la masa reposa, engrasar un molde para pan de 22 x 11 cm (8 1/2 pulg. x 4 1/2 pulg.) con aceite vegetal u otro tipo de grasa.

Utilizar una espátula de nailon húmeda para raspar las paredes del recipiente, separando la masa de las paredes y llevándola hacia el centro de la mezcla. Volver a colocar la tapa.

Seleccionar la posición de velocidad High (Alta). Encender y detener la máquina rápidamente cinco veces. Añadir más agua, 1 cucharada cada vez, únicamente si parece que la masa está muy seca. Repetir el proceso cinco veces, raspando las paredes del recipiente hasta que la masa forme una mezcla blanda y elástica.

Para ayudar a sacar la masa del recipiente, encender y apagar la máquina cinco veces (esta acción levanta la masa y la separa de las cuchillas) e invertir el recipiente rápidamente sobre el molde preparado. Dejar caer la masa en el molde y utilizar una espátula para retirar la masa restante.

Usar los dedos ligeramente enharinados o una espátula engrasada para dar forma al pan dentro del molde, presionando con cuidado para dejar la masa uniforme.

Pan multicereales crujiente *(continuación)*	Cubrir el pan con un paño de cocina limpio y seco y dejar que la masa suba hasta que alcance el borde del molde, aproximadamente entre 25 y 30 minutos. Una vez listo para hornear, realizar 3 incisiones en diagonal en la parte superior con un cuchillo de sierra. Espolvorear con 1/4 de cucharadita de semillas de sésamo. Introducir en el horno precalentado a 180 ºC (350°F) y hornear entre 40 y 50 minutos o hasta que el pan alcance una temperatura interna de 88 ºC (190°F), medida con un termómetro de lectura instantánea. Dejar enfriar en una rejilla durante 10 minutos y, a continuación, retirar del molde con cuidado. Dejar que se enfríe por completo antes de cortarlo en rebanadas.

Información nutricional por rebanada: 119 calorías (13% de grasas, 11% de proteínas, 75% de hidratos de carbono)
proteína 3 g • grasas totales 2 g • grasas saturadas 0 g • hidratos de carbono 23 g • fibra 2 g • azúcar 3 g
sodio 101 mg • colesterol 0 mg

Si no se dispone de algunos de los granos o harinas especiales mencionados anteriormente, se pueden sustituir por harina de trigo integral o cualquier otra harina especial. (Recuerde, su máquina puede moler cualquier de los cereales mencionados anteriormente hasta convertirlos en harina).

PAN DE SALVADO DE AVENA

preparación: 10 minutos • procesamiento: 30 segundos • tiempo de cocción: 30-35 minutos
rendimiento: 1 hogaza (12 rebanadas)

1 clara de huevo y 1 1/4 tazas (300 ml) de agua templada a 40-46 ºC (105°F-115°F)

2 cucharadas (30 ml) de melaza

1 sobre (1 cucharada) de levadura seca activa

1-1 1/4 tazas (80-100 g) de salvado de avena (o copos de avena)

1 1/4 tazas (150 g) de harina de trigo integral

1 taza (125 g) de harina común, sin blanquear

1 cucharadita de sal

1 cucharada de aceite de oliva suave o de pepitas de uva

Para activar la levadura, mezclar el agua templada, la melaza y la levadura. Remover rápidamente para mezclar los ingredientes. Reposar la masa 5 minutos.

Verter el salvado de avena, las harinas y la sal en el recipiente Vitamix con CUCHILLAS PARA INGREDIENTES SECOS y ajustar la tapa.

Seleccionar la Variable 1.

Poner en marcha la máquina y aumentar gradualmente la velocidad hasta la Variable 6.

Procesar hasta que se forme un hueco en el centro de la mezcla de harinas, aproximadamente 10 segundos, utilizando el empujador si es necesario para ayudar a mezclar los ingredientes.

Seleccionar la Variable 3. Poner en marcha la máquina y retirar el tapón de la tapa. Añadir la mezcla de levadura y el aceite a través de la abertura de la tapa. Detener la máquina y volver a poner el tapón en la abertura.

Seleccionar la posición de velocidad High (Alta). Encender y detener la máquina rápidamente dos veces. Detener la máquina y retirar la tapa.

Mientras la masa reposa, engrasar un molde para pan de 22 x 11 cm (8 1/2 pulg. x 4 1/2 pulg.) con aceite vegetal u otro tipo de grasa.

Utilizar una espátula de nailon húmeda para raspar las paredes del recipiente, separando la masa de las paredes y llevándola hacia el centro de la mezcla. Volver a colocar la tapa.

Seleccionar la posición de velocidad High (Alta). Encender y detener la máquina rápidamente cinco veces. Añadir más agua, 1 cucharada cada vez, únicamente si parece que la masa está muy seca. Repetir el proceso cinco veces, raspando las paredes del recipiente hasta que la masa forme una mezcla blanda y elástica.

Para ayudar a sacar la masa del recipiente, encender y apagar la máquina cinco veces (esta acción levanta la masa y la separa de las cuchillas) e invertir el recipiente rápidamente sobre el molde preparado. Dejar caer la masa en el molde y utilizar una espátula para retirar la masa restante.

Usar los dedos ligeramente enharinados o una espátula engrasada para dar forma al pan dentro del molde, presionando con cuidado para dejar la masa uniforme.

Pan de salvado de avena *(continuación)*	Cubrir el pan con un paño de cocina limpio y seco y dejar que la masa suba hasta que alcance el borde del molde, aproximadamente entre 15 y 18 minutos. Una vez listo para hornear, realizar 3 incisiones en diagonal en la parte superior con un cuchillo de sierra. Introducir en el horno precalentado a 180 ºC (350°F) y hornear entre 30 y 35 minutos o hasta que el pan alcance una temperatura interna de 88 ºC (190°F), medida con un termómetro de lectura instantánea. Dejar enfriar en una rejilla durante 10 minutos y, a continuación, retirar del molde con cuidado. Dejar que se enfríe por completo antes de cortarlo en rebanadas.

Información nutricional por rebanada: 124 calorías (13% de grasas, 14% de proteínas, 73% de hidratos de carbono) proteínas 5 g • grasas totales 2 g • grasas saturadas 0 g • hidratos de carbono 25 g • fibra 3 g • azúcar 2 g sodio 8 mg • colesterol 0 mg

FOCACCIA DE CENTENO

preparación: 15 minutos • procesamiento: 30 segundos • tiempo de cocción: 35-40 minutos
rendimiento: 1 hogaza (8-10 rebanadas)

3/4 de taza (180 ml) de agua templada a 40-46 ºC (105°F-115°F)

1 cucharada de azúcar granulado

1 sobre (1 cucharada) de levadura seca activa

1 1/2 tazas (188 g) de harina común, sin blanquear

1 taza (104 g) de harina de centeno ligera

1/2 taza (66 g) de queso suizo troceado

1 cucharadita de sal

1 cucharada de eneldo

1 cucharada de semillas de alcaravea

3/4 de taza (180 ml) de suero de leche a temperatura ambiente

Para la cobertura

2 cucharadas (30 ml) de aceite de oliva virgen extra

1 1/2 cucharaditas de sal gruesa

1/2 taza (66 g) de queso suizo troceado

1 cucharadita de eneldo

Para activar la levadura, mezclar el agua templada, el azúcar y la levadura. Remover rápidamente para mezclar los ingredientes. Reposar la masa 5 minutos.

Verter las harinas, el queso, la sal, el eneldo y las semillas de alcaravea en el recipiente Vitamix con CUCHILLAS PARA INGREDIENTES SECOS y ajustar la tapa.

Seleccionar la Variable 1.

Poner en marcha la máquina y aumentar gradualmente la velocidad hasta la Variable 10, después hasta la posición de velocidad High (Alta).

Procesar durante 15 segundos. Reducir la velocidad hasta la Variable 6 y procesar hasta que se forme un hueco en el centro de la mezcla de harinas, aproximadamente 5 segundos. Detener la máquina.

Seleccionar la Variable 1 y retirar la tapa. Poner en marcha la máquina y aumentar gradualmente la velocidad hasta la Variable 6. Añadir el suero de leche y la mezcla de levadura a través de la abertura de la tapa. Detener la máquina y volver a poner el tapón en la abertura.

Seleccionar la posición de velocidad High (Alta). Encender y detener la máquina rápidamente dos veces. Detener la máquina y retirar la tapa.

Mientras la masa reposa, engrasar un molde redondo para tarta de 23 cm (9 pulg.) con aceite vegetal u otro tipo de grasa.

Utilizar una espátula de nailon húmeda para raspar las paredes del recipiente, separando la masa de las paredes y llevándola hacia el centro de la mezcla. Volver a colocar la tapa.

Seleccionar la posición de velocidad High (Alta). Encender y detener la máquina rápidamente cinco veces. Añadir más agua, 1 cucharada cada vez, únicamente si parece que la masa está muy seca. Repetir el proceso cinco veces, raspando las paredes del recipiente hasta que la masa forme una mezcla blanda y elástica.

Para ayudar a sacar la masa del recipiente, encender y apagar la máquina cinco veces (esta acción levanta la masa y la separa de las cuchillas) e invertir el recipiente rápidamente sobre el molde preparado. Dejar caer la masa en el molde y utilizar una espátula para retirar la masa restante.

Usar los dedos ligeramente enharinados o una espátula engrasada para dar forma al pan dentro del molde, presionando con cuidado para dejar la masa uniforme.

Focaccia de centeno (*continuación*)	Cubrir el molde con un paño de cocina limpio y seco y dejar que la masa suba hasta que alcance el borde del molde, aproximadamente 30 minutos. Cuando esté lista para hornear, hacer unos hoyos con las yemas de los dedos y pintar la parte superior de la masa con aceite de oliva. Espolvorear con sal gruesa, eneldo y el queso suizo restante. Introducir en el horno precalentado a 180 ºC (350°F) y hornear entre 35 y 40 minutos o hasta que el pan alcance una temperatura interna de 88 ºC (190°F), medida con un termómetro de lectura instantánea. Dejar enfriar en una rejilla durante 10 minutos y, a continuación, retirar del molde con cuidado. Dejar que se enfríe por completo antes de cortarlo en rebanadas.

Información nutricional por rebanada: 202 calorías (32% de grasas, 15% de proteínas, 52% de hidratos de carbono)
proteínas 8 g • grasas totales 7 g • grasas saturadas 3 g • hidratos de carbono 26 g • fibra 3 g • azúcar 3 g
sodio 448 mg • colesterol 14 mg

Las masas de centeno siempre son más pegajosas y difíciles de trabajar que las masas de trigo, por lo que debemos tener paciencia y no añadir demasiada harina simplemente para evitar que sea muy pegajosa, ya que el pan sería demasiado compacto.

PRETZELS TIERNOS

preparación: 10 minutos • procesamiento: 15 segundos • tiempo de cocción: 8-10 minutos
rendimiento: 12 pretzels

3/4 de taza (180 ml) de agua templada a 40-46 ºC (105°F-115°F)

1/4 de taza (55 g) de azúcar moreno, colmada

1 sobre (1 cucharada) de levadura seca activa

1/4 de taza (30 g) de harina de trigo integral

1/2 taza (62 g) de harina común, sin blanquear

1 1/2 tazas (205 g) de harina para pan (alto contenido en gluten)

Una pizca de sal

1 huevo grande mezclado con 2 cucharadas (30 ml) de agua (para pintar la masa antes del horneado)

Sal gruesa

Para activar la levadura, mezclar el agua templada, el azúcar moreno y la levadura. Remover rápidamente para mezclar los ingredientes. Reposar la masa 5 minutos.

Verter las harinas y la sal en el recipiente Vitamix con CUCHILLAS PARA INGREDIENTES SECOS y ajustar la tapa.

Seleccionar la Variable 1.

Poner en marcha la máquina y aumentar gradualmente la velocidad hasta la Variable 6.

Procesar hasta que se forme un hueco en el centro de la mezcla de harinas, aproximadamente 5 segundos.

Seleccionar la Variable 3. Poner en marcha la máquina y retirar el tapón de la tapa. Añadir la mezcla de levadura a través de la abertura de la tapa. Detener la máquina y volver a poner el tapón en la abertura.

Seleccionar la posición de velocidad High (Alta). Encender y detener la máquina rápidamente dos veces. Detener la máquina y retirar la tapa.

Mientras la masa reposa, engrasar una bandeja de horno con aceite vegetal u otro tipo de grasa.

Utilizar una espátula de nailon húmeda para raspar las paredes del recipiente, separando la masa de las paredes y llevándola hacia el centro de la mezcla. Volver a colocar la tapa.

Seleccionar la posición de velocidad High (Alta). Encender y detener la máquina rápidamente cinco veces. Añadir más agua, 1 cucharada cada vez, únicamente si parece que la masa está muy seca. Repetir el proceso cinco veces, raspando las paredes del recipiente hasta que la masa forme una mezcla blanda y elástica.

Poner la tapa del recipiente y dejar que la masa suba hasta duplicar su tamaño, aproximadamente 15 minutos.

Colocar la masa en una superficie ligeramente enharinada y dividir en 12 partes. Con las palmas de las manos, enrollar cada parte hasta formar una cuerda de 30-46 cm (12 pulg. - 18 pulg.) de largo. Hacer una forma ovalada, enrollar los extremos y presionarlos hacia la parte superior del óvalo.

Pretzels tiernos (*continuación*)	Batir el huevo con el agua. Pintar rápidamente y con cuidado cada pretzel con la mezcla de huevo y espolvorear con sal gruesa. Introducir en el horno precalentado a 230 ºC (450°F) y hornear entre 8 y 10 minutos o hasta que se dore ligeramente. Servir caliente.

Información nutricional por pretzel: 117 calorías (8% de grasas, 13% de proteínas, 79% de hidratos de carbono)
proteínas 4 g • grasas totales 1 g • grasas saturadas 0 g • hidratos de carbono 23 g • fibra 1 g • azúcar 5 g
sodio 11 mg • colesterol 18 mg

Si desea servir los pretzels con azúcar y canela, no los espolvoree con sal gorda antes de hornearlos. Después de sacarlos del horno, píntelos con mantequilla derretida y espolvoréelos con una mezcla de azúcar y canela.

PIZZA

preparación: 15 minutos • procesamiento: 30 segundos • tiempo de cocción: 15-18 minutos
rendimiento: 1 pizza grande (8 porciones)

1 taza (240 ml) de agua templada a 40-46 ºC (105°F-115°F)

2 cucharaditas de azúcar granulado

1 sobre (1 cucharada) de levadura seca activa

2 1/2 tazas (312 g) de harina común, sin blanquear

1/2 cucharadita de sal

1 cucharada de aceite de oliva suave

2 cucharadas (15 g) de harina de maíz integral para enharinar la bandeja

Cobertura:

2 cucharadas (30 ml) de aceite de oliva

1/3 de taza (33 g) de queso parmesano rallado

1 1/3 tazas (320 g) de salsa para pizza

1 1/4 tazas (141 g) de queso mozzarella rallado

Para activar la levadura, mezclar el agua templada, el azúcar y la levadura. Remover rápidamente para mezclar los ingredientes. Reposar la masa 5 minutos.

Verter la harina y la sal en el recipiente Vitamix con CUCHILLAS PARA INGREDIENTES SECOS y ajustar la tapa.

Seleccionar la Variable 1.

Poner en marcha la máquina y aumentar gradualmente la velocidad hasta la Variable 6.

Procesar hasta que se mezclen los ingredientes y la mezcla forme un hueco en el centro, aproximadamente 5 segundos.

Detener la máquina y retirar el tapón de la tapa. Seleccionar la Variable 1. Poner en marcha la máquina y aumentar gradualmente la velocidad hasta la Variable 6. Añadir la mezcla de levadura y el aceite de oliva a través de la abertura de la tapa. Detener la máquina y volver a poner el tapón en la abertura.

Seleccionar la posición de velocidad High (Alta). Encender y detener la máquina rápidamente dos veces. Detener la máquina y retirar la tapa.

Mientras la masa reposa, enharinar ligeramente la fuente con un poco de harina de maíz.

Utilizar una espátula de nailon húmeda para raspar las paredes del recipiente, separando la masa de las paredes y llevándola hacia el centro de la mezcla. Volver a colocar la tapa.

Seleccionar la posición de velocidad High (Alta). Encender y detener la máquina rápidamente cinco veces. Añadir más agua, 1 cucharada cada vez, únicamente si parece que la masa está muy seca. Repetir el proceso cinco veces, raspando las paredes del recipiente hasta que la masa forme una mezcla blanda y elástica.

Para ayudar a sacar la masa del recipiente, encender y apagar la máquina cinco veces (esta acción levanta la masa y la separa de las cuchillas) e invertir el recipiente rápidamente sobre una superficie de trabajo limpia y ligeramente enharinada.

Cubrir la masa con un paño de cocina limpio y seco o con el recipiente invertido y dejar reposar durante 15 minutos.

Desinflar la masa con la palma de la mano, manteniendo la forma redonda. Con un rodillo, estirar desde el centro hacia fuera con movimientos uniformes en cada dirección, levantando y girando la masa 1/4 después de cada estiramiento. La forma final deberá ser de 2,5 cm (1 pulg.) más grande que la fuente. Colocar en la fuente. Enrollar los bordes para sostener el relleno.

Pizza *(continuación)*	Pintar la masa ligeramente con aceite de oliva y espolvorear queso parmesano. Añadir la salsa y extenderla con el reverso de una cuchara. Añadir los ingredientes preferidos y, a continuación, cubrir uniformemente con queso mozzarella. Introducir en la rejilla inferior del horno precalentado a 220 ºC (425°F) durante 15 a 18 minutos hasta que la corteza inferior se dore ligeramente y el queso forme burbujas. Retirar la pizza del horno, dejar reposar 5 minutos para que el queso se asiente y, a continuación, cortar en porciones.

Información nutricional por rebanada: 319 calorías (35% de grasas, 15% de proteínas, 51% de hidratos de carbono)
proteínas 12 g • grasas totales 12 g • grasas saturadas 4 g • hidratos de carbono 40 g • fibra 3 g • azúcar 6 g
sodio 320 mg • colesterol 13 mg

Estirar la masa desde el centro hacia fuera y girarla ayuda a mantener la forma redonda.

Pizza

PAN CON SEMILLAS DE AMAPOLA

preparación: 15 minutos • procesamiento: 12 segundos • tiempo de cocción: 35-40 minutos
rendimiento: 1 hogaza (12 rebanadas)

4 cucharadas (60 ml) de agua templada a 40-46 ºC (105°F-115°F)

1 sobre (1 cucharada) de levadura seca activa

1/3 de taza (80 ml) de leche

1/4 de taza (56 g) de mantequilla sin sal

1/3 de taza (80 ml) de miel

1/2 cucharadita de sal

1 huevo grande

2 1/4 tazas (281 g) de harina común sin blanquear, más una cantidad adicional para el amasado final y el estirado.

1 1/3 tazas (320 g) de relleno de semillas de amapola (receta en la página 74)

1 huevo grande más 2 cucharadas (30 ml) de leche para pintar la trenza

Para activar la levadura, mezclarla con el agua templada. Remover rápidamente para mezclar los ingredientes. Reposar la masa 5 minutos.

Calentar la leche en un cazo pequeño y añadir la mantequilla y la miel; dejar enfriar hasta que alcance una temperatura de 43-46 ºC (110°F-115°F).

Verter la harina y la sal en el recipiente Vitamix con CUCHILLAS PARA INGREDIENTES SECOS y ajustar la tapa.

Seleccionar la Variable 1.

Poner en marcha la máquina y aumentar gradualmente la velocidad hasta la Variable 6.

Procesar hasta que se forme un hueco en el centro de la mezcla, aproximadamente 5 segundos.

Seleccionar la Variable 3. Poner en marcha la máquina y retirar el tapón de la tapa. Verter el huevo, la mezcla de levadura y la mezcla de leche a través de la abertura de la tapa. Detener la máquina y volver a poner el tapón de la abertura.

Seleccionar la posición de velocidad High (Alta). Encender y detener la máquina rápidamente dos veces. Detener la máquina y retirar la tapa.

Mientras reposa la masa, engrasar ligeramente un molde grande con aceite de cocina en espray u otro tipo de grasa.

Utilizar una espátula de nailon húmeda para raspar las paredes del recipiente Vitamix. Separar la masa de las paredes del recipiente hacia el centro de la mezcla. Volver a colocar la tapa.

Seleccionar la posición de velocidad High (Alta). Encender y detener la máquina rápidamente cinco veces. Añadir más agua, 1 cucharada cada vez, únicamente si parece que la masa está muy seca. Repetir el proceso cinco veces, raspando las paredes del recipiente hasta que la masa forme una mezcla blanda y elástica.

Para sacar la masa del recipiente, encender y apagar la máquina cinco veces (esta acción levanta la masa y la separa de las cuchillas). Invertir el recipiente sobre la fuente engrasada y dejar que la masa caiga en la fuente. Invertir la masa una vez para cubrir toda la superficie; tapar con un paño de cocina limpio y dejar que suba entre 20 y 30 minutos.

Trasladar la masa a una superficie de trabajo enharinada. Estirar la masa, girándola y enharinándola con frecuencia, hasta formar un rectángulo grande de 23 cm x 38 cm (9 pulg. x 15 pulg.).

Trenza de semillas de amapola *(continuación)*

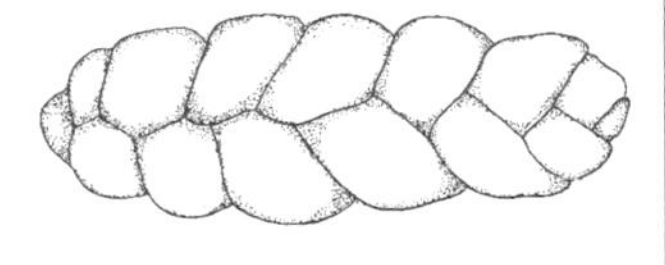

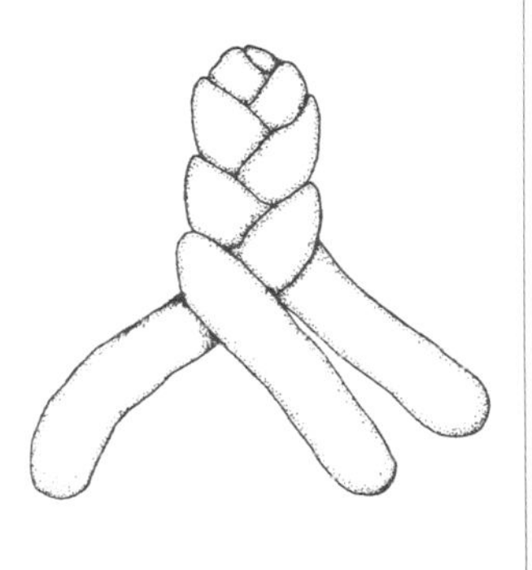

Cortar la masa a lo largo en tres partes iguales, para disponer de 3 tiras de 23 cm x 13 cm (9 pulg. x 5 pulg.) (se puede utilizar un cortador de pizza).

Espolvorear el centro de cada parte con el relleno de semillas de amapola. Humedecer los dos extremos de cada tira y uno de los lados largos con agua templada.

Enrollar cada tira a lo largo para que las semillas de amapola queden dentro del rollo. Sellar los bordes humedecidos y después los dos extremos humedecidos de las tiras.

Colocar las tres tiras en paralelo sobre una lámina de papel para hornear en una bandeja de horno (con los bordes hacia abajo). Trenzar ligeramente las tres tiras dejando espacio para que las tiras crezcan. Sellar los extremos con los dedos y con un poco más de agua y doblar la parte sellada para que quede debajo de la trenza y las tiras no se separen durante el horneado.

Cubrir con un paño de cocina limpio y seco y dejar que suba aproximadamente entre 20 y 25 minutos.

Pintar la superficie de la trenza con la mezcla de huevo y leche. Introducir en el horno precalentado a 180 ºC (350°F) y hornear entre 35 y 40 minutos o hasta que la trenza alcance una temperatura interna de 88 ºC (190°F), medida con un termómetro de lectura instantánea.

Dejar enfriar en una rejilla durante 10 minutos y, a continuación, retirar de la bandeja con cuidado. Dejar que se enfríe por completo en una rejilla antes de cortarla en rebanadas.

Información nutricional por rebanada (con relleno de semillas de amapola): 282 calorías (36% de grasas, 10% de proteínas, 54% de hidratos de carbono) • proteínas 7 g • grasas totales 12 g • grasas saturadas 4 g hidratos de carbono 39 g • fibra 2 g • azúcar 18 g • sodio 133 mg • colesterol 48 mg

PAN DE ESPELTA

preparación: 10 minutos • procesamiento: 1 minuto 30 segundos
tiempo de cocción: 35-40 minutos • rendimiento: 1 hogaza (12 rebanadas)

1 taza (240 ml) de agua templada a 40-46 ºC (105°F-115°F)

1 cucharada de miel

1 sobre (1 cucharada) de levadura seca activa

1 3/4 tazas (315 g) de espelta entera o 2 1/2 tazas (180 g) de harina de espelta

1/2 cucharadita de sal

1 cucharada de aceite de oliva suave

Para activar la levadura, mezclar el agua templada, la miel y la levadura. Remover rápidamente para mezclar los ingredientes. Reposar la masa 5 minutos.

Si se empieza con la espelta entera: colocar la espelta y la sal en el recipiente Vitamix con CUCHILLAS PARA INGREDIENTES SECOS y ajustar la tapa.

Seleccionar la Variable 1.

Poner en marcha la máquina y aumentar gradualmente la velocidad hasta la Variable 10, después hasta la posición de velocidad High (Alta).

Moler durante 1 minuto utilizando el empujador (insertado a través de la abertura de la tapa) para empujar la mezcla de harinas hacia las cuchillas. Retirar el empujador durante los últimos 5 segundos para permitir que se forme un hueco en el centro de la mezcla de harinas.

Si se empieza con la harina de espelta: colocar la harina de espelta y la sal en el recipiente Vitamix con CUCHILLAS PARA INGREDIENTES SECOS y ajustar la tapa.

Seleccionar la Variable 1.

Poner en marcha la máquina y aumentar gradualmente la velocidad hasta la Variable 6.

Procesar hasta que se forme un hueco en el centro de la mezcla de harinas, aproximadamente 5 segundos.

Seleccionar la Variable 3. Poner en marcha la máquina y retirar el tapón de la tapa. Añadir el aceite y la mezcla de levadura a través de la abertura de la tapa. Detener la máquina y volver a poner el tapón en la abertura.

Para ligar la masa, seleccionar la posición de velocidad High (Alta). Encender y detener la máquina rápidamente dos veces. Detener la máquina y retirar la tapa.

Mientras la masa reposa, engrasar un molde para pan de 22 x 11 cm (8 1/2 pulg. x 4 1/2 pulg.) con aceite vegetal u otro tipo de grasa.

Utilizar una espátula de nailon húmeda para raspar las paredes del recipiente, separando la masa de las paredes y llevándola hacia el centro de la mezcla. Volver a colocar la tapa.

Seleccionar la posición de velocidad High (Alta). Encender y detener la máquina rápidamente cinco veces. Añadir más agua, 1 cucharada cada vez, únicamente si parece que la masa está muy seca. Repetir el proceso cinco veces, raspando las paredes del recipiente hasta que la masa forme una mezcla blanda y elástica.

Pan de espelta
(continuación)

Para ayudar a sacar la masa del recipiente, encender y apagar la máquina cinco veces (esta acción levanta la masa y la separa de las cuchillas) e invertir el recipiente rápidamente sobre el molde preparado. Dejar caer la masa en el molde y utilizar una espátula para retirar la masa restante.

Usar los dedos ligeramente enharinados o una espátula engrasada para dar forma al pan dentro del molde, presionando con cuidado para dejar la masa uniforme.

Cubrir el pan con un paño de cocina limpio y seco y dejar que la masa suba hasta que alcance el borde del molde, aproximadamente entre 15 y 20 minutos. Una vez listo para hornear, realizar 3 incisiones en diagonal en la parte superior con un cuchillo de sierra.

Introducir en el horno precalentado a 180 ºC (350°F) y hornear entre 35 y 40 minutos o hasta que el pan alcance una temperatura interna de 88 ºC (190°F). Dejar enfriar en una rejilla durante 10 minutos y, a continuación, retirar del molde con cuidado. Dejar que se enfríe por completo antes de cortarlo en rebanadas.

Información nutricional por rebanada: 106 calorías (16% de grasas, 13% de proteínas, 71% de hidratos de carbono) proteínas 4 g • grasas totales 2 g • grasas saturadas 0 g • hidratos de carbono 21 g • fibra 3 g • azúcar 3 g • sodio 99 mg • colesterol 0 mg

Si se corta el pan cuando todavía está caliente, en especial el pan integral, el centro estará húmedo; dejar enfriar por completo antes de cortarlo.

PAN DE MASA MADRE (RECETA BÁSICA Y POTENCIADA)

preparación: 20 minutos • procesamiento: 30 segundos • tiempo de cocción: 30-40 minutos
rendimiento: 1 hogaza (12 rebanadas)

Receta básica

1 taza (240 ml) de fermento base de patata (receta en la página 75)

1/2 cucharadita de sal

1-1 1/2 tazas (125-188 g) de harina común, sin blanquear

Receta potenciada

1 taza (240 ml) de fermento base de patata (receta en la página 75)

1/4 de taza (60 ml) de miel

1 cucharada de mantequilla sin sal, ablandada

1/2 cucharadita de sal

1 1/3 -1 2/3 tazas (166-208 g) de harina común, sin blanquear

Elija una de las dos recetas, básica o potenciada.

Verter todos los ingredientes en el recipiente Vitamix con CUCHILLAS PARA INGREDIENTES SECOS en el orden especificado y ajustar la tapa.

Para ligar la masa, seleccionar la posición de velocidad High (Alta). Encender y detener la máquina rápidamente dos veces. Detener la máquina y retirar la tapa.

Mientras la masa reposa, engrasar un molde para pan de 20 x 10 cm (8 pulg. x 4 pulg.) con aceite vegetal u otro tipo de grasa.

Utilizar una espátula de nailon húmeda para raspar las paredes del recipiente, separando la masa de las paredes y llevándola hacia el centro de la mezcla. Volver a colocar la tapa.

Seleccionar la posición de velocidad High (Alta). Encender y detener la máquina rápidamente cinco veces. Añadir más agua, 1 cucharada cada vez, únicamente si parece que la masa está muy seca. Repetir el proceso cinco veces, raspando las paredes del recipiente hasta que la masa forme una mezcla blanda y elástica.

Para ayudar a sacar la masa del recipiente, encender y apagar la máquina cinco veces (esta acción levanta la masa y la separa de las cuchillas) e invertir el recipiente rápidamente sobre el molde preparado. Dejar caer la masa en el molde y utilizar una espátula para retirar la masa restante.

Usar los dedos ligeramente enharinados o una espátula engrasada para dar forma al pan dentro del molde, presionando con cuidado para dejar la masa uniforme.

Cubrir el molde con un paño de cocina limpio y seco y dejar que la masa suba hasta que alcance el borde del molde, aproximadamente 30 minutos. Cuando esté lista para hornear, hacer unos hoyos con las yemas de los dedos y pintar la parte superior de la masa con aceite de oliva. Espolvorear con sal gruesa, eneldo y el queso suizo restante.

Pan de masa madre (receta básica y potenciada) (*continuación*)	Introducir en el horno precalentado a 180 ºC (350°F) y hornear entre 35 y 40 minutos o hasta que el pan alcance una temperatura interna de 88 ºC (190°F), medida con un termómetro de lectura instantánea. Dejar enfriar en una rejilla durante 10 minutos y, a continuación, retirar del molde con cuidado. Dejar que se enfríe por completo antes de cortarlo en rebanadas.

Receta básica: información nutricional por rebanada: 57 calorías (3% de grasas, 12% de proteínas, 85% de hidratos de carbono) • proteínas 2 g • grasas totales 0 g • grasas saturadas 0 g • hidratos de carbono 12 g fibra 1 g • azúcar 0 g • sodio 99 mg • colesterol 0 mg

Receta potenciada: información nutricional por rebanada: 106 calorías (10% de grasas, 9% de proteínas, 81% de hidratos de carbono) • proteínas 2 g • grasas totales 1 g • grasas saturadas 1 g • hidratos de carbono 22 g fibra 1 g • azúcar 6 g • sodio 99 mg • colesterol 3 mg

BOLLOS DE BONIATO

preparación: 15 minutos • procesamiento: 30 segundos • tiempo de cocción: 20-25 minutos
rendimiento: 12 bollos

227 g de boniatos, pelados y cortados en cuartos

1 sobre (1 cucharada) de levadura seca activa

1 cucharada de azúcar granulado

1 taza (125 g) de harina común, sin blanquear

1 1/3 tazas (160 g) de harina de trigo integral y una cantidad adicional según se necesite

1/2 cucharadita de sal

2 cucharadas (28 g) de mantequilla sin sal, derretida

2 cucharadas (30 ml) de miel

1 cucharada de aceite vegetal

1 huevo grande, batido

Cocer los boniatos en un cazo con agua hasta que queden tiernos, aproximadamente 20 minutos. Escurrir y reservar 1/3 taza (80 ml) de agua de cocción. Aplastar los boniatos ligeramente y reservar. Dejar enfriar el agua de cocción hasta 46 ºC (115°F).

Para activar la levadura, mezclar 1/3 taza (80 ml) de agua de cocción, la levadura y el azúcar. Remover rápidamente para mezclar los ingredientes. Reposar la masa 5 minutos.

Verter las harinas y la sal en el recipiente Vitamix con CUCHILLAS PARA INGREDIENTES SECOS y ajustar la tapa.

Seleccionar la Variable 1.

Poner en marcha la máquina y aumentar gradualmente la velocidad hasta la Variable 10, después hasta la posición de velocidad High (Alta).

Procesar hasta que se forme un hueco en el centro de la mezcla de harinas, aproximadamente 5 segundos. Detener la máquina.

Seleccionar la Variable 3. Poner en marcha la máquina y retirar el tapón de la tapa. Añadir el boniato, la mantequilla, la miel, el aceite, el huevo y la mezcla de levadura a través de la abertura de la tapa. Detener la máquina y volver a poner el tapón en la abertura.

Para ligar la masa, seleccionar la posición de velocidad High (Alta). Encender y detener la máquina rápidamente dos veces. Detener la máquina y retirar la tapa.

Utilizar una espátula de nailon húmeda para raspar las paredes del recipiente, separando la masa de las paredes y llevándola hacia el centro de la mezcla. Volver a colocar la tapa.

Seleccionar la posición de velocidad High (Alta). Encender y detener la máquina rápidamente cinco veces. Añadir más agua, 1 cucharada cada vez, únicamente si parece que la masa está muy seca. Repetir el proceso cinco veces, raspando las paredes del recipiente hasta que la masa forme una mezcla blanda y elástica.

Engrasar ligeramente una fuente grande. Colocar la masa dentro e invertirla para cubrir toda la superficie. Cubrir la fuente con un paño de cocina limpio o con film transparente. Dejar que la masa suba en un lugar templado sin corriente de aire hasta que duplique su tamaño, aproximadamente 20 minutos.

Bollos de boniato
(continuación)

Mientras la masa reposa, engrasar un molde cuadrado para tarta de 23 cm (9 pulg.) con aceite vegetal u otro tipo de grasa. Amasar. Trasladar la masa a una superficie ligeramente enharinada y amasar ligeramente hasta que quede lisa. Cortar la masa en 12 partes iguales. Formar una bola con cada parte y colocarlas en la fuente a poca distancia unas de otras.

Cubrir la fuente con un paño de cocina limpio y seco o con film transparente y dejar que suba unos 20 minutos. Introducir en el horno precalentado a 190 ºC (375°F) y hornear entre 20 y 25 minutos o hasta que se doren ligeramente, girando la fuente una vez para que se doren de manera uniforme. Dejar enfriar en una rejilla.

Información nutricional por bollo: 150 calorías (24% de grasas, 11% de proteínas, 66% de hidratos de carbono)
proteínas 4 g • grasas totales 4 g • grasas saturadas 2 g • hidratos de carbono 25 g • fibra 3 g • azúcar 5 g
sodio 113 mg • colesterol 23 mg

PAN DE TRIGO INTEGRAL

preparación: 10 minutos • procesamiento: 35 segundos • tiempo de cocción: 35 minutos
rendimiento: 1 hogaza (12 rebanadas)

1 sobre (1 cucharada) de levadura seca activa

1 1/4 tazas (300 ml) de agua templada a 40-46 ºC (105°F-115°F)

1 cucharada de miel

1 1/2 tazas (270 g) de trigo integral o 2 1/4 tazas (270 g) de harina de trigo integral

1 cucharadita de sal

1 cucharada de aceite de oliva suave o de pepitas de girasol

1 cucharadita de zumo de limón

1 clara de huevo batida con 1 cucharada de agua, opcional (para pintar la masa antes de hornear)

Para activar la levadura, mezclar el agua templada, la miel y la levadura. Remover rápidamente para mezclar los ingredientes. Reposar la masa 5 minutos.

Si se empieza con el trigo integral: verter el trigo y la sal en el recipiente Vitamix con CUCHILLAS PARA INGREDIENTES SECOS y ajustar la tapa.

Seleccionar la Variable 1.

Poner en marcha la máquina y aumentar gradualmente la velocidad hasta la Variable 10, después hasta la posición de velocidad High (Alta).

Moler el trigo durante 1 minuto. (No moler en exceso). Detener la máquina y dejar que la harina se enfríe durante unos minutos.

Si se empieza con la harina de trigo integral: verter la harina y la sal en el recipiente Vitamix con CUCHILLAS PARA INGREDIENTES SECOS y ajustar la tapa.

Seleccionar la Variable 1.

Poner en marcha la máquina y aumentar gradualmente la velocidad hasta la Variable 6.

Procesar hasta que se forme un hueco en el centro de la mezcla, aproximadamente 5 segundos.

Seleccionar la Variable 3. Poner en marcha la máquina y retirar el tapón de la tapa. Verter el aceite, el zumo de limón y la mezcla de levadura a través de la abertura de la tapa. Detener la máquina y volver a poner el tapón en la abertura.

Seleccionar la posición de velocidad High (Alta). Encender y detener la máquina rápidamente dos veces. Detener la máquina y retirar la tapa.

Mientras la masa reposa, engrasar un molde para pan de 22 x 11 cm (8 1/2 pulg. x 4 1/2 pulg.) con aceite vegetal u otro tipo de grasa.

Utilizar una espátula de nailon para raspar las paredes del recipiente Vitamix. Separar la masa de las paredes del recipiente hacia el centro de la mezcla. Volver a colocar la tapa.

Seleccionar la posición de velocidad High (Alta). Encender y detener la máquina rápidamente cinco veces. Añadir más agua, 1 cucharada cada vez, únicamente si parece que la masa está muy seca. Repetir el proceso cinco veces, raspando las paredes del recipiente hasta que la masa forme una mezcla blanda y elástica.

Pan de trigo integral
(continuación)

Para sacar la masa del recipiente, encender y apagar la máquina cinco veces (esta acción levanta la masa y la separa de las cuchillas). Invertir el recipiente sobre el molde preparado y dejar que la masa caiga sobre este. Utilizar una espátula de nailon húmeda para retirar la masa restante.

Utilizar una espátula de nailon húmeda (o los dedos ligeramente enharinados) para dar forma al pan. Dejar que la masa suba, cubierta con un paño de cocina limpio y seco, hasta que alcance el borde del molde, aproximadamente entre 20 y 25 minutos.

Si se desea, pintar el pan rápidamente con la mezcla de huevo y realizar tres o cuatro incisiones en diagonal de aproximadamente 0,6 cm (1/4 pulg.) con un cuchillo de sierra afilado.

Introducir en el horno precalentado a 180 ºC (350°F) y hornear durante 35 minutos o hasta que el pan alcance una temperatura interna de 88 ºC (190°F), medida con un termómetro de lectura instantánea.

Dejar enfriar en una rejilla durante 10 minutos y, a continuación, retirar del molde con cuidado. Dejar que se enfríe por completo antes de cortarlo en rebanadas.

Información nutricional por rebanada: 102 calorías (13% de grasas, 13% de proteínas, 74% de hidratos de carbono) proteínas 3 g • grasas totales 2 g • grasas saturadas 0 g • hidratos de carbono 20 g • fibra 3 g • azúcar 2 g sodio 203 mg • colesterol 0 mg

BAGUETTE DE CEREALES INTEGRALES

preparación: 15 minutos • procesamiento: 35 segundos • tiempo de cocción: 30-40 minutos
rendimiento: 1 hogaza (16-18 rebanadas)

1 taza (240 ml) de agua templada a 40-46 ºC (105°F-115°F), uso dividido

1 sobre (1 cucharada) de levadura seca activa

1 1/4 tazas (150 g) de harina de trigo integral

3/4 de taza (103 g) de harina para pan

1 1/2 cucharaditas de sal

2 cucharadas (21 g) de semillas de lino

2 cucharadas (18 g) de pipas de girasol

1 cucharada de pipas de calabaza o 1 cucharada de mijo

1 cucharada de germen de trigo

1 cucharada de aceite de oliva

2 cucharadas (15 g) de harina de maíz entero

1 huevo batido con 1 cucharadita de agua (para pintar la masa antes del horneado)

Para activar la levadura, mezclar 1/2 taza (120 ml) de agua templada con la levadura. Remover rápidamente para mezclar los ingredientes. Reposar la masa 5 minutos.

Verter la harina de trigo integral, la harina para pan, la sal, las semillas de lino, las pipas de girasol, las pipas de calabaza O el mijo y el germen de trigo en el recipiente Vitamix con CUCHILLAS PARA INGREDIENTES SECOS.

Seleccionar la Variable 1.

Poner en marcha la máquina y aumentar gradualmente la velocidad hasta la Variable 6.

Procesar hasta que se forme un hueco en el centro de la mezcla de harinas, aproximadamente 5 segundos. Detener la máquina.

Seleccionar la Variable 3. Poner en marcha la máquina y retirar el tapón de la tapa. Añadir la mezcla de levadura y la 1/2 taza (120 ml) de agua templada restante a través de la abertura de la tapa. Detener la máquina y volver a poner el tapón en la abertura.

Para ligar la masa, seleccionar la posición de velocidad High (Alta). Encender y detener la máquina rápidamente dos veces. Detener la máquina y retirar la tapa.

Mientras la masa reposa, engrasar una fuente de tamaño mediano con aceite de oliva y espolvorear harina de maíz en una bandeja de horno.

Utilizar una espátula de nailon húmeda para raspar las paredes del recipiente, separando la masa de las paredes y llevándola hacia el centro de la mezcla. Volver a colocar la tapa.

Seleccionar la posición de velocidad High (Alta). Encender y detener la máquina rápidamente cinco veces. Añadir más agua, 1 cucharada cada vez, únicamente si parece que la masa está muy seca. Repetir el proceso cinco veces, raspando las paredes del recipiente hasta que la masa forme una mezcla blanda y elástica.

Para ayudar a sacar la masa del recipiente, encender y apagar la máquina cinco veces (esta acción levanta la masa y la separa de las cuchillas) e invertir el recipiente rápidamente sobre la fuente preparada, utilizando una espátula húmeda para retirar la masa restante. Invertir la masa para se cubra bien con la mezcla de la fuente. Tapar con film transparente y dejar que suba hasta prácticamente triplicar su tamaño, aproximadamente 1 hora.

Baguette de cereales integrales *(continuación)*

Aplastar la masa ligeramente y trasladarla a una superficie de trabajo enharinada. Estirar en forma rectangular de 30 x 15 cm (12 pulg. x 6 pulg.) con un rodillo enharinado. Estirar desde el extremo largo hacia abajo, presionando los bordes y añadiendo agua para sellarlos.

Colocar la masa con los bordes hacia abajo sobre la bandeja de horno preparada. Cubrir con un paño de cocina limpio y seco y dejar que la masa suba hasta duplicar su tamaño, aproximadamente 45 minutos.

Pintar la parte superior con la mezcla de huevo y realizar tres o cuatro incisiones en diagonal de aproximadamente 0,6 cm (1/4 pulg.) con un cuchillo de sierra afilado.

Introducir en el horno precalentado a 220 ºC (425°F) y hornear entre 30 y 40 minutos o hasta que el pan alcance una temperatura interna de 88 ºC (190°F), medida con un termómetro de lectura instantánea. Dejar enfriar en una rejilla durante 10 minutos y, a continuación, sacarlo de la bandeja de horno. Dejar que se enfríe por completo antes de cortarlo en rebanadas.

Información nutricional por rebanada: 74 calorías (23% de grasas, 16% de proteínas, 62% de hidratos de carbono)
proteínas 3 g • grasas totales 2 g • grasas saturadas 0 g • hidratos de carbono 12 g • fibra 2 g • azúcar 0 g
sodio 202 mg • colesterol 0 mg

Una espátula metálica es útil para sacar el pan de la bandeja del horno.

PAN DE TRIGO INTEGRAL, AVENA Y SEMILLAS DE LINO

preparación: 10 minutos • procesamiento: 40 segundos • tiempo de cocción: 30-35 minutos
rendimiento: 1 hogaza (12 rebanadas)

1 taza (240 ml) de agua templada a 40-46 ºC (105°F-115°F)

2 cucharadas (30 ml) de miel

1 sobre (1 cucharada) de levadura seca activa

2 cucharadas (10 g) de copos de avena (naturales, no instantáneos)

2 cucharadas (20 g) de semillas de lino

3/4 de taza (135 g) de trigo integral o 1 taza (120 g) de harina de trigo integral

1 1/4 tazas (171 g) de harina para pan

1 cucharadita de sal

1 cucharada de aceite de oliva suave

Para activar la levadura, mezclar el agua templada, la miel y la levadura. Remover rápidamente para mezclar los ingredientes. Reposar la masa 5 minutos.

Si se empieza con el trigo integral, verter la avena, las semillas de lino y el trigo integral en el recipiente Vitamix con CUCHILLAS PARA INGREDIENTES SECOS y ajustar la tapa.

Seleccionar la Variable 1.

Poner en marcha la máquina y aumentar gradualmente la velocidad hasta la Variable 10, después hasta la posición de velocidad High (Alta).

Moler durante 30 segundos.

Detener la máquina. Verter la harina para pan y la sal en el recipiente Vitamix y ajustar la tapa.

Seleccionar la Variable 1.

Poner en marcha la máquina y aumentar gradualmente la velocidad hasta la Variable 10, después hasta la posición de velocidad High (Alta).

Procesar durante 30 segundos utilizando el empujador (insertado a través de la abertura de la tapa) para empujar la mezcla de harinas hacia las cuchillas. Retirar el empujador durante los últimos 5 segundos para permitir que se forme un hueco en el centro de la mezcla de harinas.

Si se empieza con la harina de trigo integral, verter la avena, las semillas de lino, la harina de trigo integral, la harina para pan y la sal en el recipiente Vitamix con CUCHILLAS PARA INGREDIENTES SECOS y ajustar la tapa.

Seleccionar la Variable 1.

Poner en marcha la máquina y aumentar gradualmente la velocidad hasta la Variable 10, después hasta la posición de velocidad High (Alta).

Procesar durante 30 segundos utilizando el empujador (insertado a través de la abertura de la tapa) para empujar la mezcla de harinas hacia las cuchillas. Retirar el empujador durante los últimos 5 segundos para permitir que se forme un hueco en el centro de la mezcla de harinas.

Seleccionar la Variable 3. Poner en marcha la máquina y retirar el tapón de la tapa. Añadir el aceite y la mezcla de levadura a través de la abertura de la tapa. Detener la máquina y volver a poner el tapón en la abertura.

Pan de trigo integral, avena y semillas de lino *(continuación)*

Seleccionar la posición de velocidad High (Alta). Encender y detener la máquina rápidamente dos veces. Detener la máquina y retirar la tapa.

Mientras la masa reposa, engrasar un molde para pan de 20 x 10 cm (8 pulg. x 4 pulg.) con aceite vegetal u otro tipo de grasa.

Utilizar una espátula de nailon húmeda para raspar las paredes del recipiente, separando la masa de las paredes y llevándola hacia el centro de la mezcla. Volver a colocar la tapa.

Seleccionar la posición de velocidad High (Alta). Encender y detener la máquina rápidamente cinco veces. Añadir más agua, 1 cucharada cada vez, únicamente si parece que la masa está muy seca. Repetir el proceso cinco veces, raspando las paredes del recipiente hasta que la masa forme una mezcla blanda y elástica.

Para ayudar a sacar la masa del recipiente, encender y apagar la máquina cinco veces (esta acción levanta la masa y la separa de las cuchillas) e invertir el recipiente rápidamente sobre el molde preparado. Dejar caer la masa en el molde y utilizar una espátula húmeda para retirar la masa restante.

Usar los dedos ligeramente enharinados o una espátula engrasada para dar forma al pan dentro del molde, presionando con cuidado para dejar la masa uniforme.

Cubrir el pan con un paño de cocina limpio y seco y dejar que la masa suba hasta que alcance el borde del molde, aproximadamente entre 20 y 25 minutos. Una vez listo para hornear, realizar 3 incisiones en diagonal en la parte superior con un cuchillo de sierra.

Introducir en el horno precalentado a 190 ºC (375°F) y hornear entre 30 y 35 minutos o hasta que el pan alcance una temperatura interna de 88 ºC (190°F). Dejar enfriar en una rejilla durante 10 minutos y, a continuación, retirar del molde con cuidado. Dejar que se enfríe por completo antes de cortarlo en rebanadas.

Información nutricional por rebanada: 130 calorías (15% de grasas, 12% de proteínas, 73% de hidratos de carbono)
proteína 4 g • grasas totales 2 g • grasas saturadas 0 g • hidratos de carbono 24 g • fibra 3 g • azúcar 3 g
sodio 199 mg • colesterol 0 mg

Si se corta el pan cuando todavía está caliente, en especial el pan integral, el centro estará húmedo; dejar enfriar por completo antes de cortarlo.

adobos secos

Utilizar condimentos secos

Los adobos secos añaden una dimensión de sabor a los alimentos cocinados a la parrilla. Explore nuestras combinaciones favoritas y siga algunas pautas para obtener mejores resultados.

- Los adobos secos añaden un toque de sabor y funcionan bien con alimentos fritos, asados a la parrilla o en horno. Son fantásticos con tofu, pescado, chuletas de cerdo, pechuga de pollo y verdura.
- Guarde los adobos en un tarro de cristal hermético y colóquelos en un lugar fresco. Usar al gusto.
- Tres o cuatro cucharadas de condimento seco son suficientes para cocinar aproximadamente 1 kg de comida.
- Para usar el condimento, espolvoréelo sobre carne, pescado o verdura y frótelo con las manos sobre la superficie. O coloque el condimento en una bolsa de plástico grande, añada los ingredientes y agítelo para cubrirlos con el condimento. A continuación, deje reposar la comida en la nevera durante varias horas o toda la noche antes de cocinarla.
- Para potenciar el sabor de los alimentos a la parrilla, condimente generosamente la carne, el pescado u otro alimento de su elección frotándolo por ambos lados. Cúbralo con film transparente y déjelo reposar en la nevera durante 30 minutos. Cocine los alimentos condimentados en la parrilla.

Notas importantes:

Moler ingredientes secos durante más de dos minutos puede dañar la máquina. El uso habitual puede provocar deterioros estéticos en el recipiente y desafilar las cuchillas con el tiempo.

Al moler algunas hierbas, estas pueden desprender aceites volátiles que pueden decolorar el recipiente de forma permanente. Otras hierbas tienen aromas muy intensos que pueden permanecer en el recipiente y afectar al sabor de otros alimentos. La molienda de algunas hierbas y especias también puede causar que las cuchillas se desafilen con el tiempo o que se agriete el recipiente.

CONDIMENTO PARA BARBACOA

preparación: 10 minutos • procesamiento: 45 segundos • rendimiento: 1 taza (240 g)

1 cucharada de sal marina

1/4 de taza (55 g) de azúcar moreno

1/4 de taza (28 g) de pimentón dulce

2 cucharadas (24 g) de pimienta negra en grano

1 cucharada de ajo deshidratado en copos

1 cucharada de cebolla deshidratada en copos

1 chile pasilla entero deshidratado, sin semillas y cortado por la mitad

1/2 cucharadita de semillas de apio

Verter todos los ingredientes en el recipiente Vitamix con CUCHILLAS PARA INGREDIENTES SECOS en el orden especificado y ajustar la tapa.

Seleccionar la Variable 1.

Poner en marcha la máquina y aumentar gradualmente la velocidad hasta la Variable 10, después hasta la posición de velocidad High (Alta).

Procesar durante 45 segundos. Utilizar inmediatamente o guardar en un recipiente hermético con sus especias hasta su uso.

NOTA: Añade un toque de especias y picante a todo, desde costillas a salmón.

Información nutricional por ración de 1 cucharadita: 8 calorías (11% de grasas, 7% de proteínas, 82% de hidratos de carbono) • proteínas 0 g • grasas totales 0 g • grasas saturadas 0 g hidratos de carbono 2 g • fibra 0 g • azúcar 1 g • sodio 71 mg • colesterol 0 mg

All Purpose Barbecue Rub

CONDIMENTO CAJÚN

preparación: 10 minutos • procesamiento: 30 segundos • rendimiento: 1 taza (240 g)

1/4 de taza (67 g) de sal marina gruesa

3 cucharadas (21 g) de pimentón dulce

2 cucharadas (17 g) de ajo en polvo

2 cucharadas (14 g) de cebolla en polvo

2 cucharadas (5 g) de tomillo deshidratado

2 cucharadas (6 g) de orégano deshidratado

1 cucharada de pimienta negra molida o 1 cucharadita de pimienta negra en grano

1 cucharada de pimienta blanca molida o 1 cucharadita de pimienta blanca en grano

2 cucharaditas de hojas de salvia deshidratadas

2 cucharaditas de pimienta cayena o 1 chile tailandés deshidratado

Verter todos los ingredientes en el recipiente Vitamix con CUCHILLAS PARA INGREDIENTES SECOS en el orden especificado y ajustar la tapa.

Seleccionar la Variable 1.

Poner en marcha la máquina y aumentar gradualmente la velocidad hasta la Variable 10, después hasta la posición de velocidad High (Alta).

Procesar durante 30 segundos utilizando el empujador si es necesario para empujar los ingredientes hacia las cuchillas. Utilizar inmediatamente o guardar en un recipiente hermético con sus especias hasta su uso.

Información nutricional por ración de 2 cucharadas (30 g): 31 calorías (15% de grasa, 14% de proteína, 71% de hidratos de carbono) • proteínas 1 g • grasas totales 1 g • grasas saturadas 0 g • hidratos de carbono 7 g fibra 3 g • azúcar 1 g • sodio 1683 mg • colesterol 0 mg

CONDIMENTO SECO DE CAFÉ

preparación: 15 minutos • procesamiento: 45 segundos • rendimiento: 1/2 taza (120 g)

1 1/2 cucharaditas de sal marina

4 cucharaditas de café molido o 1 cucharada de café en grano

1 chile pasilla entero deshidratado, sin semillas

2 cucharadas (28 g) de azúcar moreno

1/2 cucharadita de pimienta negra molida o 1/4 de cucharadita de pimienta negra en grano

1/2 cucharadita de cebolla en polvo

1/2 cucharadita de ajo en polvo

1/4 de cucharadita de pimienta cayena

1/4 de cucharadita de semillas de cilantro

1/4 de cucharadita de cúrcuma

Verter todos los ingredientes en el recipiente Vitamix con CUCHILLAS PARA INGREDIENTES SECOS en el orden especificado y ajustar la tapa.

Seleccionar la Variable 1.

Poner en marcha la máquina y aumentar gradualmente la velocidad hasta la Variable 10, después hasta la posición de velocidad High (Alta).

Procesar durante 45 segundos. Utilizar inmediatamente o guardar en un recipiente hermético con sus especias hasta su uso.

Información nutricional por ración de 1 cucharadita: 7 calorías (8% de grasa, 6% de proteína, 86% de hidratos de carbono) • proteínas 0 g • grasas totales 0 g • grasas saturadas 0 g hidratos de carbono 2 g • fibra 0 g • azúcar 1 g • sodio 71 mg • colesterol 0 mg

El café de este condimento aporta a la comida un sabor suntuoso e intenso. Ideal para condimentar ternera.

CONDIMENTO SECO PARA CARNE

preparación: 10 minutos • procesamiento: 45 segundos • rendimiento: 1/2 taza (67 g)

3 cucharadas (41 g) de azúcar moreno

1 1/2 cucharadas de sal marina gruesa

1 cucharada de semillas de cilantro

1 cucharadita de pimienta negra en grano

1 1/2 cucharaditas de ajo en polvo

1 1/2 cucharaditas de cebolla en polvo

1 1/2 cucharaditas de tomillo deshidratado

1 cucharadita de pimienta inglesa en grano o
1 1/2 cucharaditas de pimienta inglesa molida

1 cucharadita de canela molida

1/2 o 1 cucharadita de pimienta cayena o
1 chile tailandés deshidratado

Verter todos los ingredientes en el recipiente Vitamix con CUCHILLAS PARA INGREDIENTES SECOS en el orden especificado y ajustar la tapa.

Seleccionar la Variable 1.

Poner en marcha la máquina y aumentar gradualmente la velocidad hasta la Variable 10, después hasta la posición de velocidad High (Alta).

Procesar durante 45 segundos. Utilizar inmediatamente o guardar en un recipiente hermético con sus especias hasta su uso.

Información nutricional por ración de 1 cucharadita: 9 calorías (6% de grasa, 4% de proteínas, 90% de hidratos de carbono) • proteínas 0 g • grasas totales 0 g • grasas saturadas 0 g hidratos de carbono 2 g • fibra 0 g • azúcar 2 g • sodio 443 mg • colesterol 0 mg

"NUEVO" CONDIMENTO DE LA BAHÍA

preparación: 10 minutos • procesamiento: 1 minuto • rendimiento: 1 1/4 tazas (300 g)

1/2 taza (134 g) de sal marina gruesa

1/2 taza (56 g) de pimentón dulce

2 cucharadas (13 g) de semillas de apio

1 cucharada de pimienta inglesa en grano

1 cucharada de pimienta negra en grano

1 cucharada de mostaza deshidratada molida

1 cucharada de jengibre molido

1 cucharada de canela molida

1 cucharada de cayena molida

1/2 cucharada de semillas de cardamomo

1/2 cucharada de clavos

10 hojas de laurel

Verter todos los ingredientes en el recipiente Vitamix con CUCHILLAS PARA INGREDIENTES SECOS en el orden especificado y ajustar la tapa.

Seleccionar la Variable 1.

Poner en marcha la máquina y aumentar gradualmente la velocidad hasta la Variable 10, después hasta la posición de velocidad High (Alta).

Procesar durante 1 minuto utilizando el empujador si es necesario para empujar los ingredientes hacia las cuchillas. Utilizar inmediatamente o guardar en un recipiente hermético con sus especias hasta su uso.

Información nutricional por ración de 1 cucharadita: 6 calorías (31% de grasa, 14% de proteínas, 55% de hidratos de carbono) • proteínas 0 g • grasas totales 0 g • grasas saturadas 0 g hidratos de carbono 1 g • fibra 1 g • azúcar 0 g • sodio 449 mg • colesterol 0 mg

Este condimento es lo suficientemente versátil como para añadirlo al agua de cocción de gambas y cangrejos, marinar pescado o incluso mezclarlo con mantequilla para aderezar langostas y gambas.

CONDIMENTO CON PIMENTÓN PARA CARNE DE AVE

preparación: 15 minutos • procesamiento: 1 segundo • rendimiento: 3/4 de taza (180 g)

1/3 de taza (9 g) de mejorana deshidratada

1/4 de taza (28 g) de pimentón dulce

1 chile pasilla deshidratado, sin semillas

2 cucharadas (14 g) de cebolla en polvo

2 cucharadas (36 g) de cáscara de limón deshidratada

1/4 de taza (24 g) de hojas de salvia deshidratadas

1 cucharada de sal marina o de sal gruesa

1 cucharada de pimienta negra en grano

1/2 cucharada de semillas de apio

Verter todos los ingredientes en el recipiente Vitamix con CUCHILLAS PARA INGREDIENTES SECOS en el orden especificado y ajustar la tapa.

Seleccionar la Variable 1.

Poner en marcha la máquina y aumentar gradualmente la velocidad hasta la Variable 10, después hasta la posición de velocidad High (Alta).

Procesar durante 1 minuto. Utilizar inmediatamente o guardar en un recipiente hermético con sus especias hasta su uso.

Información nutricional por ración de 1 cucharadita: 7 calorías (22% de grasa, 13% de proteínas, 65% de hidratos de carbono) • proteína 0 g • grasas totales 0 g • grasas saturadas 0 g hidratos de carbono 1 g • fibra 1 g • azúcar 0 g • sodio 94 mg • colesterol 0 mg

Un adobo perfecto para todos los días.

MEZCLA DE ESPECIAS PARA PASTEL DE CALABAZA

preparación: 10 minutos • procesamiento: 45 segundos • rendimiento: 2 cucharadas (30 g)

- 1 cucharada de canela molida
- 1 cucharadita de jengibre molido
- 6 clavos
- 3 granos de pimienta inglesa
- 1/2 cucharadita de macia molida
- 1/2 cucharadita de nuez moscada recién rallada

Verter todos los ingredientes en el recipiente Vitamix con CUCHILLAS PARA INGREDIENTES SECOS en el orden especificado y ajustar la tapa.

Seleccionar la Variable 1.

Poner en marcha la máquina y aumentar gradualmente la velocidad hasta la Variable 10, después hasta la posición de velocidad High (Alta).

Procesar durante 45 segundos. Utilizar inmediatamente o guardar en un recipiente hermético con sus especias hasta su uso.

NOTA: esta mezcla puede manchar ligeramente el recipiente.

Información nutricional por ración de 1 cucharadita: 6 calorías (22% de grasa, 5% de proteínas, 73% de hidratos de carbono) • proteínas 0 g • grasas totales 0 g • grasas saturadas 0 g hidratos de carbono 1 g • fibra 1 g • azúcar 0 g • sodio 1 mg • colesterol 0 mg

Esta mezcla es tan popular que querrá añadirla a todos sus platos, desde pasteles de manzana a puré de patatas y, por supuesto, a la clásica tarta de calabaza. Con su máquina Vitamix, es fácil aprovechar la frescura de los ingredientes aromáticos, por lo puede hacer cantidades pequeñas de cada vez para potenciar el sabor.

CONDIMENTO SECO DULCE Y SALADO

preparación: 10 minutos • procesamiento: 30 segundos • rendimiento: 1/4 de taza (60 g)

- 2 cucharaditas de azúcar moreno
- 2 cucharaditas de mostaza seca
- 1 cucharadita de cebolla en polvo
- 1/2 cucharadita de sal gruesa
- 6 granos de pimienta blanca o 1/4 de cucharadita de pimienta blanca molida

Verter todos los ingredientes en el recipiente Vitamix con CUCHILLAS PARA INGREDIENTES SECOS y ajustar la tapa.

Seleccionar la Variable 1.

Poner en marcha la máquina y aumentar gradualmente la velocidad hasta la Variable 10, después hasta la posición de velocidad High (Alta).

Procesar durante 30 segundos. Utilizar inmediatamente o guardar en un recipiente hermético con sus especias hasta su uso.

Información nutricional por ración de 1 cucharadita: 7 calorías (24% de grasa, 10% de proteínas, 66% de hidratos de carbono) • proteínas 0 g • grasas totales 0 g • grasas saturadas 0 g hidratos de carbono 1 g • fibra 0 g • azúcar 1 g • sodio 47 mg • colesterol 0 mg

CONDIMENTO SECO DE CURRY DE TRINIDAD

preparación: 10 minutos • procesamiento: 45 segundos • rendimiento: 1/2 taza (120 g)

3 cucharadas (15 g) de semillas de cilantro

3 cucharadas (20 g) de cúrcuma molida

2 cucharadas (24 g) de pimienta negra en grano

1 cucharada de sal gruesa

1 cucharada de semillas de comino

1 cucharadita de pimienta inglesa en grano

1 cucharadita de semillas de cardamomo

1 cucharadita de nuez moscada recién rallada

1 cucharadita de canela molida

3/4 de cucharadita de jengibre molido

2 chiles tailandeses, sin semillas

Verter todos los ingredientes en el recipiente Vitamix con CUCHILLAS PARA INGREDIENTES SECOS en el orden especificado y ajustar la tapa.

Seleccionar la Variable 1.

Poner en marcha la máquina y aumentar gradualmente la velocidad hasta la Variable 10, después hasta la posición de velocidad High (Alta).

Procesar durante 45 segundos. Utilizar inmediatamente o guardar en un recipiente hermético con sus especias hasta su uso.

NOTA: esta mezcla puede manchar ligeramente el recipiente.

Información nutricional por ración de 1 cucharadita: 21 calorías (29% de grasa, 11% de proteínas, 60% de hidratos de carbono) • proteína 1 g • grasas totales 1 g • grasas saturadas 0 g hidratos de carbono 4 g • fibra 2 g • azúcar 0 g • sodio 284 mg • colesterol 0 mg

CONDIMENTO SECO PARA ADOBO

preparación: 10 minutos • procesamiento: 1 minuto • rendimiento: 1 taza (240 g)

1/4 de taza (34 g) de ajo en polvo

1/4 de taza (28 g) de cebolla en polvo

3 cucharadas (9 g) de orégano deshidratado

2 cucharadas (12 g) de semillas de comino

2 cucharadas (29 g) de sal gruesa

2 cucharadas (24 g) de pimienta negra en grano

1 cucharada de cáscara de limón deshidratada

Verter todos los ingredientes en el recipiente Vitamix con CUCHILLAS PARA INGREDIENTES SECOS en el orden especificado y ajustar la tapa.

Seleccionar la Variable 1.

Poner en marcha la máquina y aumentar gradualmente la velocidad hasta la Variable 10, después hasta la posición de velocidad High (Alta).

Procesar durante 1 minuto. Utilizar inmediatamente o guardar en un recipiente hermético con sus especias hasta su uso.

Información nutricional por ración de 1 cucharadita: 7 calorías (11% de grasas, 14% de proteínas, 74% de hidratos de carbono) • proteínas 0 g • grasas totales 0 g • grasas saturadas 0 g hidratos de carbono 1 g • fibra 0 g • azúcar 0 g • sodio 141 mg • colesterol 0 mg

Una mezcla latinoamericana de especias para uso general, perfecta para carnes y para espolvorear sobre legumbres o verduras asadas.

Guía de resolución de problemas

Si es principiante, es posible que le abrume la cantidad de variables a la hora de elaborar pan de levadura y puede que se pregunte qué debe hacer si las cosas no salen como se indican en la receta. Es cierto que la elaboración de pan con levadura no es una ciencia exacta, pero también es cierto que es bastante tolerante. Aquí incluimos la respuesta a algunas de las preguntas que puede tener.

¿Cómo puedo saber si se ha activado la levadura?

Los sobres de levadura seca activa tienen fecha de caducidad, por lo que puede saber durante cuánto tiempo estará activa. Pero si compra levadura a granel, no siempre es fácil averiguarlo. Puede probar la levadura activándola, un paso sencillo incluido en muchas recetas de pan. Al disolver la levadura en agua templada, añada entre 1 y 3 cucharaditas de azúcar o miel, según sea adecuado para la receta. (Si ninguna de las dos opciones es adecuada, puede añadir 1 cucharadita sin que afecte al sabor del pan). Deje la mezcla reposar entre 5 y 15 minutos o hasta que forme burbujas; las burbujas son la prueba de que la levadura sigue estando fresca y activa.

¿Cómo se manejan las interrupciones en el proceso de elaboración del pan?

No debemos preocuparnos por las interrupciones breves de hasta media hora. Si acaba de disolver la levadura, tápela y déjela a temperatura ambiente, no es perjudicial dejar que fermente un rato. Si está mezclando o amasando la masa, tápela con film transparente para que no se seque.

Si no es el momento adecuado para dar forma al pan cuando la masa se ha duplicado, aplástela y deje que suba otra vez a temperatura ambiente. Puede aplastar dos o tres veces y aún así conseguir un pan excelente.

Puede posponer los últimos pasos (dar forma, dejar subir por segunda vez y hornear) dejando la masa tapada con film transparente en la nevera durante la primera fermentación. Puede conservarlo en la nevera varias horas; el proceso de fermentación continuará, aunque a un ritmo mucho más lento. Cuando esté listo, deje que la masa termine de subir en lugar templado.

¿Cómo puedo saber si la masa tiene suficiente harina?

Si no está seguro de haber añadido suficiente harina a la masa (recuerde que el exceso de harina produce panes muy secos), coloque el recipiente invertido sobre la masa y deje que repose durante aproximadamente 15 minutos. Si después de ese tiempo la masa está muy pegajosa y se ha extendido hacia los lados en lugar de subir, añada más harina.

Guía de resolución de problemas *(continuación)*

¿Qué pasa si la masa sube demasiado?

Si ha dejado que la masa fermente durante demasiado tiempo, subirá mucho. La solución es aplastarla, amasarla un poco para liberar el aire atrapado y dejar que vuelva a subir. La masa demasiado fermentada parece que ha aumentado su tamaño original más del doble. La superficie es fina y transparente con burbujas justo por debajo.

Si se deja el tiempo suficiente, es posible que se desinfle sola, en cuyo caso no es necesario aplastarla y volver a dejar que suba. Se puede utilizar la misma técnica si se ha dejado subir demasiado la masa con la forma de pan ya aplicada. Amásela ligeramente para liberar el aire atrapado, vuelva a darle forma y deje que suba otra vez, pero obsérvela atentamente, ya que una vez se le da forma, la masa sube más rápido.

¿Qué pasa si la parte inferior de los panes no se ha dorado lo suficiente cuando los saco de los moldes?

Si prefiere una corteza más dorada, puede volver a meter los panes en el horno, bien en los moldes, bien directamente en la rejilla del horno. Unos pocos minutos más producirán una corteza más oscura y crujiente.

Notas